Brilliant
Adobe®
Photoshop CS4

PEARSON
Prentice
Hall

Harlow, England • London • New York • Boston • San Francisco • Toronto
Sydney • Tokyo • Singapore • Hong Kong • Seoul • Taipei • New Delhi
Cape Town • Madrid • Mexico City • Amsterdam • Munich • Paris • Milan

Pearson Education Limited
Edinburgh Gate
Essex CM20 2JE
England

and Associated Companies throughout the world

Visit us on the World Wide Web at:
www.pearsoned.co.uk

Original edition, entitled ADOBE® PHOTOSHOP CS4 PROFESSIONAL ON DEMAND, 1ˢᵗ edition, 078973835X by JOHNSON, STEVE; PERSPECTION, INC., published by Pearson Education, Inc., publishing as Que/Sams. Copyright 2009 Perspection, Inc.

ISBN: 978-0-273-72265-6

British Library Cataloguing-in-Publication Data
A catalogue record for this book is available from the British Library

10 9 8 7 6 5 4 3 2 1
12 11 10 09 08

Printed and bound in the United States of America

The publisher's policy is to use paper manufactured from sustainable forests.

Brilliant Guides

What you need to know and how to do it

When you're working on your computer and come up against a problem that you're unsure how to solve, or want to accomplish something in an application that you aren't sure how to do, where do you look?? Manuals and traditional training guides are usually too big and unwieldy and are intended to be used as an end-to-end training resource, making it hard to get to the info you need right away without having to wade through pages of background information that you just don't need at that moment – and helplines are rarely that helpful!

Brilliant guides have been developed to allow you to find the info you need easily and without fuss and guide you through the task using a highly visual, step-by-step approach – providing exactly what you need to know when you need it!!

Brilliant guides provide the quick easy-to-access information that you need, using a detailed index and troubleshooting guide to help you find exactly what you need to know, and then presenting each task on one or two pages. Numbered steps then guide you through each task or problem, using numerous screenshots to illustrate each step. Added features include "See Also…" boxes that point you to related tasks and information in the book, whilst "Did you know?…" sections alert you to relevant expert tips, tricks and advice to further expand your skills and knowledge.

In addition to covering all major office applications, and related computing subjects, the *Brilliant* series also contains titles that will help you in every aspect of your working life, such as writing the perfect CV, answering the toughest interview questions and moving on in your career.

Brilliant guides are the light at the end of the tunnel when you are faced with any minor or major task!

Acknowledgements

Perspection, Inc.

Brilliant Adobe Photoshop CS4 has been created by the professional trainers and writers at Perspection, Inc. to the standards you've come to expect from Que publishing. Together, we are pleased to present this training book.

Perspection, Inc. is a software training company committed to providing information and training to help people use software more effectively in order to communicate, make decisions, and solve problems. Perspection writes and produces software training books, and develops multimedia and Web-based training. Since 1991, we have written more than 90 computer books, with several bestsellers to our credit, and sold over 5 million books.

This book incorporates Perspection's training expertise to ensure that you'll receive the maximum return on your time. You'll focus on the tasks and skills that increase productivity while working at your own pace and convenience.

We invite you to visit the Perspection web site at:

www.perspection.com

Acknowledgements

The task of creating any book requires the talents of many hard-working people pulling together to meet impossible deadlines and untold stresses. We'd like to thank the outstanding team responsible for making this book possible: the writer, Steve Johnson; the technical editor and contributor, Toni Bennett; the production editors, James Teyler and Beth Teyler; proofreaders, Toni Bennett and Beth Teyler; and the indexer, Katherine Stimson.

At Que publishing, we'd like to thank Greg Wiegand and Laura Norman for the opportunity to undertake this project, Cindy Teeters for administrative support, and Sandra Schroeder for your production expertise and support.

Perspection

About The Author

Steve Johnson has written more than 45 books on a variety of computer software, including Adobe Photoshop CS3 and CS2, Adobe Flash CS3, Dreamweaver CS3, Microsoft Office 2007 and 2003, Microsoft Windows Vista and XP, Microsoft Office 2008 for the Macintosh, and Apple Mac OS X Leopard. In 1991, after working for Apple Computer and Microsoft, Steve founded Perspection, Inc., which writes and produces software training. When he is not staying up late writing, he enjoys playing golf, gardening, and spending time with his wife, Holly, and three children, JP, Brett, and Hannah. Steve and his family live in Pleasanton, California, but can also be found visiting family all over the western United States.

Contents

W Workshops: Putting It All Together   503

Introduction

Welcome to *Brilliant Adobe Photoshop CS4*, a visual quick reference book that shows you how to work efficiently with Photoshop CS4. This book provides complete coverage of basic to advanced Photoshop skills.

How This Book Works

You don't have to read this book in any particular order. We've designed the book so that you can jump in, get the information you need, and jump out. However, the book does follow a logical progression from simple tasks to more complex ones. Each task is presented on no more than two facing pages, which lets you focus on a single task without having to turn the page. To find the information that you need, just look up the task in the table of contents or index, and turn to the page listed. Read the task introduction, follow the step-by-step instructions in the left column along with screen illustrations in the right column, and you're done.

What's New

If you're searching for what's new in Photoshop CS4, just look for the icon: **New!**. The new icon appears in the table of contents and throughout this book so you can quickly and easily identify a new or improved feature in Photoshop CS4. A complete description of each new feature appears in the New Features guide in the back of this book.

Keyboard Shortcuts

Most menu commands have a keyboard equivalent, such as Ctrl+P (Win) or ⌘+P (Mac), as a quicker alternative to using the mouse. A complete list of keyboard shortcuts is available on the Web at *www.perspection.com*.

How You'll Learn

How This Book Works

What's New

Keyboard Shortcuts

Step-by-Step Instructions

Real World Examples

Workshops

Adobe Certified Expert

Get More on the Web

Step-by-Step Instructions

This book provides concise step-by-step instructions that show you "how" to accomplish a task. Each set of instructions includes illustrations that directly correspond to the easy-to-read steps. Also included in the text are time-savers, tables, and sidebars to help you work more efficiently or to teach you more in-depth information. A "Did You Know?" provides tips and techniques to help you work smarter, while a "See Also" leads you to other parts of the book containing related information about the task.

Easy-to-follow introductions focus on a single concept.

Illustrations match the numbered steps.

Numbered steps guide you through each task.

See Also points you to related information in the book.

Did You Know? alerts you to tips, techniques and related information.

Real World Examples

This book uses real world examples files to give you a context in which to use the task. By using the example files, you won't waste time looking for or creating sample files. You get a start file and a result file, so you can compare your work. Not every topic needs an example file, such as changing options, so we provide a complete list of the example files used through out the book. The example files that you need for project tasks along with a complete file list are available on the Web at *www.perspection.com*.

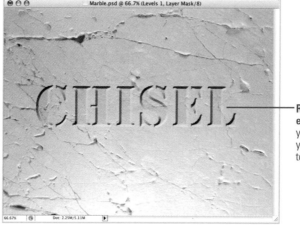

Real world examples help you apply what you've learned to other tasks.

Workshops

This book shows you how to put together the individual step-by-step tasks into in-depth projects with the Workshop. You start each project with a sample file, work through the steps, and then compare your results with project results file at the end. The Workshop projects and associated files are available on the Web at *www.perspection.com*.

Workshops

Introduction

The Workshop is all about being creative and thinking outside of the box. These workshops will help your right-brain soar, while making your left-brain happy by explaining why things work the way they do. Exploring Photoshop's possibilities is great fun; however, always stay grounded with the knowledge of how things work. Knowledge is power.

Getting and Using the Project Files

Each project in the Workshop includes a start file to help you get started with the project, and a final file to provide you with the results so you can see how well you accomplished the task.

Before you can use the project files, you need to download them from the Web. You can access the files at *www.perspection.com*. After you download the files, uncompress them into a folder on your hard drive.

Project 1: Scaling an Image Using Content-Aware

Skills and Tools: Content-Aware Scale, Refine Edge, and Blending Mode

One of the exciting new features in Photoshop CS4 is Content-Aware Scaling. This command looks for the focal point in your image and then identifies pixel areas that are less important and adds or subtracts pixels in those areas as necessary as you scale the image, leaving the focal point unchanged (unless you go too far).

The Project

In this project, you'll use the Content-Aware Scaling feature along with other refining tools to modify and enhance a photograph.

The Process

1. Open the file Red_Rock_Canyon_start.psd in Photoshop and then save it as my_Red_Rock_Canyon.psd.

2. Be sure you're not working on a locked layer (like the Background). If necessary, double click on the word 'Background' and rename it. Duplicate the layer by dragging it on to the New Layer icon or using Ctrl+J (Win) Command+J (Mac). Duplicating the layer will enable you to

501

The **Workshop** walks you through in-depth projects to help you put Photoshop to work.

Adobe Certified Expert

This book prepares you fully for the Adobe Certified Expert (ACE) exam for Adobe Photoshop CS4. Each Adobe Certified Expert certification level has a set of objectives, which are organized into broader skill sets. To prepare for the certification exam, you should review and perform each task identified with a Adobe Certified Expert objective to confirm that you can meet the requirements for the exam. Throughout this book, content that pertains to an objective is identified with the Adobe Certified Expert logo and objective number next to it.

Adobe Certified Expert

About the Adobe Certified Expert (ACE) Program

The Adobe Certified Expert (ACE) program is for graphic designers, Web designers, systems integrators, value-added resellers, developers, and business professionals seeking official recognition of their expertise on Adobe products.

What Is an ACE?

An Adobe Certified Expert is an individual who has passed an Adobe Product Proficiency Exam for a specific Adobe software product. Adobe Certified Experts are eligible to promote themselves to clients or employers as highly skilled, expert-level users of Adobe software. ACE certification is a recognized worldwide standard for excellence in Adobe software knowledge. There are three levels of ACE certification: Single product certification, Specialist certification, and Master certification. To become an ACE, you must pass one or more product-specific proficiency exam and sign the ACE program agreement. When you become an ACE, you enjoy these special benefits:

- Professional recognition
- An ACE program certificate
- Use of the Adobe Certified Expert program logo

What Does This Logo Mean?

It means this book will prepare you fully for the Adobe Certified Expert exam for Adobe Photoshop CS4. The certification exam has a set of objectives, which are organized into broader skill sets. Throughout this book, content that pertains to an ACE objective is identified with the following Adobe Certified Expert logo and objective number below the title of the topic:

525

Logo indicates a task fulfills one or more Adobe Certified Expert objectives.

Get More on the Web

In addition to the information in this book, you can also get more information on the Web to help you get up to speed faster with Photoshop CS4. Some of the information includes:

Transition Helpers

◆ **Only New Features.** Download and print the new feature tasks as a quick and easy guide.

Productivity Tools

◆ **Keyboard Shortcuts.** Download a list of keyboard shortcuts to learn faster ways to get the job done.

More Content

◆ **Photographs.** Download photographs and other graphics to use in your Photoshop documents.

◆ **More Content.** Download new content developed after publication.

You can access these additional resources on the Web at *www.perspection.com.*

Keyboard Shortcuts

Adobe Photoshop CS4 is a powerful program with many commands, which some-times can be time consuming to access. Most menu commands have a keyboard equivalent, known as a **keyboard shortcut**, as a quicker alternative to using the mouse. For example, if you want to open a new document in Photoshop, you click the File menu, and then click New, or you can abandon the mouse and press Ctrl+N (Win) or ⌘+N (Mac) to use shortcut keys. Using shortcut keys reduces the use of the mouse and speeds up operations. If a command on a menu includes a keyboard shortcut to the right of the command name, you can perform the action by pressing and holding the first key, and then pressing the second key to perform the command quickly. In some cases, a keyboard shortcut uses one key or three keys. For three keys, simply press and hold the first two keys, and then press the third key. Keyboard shortcuts provide an alternative to using the mouse and make it easy to per-form repetitive commands.

Finding a Keyboard Shortcut

Photoshop contains keyboard shortcuts for almost every command and task in the program. To help you find the keyboard shortcut you're looking for, the shortcuts are organized in categories and listed with page numbers.

Actions, 21
Adobe Bridge, 23
Animations, 21
Blending Modes, 16
Brushes, 18
Channel Palettes, 16
Color, 17
Dialog Boxes, 21
Display, 8
Edit, 3
File (Documents), 2
Filters, 18

History, 20
Image, 13
Layers, 13
Paths, 19
Photoshop, 2
Quick Masks, 19
Selecting, 10
Tools, 3
Transform, 21
Type, 10
View, 8

If you're searching for new keyboard shortcuts in Adobe Photoshop CS4, just look for the letter: **N**. The **N** appears in the Keyboard Shortcuts table so you can quickly and easily identify new shortcuts.

Additional content is available on the Web.

Getting Started with Photoshop CS4

Introduction

Adobe Photoshop CS4 is a graphics design and image enhancement program that runs seamlessly on both Windows and Macintosh platforms. Adobe Photoshop comes in two editions: Photoshop CS4 and Photoshop CS4 Extended. Photoshop CS4 Extended edition has all the same features included in the standard edition. However, the Extended edition contains additional features geared towards creating more sophisticated content. Adobe Photoshop CS4 and Photoshop CS4 Extended are stand-alone programs, but they're also part of Adobe's Creative Suite of professional programs that work together to help you create designs in print, on the Web, or on mobile devices. All Creative Suite 4 programs also include additional Adobe programs—Bridge, Version Cue, Device Central, and Extension Manager—to help you manage and work with files.

Creative artists from Hollywood, brochure designers, as well as casual users turn to Photoshop for its proven ability to create special effects and image composites. Photoshop's ability to manipulate digital images, restore old photographs, as well as create digital artwork from scratch, has made Photoshop the undisputed leader in the digital industry. When it comes to digital imaging, Photoshop is literally the best software the computer industry has to offer.

Photoshop accepts images created with any digital camera, or traditional photographic film images converted to digital format through the use of a scanner. Once an image is opened in Photoshop, the designer can manipulate the image thousands of ways, from correcting color, reducing dust and scratches in an old image, removing a tree, or adding a missing friend.

What You'll Do

Install and Start Photoshop

View the Photoshop Window

Work with Panels

Work with Photoshop Tools

Create a New Document

Select Color Modes and Resolution

Create a New Document for Video Using Presets

Work with Non-Square Pixels

Open Images

Import Raw Data and Insert Images

Work with Smart Objects

Change Image Size and Resolution

Check for Updates and Patches

Get Help While You Work

Save a Document

Use the Status Bar

Close a Document

Finish Up

Installing Photoshop

To perform a standard program install, insert the Photoshop CS4 DVD into the DVD player on your computer or download the software online and start the setup program, following the onscreen instructions. Make sure to have your serial number handy because you'll be asked to enter it during the installation process. If you're updating from a previous version of Photoshop, you'll be required to verify the older version by instructing Photoshop where to find the previous version on your hard drive, or by inserting the previous version's install disk. Adobe, in an attempt to thwart software piracy, now requires online or phone activation of the program. The process can be postponed for 30 days. However, at the end of 30 days, the Photoshop program will shut down if it has not been properly activated. You can't blame Adobe for attempting to protect their products, since some surveys suggest there are more pirated than purchased versions of Photoshop in use.

Install Photoshop CS4 in Windows

1. Insert the Photoshop CS4 DVD into your DVD ROM drive, or download the software online to your hard disk.

2. If necessary, double-click the DVD icon or open the folder with the downloaded software, and then double-click the setup icon.

3. Follow the onscreen instructions.

IMPORTANT *During the installation process, Photoshop requires you to activate the program. Activation (using the Internet or by phone), must be accomplished within 30 days of installation, or Photoshop will cease to function.*

Did You Know?

The DVD comes with bonus content. The Resources and Extras DVD included with Adobe CS4 products includes bonus content and files in the Goodies folder. Check it out! For more free online resources, go to *www.adobe.com* and visit Adobe Studio Exchange.

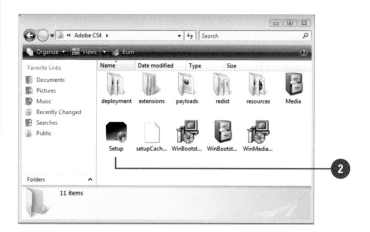

Install Photoshop CS4 in Macintosh

1 Insert the Photoshop CS4 DVD into your DVD ROM drive, or download the software online to your hard disk.

2 If necessary, double-click the DVD icon or open the folder with the downloaded software, and then double-click the setup icon.

3 Follow the onscreen instructions.

Did You Know?

You can create a shortcut on the Macintosh. Drag and drop the Photoshop program to the bottom of the monitor screen, and then add it to the shortcuts panel.

Photoshop CS4 System Requirements

Hardware/Software	Minimum (Recommended)
WINDOWS	
Computer Processor	1.8 GHz or faster processor
Operating System	Microsoft Windows XP SP2 (3) or Vista SP1
Hard Drive	1 GB of available space
Available RAM	512 MB (1 GB recommended)
Video Card	16-bit (GPU-equipped video card for OpenGL features)
Monitor Resolution	1024 x 768 (1280 x 800 or dual monitors)
DVD-ROM drive	Any type
MACINTOSH	
Computer Processor	Power PC G5 or multi-core Intel-based Macs
Operating System	Macintosh OS X 10.4.11 or higher
Hard Drive	2 GB of available space
Available RAM	512 MB (1 GB recommended)
Video Card	16-bit (GPU-equipped video card for OpenGL features)
Monitor Resolution	1024 x 768 (1280 x 800 or dual monitors)
DVD-ROM drive	Any type (SuperDrive for DVD burning)
Additional	
QuickTime 7.2	Required for multimedia features

Starting Photoshop

You can launch Photoshop like any other program. After you launch Photoshop, the program checks for updates to Photoshop and related CS4 software—including Adobe Bridge, and Adobe Help Viewer—using the Adobe Updater. If you want to access the Adobe Updater at any time, you can choose Updates from the Help menu. Once inside this dialog box, you can click on Preferences to set Adobe Updater Preferences options. You can choose to check for updates weekly or monthly and you can also specify whether you want Adobe to automatically download updates or ask before performing the download. See "Checking for Updates and Patches" on page 24 for information on using the Adobe Updater Preferences dialog box.

Start Photoshop CS4 in Windows

1. Click **Start** on the taskbar.

2. Point to **All Programs** (which changes to Back).

3. Point to an Adobe Collection CS4 menu, if needed.

4. Click **Adobe Photoshop CS4**.

5. If you're starting Photoshop CS4 for the first time, perform the following:

   ◆ Enter your serial number, and then click **OK** to continue.

   ◆ Click **OK** to complete the activation process.

   ◆ Fill in the registration form, and then click **Register Now**.

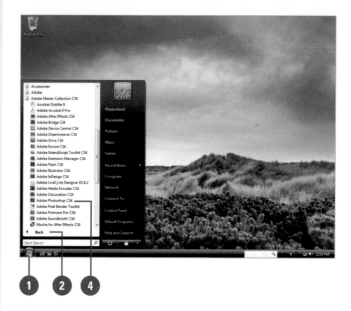

Did You Know?

You can create and use a shortcut icon on your desktop to start Photoshop (Win). Click Start on the taskbar, point to All Programs, right-click Adobe Photoshop CS4, point to Send To, and then click Desktop (Create Shortcut). Double-click the shortcut icon on your desktop to start Photoshop.

Start Photoshop CS4 in Macintosh

1 Open the **Applications** folder (located on the main hard drive).

2 Double-click the **Adobe Photoshop CS4** folder.

3 Double-click the **Adobe Photoshop CS4** program icon.

4 If you're starting Photoshop CS4 for the first time, perform the following:

◆ Enter your serial number, and then click **OK** to continue.

◆ Click **OK** to complete the activation process.

◆ Fill in the registration form, click **Register Now**.

Did You Know?

You can create a shortcut on the Macintosh. Drag and drop the Photoshop application to the bottom of the monitor screen, and then add it to the dock.

You can create and use a keyboard shortcut to start Photoshop (Win). Click Start on the taskbar, point to All Programs, right-click Adobe Photoshop CS4, and then click Properties. In the Shortcut Key box, type or press any letter, number, or function key, such as P, to which Windows adds Ctrl+Alt. Click OK to create the keyboard shortcut. From anywhere in Windows, press the keyboard shortcut you defined (Ctrl+Alt+P) to start Photoshop.

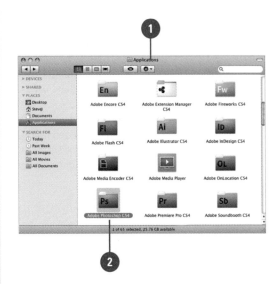

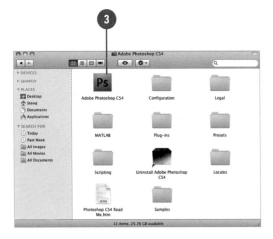

Shortcut for Photoshop CS4

Viewing the Photoshop Window

Options Bar
Displays options for the
active tool.

Toolbox
Gives you
access to
all of the
drawing,
painting, and
selection
tools.

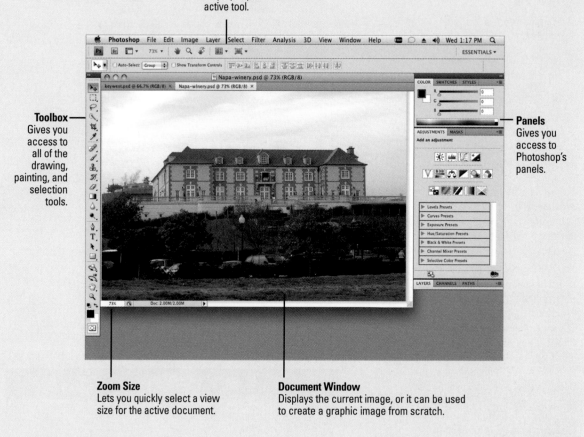

Panels
Gives you
access to
Photoshop's
panels.

Zoom Size
Lets you quickly select a view
size for the active document.

Document Window
Displays the current image, or it can be used
to create a graphic image from scratch.

Showing and Hiding Panels

Panels give you easy access to many task-specific commands and operations from color control to vector path information. By default, the main panel display is located along the right side of your window. You can use the Window menu or click a panel tab within a group to display it, and then select options on the panel or choose panel-specific commands from the Panel Options menu to perform actions. Instead of continually moving, resizing, or opening and closing windows, you can use the header bar with the panel tabs to collapse or expand individual panels within a window to save space.

Open and Close a Panel

1. Click the **Window** menu.

2. Click a panel name, such as Color, Layers, Navigator, Options, or Tools.

   TIMESAVER *To close a panel, or a single tab, click the Options menu and then click Close Tab Group or Close (for a single tab). On the Mac, you can also click the Close button on the panel.*

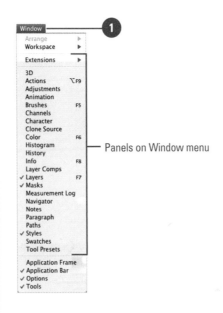

Panels on Window menu

Collapse or Expand a Panel

1. To collapse or expand an open panel, click the dark gray area or double-click a title tab on the header bar of the panel.

   If the panel is in icon mode, click on the icon to expand it. To reduce the panel back to icon mode, click on the double right-facing arrows in the dark gray area or click once on the title tab.

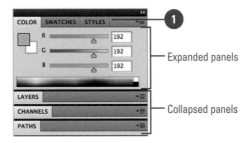

Expanded panels

Collapsed panels

Working with Panels

 PS 1.1

The movable panels are organized into groups, such as Color/Swatches/Styles and History/Actions, to save screen space and help with workflow. You can also add or subtract specific panels within a group to customize your workspace. A panel appears with a header, which includes the tab titles and three options: the Collapse to Icons button, the Close button, and an Options menu. The Options menu provides you with panel commands. The entire set of panels includes a double arrow at the top you can use to collapse and expand the entire panel back and forth between icons and full panels.

Add a Panel

1. Select a panel by clicking on the named panel, or click the **Window** menu, and then click the panel name you want to display.

2. Drag the panel into another group.

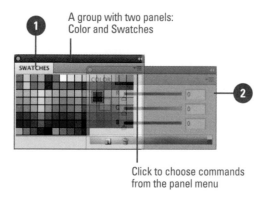

A group with two panels: Color and Swatches

Click to choose commands from the panel menu

Subtract a Panel

1. Select a panel by clicking on the named panel or click the **Window** menu, and then click the panel name you want to display.

2. Drag the panel out of the group.

3. Drop it onto the desktop (Mac) or Photoshop window (Win).

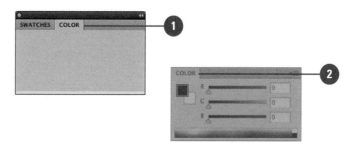

For Your Information

Hiding Panels While You Work

If Photoshop's panels get in the way, just press the Tab key to temporarily hide all the panels. Or, you can hold down the Shift key, and then press the Tab key to hide the panels, but leave the Toolbox and Options bar. Press the Tab key again to restore all the panels to their most recent positions.

Collapse and Expand the Panel Set Between Icons and Panels

◆ To collapse the panel set to icons with text, click the double arrow pointing right (Collapse to Icons) at the top of the panels.

◆ To expand the panel set from icons with text to full panels, click the double arrow pointing left (Expand Panels) at the top of the panels.

◆ To have an expanded panel icon automatically collapse or hide when you click away, right-click (Win) or Control-click (Mac) a panel, and then click **Auto-Collapse Icon Panels** or **Auto-Show Hidden Panels** (New!).

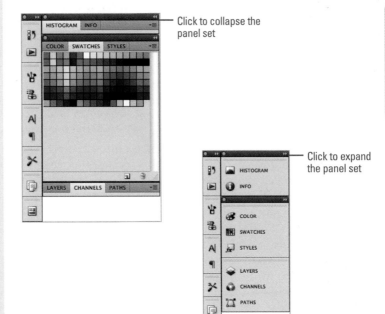

Click to collapse the panel set

Click to expand the panel set

Use the Panel Options Menu

1 Open or expand a panel.

2 Click the **Options** button on the right side of the panel header bar.

3 Click a command from the list (commands vary). Common commands include:

◆ **Close.** Closes the currently displayed tab in the panel.

◆ **Close Tab Group.** Closes all the tabs in the panel.

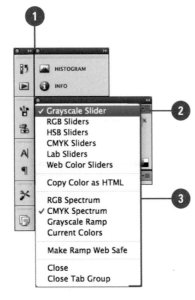

Working with Photoshop Tools

Adobe Certified Expert   PS 1.2

Photoshop has an abundance of tools that give a Photoshop designer tremendous control over any creative designing problems that may crop up. For example, the Photoshop toolbox contains 8 selection tools (you can never have enough selection tools), 10 painting or shape tools, 4 type tools, and 12 tools dedicated to restoring and retouching images. Add to that collection, slicing, sampling, and viewing tools and you have a total of 70 tools. When you work on a document, it's important to know what tools are available, and how they can help in achieving your design goals. Photoshop likes to save space, so it consolidates similar tools under one button. To access multiple tools, click and hold on any toolbox button that contains a small black triangle, located in the lower right corner of the tool button. Take a moment to explore the Photoshop toolbox and get to know the tools.

The Photoshop toolbox contains the tools needed to work through any Photoshop job, but it's not necessary to click on a tool to access it. Simply using a letter of the alphabet can access all of Photoshop's tools. For example, pressing the V key switches to the Move tool, and pressing the W key switches to the Magic Wand tool. In addition, if a button has more than one tool available, such as the Gradient and Paint Bucket buttons, pressing the Shift key along with the tool's shortcut lets you cycle through the tool's other options. You can quicker move between tools using Spring-loaded keys (**New!**). Rather than go back to the toolbox when you want to switch tools, just hold down the shortcut letter key for the new tool, use the tool, and then let go of the shortcut key and you'll be back using the first tool.

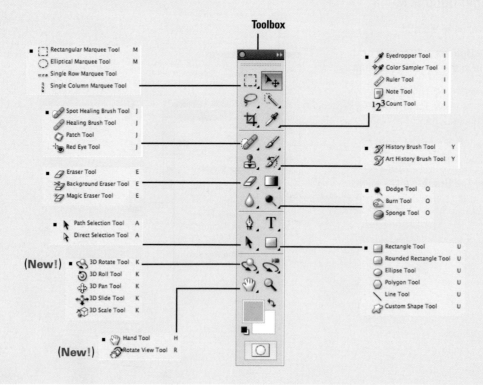

Toolbox

- Rectangular Marquee Tool   M
  Elliptical Marquee Tool   M
  Single Row Marquee Tool
  Single Column Marquee Tool

- Spot Healing Brush Tool   J
  Healing Brush Tool   J
  Patch Tool   J
  Red Eye Tool   J

- Eraser Tool   E
  Background Eraser Tool   E
  Magic Eraser Tool   E

- Path Selection Tool   A
  Direct Selection Tool   A

(New!) - 3D Rotate Tool   K
  3D Roll Tool   K
  3D Pan Tool   K
  3D Slide Tool   K
  3D Scale Tool   K

- Hand Tool   H
(New!) Rotate View Tool   R

- Eyedropper Tool   I
  Color Sampler Tool   I
  Ruler Tool   I
  Note Tool   I
  Count Tool   I

- History Brush Tool   Y
  Art History Brush Tool   Y

- Dodge Tool   O
  Burn Tool   O
  Sponge Tool   O

- Rectangle Tool   U
  Rounded Rectangle Tool   U
  Ellipse Tool   U
  Polygon Tool   U
  Line Tool   U
  Custom Shape Tool   U

You can refer to Adobe Photoshop CS4 Keyboard Shortcuts (available for download on the Web at *www.perspection.com*) for more information on all the letter assignments for the various tools. To really get efficient in Photoshop, you need to learn to use both hands. Use one hand for your mouse or drawing tablet, and the other on the keyboard to make quick changes of tools and options.

Using the Options Bar

The Options bar displays the options for the currently selected tool. If you are working with the Shape Marquee tools, your options include Feather, Style, Width, and Height. When working with the Brush tools, available tool options include Size, Mode, Opacity, and Tolerance. The Airbrush mode of the Brush tool also includes Flow. The Pencil tool options include Auto Erase along with the standard Brush tool options. The Standard Shape tool Options bar includes Fill Pixels, Weight, Radius, Style, and Color. The important thing to remember is that the Options bar is customized based on the tool you have selected. For more information on these options, refer to Chapters 4, 6, and 9.

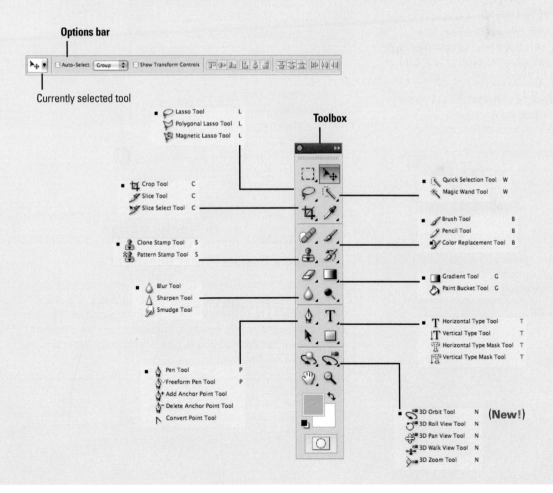

Creating a New Document

Creating a new Photoshop document requires more thought than creating a new word processing document. For example, there are resolution and color mode considerations to keep in mind. You can create as many new documents as you need for your current project. However, since opening more than one document takes more processing power, it's probably best to work on only one new document at a time. Once a new document is created, you have access to all of Photoshop's design and manipulation tools to create anything you can imagine.

Create a New Document

1. Click the **File** menu, and then click **New**.

2. Type a name for the document.

   IMPORTANT *Typing a name does not save the document. You still need to save your document after you create it.*

3. Click the **Preset** list arrow, and then select a preset document, or choose your own options to create a custom document.

   ◆ **Width and Height.** Select from various measurements, such as points, centimeters, or inches.

   ◆ **Resolution.** Select a resolution, such as 72 pixels/inch (ppi) for online use and 300 ppi for print.

   ◆ **Color Mode.** Select a color mode, such as RGB for color and Grayscale for black/white.

   ◆ **Background Contents.** Select a background color or a transparent background.

4. Click **OK**.

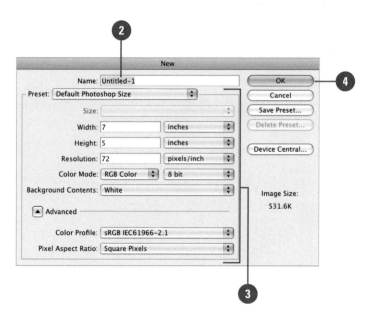

For Your Information

Creating a Custom Preset Document

You may find that you use the same new document size over and over again. To save time, you can save the settings as a preset. In the New dialog box, click the Preset list arrow, click a setting, and then change the various options to customize your new document. To name your customized preset, type a name in the Name box, and then click Save Preset.

Selecting Color Modes and Resolution

Selecting a Color Mode

A **color mode**, also known as **color space**, determines how Photoshop displays and prints an image. You choose a different color mode (based on models used in publishing) for different tasks. You can choose a color mode when you create a new document or change a color mode for an existing document. The common color modes include:

Grayscale.   Best for printing black-and-white and duotone images. This mode uses one channel and has a maximum of 256 shades of gray.

RGB (Red, Green, and Blue).   Best for online and multimedia color images. Red, green, and blue are also the primary colors on a monitor.

CMYK (Cyan, Magenta, Yellow, and Black).
Best for commercial printing of color images.

LAB (Luminosity, A and B channels).   Best for performing image correction. This mode puts all grayscale information on the L channel and splits the colors to the A and B channels.

For more information on color, see Chapter 8, "Understanding Colors and Channels."

Selecting Image Resolution

Photoshop works primarily with raster documents. **Raster** documents are images composed of pixels. A **pixel** is a unit of information that holds the color and detail information of the image. Think of a Photoshop document as a brick wall, with the individual bricks in the wall representing the individual pixels in the image. Documents opened in Photoshop have a specific resolution. The **resolution** of the image, along with its width and height, represents how many pixels the image contains. Since pixels (the bricks in the wall) represent information, the more pixels a document contains, the more information Photoshop has to manipulate or enhance the image.

A typical 17-inch monitor displays pixels at a resolution of 1,024 x 768 pixels per inch. You can figure out how many pixels are present on a 17-inch monitor by multiplying 1,024 x 768, which equals 786,432 pixels on the screen. The resolution is equal to how many pixels fit into each monitor inch, otherwise known as **ppi** (pixels per inch). A typical monitor displays pixels at 72 pixels per inch.

To determine the size of an image in inches, we divide the pixels by the ppi. For example, an image 1,024 pixels wide at 72 ppi would be 14.2 inches wide (1,024 / 72 = 14.2). To determine the pixels present in an image, you multiple the size by the ppi. For example, a 3 inch image at 72 ppi would have a total of 216 pixels (3 x 72 = 216). As the image resolution drops, so does the output quality of the image. **Pixelization** occurs when the resolution is so low that the edges of the pixel begin to appear. The higher the resolution (more pixels), the sharper your image will be. However, the higher the resolution, the larger the file size will become. To optimize your image file size, you need to use the correct resolution for the specific task. Use 72 ppi for web pages, CD-ROMs, and multimedia; use 150 ppi for inkjet printers, 200 ppi for photo printers, and 300 ppi for commercial printing.

When working with images, it's always a good idea to start with a larger image size. You can always reduce the size of the image (subtract pixels) without losing any quality. If you need to enlarge an image, you run the risk of losing image quality. When you enlarge an image, the number of pixels doesn't increase as the image does, so the pixels become larger, which results in a rougher, or more pixelated, image.

Creating a New Document Using Presets

PS 10.4

When you create documents for specific purposes, such as, web, film, video, or for use on a mobile device, you know the importance of creating documents that will perfectly match the output requirements of the intended file destination. The preset file sizes available in the Preset menu let you create images at a size and pixel aspect ratio that compensate for scaling when you incorporate them into various output modes. When you work with the Preset menu, the guesswork involved in creating compatible photo, web, mobile device, film and video documents in Photoshop is a thing of the past.

Create a New Document Using Presets

1. Click the **File** menu, and then click **New**.

2. Click the **Preset** list arrow, and then select from the available presets:

   - Photo
   - Web
   - Mobile & Devices
   - Film & Video
   - Custom

3. Click the **Size** list arrow, and then select the preset you want. The options vary depending on the type of document you want to create.

   - **Photo.** For example, Landscape 4 x 6.

   - **Web.** For example, 640 x480.

   - **Mobile & Devices.** For example, 176 x 208.

   - **Film & Video.** For example, HDTV 1080p/29.97.

4. If you want, adjust the available options.

5. Click **OK**.

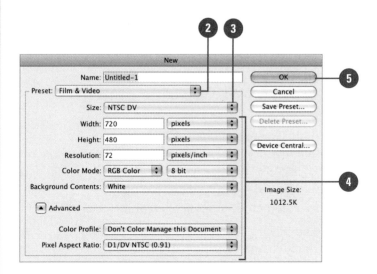

For Your Information

Using a Video Preview Option

Photoshop now includes a Video Preview option that lets you preview your documents on a display device such as a standard or DVD screen. The device must be attached to your computer through the use of a FireWire port. Once the device is attached, open a document, click the File menu, point to Export, and then click Send Video Preview to Device. To set output options before viewing your document on the device, click the File menu, point to Export, and then click Video Preview. The Video Preview option supports RGB, grayscale, and indexed color images, in either 8 or 16 bits per channel. You can adjust the aspect ratio for proper display of images. First, select the aspect ratio of the display device, either Standard (4:3) or Widescreen (16:9), and then select a placement option, such as Center or Crop to 4:3, for the image. To maintain an image's (nonsquare) pixel aspect ratio, select the Apply Pixel Aspect Ratio to Preview check box.

Working with Non-Square Pixels

Images displayed on a computer monitor are made up of square pixels. Conversely, an image displayed on a video monitor is not composed of pixels at all. Non-square pixels are most commonly used by encoding devices for video production. When importing an image created by a square-pixel graphics program into a video editing program such as Adobe Premiere, the square pixels are automatically scaled to non-square pixels for video encoding. This scaling results in a distorted image. By default, non-square pixel documents open with Pixel Aspect Ratio Correction enabled. This enables you to preview how the image will appear on an output device such as a video monitor, and see how it will appear when exported to an analog video device. In keeping with an ever-changing industry, Adobe includes the following Pixel Aspect Ratio options: DVCPRO HD 1080 (1.5) and HDV 1080/DVCPRO HD 720 (1.33).

Work with Non-Square Pixels

1. Click the **File** menu, and then click **New**.

2. On the bottom of the New dialog box, click the **Pixel Aspect Ratio** list arrow, select any of the non-square pixel settings, and then click **OK**.

3. Click the **Window** menu, point to **Arrange**, and then click **New Window** to create a new window for the active document.

4. Click the **Window** menu, point to **Arrange**, and then click **Tile** to view both images side-by-side.

5. Select the new window.

6. Click the **View** menu, and then click **Pixel Aspect Ratio** to toggle between corrected view and uncorrected view. (The default is corrected.)

   The original window shows the corrected aspect ratio, and the new window displays the same document without pixel aspect ratio correction.

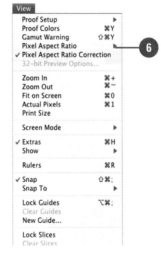

Image with a non-square pixel ratio

Opening Images

Photoshop lets you open image files created in different formats, such as TIFF, JPEG, GIF, and PNG, as well as Photoshop documents in the PSD or PSB formats. If you want to simply open an image or Photoshop document, the Open dialog box is the most efficient way. However, if you need to manage, organize, or process files, Adobe Bridge is the way to go. You open an existing Photoshop document or image file the same way you open documents in other programs. However, you have two Open dialog box display options: Adobe or OS.

Open an Image

1 Click the **File** menu, and then click **Open** to display all file types in the file list of the Open dialog box.

> **TIMESAVER** *Point to the Open Recent command on the File menu to quickly open a recent file.*

2 To use a different Open dialog box display, click **Use Adobe Dialog** or click **Use OS Dialog**.

3 Click the **Files of Type** (Win) or **Enable** (Mac) list arrow, and then select a format.

4 Click the the **Look In** (Win) or **Where** (Mac) list arrow, and then choose the location where the image you want to open is stored.

5 Click the image file you want to open.

> **TIMESAVER** *Press and hold the Shift key to select multiple contiguous files to open in the Open dialog box.*

6 Click **Open**.

See Also

See "Understanding File Formats" on page 381 for information on the different file formats.

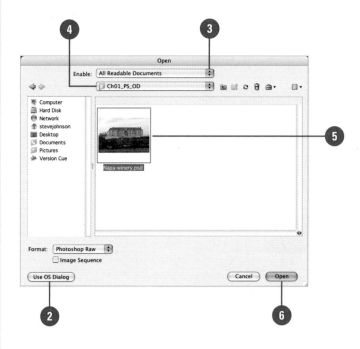

For Your Information

Opening a File as Another Format

The Open As command on the File menu allows you to open a file in Photoshop that was saved incorrectly (with the wrong extension) or is being moved between Windows and Macintosh systems. Click the File menu, click Open As, select the file you want to open (if you do not see the file you want, choose the option to display all files), select the correct format from the Open As (Win) or Format (Mac) list arrow, and then click Open. If the file does not open, then the chosen format may not match the file's real format, or the file may be damaged.

Inserting Images in a Document

You can use Photoshop's Place command to insert artwork into an open document. To increase your control of the new image information, Photoshop places the new image into a separate layer. Photoshop lets you place files saved in PDF, Adobe Illustrator, and EPS formats. When you first place a vector-based image into Photoshop, you have the ability to modify the width, height, and rotation while retaining the vector format of the file. However, since Photoshop is primarily a raster program, when you finalize your changes, Photoshop rasterizes the file information (converts the vector data into pixels), and saves it as a Smart Object, which means you can no longer edit the placed document as you would a vector shape or path. However, you can still open up the Smart Object in the original file, and make changes to update it.

Insert an Image in a Document Using the Place Command

1 Open a Photoshop document.

2 Click the **File** menu, and then click **Place**.

3 Select the document you want to place into the active document.

4 Click **Place**.

Photoshop places the image in a new layer, directly above the active layer, and then encloses it within a transformable bounding box.

5 Control the shape by manipulating the corner and side nodes of the freeform bounding box.

6 Press Enter (Win) or Return (Mac) to rasterize the image at the resolution of the active document.

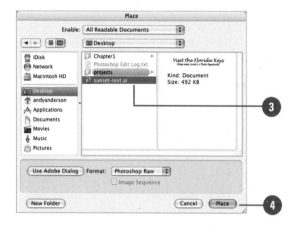

Did You Know?

You can scan images into Photoshop. With the scanner hardware and software connected and installed (including the Twain plug-in), click the File menu, point to Import, click Twain, set scan settings, and then click Scan.

Freeform bounding box

New layer placed

Importing Raw Data from a Digital Camera

PS 1.6, 7.1, 7.2, 7.3, 7.5

Raw image file formats are available with most mid- to high-end digital cameras and contain information about how the image was taken. The raw format turns off all camera adjustments, and saves the image information to a digital memory card. When you open a raw file, Photoshop opens Camera Raw, allowing you to adjust image details. If you're not sure what to do, you can click Auto to have Camera Raw do it or drag color sliders to adjust options manually. You can adjust color tones, reduce noise, correct for lens defects, add post-crop vignetting (**New!**) and retouch images with the Heal, Clone and Red Eye tools. To adjust color tones, you can make changes to exposure, highlights recovery, fill light, brightness, contrast and saturation—with Vibrance and Saturation. Raw images are larger; however, the increase in file size is actually more information that can be used by Camera Raw. In addition, raw images can be converted into 16-bit mode, which provides more control over adjustments such as tonal and color correction. Once processed, raw images can be saved in the DNG (Digital Negative), TIFF, PSD, PSB, or JPEG formats. When a raw file is placed as a Smart Object, Photoshop embeds the raw data within the document, allowing you to change the raw settings and update the converted layer.

Import a Camera Raw File

1. Click the **File** menu, and then click **Open**.

   ◆ To place a raw file as a Smart Object, click the **File** menu, and then click **Place**.

2. Click the **Files of Type** (Win) or **Enable** (Mac) list arrow, and then click **Camera Raw**.

3. Select a single raw image file, or Ctrl (Win) or ⌘ (Mac)+ click to select more than one file.

4. Click **Open**.

   The Camera Raw dialog box opens, displaying the Basic tab.

5. Click any of the tabs—**Basic, Tone Curve, Detail** (Sharpen & Noise Reduction), **HSL / Grayscale, Split Toning, Lens Correction, Camera Calibrations,** or **Presets**—to change the options you want.

6. To automatically make tonal adjustments, click **Auto** on the Basic tab, and then make any other manual adjustments.

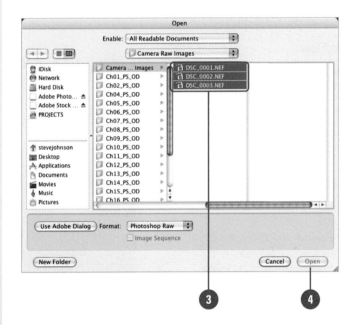

7 Use the following tools to modify the image:

◆ Use the **Zoom**, **Hand**, **Rotate**, **Crop**, and **Straighten** tools to change the size, orientation, and position of the image.

◆ Use the **White Balance** tool to set the image white balance or the **Color Sampler** tool to sample a color from the image.

◆ Use the **Spot Removal** or **Red Eye Removal** tool to fix the image.

◆ Use the **Adjustment Brush** or **Gradient Filter** tool (**New!**) to make adjustments to exposure, brightness, contrast, saturation, clarity, sharpness, and color.

8 There are two areas of the screen related to image view:

◆ **Image Preview.** If checked, displays current version of image with all changes that have been made.

◆ **Zoom Level.** Changes to the level of image magnification can be made here.

9 Click the filename to change the (color) Space, (bit) Depth, Size, and Resolution of the image.

10 Click **Save Image(s)** to specify a folder destination, file name, and format for the processed images.

11 Select the images you want to synchronize (apply settings) in the Filmstrip (if desired, click **Select All**), and then click **Synchronize**.

12 Click the **Camera Raw Menu** button to **Load**, **Save**, or **Delete** a specific set of Raw settings.

13 When you're done, click **Done** to process the file, but not open it, or click **Open Image(s)** to process and open it in Photoshop. Hold Alt (Win) or Option (Mac) to use **Open Copy** or **Reset**.

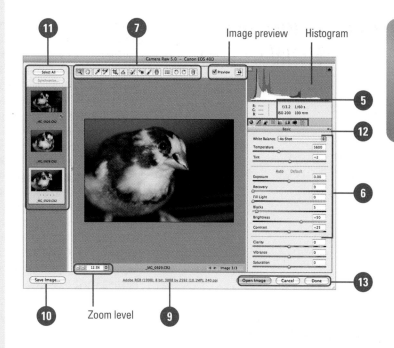

Image preview   Histogram

Zoom level

Basic tab

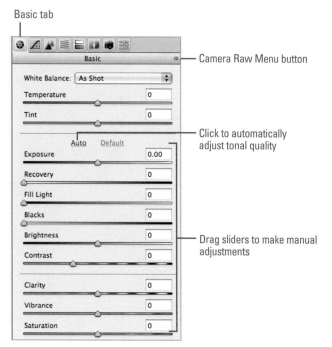

Camera Raw Menu button

Click to automatically adjust tonal quality

Drag sliders to make manual adjustments

Working with Smart Objects

 PS 7.1, 10.1, 10.2

A **Smart Object** is a container in which you can embed raster (e.g., PSD, JPEG, TIFF) or vector (e.g., AI, PDF, EPS) image data from another Photoshop or Adobe Illustrator file that retains all its original character- istics and remains fully editable. A Smart Object can be scaled, rotated, and warped nondestructively without losing original image data. Smart Objects store source data with the original object, so you can work on a representation of the image without changing the original—resulting in one file embedded within another. For example, when an Illustrator Smart Object is double-clicked in the Layers panel, Photoshop starts Illustrator and opens a working copy of the artwork. When you make changes in Illustrator and then save the file, Photoshop automatically re-rasterizes the file. If you duplicate a Smart Object, Photoshop stores only one copy of the source data while creating a second instance of the composite data, thus saving valuable disk space. When you edit one Smart Object, Photoshop updates all the copies. In addition, you can link Smart Objects to their layer mask (**New!**) so they can be move together. You can create Smart Objects by converting selected layers, pasting Illustrator data from the clipboard, using the Place command to insert a file, or using the Open As Smart Object command.

Work with Smart Objects

1. Use one of the following to create a Smart Object:

   ◆ Click the **File** menu, click **Open As Smart Object**, select a file, and then click **Open**.

   ◆ Click the **File** menu, and then click **Place** to import into an open Photoshop document.

   ◆ Select a layer, click the **Layer** menu, point to **Smart Objects**, and then click **Convert To Smart Object**.

2. If you use **Place** to import a Smart Object, use the bounding box to modify the image to the shape you want.

3. Press Enter (Win) or Return (Mac) to convert the image to a Smart Object (in the Layers panel).

4. To make a copy, drag the Smart Object layer to the New Layer button.

5. Double-click the thumbnail of the original or copy to open the editor for the Smart Object.

Copy of Smart Object

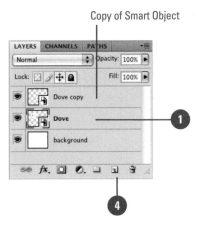

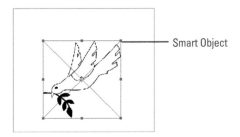

Smart Object

6 Make the desired changes to the image, save, and then close the editor window.

7 When you're done working with a Smart Object, use any of the following:

◆ **Convert to normal layer.** Select the layer, click the **Layer** menu, point to **Rasterize**, and then click **Smart Object**.

◆ **Export contents.** Select the layer, click the **Layer** menu, point to **Smart Objects**, and then click **Export Contents**.

Photoshop saves the contents in its original format, or PSB if it was created from a layer.

◆ **Replace contents.** Select the layer, click the **Layer** menu, point to **Smart Objects**, click **Replace Contents**, select a file, and then click **Open**.

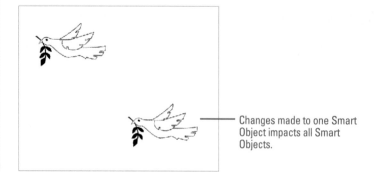

Changes made to one Smart Object impacts all Smart Objects.

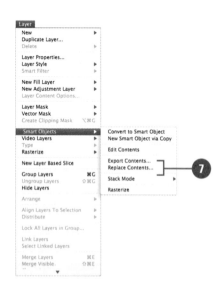

Did You Know?

You can't alter pixel data. If you want to use painting, dodging, burning, or cloning tools, you need to convert the Smart Object layer to a normal layer.

You can apply a filter to a Smart Object. When you apply a filter to a Smart Object, the filter becomes a Smart Filter. Smart Filters appear in the Layers panel below the Smart Object layer, where you can show or hide them independently; they are nondestructive. You can apply any filter, except Liquify and Vanishing Point.

You can convert a 3D layer to a Smart Object (Extended). Select the 3D layer in the Layers panel, click the Options menu, and then click Convert to Smart Object. To reedit the 3D content, double-click the Smart Object layer.

Changing Image Size and Resolution

 PS 1.4

You can modify the size and resolution of a document after opening. However, be aware that changing the size and/or the resolution of an image forces Photoshop to add or subtract pixels from the image in a process called **interpolation**. For example, when you change the resolution of an image from 72 ppi (pixels per inch) to 144 ppi, Photoshop must add more pixels. Conversely, if you reduce the resolution, Photoshop must remove pixels. The image interpolation method determines how Photoshop completes this process. You can use the Nearest Neighbor method for the fastest way, but it produces the poorest visual image. Or, you can use the Bicubic Sharper method, which takes the longest to perform, but produces the best visual results.

Change Image Size

1 Open an image.

2 Click the **Image** menu, and then click **Image Size**.

3 Select the **Resample Image** check box.

4 Click the **Resample Image** list arrow, and then select an option:

- ◆ **Nearest Neighbor.** Best for quick results with low quality.

- ◆ **Bilinear.** Best for line art.

- ◆ **Bicubic.** Default, best for most purposes with high quality.

- ◆ **Bicubic Smoother.** Best for enlarging an image.

- ◆ **Bicubic Sharper.** Best for reducing an image.

5 To maintain image proportions, select the **Constrain Proportions** check box.

6 Enter the desired sizes in the image size boxes.

If you choose to constrain proportions in step 5, when you change a size, the other boxes will adjust automatically.

7 Click **OK**.

Icon indicates constrained proportions

Image Size

Pixel Dimensions: 3.96M

Width: 1440 pixels

Height: 960 pixels

Document Size:

Width: 6 inches

Height: 4 inches

Resolution: 240 pixels/inch

☑ Scale Styles
☑ Constrain Proportions
☑ Resample Image:

Bicubic (best for smooth gradients)

OK   Cancel   Auto...

For Your Information

Using a Large Canvas Size

Photoshop supports documents up to 300,000 pixels in either dimension, with up to 56 channels per file. Photoshop offers three file formats for saving documents greater than 2 GB: PSB, Photoshop RAW, and TIFF. It's important to note that most programs, including older versions of Photoshop (before the CS version), support a maximum file size of 2 GB.

Change Image Resolution

1. Open an image.

2. Click the **Image** menu, and then click **Image Size**.

3. Clear the **Resample Image** check box.

4. Enter a resolution, which automatically adjusts the Width and Height fields.

5. Click **OK**.

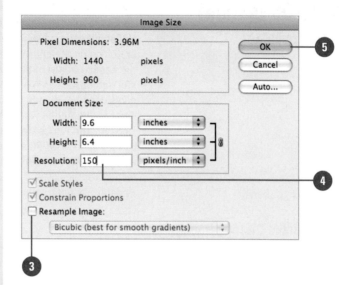

Checking for Updates and Patches

As time passes, Photoshop—like any other program—will change. There are two types of changes to a program: updates and patches. Updates are improvements to a program such as a new feature, option, or command. Patches are software fixes for problems discovered after the public release of the program. The good news is that both updates and patches are free, and once downloaded, are self-installing. Adobe gives you two ways to check for changes. You can check manually by going to the Adobe web site, or automatically through the Adobe Updater. The Adobe Updater Preferences dialog box allows you to set update options for Photoshop and other installed Adobe products, such as Bridge. You can set the update preferences to check for updates monthly or weekly and automatically download them, or have Adobe Updater ask before performing the download.

Check for Updates Directly from the Internet

① Open your Internet browser.

② Go to the following Web address: *www.adobe.com/downloads/ updates/*

③ Click the list arrow, and then click the **Photoshop - Macintosh** or **Photoshop - Windows**.

④ Click **Go**.

Any updates or patches appear in a list.

⑤ Based on your operating system, follow the onscreen instructions to download and install the software.

IMPORTANT *Checking on your own requires a computer with a connection to the Internet. Since some of the updates can be rather large, it's recommended you have high-speed access; 56k is good, but DSL or cable modem is better.*

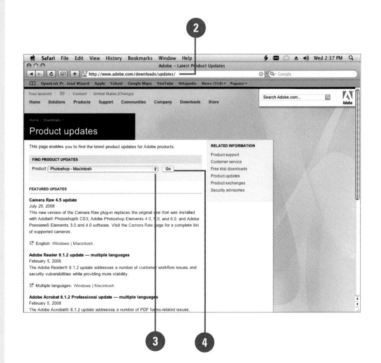

Check for Updates from the Photoshop Help Menu

1 Start Adobe Photoshop, if necessary.

2 Click the **Help** menu, and then click **Updates**.

Photoshop automatically connects you to the Internet, and checks for updates. If there are any updates available, Adobe downloads and installs them.

IMPORTANT *Remember, these files can be quite large. So, if you're running with a slow Internet connection speed, you might want to perform downloading files at a low traffic time. Also, by making sure you don't have other programs running, you can maximize your system's resources for the downloading of files.*

When the check or download is complete, the Adobe Updater dialog box opens.

3 To change Adobe Updater preferences, click **Preferences**, select the **Automatically Check For Adobe Updates** check box, select the update and program options you want, and then click **OK**.

4 Click **Quit**.

Select to update an application.

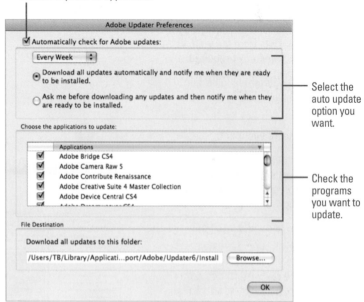

Select the auto update option you want.

Check the programs you want to update.

Getting Help While You Work

At some time, everyone has a question or two about the program they are using. Photoshop Help uses a Community Help site (**New!**) on the web at *adobe.com* (which is updated regularly) to help you find the information you need. When you start Photoshop Help, your browser opens, displaying a web site with Photoshop help categories and topics. You can search the Photoshop Help site by using keywords or phrases or browsing through a list of categories and topics to locate specific information. When you perform a search using keywords or phrases, a list of possible answers is shown to you from adobe.com, with the most likely answer to your question at the top of the list. Along with help text, some help topics include links to text and video tutorials. In addition, comments and ratings from users are available to help guide you to an answer.

Get Help Information

1. Click the **Help** menu, and then click **Photoshop Help**.

   TIMESAVER *Press F1.*

   Your browser opens, displaying Photoshop Help from the web. An Internet connected is required.

2. Click Help categories (plus sign icons) until you display the topic you want.

3. Click the topic you want.

4. Read the topic, and if necessary, click any hyperlinks to get information on related topics or definitions.

5. When you're done, close your browser.

Did You Know?

You can get help with Photoshop through the Internet. Click the Help menu, and then click Photoshop Online (requires an Internet connection) to display Photoshop help resources from all over the Web.

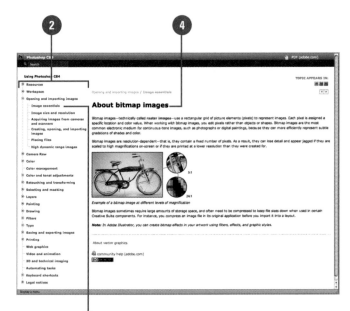

26

Search for Help Information

1 Click the **Help** menu, and then click **Photoshop Help**.

Your browser opens, displaying Photoshop Help from the web. An Internet connected is required.

2 Type one or more keywords in the Search box, and then press Enter (Win) or Return (Mac).

Your browser displays an Adobe web site with a list of topics that match the keywords you entered in the Search box.

3 Click the link to the topic you want from the search list of results.

4 Read the topic, and then if you want, click any hyperlinks to get information on related topics or definitions.

5 When you're done, close your browser.

Did You Know?

You can find out what's new in Photoshop. Click the Help menu, click Photoshop Help, click the plus sign (+) next to Resources, and then click What's New.

You can print out the selected Help topic. Open the Help screen in your browser, select the Help topic you want to print, select the Print command, specify print options, and then click Print (Win) or OK (Mac).

You can move backward and forward between help topics. Click the Previous or Next button on the right side of the Help web page.

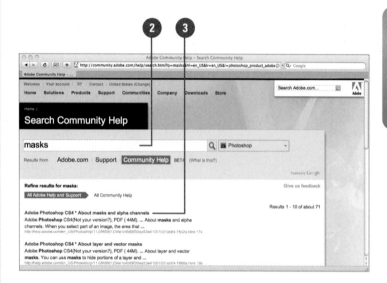

Check What's New

Saving a Document

PS 9.6

When you finish working on your Photoshop document, you need to save it before you close the document or exit Photoshop. While this may seem like a simple task, there are questions that must be asked before saving a file, like *What is the intended final output of the image?* For example, if the document is destined for the Internet, you'll probably save the document using the JPEG, GIF, or PNG formats. Each output device, whether monitor or paper-based, requires a specific format, and it's best to know this information at the beginning of the creation process. Knowing the eventual destination of an image helps you create the design with the output in mind.

Save a Document

1. Click the **File** menu, and then click **Save**.

2. Enter a name for the file in the File Name (Win) or Save As (Mac) box.

3. Click the **Format** list arrow, and then select a format.

4. Click the **Save In** (Win) or **Where** (Mac) list arrow, and then choose where to store the image.

5. Select from the available Save options:

   ◆ **As A Copy.** Saves a copy of the file while keeping the current file on your desktop.

   ◆ **Alpha Channels.** Saves or removes alpha channel information for the image.

   ◆ **Layers.** Maintains all layers in the image. If this option is cleared or unavailable, all visible layers are flattened or merged (depending on the selected format).

   ◆ **Notes.** Saves notes with the image.

   ◆ **Spot Colors.** Saves or removes spot channel information for the image.

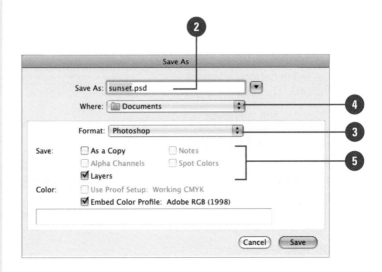

6 Select from the available Color options:

- ◆ **Use Proof Setup.** Creates a color-managed document.

- ◆ **Embed ICC Profile** (Win) or **Color Profile** (Mac). Embeds proof profile information in an untagged document. If the document is tagged, the profile is embedded by default.

7 Select from other available options (Win):

- ◆ **Thumbnail.** Saves thumbnail data for the file.

  To use this option, you need to select Ask When Saving for the Image Previews option in the File Handling area of the Preferences dialog box.

- ◆ **Use Lower Case Extension.** Makes the file extension lowercase.

8 Click **Save**, and then click **OK**, if necessary, to maximize the compatibility of the file save.

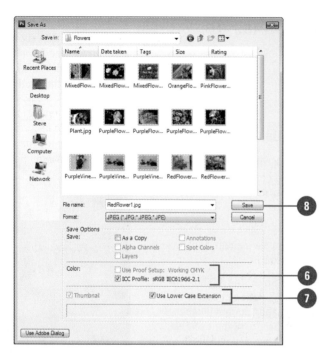

See Also

See "Saving a Document with a Different File Format" on page 382 for information on the save options.

See "Understanding File Formats" on page 381 for information on the different file formats.

For Your Information

Understanding the Save Commands

When you use the Save command from the File menu to save an existing document, Photoshop performs the save without opening a dialog box. That means the original document file has been replaced with the current state of the image. To preserve the original document, use the Save As command from the File menu, and then give the document a new name. For example, a file originally named landscape.psd could be saved as landscape_1.psd. You could keep creating new files with new names using the Save As command as you make changes, or you could use Layer Comps or Version Cue to keep track of different versions of the same file.

Using the Status Bar

To work efficiently in Photoshop you need information about the active document. Details about the document's size, resolution, color mode, and current size all help in the design and preparation of the final image. Photoshop displays current information about the active document through the Status Bar, located at the bottom of the document window.

Use the Status Bar

1. Click the **black triangle** near the Status bar info box, point to **Show**, and then select from the following options:

   ◆ **Version Cue.** Indicates whether Version Cue file management has been enabled.

   ◆ **Document Sizes.** The left number indicates the flattened size of the image file, and the right number indicates the size of the open file, based on layers and options.

   ◆ **Document Profile.** Displays information on the color profile assigned to the document.

   ◆ **Document Dimensions.** Represents the width and height of the image.

   ◆ **Measurement Scale.** Shows the scale of the document.

   ◆ **Scratch Sizes.** The left number indicates the scratch disk space required by Photoshop, and the right number indicates the available scratch disk space.

   ◆ **Efficiency.** Displays a percentage that represents Photoshop efficiency based on available RAM and scratch disk space.

   ◆ **Timing.** Records the amount of time required to perform the last command or adjustment.

   ◆ **Current Tool.** Displays the current tool.

   ◆ **32-bit Exposure.** Lets you control the overall image exposure.

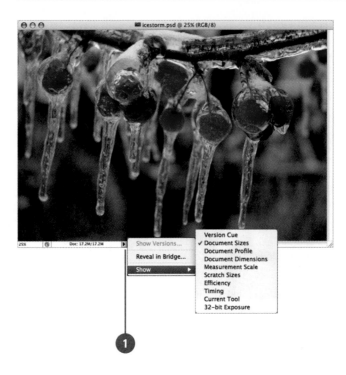

Closing a Document

To conserve your computer's resources, close any Photoshop documents you are not working on. You can close open documents one at a time (choose Close from the File menu or click the Close button on the Document tab (**New!**)), or you can use one command to close all open documents without closing the program (choose Close All from the File menu). Either way, if you try to close a document without saving, a dialog box appears, prompting you to save your changes.

Close a Document

1 Click the **Close** button on the Document tab or click the **File** menu, and then click **Close**.

> **TIMESAVER** *Press Ctrl+W (Win) or ⌘+W (Mac) to close the active document.*

2 If necessary, click **Yes** to save your changes.

Did You Know?

You can close all documents in one step. Click the File menu, and then click Close All. If necessary, click Yes to save your changes for each document. You can also press Alt+Ctrl+W (Win) or Option+⌘+W (Mac) to close all documents.

You can close documents and open the Bridge in one step. If you wish to close the open document or documents and then open the Bridge, click the File menu, and then click Close And Go To Bridge.

1 Close button on the Document tab

Finishing Up

Now that you've decided how you want to save your document, it's time to leave Photoshop. You'll want to make sure that all of your documents have been properly saved and closed before you exit Photoshop. Photoshop performs a bit of memory management, saves the current location of the panels and toolbox, and then quits.

Exit Photoshop from Windows

① Click the **File** menu.

② Click **Exit**.

TIMESAVER *Click the Close button on the program window or press Ctrl+Q to exit Photoshop.*

③ If necessary, click **Yes** to save your changes.

Photoshop closes and you are brought back to your desktop.

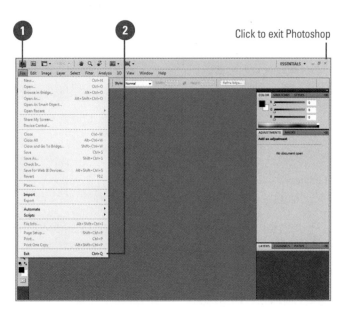

Click to exit Photoshop

Quit Photoshop from Macintosh

① Click the **Photoshop** menu.

② Click **Quit Photoshop**.

TIMESAVER *Press ⌘+Q to exit Photoshop.*

③ If necessary, click **Yes** to save your changes.

Photoshop closes and you are brought back to your desktop.

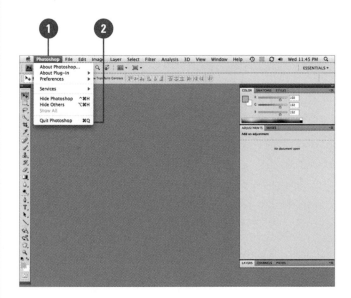

Understanding Navigation and Measurement Systems

2

Introduction

When you go on a road trip, you need two things to make the trip a success: good navigational aids (maps), and an understanding of how to measure distances between two points on a road map (1 inch typically equals 100 miles). When you are working with Adobe Photoshop, one of the keys to making the journey a success is to understand the navigational and measurement aids available. Photoshop lets you choose a measurement system to fit a specific project. For example, if you're working on images destined for the Web or a monitor, you'll be using pixels as a measurement system.

Conversely, if you're outputting to paper, or possibly a 4-color press, you'll likely choose inches or picas. Selecting between different measurement systems does not impact the quality of the final image, only how you measure distance. Trust me on this one; understanding how to measure distance helps to make the journey an enjoyable experience (I know from experience).

Having problems squinting at the small details of a photographic image? Using the Zoom tool is a great way to get you focused where you need to be. Zooming into a specific section of a document makes touching up the fine details just that much easier. In addition, the Info panel gives you up-to-date information on the exact position of the cursor inside the document, as well as detailed color information that can be indispensable in color-correcting an image.

The ability to create text annotations allows you to record document information that might be vital to the processing of the image and pass it on to anyone who opens the document. Photoshop's navigation and measurement systems are more than just information; they represent control of the document and control of the creative process.

What You'll Do

Change the View Size and Area with the Navigator Panel

Change the Color of the Navigator Panel View Box

Change the Screen Display Mode

Change the View with the Zoom Tool

Increase or Decrease Magnification

Move Images in the Document Window

Work with Multiple Documents

Work with One Image in Multiple Windows

Move Layers Between Two Open Documents

Create Notes

Work with the Info Panel

Change How the Info Panel Measures Color

Work with Rulers

Create Tool Presets

Changing the View Size with the Navigator Panel

PS 1.3

Photoshop's Navigator panel gives you an overall view of the image and the ability to navigate through the document or change the zoom size. Viewing images at different sizes gives you the ability to focus on small elements of the design without actually changing the image in any way. Once small areas of an image are enlarged, it's easier for you to make minute changes. Zoom size determines the visible size of an image; the zoom percentage can be seen in the document window. Zooming in (enlarging the image) by using the handy magnifying glass lets you work on and manipulate fine details, and then you can zoom out (reduce the image) to view how the changes impact the entire image. The Navigator panel contains a thumbnail view of the image, and under the thumbnail are easy-to-use controls that let you adjust the zoom of the image. In addition, changes made in the Navigator panel are immediately viewable in the active document window (what you see is what you get).

Change the View Size with the Navigator Panel

1. Select the **Navigator** panel.

2. Use one of the following methods to change the view size:

   ◆ Drag the triangular slider to the right to increase the zoom or to the left to decrease the zoom.

   ◆ Click the small and large mountain icons, located to the left and right of the triangular slider, to decrease or increase the zoom.

   ◆ Enter a value from .33% to 1600% into the Zoom box.

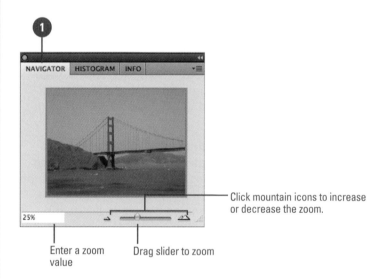

Click mountain icons to increase or decrease the zoom.

Enter a zoom value

Drag slider to zoom

Did You Know?

There are additional ways to zoom in using the Navigator panel. In the View box, hold down the Ctrl key, and then drag to resize the active document.

You can constrain the view box to drag horizontally or vertically. Hold down the Shift key, and then drag the view box horizontally or vertically.

For Your Information

Navigator Panel Shortcut

You can control the view of the document through a great shortcut. Simply click once in the Zoom input box on the Navigator panel, and then use the Up/Down arrow keys to increase or decrease the zoom value of the document 1% at a time. Not fast enough for you? Then hold down the Shift key, and use the Up/Down arrow keys to change the zoom size 10% at a time. Press the Enter key to see your changes reflected in the active document window.

Changing the View Area with the Navigator Panel

Zoomed images are typically larger than the size of the document window. When this happens, Photoshop adds navigational scroll bars to the bottom and the right of the document window. However, using scroll bars is not the only way to change your position within the image; the Navigator panel gives you a visible approach to changing the viewable area of the image. The view box in the Navigator panel represents the visible boundaries of the active document window, which is the viewable area of the image.

Change the View Area with the Navigator Panel

1 Select the **Navigator** panel.

2 Drag the view box in the thumbnail of the active image.

3 Click within the thumbnail.

The position of the view box changes, which also changes the viewable area of the image in the document window.

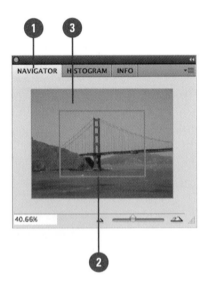

Did You Know?

You can show the Navigator panel. If the Navigator panel is not visible, click the Window menu, and then click Navigator.

You can change Zoom size of an image using the Navigator thumbnail. Hold down the Ctrl key (Win) or the ⌘ key (Mac), and then drag in the thumbnail. When you release your mouse, the selected area expands. It's just like using the Zoom tool, except you're dragging in the Navigator's thumbnail. Conversely, if you drag a second time (this time using a larger rectangle), the image zooms out.

Changing the Color of the Navigator Panel View Box

The colored box in the Navigator panel (proxy preview area) defines the viewable area of the image. It's important for the colored lines of the view box to stand out clearly against the image. The default color of the view box is a light red; however, some documents contain images that are predominantly the same color as the colored lines of the viewable area, making the viewing area difficult to identify. By changing the color of the lines, you can make sure they stand out against the image. This may seem like a small thing, but choosing a color that contrasts with my image significantly cuts down on my frustration level when I'm attempting to identify the viewable area.

Change the View Box Color

1 Select the **Navigator** panel.

2 Click the **Navigator Options** button, and then click **Panel Options**.

3 Click the **Color** list arrow, and then click a predefined color, or click **Custom** to select a color from the Color Picker dialog box.

4 Click **OK**.

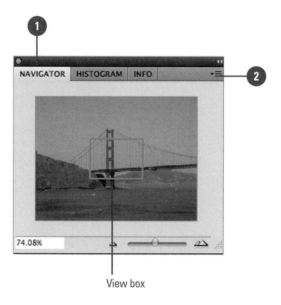

View box

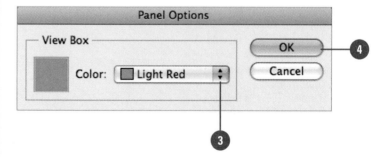

Did You Know?

You can increase the size of the Navigator panel's thumbnail.
Drag the lower right corner of the Navigator panel to expand the size of the panel. As the Navigator panel increases in size, so does the thumbnail.

Changing the Screen Display Mode

In Photoshop, the Screen Display mode determines the background displayed behind the active image. For example, you can choose a Screen Mode that changes the background to black, and then hides all the panels. Since monitor backgrounds,, combined with Photoshop's panels, add distracting colors to your workspace, changing the Screen Mode gives you a chance to isolate your image against a solid color background. Viewing your images against a black or gray background helps your eyes identify the true colors within an image.

Change the Screen Mode

1 Click **Change Screen Mode** button to toggle between screen modes or click the **Change Screen Mode** button arrow, and then select the mode you want:

◆ **Standard Screen Mode.** Displays the image against a gray, black, or custom color background (Win), or with the visible desktop (Mac). All menus and panels are visible.

◆ **Full Screen Mode with Menu Bar.** Centers the image, and displays it against a gray, black, or custom color background.

◆ **Full Screen Mode.** Centers the image, and displays it against a gray, black, or custom color background. (Default: Black)

TIMESAVER *Press F to toggle between the screen modes.*

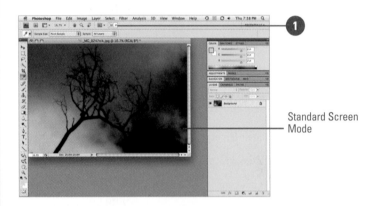

Standard Screen Mode

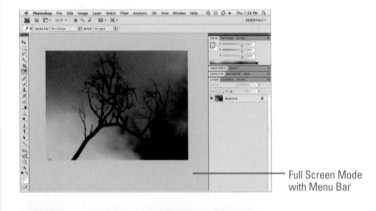

Full Screen Mode with Menu Bar

Full Screen Mode

Did You Know?

You can temporarily hide all of the panels and toolbox. Press the Tab key to hide the toolbox and panels. Press the Tab key a second time to display the hidden toolbox and panels. Hold down the Shift key, and then press the Tab key to hide the panels, but not the Toolbox or Options bar. In Interface preferences, you can choose to have either a border, a drop shadow or no effect for each screen mode (**New!**).

Changing the View with the Zoom Tool

Working with the Zoom tool gives you one more way to control exactly what you see in Photoshop. Just like the Navigator panel, the Zoom tool does not change the active image, but allows you to view the image at different magnifications. The Zoom tool is located towards the bottom of Photoshop's toolbox, and resembles a magnifying glass. The maximum magnification of a Photoshop document is 1600%, and the minimum size is 1 pixel. Increasing the magnification of an image gives you control over what you see and gives you control over how you work. Large documents are difficult to work with and difficult to view. Many large documents, when viewed at 100%, are larger than the maximum size of the document window, requiring you to reduce the zoom in order to view the entire image.

Zoom In the View of an Image

1. Select the **Zoom** tool on the toolbox.

2. Use one of the following methods:

   ◆ **Click on the document.**

   The image increases in magnification centered on where you clicked.

   ◆ **Drag to define an area with the Zoom tool.**

   The image increases in magnification based on the boundaries of the area you dragged. When you zoom in to 500% or more magnification, a Pixel Grid (**New!**) will appear, making it easy to make pixel-specific modifications.

   ◆ **Bird's Eye View (New!).**

   If you are zoomed into an image, you can press and hold the H key, click with your mouse and zoom out. Then reposition the viewing rectangle to the next spot you want to zoom into and it will zoom you into that specific spot.

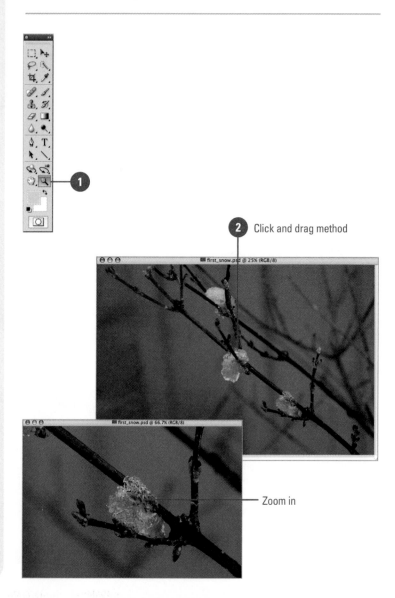

2 Click and drag method

Zoom in

Zoom Out the View of an Image

1. Select the **Zoom** tool on the toolbox.

2. Hold down the Alt (Win) or Option (Mac) key, and then click on the screen to reduce the zoom of the active document.

   The zoom reduction centers on where you click on the active document.

   IMPORTANT *Since images viewed in Photoshop are composed of pixels (like bricks in a wall), the only way to really see what the printed results of your artwork will look like is to view the image (even if it is too big for the screen) at 100%.*

Did You Know?

You can zoom in or out using shortcut keys regardless of what tool you're currently using. To zoom in, press Ctrl+Spacebar (Win) or ⌘+Spacebar (Mac) and click or drag to define an area. To zoom out, press Ctrl+Spacebar+Alt (Win) or ⌘+Spacebar+Option (Mac) and click or drag to define an area.

You can always display a clear view. When you zoomed into your image at 33% or 66% in previous versions of Photoshop, you would get a jaggy preview. Now, no matter what magnification size you choose, the preview is crisp and clear (**New!**).

Zoom out

Increasing or Decreasing Magnification

Adobe Certified Expert PS 1.3

Increase the Magnification of an Image

1. Click the **Zoom In** or **Zoom Out** buttons on the Options bar, and then click in the document window to increase or decrease the zoom.

2. Select the **Resize Windows To Fit** check box on the Options bar to resize the active document to fit the zoomed window.

3. Select the **Zoom All Windows** check box to zoom all open windows to the same magnification.

4. Click **Actual Pixels**, **Fit Screen**, **Fill Screen**, or **Print Size** on the Options bar to quickly zoom the screen to a preset size.

   TIMESAVER *It's possible to change the zoom of a document without ever leaving the keyboard. Hold the Ctrl (Win) or ⌘ (Mac) key, and then press the plus "+", or minus "-" keys. The plus key increases the zoom size, and the minus key decreases the zoom size.*

Did You Know?

You can zoom in on more than one document. If you have more than one open document, click Zoom All Windows on the Options bar.

Since easily changing the magnification of an image is fundamental to an optimal workflow, Photoshop gives you several ways to accomplish zooming. One way to zoom is using the options on the Options bar. To access the Zoom tool options, you must have the Zoom tool selected. Photoshop gives you two handy zoom preset values. To automatically zoom the document to 100%, double-click the Zoom tool. To automatically fit the image into the Photoshop workspace, double-click the Hand tool.

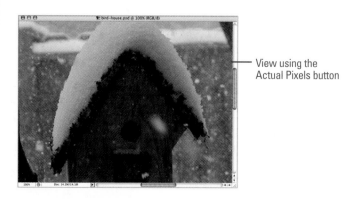

View using the Actual Pixels button

View using the Fit On Screen button

View using the Print Size button

Moving Images in the Document Window

One of those little used, but handy, tools is Photoshop's Hand tool. The Hand tool (so named because it resembles an open hand) lets you quickly move the active image within the document window without ever using the scroll bars. For example, you've zoomed the image beyond the size that fits within the document window and you need to change the visible portion of the document. It's a simple operation, but a handy one to know. If you have OpenGL on your computer, you can use the Rotate View tool (**New!**) to tilt the canvas for a more comfortable working angle, which is helpful when working with drawing tablets.

Move an Image in the Document Window

1. Select the **Hand** or **Rotate View** tool on the toolbox.

2. Drag in the active document to move or rotate the image.

   When you rotate the image to a different canvas angle, a compass appears to indicate north in the image regardless of the current canvas angle.

   ◆ To rotate a specific angle, enter a value in the Rotation Angle field.

3. To restore the image back to the normal canvas angle from a rotation, click **Reset View**.

Did You Know?

You can quickly access the Hand tool whenever you need it. Hold down the Spacebar to temporarily change to the Hand tool. Drag in the active document to the desired position, and then release the Spacebar. You're instantly returned to the last-used tool. It's important to note that you cannot use the Spacebar to access the Hand tool if you are currently using the Type tool.

2 Rotate View tool   Hand tool 2

Working with Multiple Documents

When you open multiple documents, you can use the Window menu or tabs (**New!**) at the top of the Document window to switch between them. You can click a tab name to switch and activate the document. By default, tabs are displayed in the order in which you open or create documents. However, you can change the order. When you want to move or copy information between documents, it's easier to display several Document windows at the same time and move them around (**New!**). The Arrange Documents menu (**New!**) makes it easy to display open document windows on the screen for better views.

Work with Multiple Documents

1. Open more than one document.

2. Click a tab name to switch to the document.

   TIMESAVER *Press Ctrl+Tab or Ctrl+Shift+Tab to cycle to a tab.*

   ◆ You can also click the **Window** menu, and then click a document name at the bottom of the menu.

3. Click the **Arrange Documents** menu on the Application bar, and then select an arrangement button icon:

   ◆ **Consolidate All.** Displays the active document.

   ◆ **Tile All In Grid.** Displays all open documents in a grid.

   ◆ **Tile All Vertically.** Displays all open documents vertically.

   ◆ **Tile All Horizontally.** Displays all open documents horizontally.

   ◆ **2-Up, 3-Up, 4-Up, 5-Up, or 6-Up.** Displays the number of documents in a pattern.

4. To move a document window around, do any of the following:

   ◆ To rearrange the order of documents (**New!**), drag a window's' tab to a new location.

   ◆ To dock or undock a document window (**New!**), drag the window's tab out of the group or into the group.

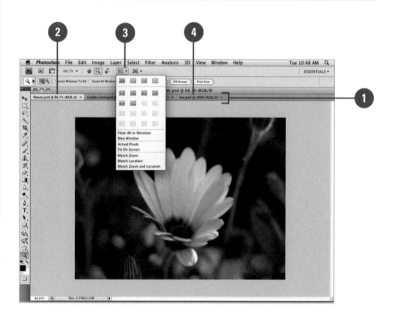

Results of 3-Up document arrangement

Working with One Image in Multiple Windows

 PS 1.2

There are times when you're working on an image in Photoshop, and you need to see two separate views of the image. For example, you're working on retouching a photo and you need a zoomed-in view to do fine detail work. At the same time, you want to see a normal view to get an idea of how the retouching is affecting the full-sized image. Being able to view one image at two different magnifications is a valuable tool. You can also use the Arrange Documents menu to rearrange open document windows on the screen for better views.

Create Two Views of One Image

1. Open a document.

2. Click the **Arrange Documents** menu, and then click **New Window**.

   A copy of the active document is created in a new window.

3. If you want to arrange multiple documents, click the **Arrange Document** menu, and then select and arrangement button icon (see the *For Your Information* for more details).

4. Select the **Zoom** tool on the toolbox, and then increase the zoom of the new document to the desired level.

5. Select an editing or painting tool, and then begin work on the new image in the zoomed window.

   The effects of your work instantly display in the normal image window.

6. When you're done with the new window, click the **Close** button.

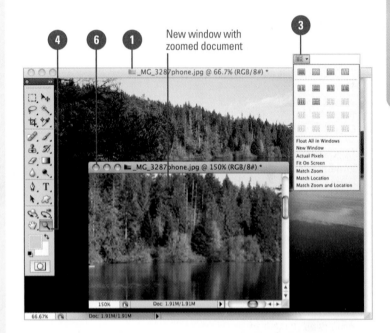

New window with zoomed document

Did You Know?

You can prevent the zoomed window from expanding. With the Zoom tool selected, move into the Options bar and deselect Resize Windows To Fit.

Moving Layers Between Two Open Documents

Photoshop has a lot of tricks up its electronic sleeves, and one of the handiest is the ability to move layers between open documents. For example, you have an image of a landscape and sky, but you don't like the sky, so you erase it. You then open another document with a sky that suits the design of your document. It's a simple matter to move the layer containing the preferred sky into any other open document.

Move Layers Between Documents

1. Open two or more documents.

2. Click on the document containing the layer you want to move to make it the active document.

3. Select the **Move** tool on the toolbox.

4. Drag the layer you want to move from the open document window into the second document.

    IMPORTANT *If the document you're moving a layer into contains more than one layer, Photoshop places the layer you're moving directly above the active layer in the second document. If the layer is in the wrong stacking order, drag it up and down in the Layers panel until it's correctly positioned.*

Did You Know?

You can also drag a layer thumbnail onto a document. Drag the layer thumbnail from the Layers panel into the document window of the second document.

From the Experts Corner

Removing the Excess

If you're dragging a layer from a document that contains more pixels than the document you're moving it into, the areas of the image outside the viewable area of the document are still there, taking up file space. To delete them, first position the image exactly where you want, click the Select menu, and then click Select All. Select the Image menu, and then click Crop. That's it. All the image information outside the viewable window is removed.

Creating Notes

Notes can be found everywhere—you see them stuck to the side of refrigerators, bulletin boards, and even covering your computer monitor. Notes remind you of important tasks and events. When you work in Photoshop, the ability to save notes can help you remember an important part of the design, or they can instruct another designer in the how's and why's of your document. For example, you can attach specific instructions in the form of Photoshop Notes to your service bureau on the printing of a document to obtain the best output. Text input is done through the Notes panel (**New!**). When you place a note, it doesn't become part of the image, but it is saved with the image.

Create a Note

1. Select the **Note** tool on the toolbox.

2. Click on the active document or the canvas to create a blank note.

3. Enter the text for your note.

   TIMESAVER *Click the note icon to select it and click again to deselect the note. You can also right-click a note icon to access a shortcut menu with note commands.*

4. Click the **Next** or **Previous** button to scroll through multiple notes one at a time.

5. Click the **Close** button.

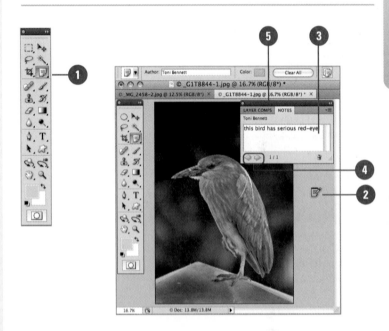

Did You Know?

You can change the Author and the default color of a Note. Select a note, and then use the Author and color options on the Options bar to create a personalized note. You can show and hide note icons by choosing View/Extras/Notes.

Working with Notes

Action	Keystrokes
Deselect a note	Click on the selected note to deselect.
Reopen a note	Click on the Note icon and use the Notes panel to edit the text, if desired.
Delete a note	Choose the specific note from the Notes panel, and then press Delete or select the Note and drag it to the Trash can in the Notes panel.

Working with the Info Panel

Photoshop's Info panel gives you a wealth of data on the current document's color space, as well as information on the x and y (horizontal/vertical) position of your mouse cursor within the active document window. In addition, when you're using one of Photoshop's drawing or measuring tools, the Info panel gives you up-to-date information on the size of the object you're creating. Photoshop works with black, white, shades of gray, and every color in-between. By creating color markers you can identify the location of specific color points within an image, which is indispensable for performing color correction. The Info panel also displays color information about the marked color and on how the color has shifted after you've made changes.

Create a Specific Size Object

① Select the **Info** panel.

② Select a drawing tool on the toolbox.

③ Drag in the document window to create a shape.

④ Release the mouse when the Info panel displays the correct dimensions.

> **IMPORTANT** *The bottom of the Info panel now displays tips on how to use the current tool, and the current size of the working document.*

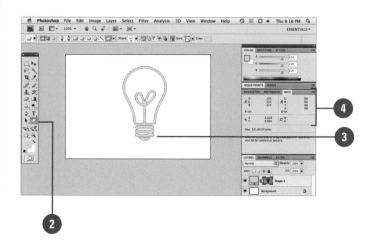

Create a Color Marker

① Select the **Info** panel.

② Select the **Eyedropper** tool on the toolbox.

③ In the document, hold down the Shift key, and then click once to create a color marker. You can have a maximum of four Color Markers in a single document.

Repositioning a marker is easy, simply press the Ctrl (Win) or ⌘ (Mac) key, and then click and drag the marker to a new position, or drag it off the document window to delete it.

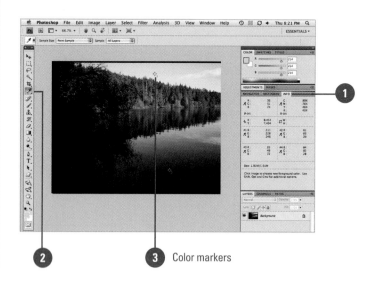

③ Color markers

Changing How the Info Panel Measures Color

Knowledge of the colors used in a document is important, but so is a thorough understanding of the color mode of the document. Different documents require different color modes. For example, images displayed on a monitor use the RGB (Red, Green, and Blue) color mode, and images sent to a 4-color press use CMYK (Cyan, Magenta, Yellow, and Black). Not only does the Info panel measure color, it also measures color in specific color modes.

Change How the Info Panel Measures Color

1. Select the **Info** panel.

2. Click the **Info Options** button, and then click **Panel Options**.

3. Click the **Mode** list arrows for First Color and Second Color Readout, and then select from the available options.

4. Click **OK**.

   The Info panel now measures color based on your selections.

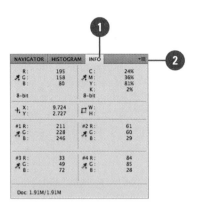

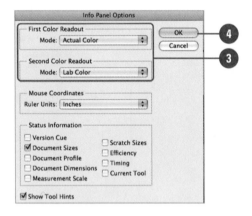

Did You Know?

The Info panel now allows you to display information such as: Document Sizes, Efficiency, Scratch Sizes, and more. Simply click the Info Options button, and then select from the available options. The Info panel also displays whether the image is using 8-, 16-, or 32-bit color channels.

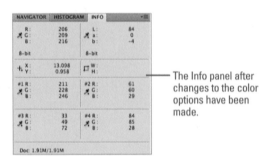

The Info panel after changes to the color options have been made.

Working with Rulers

Carpenters know that precise measurements are essential to making things fit, so they have a rule: Measure Twice, Cut Once. The designers of Photoshop also know that measurements are essential and give you several measuring systems—among them are the rulers. Rulers are located on the top and left sides of the active document window, and serve several purposes. They let you measure the width and height of the active image, they let you place guides on the screen to control placement of other image elements, and they create markers that follow your cursor as you move. As you can see, rulers are critical in the design of a document by helping you correctly align image design elements. As a matter of fact, if you're not working on a flat screen or LCD monitor, the curvature of your monitor can give you a false impression of the vertical and horizontal measurements. By using guides, you have access to precise alignment systems. To use the Ruler guides, the rulers must first be visible.

Change Ruler Options

1. Click the **Edit** (Win) or **Photoshop** (Mac) menu, point to **Preferences**, and then click **Units & Rulers**.

2. Select Ruler measurements and Type from the available options.

3. Click **OK**.

   IMPORTANT *If the Rulers are not visible in the active document, click the View menu, and then click Rulers.*

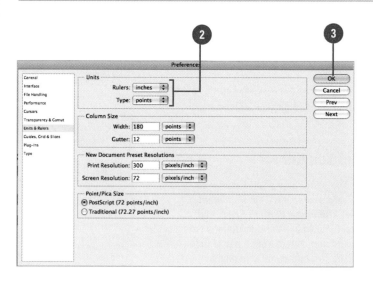

Did You Know?

You can choose what type of Point/Pica size to use. Click Postscript (72 points/inch) or click Traditional (72.27 points/inch). Postscript is more widely used, and Photoshop defaults to this option.

See Also

See "Working with Units & Rulers" on page 62 for more information on setting Units and Rulers preferences.

Use Ruler Guides

1. Click the **View** menu, and then click **Rulers** to display the ruler bars within the document window.

2. Move to the vertical or horizontal Ruler bar, and then click and drag into the document.

3. Return to the Ruler bar and continue to drag until you have all your guides properly set.

4. Click the **View** menu, and then click **Lock Guides** to lock the existing guides in place, or click **Clear Guides** to remove all guides.

5. Click the **Move** tool on the toolbox to drag existing guides to a new position (make sure Lock Guides is not selected).

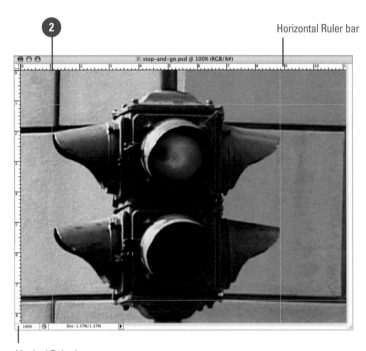

Horizontal Ruler bar

Vertical Ruler bar

Did You Know?

You can remove one guide at a time. Make sure Lock Guides is clear, and then click the Move tool. Drag the existing guide you want removed back to the corresponding Ruler bar.

You can switch guides on the fly. If you're dragging a vertical or horizontal guide onto the document window, when in fact you wanted the opposite guide, press the Alt (Win) or Option (Mac) key, while still dragging the guide. Vertical guides become horizontal, and horizontal guides become vertical.

See Also

See "Working with Guides, Grid & Slices" on page 64 for more information on setting guide preferences.

Creating Tool Presets

Photoshop provides you with a variety of tools to modify images. Each tool provides additional options you can choose from on the Options bar. If you frequently use the same tool with specific settings, you can save and reuse tool settings to save time in the future. You can load, edit, and create libraries of tool presets using the Tool Preset picker on the Options bar, the Tool Presets panel, or the Preset Manager.

Create and Use Tool Presets

1. Click the tool and set the options on the Options bar you want to save.

2. Click the **Tool Preset** button arrow next to the tool on the left side of the Options bar.

3. Click the **Create New Tool Preset** button.

4. Enter a name for the tool preset.

5. Click **OK**.

6. To use the tool preset, use one of the following:

   ◆ **Tool Preset button.** Click the Tool Preset picker on the Options bar, and then select the tool preset you want.

   ◆ **Tool Panel.** Click the Window menu, click Tool Preset, and then select the tool preset you want.

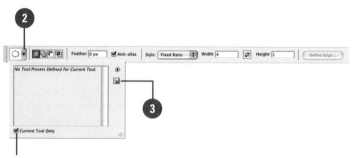

Select to display tool presets for current tool only

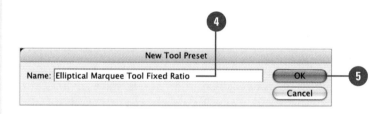

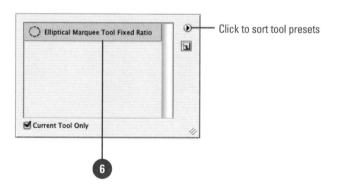

Click to sort tool presets

Did You Know?

You can change the list of tool presets. Click the triangle on the Tool Preset picker, and then click the display option you want: Sort By Tool, Show All Tool Presets, Show Current Tool Presets, or Text Only, Small List, or Large List.

Customizing the Way You Work

3

Introduction

No description of Adobe Photoshop would be complete without that well-known, but little utilized area called Preferences. Photoshop preferences serve several purposes. They help customize the program to your particular designing style, and they help you utilize available computer resources to increase the overall performance of the program.

By modifying File Handling preferences, such as appending a file extension on the file, or being asked when saving a layered TIFF file, you can streamline the file saving process. In addition, you can change the way your cursors look. For example, do you want your paintbrush to look like a paintbrush when you paint, do you prefer a precision crosshair or the actual brush size shape, or the shape with a crosshair?

As you use Photoshop, you'll come to realize the importance of working with units and rulers. Precision is the name of the game when you are working with images. What about the color of your guides, grids, and slices? No big deal, you say. Well, if you've ever tried viewing a blue guide against a blue-sky image, you know exactly why guide color is important. By working through preferences such as Image Cache, Scratch Disks, and RAM (Random Access Memory), speed increases of up to 20% can be achieved.

In addition, customizing the program helps make you more comfortable, and studies show that the more comfortable you are as a designer, the better your designs. Plus, being comfortable allows you to work faster, and that means you'll accomplish more in the same amount of time. What does setting up preferences do for you? They make Photoshop run faster (up to 20%), you work more efficiently, and your designs are better. That's a pretty good combination. Photoshop doesn't give you Preferences to confuse you, but to give you choices, and those choices give you control.

What You'll Do

Optimize Photoshop

Set General Preferences

Modify File Handling Preferences

Work with Interface Preferences

Work with Cursors Preferences

Control Transparency & Gamut Preferences

Work with Units & Rulers

Work with Guides, Grid & Slices

Select Plug-Ins

Select Scratch Disks

Allocate Memory & Image Cache

Work with Type

Manage Libraries with the Preset Manager

Customize the Workspace

Define Shortcut Keys

Create a Customized User Interface

Use Drawing Tablets

Optimizing Photoshop

Photoshop is a powerful program, and as such, requires a tremendous amount of computing power. When working on large documents, a poorly optimized Photoshop program will mean longer processing times for your files. That's the bad news if you have a deadline to meet. The good news is that Photoshop can be configured to run more efficiently. To optimize Photoshop, click the Edit (Win) or Photoshop (Mac) menu, point to Preferences, and then click Performance. The Performance preferences dialog box contains options that will help maximize the performance of Photoshop.

History States

History States control the number of undos available. In fact, you can have up to 1,000 undos (ever wonder who would make so many mistakes that they would need 1,000 undos?). Unfortunately, increasing the number of History States will ultimately increase the amount of RAM Photoshop uses to manage the History panel. Assigning more RAM to manage History means less memory for Photoshop to perform other operations, and will reduce the performance of the program. If you are experiencing problems with slow performance, lowering the number of History States frees up more RAM, and permits Photoshop to operate more efficiently.

Scratch Disk

When your computer doesn't have enough RAM to perform an operation, Photoshop uses free space on any available drive, known as a **Scratch Disk**. Photoshop requires 5 times the working size of the file in contiguous hard drive space. For example, if the working size of your file is 100 MB, you will need 500 MB of contiguous

History States

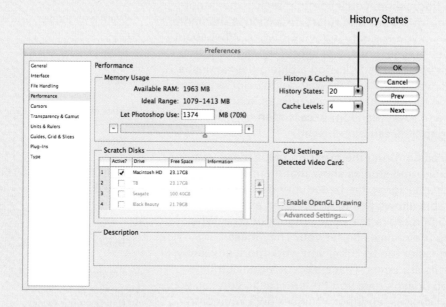

hard drive space, or you will receive an error message: Out of Scratch Disk Space (I hate it when that happens). Using additional hard drives gives Photoshop the ability to divide the processing load and increase performance. Photoshop detects and displays all available internal disks in the Preferences dialog box. Scratch disks must be physically attached to your computer (avoid networks and removable media, such as zip drives, or rewriteable CDs or DVDs). For maximum speed, avoid USB, and use 4- or 6-pin FireWire drives. Benchmark tests show FireWire drives provide up to a 20% speed improvement when used as Scratch Disks. Think of saving one hour out of every five, or one full day out of every five. That's not too bad. For best results, select a scratch disk on a different drive than the one used for virtual memory or any large files you're editing.

Memory & Image Cache

Photoshop functions in RAM (actually all applications work within RAM). To run efficiently, Photoshop requires 5 times the working size of the open document in available memory (some tests indicate 6 to 8 times). Strictly speaking, the more RAM you can assign to Photoshop, the more efficiently the program operates, especially when opening large documents.

RAM usage is determined by the working size of the document, not its open size. As you work on a document, you will eventually add additional layers to separate and control elements of the image. As you add these new layers, the working size of the file increases.

RAM memory allocation

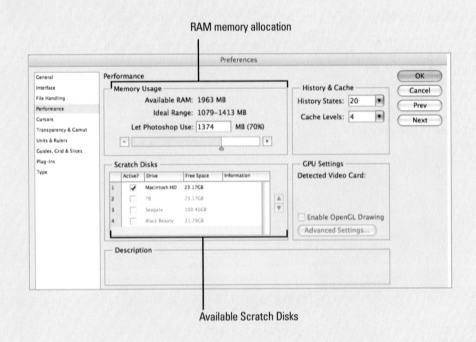

Available Scratch Disks

Setting General Preferences

  PS 1.3

Photoshop's General preferences help you configure some of the more common features of the program. Image interpolation settings, as well as the History log, are set up in General preferences. Other options, such as beeping when an operation is finished, auto-updating open documents, and using the Shift key for tool switching, can all be turned on or off in the Options area. The History Log lets you save all the History States performed on a particular document. For example, when you open an image, all the adjustments and actions performed are saved in a text file. This gives you access to valuable information, and lets you reproduce the steps performed on one image to correct another.

Work with General Options

1 Click the **Edit** (Win) or **Photoshop** (Mac) menu, and then point to **Preferences**.

2 Click **General**.

3 Click the **Color Picker** list arrow, and then select Adobe or another operating system (Windows or Macintosh).

4 Click the **Image Interpolation** list arrow, and then select Nearest Neighbor (Faster), Bilinear, or one of the Bicubic options.

5 Select the various options you want to use:

◆ **Auto-Update Open Documents.** Creates a link between the open image and the image file on disk.

◆ **Beep When Done.** Makes a sound when an operation is complete.

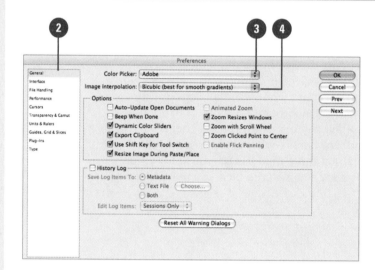

◆ **Dynamic Color Sliders.** Previews color effects within the slider bars.

◆ **Export Clipboard.** Transfers a copied image to the operating systems clipboard.

◆ **Use Shift Key For Tool Switch.** Allows you to use the keyboard shortcut when two tools share the same slot in the toolbox.

◆ **Resize Image During Paste/ Place.** Allows you to resize an image during a Paste or Place.

◆ **Animated Zoom. (New!)** Enables continuous-motion, smooth zooming in and out of your document. Must have OpenGL on your computer.

◆ **Zoom Resizes Windows.** Forces the image window to resize when zoom is selected.

◆ **Zoom With Scroll Wheel.** Determines whether zooming or scrolling is the default operation of the scroll wheel.

◆ **Zoom Clicked Point to Center. (New!)** Centers the zoom view on the clicked location.

◆ **Enable Flick Panning. (New!)** Enables quick mouse movement over the image instead of holding down the mouse.

6 Select the History Log options you want to use.

7 Click **OK**.

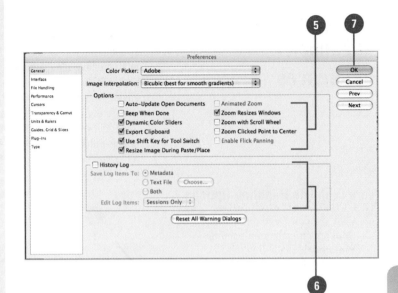

Did You Know?

You can turn a text box into a slider. You can use any text box which displays a numerical value, such as font size, like a slider. Point to the name of the box (which changes the cursor to a hand with arrows), and then move the mouse left to decrease or right to increase the displayed number.

Modifying File Handling Preferences

Sooner or later, you'll have to save the file (document) you've created in Photoshop. The final output of any document is contained within a specific file format such as TIFF, EPS, JPEG, or BMP. In fact, Photoshop lets you save files using over 15 different formats. The File Handling preferences provide several options that modify what information is saved with a file. Image previews are typically very small, adding very little to the file size of the saved document. Once saved you may want to open, print, and possibly even modify the document using other image-editing applications. The File compatibility options help you save a file that will be transportable to other applications.

Work with File Handling Options

1. Click the **Edit** (Win) or **Photoshop** (Mac) menu, and then point to **Preferences**.

2. Click **File Handling**.

3. Select the File Saving Options you want to use:

   ◆ **Image Previews.** Select from: Always Save, Never Save, or Ask When Saving.

   ◆ **Icon.** Saves previews of the images (Mac).

   ◆ **Full Size.** Saves full-size previews for use as FPO (For Placement Only) objects in Desktop layout programs (Mac).

   ◆ **Mac Thumbnail.** Saves previews viewable when using the Mac File Open command (Mac).

   ◆ **Win Thumbnail.** Saves previews viewable when using the Win File Open command (Mac).

   ◆ **Append File Extension.** Lets you choose whether or not to append the file extension (Mac).

   ◆ **Use Lower Case.** Choose to have upper or lower case extensions.

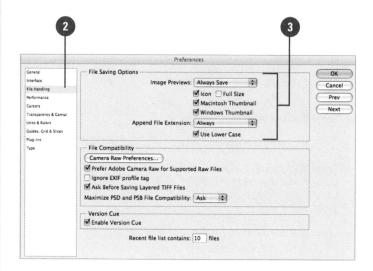

4 Select the File Compatibility options you want to use:

◆ **Camera Raw Preferences** Click to choose from options such as default image settings, cache size, DNG file handling, and whether or not to open JPEG and TIFF files with Camera Raw.

◆ **Prefer Adobe Camera Raw for Supported Raw Files.** Open supported raw files in Camera Raw.

◆ **Ignore EXIF Profile Tag.** Ignores color space metadata attached to digital camera images.

◆ **Ask Before Saving Layered TIFF Files.** Lets you create multi-layered documents, and then save them using the TIFF format.

This is a distinct advantage when you need to use multi-layered files and you don't want to save them using Photoshop's proprietary format (PSD).

◆ **Maximize PSD and PSB File Compatibility.** Lets you save PSD files that can be opened in earlier versions of the program and PSB (Large Document Format) files.

5 Select the **Enable Version Cue** check box to enable Adobe Version Cue in your work process.

6 Enter the number of files (up to 30) to keep in the Recent File List box.

7 Click **OK**.

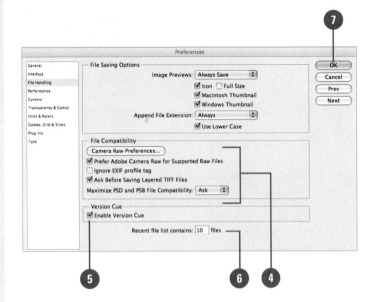

See Also

See "Understanding File Formats" on page 381 for information on some of the various file formats available in Photoshop.

Working with Interface Preferences

PS 1.1, 1.2

Working with the Interface preferences gives you control over whether Photoshop displays or hides user interface features. You can display some user interface elements in color. For example, you can show the Application icon in color or grayscale, show channels in color, or show selected menu items in user-defined colors. Interface preferences also allow you to show descriptive labels when your cursor is placed over an option, automatically collapse icon panels when you click away, and remember panel locations for the next use. You can also change the size of the text font on the Options bar, panels, and tool tips.

Work with Interface Options

1 Click the **Edit** (Win) or **Photoshop** (Mac) menu, point to **Preferences**, and then click **Interface**.

2 Select the Interface options:

◆ **Screen Modes.** Choose background and border colors for the three screen modes.

◆ **Use Grayscale Application Icon.** Shows the application icon in grayscale or color.

◆ **Show Channels In Color.** Allows you to view channels in the Channels panel in color.

◆ **Show Menu Colors.** Displays menu items in user-defined colors.

◆ **Show Tool Tips.** Shows labels when your cursor is placed over an option.

◆ **Auto-Collapse Iconic Panels.** Automatically collapses icon panels when you click away.

◆ **Remember Panel Locations.** Saves the panel locations.

◆ **Auto-Show Hidden Panels. (New!)** Hidden panels will temporarily appear when you move your cursor to the edge of the application window.

◆ **UI Text Options.** Click the UI Language list arrow to choose a default language, and then click the Font Size list arrow to select a size for interface fonts.

3 Click **OK**.

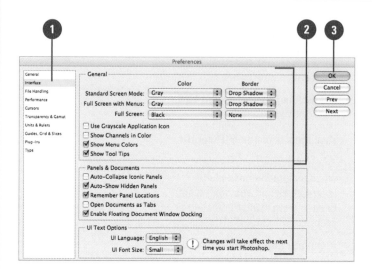

Working with Cursors Preferences

We communicate with Photoshop using various devices, such as a drawing tablet, mouse, touch screen, track pad, or keyboard. Photoshop communicates with us using visual cues, the most prominent one being the shape of the cursor. For example, when a cursor looks like an I-beam, this typically means it's time to enter text, or when the cursor looks like a magnifying glass, clicking on the image expands the view size. Working with the Cursors preferences gives you control over how Photoshop communicates with you.

Work with Cursors Options

1. Click the **Edit** (Win) or **Photoshop** (Mac) menu, and then point to **Preferences**.

2. Click **Cursors**.

3. Select the Painting Cursors options you want to use:

   ◆ **Standard.** Painting cursors look like their toolbox icons.

   ◆ **Precise.** Painting cursors appear as crosshairs.

   ◆ **Normal Brush Tip.** Painting cursors appear with the shape of the active brush tip.

   ◆ **Full Size Brush Tip.** Shows the full size of the brush tip, including feathered edges.

   ◆ **Show Crosshair In Brush Tip.** Displays a crosshair in the center of the brush tip.

4. Select the Other Cursors options you want to use:

   ◆ **Standard.** Painting cursors look like their toolbox icons.

   ◆ **Precise.** Painting cursors appear as crosshairs.

   ◆ **Brush Preview.** Choose a color for brush editing preview.

5. Click **OK**.

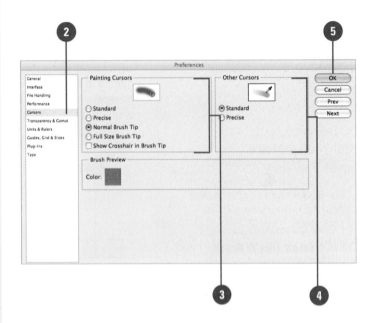

For Your Information

Toggling Between Precise and Standard Tools

Pressing the Caps Lock key while using a painting cursor toggles the tool between the precise and brush size options, and pressing the Caps Lock key when using any other cursor toggles between standard and precise options.

Controlling Transparency & Gamut Preferences

The Transparency & Gamut preferences control how Photoshop displays transparent areas of a document (commonly called the checkerboard), as well as the color and opacity of areas of an image that fall outside of the CMYK (Cyan, Magenta, Yellow, and Black) color mode. It's important to understand that transparency in Photoshop does not always translate into transparency after you save the file. For example, the JPEG format is used primarily for images saved for the Internet, and does not support transparency. When you save the file, Photoshop will fill the transparent areas of the image with a matte color (the default is white). In addition, the Gamut Warning may be activated because a monitor displays color information using RGB, and has more available saturation values than a CMYK document. Using a different ink or spot colors can sometimes fix an out-of-gamut color. For transparency it's important to remember that unless you're printing the document directly in Photoshop, it's the format you choose that determines if the transparent areas will be saved, and the Gamut Warning is there to warn you of any areas that may not print the way you expect.

Control Transparency & Gamut Options

1. Click the **Edit** (Win) or **Photoshop** (Mac) menu, and then point to **Preferences**.

2. Click **Transparency & Gamut**.

3. Select the Transparency Settings options you want to use:

   ◆ **Grid Size.** Allows you to select a transparency grid size.

   ◆ **Grid Colors.** Allows you to choose the color scheme for the transparency grid.

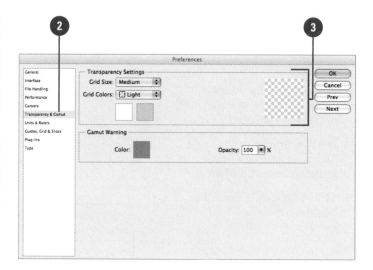

④ Select the Gamut Warning options you want to use:

◆ **Color.** Choose a color to mask areas of an image that move out of the CMYK color space.

◆ **Opacity.** Enter a value from 0% to 100%.

Opacity determines how much of the Color Overlay masks the original image pixels.

For example, if you choose the color gray, and an opacity of 100%, areas of an image that fall outside of the CMYK color space will be masked with gray.

⑤ Click **OK**.

IMPORTANT *To activate the gamut warning option, open a document in Photoshop, click the View menu, and then click Gamut Warning. Out of Gamut areas of the image will display with the color and opacity chosen in the Transparency & Gamut preferences.*

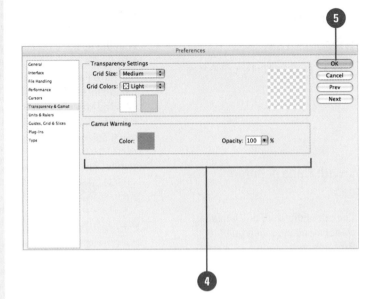

Working with Units & Rulers

While changing the measurable units and rulers do not affect output quality, they do help to measure information in a document consistent with the specific output device. Ruler Units give you precise information on the width and height of the active document. The Column Size measurements provide information that Photoshop needs to create documents with columns, such as newspapers, magazines, brochures, etc. The New Document Preset Resolutions area lets you select specific resolution values when creating new documents. Insert the values you'll use most often in the creation of a new Photoshop document.

Work with Units & Rulers Options

1 Click the **Edit** (Win) or **Photoshop** (Mac) menu, and then point to **Preferences**.

2 Click **Units & Rulers**.

3 Select the Units options you want to use:

   ◆ **Rulers.** Sets a default measuring system for the Ruler bar.

   For example, pixels would be most common for images displayed on a monitor, and picas or inches most common for output to press or printer.

   ◆ **Type.** Use to measure type with pixels, points, or millimeters.

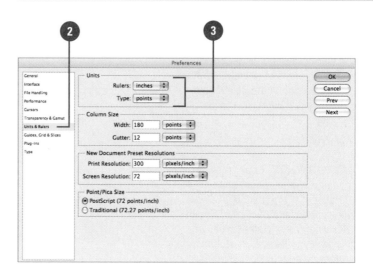

Did You Know?

You can switch between ruler measurements without going to Preferences. To change the default measurement system of the Ruler bar, simply move into the Ruler bar, and then right-click your mouse. A list of available measurement options will be instantly available.

4 Select the Column Size settings you want to use:

- ◆ **Width.** Choose a measurement system and numerical value for column width.

- ◆ **Gutter.** Choose a measurement system and numerical value for gutter (the space between the columns).

  When you choose a measurement system (points, inches, or centimeters), Photoshop changes the value to correspond to the type of measurement system.

5 Select the New Document Preset Resolutions settings you want to use:

- ◆ **Print Resolution.** Select a print resolution and measurement value for default printing.

- ◆ **Screen Resolution.** Select a print resolution and measurement value for default screen display.

6 Click the **PostScript** or **Traditional** option measuring systems for Photoshop's type tool (PostScript is the most widely used).

7 Click **OK**.

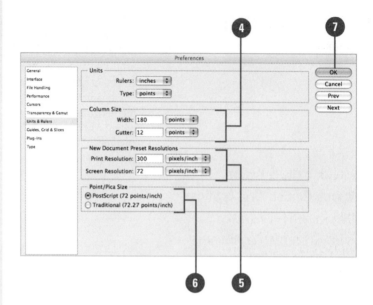

Working with Guides, Grid & Slices

The Guides, Grid & Slices preferences help keep a multi-layered document in proper order. For example, using Guides can help you line up buttons on a web interface, or make sure specific design elements are precisely placed within the document window. The Guides option lets you select the color and style of the guides placed within a Photoshop document. Guides are placed within the image by dragging them from the horizontal or vertical Ruler bars in the active document. The Grid options let you decide on a color, style, and layout for Photoshop's grid system. The Slices option defines the visible color of a slice, and whether Photoshop displays a number value for each slice.

Work with Guides, Grid & Slices Options

1 Click the **Edit** (Win) or **Photoshop** (Mac) menu, and then point to **Preferences**.

2 Click **Guides, Grid & Slices**.

3 Select the Guides options you want to use:

- ◆ **Color.** Select a default color for displaying guides.

- ◆ **Style.** Select a default (Lines or Dashed Lines) for displaying guidelines.

4 Select the Smart Guides options you want to use:

- ◆ **Color.** Select a color for use with Smart Guides.

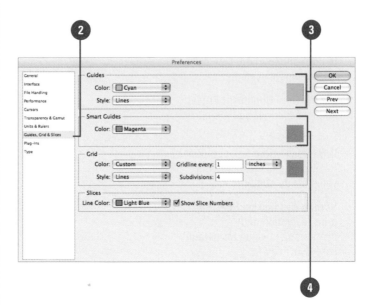

Did You Know?

You can change a horizontal guide into a vertical guide, and vice versa. Move into the Ruler bar and drag a guide into the document window. Before releasing the mouse, hold down the Alt (Win) or Option (Mac) key. The guide automatically switches directions.

5 Select the Grid options you want to use:

◆ **Color.** Select a default color for displaying grids.

◆ **Style.** Select a default style (Lines, Dashed Lines, or Dots) for displaying the grid.

◆ **Gridline Every.** Enter a value for how often the grid lines appear within the active document.

◆ **Subdivisions.** Enter a value for how many subdivisions (lines) appear between each main gridline.

6 Select the Slices options you want to use:

◆ **Line Color.** Select a default line color for displaying document slices.

◆ **Show Slice Numbers.** Select the check box to display a number for each slice in the upper left corner of the slice.

IMPORTANT *When you select a line color, choose a color that is different than the grid and guide line colors. That way you can easily identify grids and guides for user-created lines.*

7 Click **OK**.

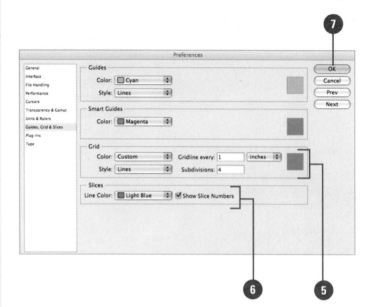

Did You Know?

You can change color choices for Guides, Grid & Slices. Not satisfied with the color choices offered by the color and style menus? Click on the Color boxes located on the right side of the Preferences dialog box, and select any color from the Color Picker.

Selecting Plug-Ins

The Plug-ins preferences give you the ability to organize your plug-ins by saving them in one or more folders. These additional folders are typically used to hold third-party plug-ins. When selected, plug-ins contained within the folder will be available from Photoshop's Filter menu. Organizing your plug-ins into folders helps keep your projects focused and reduces the clutter of plug-ins when you select them from the Filter menu.

Work with Plug-Ins Options

1. Click the **Edit** (Win) or **Photoshop** (Mac) menu, and then point to **Preferences**.

2. Click **Plug-Ins**.

3. Select the **Additional Plug-Ins Folder** check box if you have additional plug-ins stored outside the default Photoshop plug-ins folder.

   IMPORTANT *The first time you select this option, Photoshop asks you where the plug-ins are stored.*

4. If you change the location of your additional plug-ins folder, you can always click **Choose** and navigate to it.

5. Choose options for Extension Panels. (**New!**)

   Check **Allow Extensions to Connect to the Internet** and/or **Load Extension Panels** if you want to use new features such as Kuler or Connections. (**New!**)

6. Click **OK**.

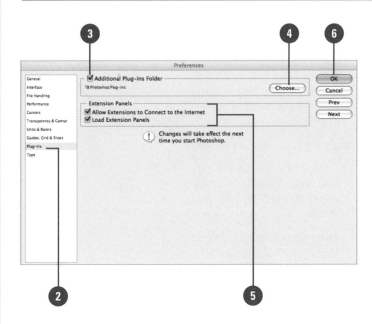

Selecting Scratch Disks

The Performance preferences are available to help you get the best performance out of your computer by letting you choose one or more hard drives for scratch operations. When your computer doesn't have enough RAM to perform an operation, Photoshop uses free space on any available drive, known as a Scratch Disk. Photoshop runs faster when you divide the Scratch Disk workload. Scratch operations are performed on your hard drive and take place when Photoshop is using one of its many filters and adjustments. Photoshop detects and displays all available disks in the Performance preferences dialog box, where you can select the disks you want to use. By assigning additional hard drives to the task, you speed up Photoshop's overall performance. Scratch Disk changes take effect the next time you start Photoshop.

Work with Scratch Disks Options

1. Click the **Edit** (Win) or **Photoshop** (Mac) menu, and then point to **Preferences**.

2. Click **Performance**.

3. Select the check box next to the scratch disk you want to use or clear the check box to remove it.

   IMPORTANT *Photoshop holds scratch disk space as long as the application is open. To delete scratch disk space you must close Photoshop.*

4. Click **OK**.

Allocating Memory & Image Cache

PS 1.3

The Memory Usage and History & Cache preferences give you control over how much RAM is assigned to Photoshop, and how much memory is allocated to screen redraws (Image Cache). Photoshop, being a high-performance application, requires a fairly large amount of RAM. Adjusting these options can help increase Photoshop's overall speed performance. Photoshop uses many operations that affect RAM: History States, Undo, Clipboard, and Cache. When you modify the Memory Usage settings, you are increasing or decreasing the amount of RAM Photoshop uses for various tasks. Experimentation is the key here. Try different settings and record Photoshop's performance. By fine-tuning Photoshop's engine, you increase its overall speed, and you'll get more design miles to the gallon.

Allocate Memory & Image Cache Options

1. Click the **Edit** (Win) or **Photoshop** (Mac) menu, and then point to **Preferences**.

2. Click **Performance**.

3. Select the History & Cache options you want to use:

    ◆ **Cache Levels.** Select a number from 1 to 8.

    ◆ **History States.** Enter the amount of History States steps you want to keep as undos; you can enter up to 1,000.

    IMPORTANT *History States impact Photoshop's performance by holding the History States using a combination of RAM and Scratch Disk space. The more History States used, the more RAM is required. Using an extensive number of History States can impact Photoshop's performance.*

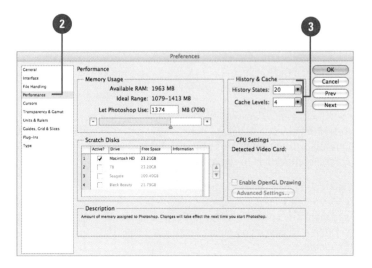

See Also

See "Installing Photoshop," on page 2 for information on RAM and other system needs.

For Your Information

Setting the Cache Levels

Cache Levels are screen redraws, or how many versions of the current active document Photoshop saves. When you're working on large documents, more Cache Levels help speed up the redraw function, and make image manipulation proceed faster. However, they are held primarily in RAM, so the more Cache Levels you choose, the less RAM is available for other Photoshop functions.

4 Enter the percentage of RAM used in the Let Photoshop Use box.

Photoshop needs about 5 times the size of the open document of unused RAM to operate efficiently.

IMPORTANT *Any changes made for allocating memory and image caching will take place the next time you start Photoshop. Please see the message at the bottom of the screen.*

5 GPU Settings (**New!**). If you have a video card installed with a GPU (Graphics Processing Unit), the name of your video card will appear under Detected Video Card. Check **Enable OpenGL Drawing** (GL stands for Graphics Library) to make the enhanced speed and smoothness of CS4 graphic rendering and navigation available to you.

6 Click **OK**.

IMPORTANT *Never select 100% Memory Usage. Selecting 100% gives Photoshop your entire available RAM, leaving nothing for the operating system or any other open programs. If you are experiencing more than your usual share of Photoshop crashes, experiment with reducing memory usage.*

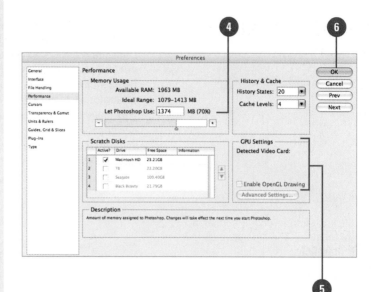

Working with Type

Although Photoshop is not by definition a typesetting application, such as Adobe InDesign, it does have some very powerful type features. For example, Adobe Photoshop allows you to output PostScript text to a printer with a PostScript option. This way you will not need to place Photoshop images into type-intensive applications, such as InDesign or Illustrator, just to create a few lines of text. In addition, Photoshop's type menu lets you see fonts exactly as they will print or display. For designers who use a lot of fonts, this WYSIWYG (What You See Is What You Get) font menu is a timesaver. You can use Type preferences to help you select the type and font options you want to use.

Work with Type Options

1. Click the **Edit** (Win) or **Photoshop** (Mac) menu, and then point to **Preferences**.

2. Click **Type**.

3. Select the Type options you want to use:

   ◆ **Use Smart Quotes.** Select to use left and right quotation marks.

   ◆ **Show Asian Text Options.** Select to display Japanese, Chinese, and Korean type options in the Character and Paragraph panels.

   ◆ **Enable Missing Glyph Protection.** Select to automatically select incorrect, unreadable characters between roman and non-roman (Japanese or Cyrillic) fonts.

   ◆ **Show Font Names In English.** Select to display non-roman fonts using their roman names.

   ◆ **Font Preview Size.** Select to display fonts on the menu in small, medium, or large size.

4. Click **OK**.

   IMPORTANT *Photoshop uses PostScript measuring systems to size fonts. Therefore a 72-point font will print 1 inch tall. This lets you know how big the fonts will appear when output to print.*

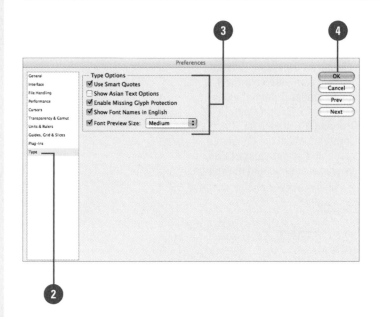

Managing Libraries with the Preset Manager

The Preset Manager gives you one place to manage brushes, swatches, gradients, styles, patterns, contours, custom shapes, and preset tools. The Preset Manager can be used to change the current set of preset items and create new libraries of customized sets. Once a library is loaded in the Preset Manager, you can access the library's items in all locations where the preset is available. Changes made in the Preset Manager are global and are applied every time you open Photoshop. When you save a new preset, the name appears in the dialog box for the specific option you selected.

Create a New Preset

① Click the **Edit** menu, and then click **Preset Manager**.

② Click the **Preset Type** list arrow, and then select the options.

③ Click the **Options** list arrow, and then select from the available presets to add them to the current item list.

④ To remove any items in a new preset, click a thumbnail, and then click **Delete**.

⑤ To reorganize their order, click and drag the thumbnails to new positions within the view window.

⑥ To change a preset name, click a thumbnail, click **Rename**, change the name, and then click **OK**.

⑦ Click a thumbnail, and then click **Save Set**.

⑧ Enter a new set name, and then select a location to store the set.

⑨ Click **Save**, and then click **Done**.

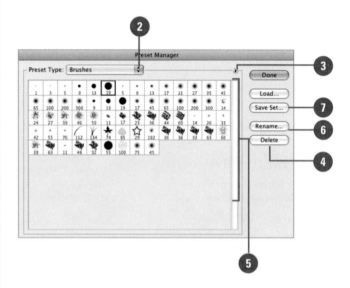

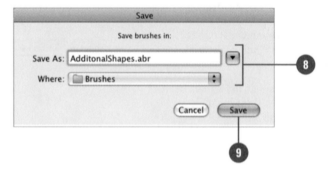

Did You Know?

You can save specific items in the view window as a preset. Press Ctrl+click (Win) or ⌘+click (Mac) on only those items you want in the new set, and then click Save Set.

Customizing the Workspace

 PS 1.1

The Photoshop workspace consists of a document surrounded by an Application frame (Mac only), Application bar, Options bar, toolbox, and over 20 floating panels, including new 3D, Adjustments, Masks, and Notes panels (**New!**). Depending on how you work, your workspace may reflect any combination of the above. For example, when you work with text, you would need the Character and Paragraph panels, but you might not need the Styles or Histogram panel. To work efficiently, each job requires a specific organization of the workspace. Rather than making you redesign your workspace every time you begin a new project, Photoshop gives you ways to create and save your own customized workspaces.

Create a Customized Workspace

1. Arrange the panels into a specific working order.

2. Click the **Window** menu, point to **Workspace**, and then click **Save Workspace**.

3. Type a name for the workspace.

4. Select check boxes to save Panel Locations, Keyboard Shortcuts, or Menus.

5. Click **Save**.

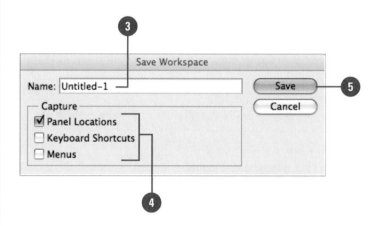

Delete a Customized Workspace

1. Click the **Window** menu, point to **Workspace**, and then click **Delete Workspace**.

2. Click the **Workspace** list arrow, and then click the workspace you want to delete, or click **All**.

3. Click **Delete**, and then click **Yes** to confirm the deletion.

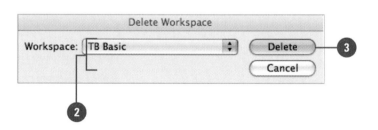

Did You Know?

You cannot delete the Workspace in which you are currently working. You must switch to another workspace first.

Defining Shortcut Keys

 PS 1.1

A wise man once wrote "time is money," and Photoshop is a program that can consume a lot of time. That's why the Photoshop application uses keyboard shortcuts. **Keyboard Shortcuts**, as their name implies, let you perform tasks in a shorter period of time. For example, if you want to open a new document in Photoshop, you can click the File menu, and then click New, or you can abandon the mouse and press Ctrl+N (Win) or ⌘+N (Mac) to use shortcut keys. Using shortcut keys reduces the use of the mouse and speeds up operations. In fact, a recent study in the American Medical Journal suggested that the use of shortcut keys significantly cuts down on repetitive stress, and reduces instances of carpal tunnel syndrome. Photoshop raises the bar by not only giving you hundreds of possible shortcut keys, but also actually allowing you to define your own shortcuts.

Create a Keyboard Shortcut

1. Click the **Edit** menu, and then click **Keyboard Shortcuts**.

2. Click an arrow (left column) to expand the menu that contains the command for which you want to create a shortcut.

3. Select an item from the Commands list.

4. Use the keyboard to create the new shortcut. For example, press Ctrl+N (Win) or ⌘+N (Mac).

5. Click **Accept**.

6. Click **OK**.

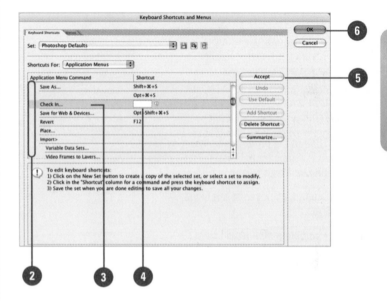

Did You Know?

You can save time using shortcut keys. According to several time and motion studies, using shortcut keys can actually save a computer user 1 hour out of every 8 in a work day.

For Your Information

Working with Shortcuts

In addition to adding shortcuts, you can delete any of them you don't want and even print out a summary of shortcuts defined in Photoshop. Shortcuts can be used for the Application and Panel menus, as well as for your tools in the toolbox. Click the Edit menu, click Keyboard Shortcuts, and then use the appropriate buttons, such as Add Shortcut, Delete Shortcut, or Summarize, to perform the tasks you want.

Creating a Customized User Interface

PS 1.1

Photoshop's pull-down menus actually contain hundreds of options (yes, I did say hundreds). If you find navigating through menus a hassle, then Adobe has the answer to your problem with a customizable user interface. In Photoshop, you have the ability to choose what menu items appear on the pull-down menus and you can even colorize certain menu items for easier visibility. For example, if you're curious about all the new features in Photoshop CS4, you can choose a drop-down menu system with all the new features highlighted. Photoshop includes nine predefined user interface sets, known as workspaces, just to get you started in the right direction. You can access these workspaces—such as Essentials, Basic, and What's New in CS4—by using the Workspace menu (**New!**) on the Application bar or Workspace submenu on the Window menu.

Use a Predefined User Interface

① Click the **Window** menu, and then point to **Workspace**.

TIMESAVER *Click the Workspace menu (**New!**) (which displays the name of the current workspace) on the menu bar.*

② Click one of the predefined sets, such as: Automation, Web, Painting, or What's New in CS4.

③ If prompted, click **Yes** to apply the changes.

The Photoshop menus will now display with highlighted options based on your selection.

Did You Know?

You can restore menus to the original settings. To restore all of the Photoshop menu settings to the original values, click the Window menu, choose Workspace, then scroll to the bottom and choose Keyboard Shortcuts & Menus. From there, you can choose Photoshop Defaults in the Set drop-down menu to revert to default menus.

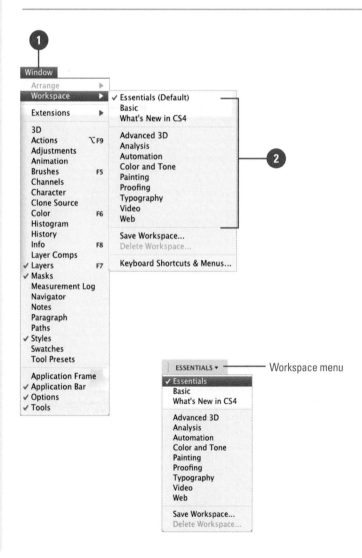

Workspace menu

Create a Customized User Interface

1. Click the **Window** menu, point to **Workspace**, and then click **Keyboard Shortcuts & Menus**.

2. Click the **Menus** tab.

3. To create a new set based on the current active set, click the **Create New Set** button, enter a name, and then click **Save**.

4. Click the **Set** list arrow, and then select a listing of modified User Interfaces.

5. Click the **Menu For** list arrow, and then click **Application Menus** or **Panel Menus** with the items you want to modify.

6. Click an arrow (left column) to expand the menu that contains the command you want to modify.

7. Click the **Visibility** icon associated with a command to show or hide the command.

8. Click the **Color** list arrow, and select a color for the selected command.

9. Click the **Save All Changes** button to save the new customized User Interface.

10. Click **OK**.

Did You Know?

You can delete a user interface set. Click the Windows menu, point to Workspace, click Keyboard Shortcuts & Menus, click the Menus tab, click the Set list arrow, click the set you want, and then click the Delete button.

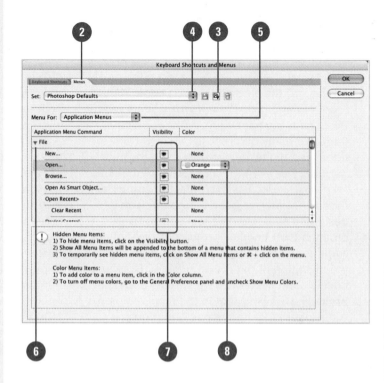

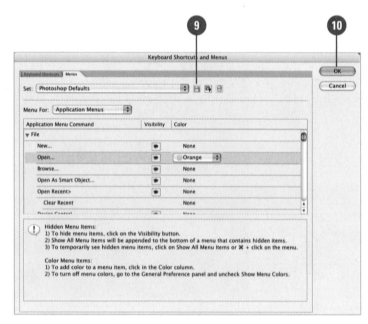

Using Drawing Tablets

When you design on a computer, you're leaving the natural world of oil, watercolor, and canvas, for the electronic world of computer monitors and pixels (don't worry, it's a relatively painless transition). Without a doubt, there are many differences between traditional and digital design; however, it's not necessary to abandon all aspects of the natural media world. For example, the computer mouse has always been a problem with designers who miss the feel and control of a brush in their hands. Fortunately, technology came to the rescue several years ago, with the invention of the drawing tablet. Drawing tablets combine a drawing surface and a brush-like drawing tool in the form of a pen. A designer picks up the pen and moves it across the drawing tablet surface. In turn, the drawing tablet interprets those movements as brush strokes. Not only does Photoshop fully support drawing tablet technology, it also interprets the particular drawing style of the designer. For example, pushing harder with the brush against the drawing tablet instructs Photoshop to create a wider stroke, or to apply more color. Drawing tablets have helped to translate the control of working with real art brushes on canvas, into the world of the digital designer. Of all the manufacturers, Wacom stands out as the leader in drawing tablet technology. Wacom returns the feel of designing with a brush to the digital designer's world, and the software required to power the tablet works seamlessly with Photoshop and the Windows or Macintosh operating systems. To check out which tablet might be right for your needs, point your browser to *www.wacom.com* and check out the available options.

Wacom tablet

Drawing pen

Mastering the Art of Selection

4

Introduction

Mastering Adobe Photoshop requires skill in many diverse areas. While modifying an image's color, enhancing an old photograph, or removing dust and scratches may require different skills, they have one common thread—selection. Without a selection, any changes you apply are made to the whole image. For example, if you choose to paint a black stroke, you would select the Paintbrush tool, choose the color black, and begin painting. Photoshop will let you apply black paint to any and all portions of the image. Selections are your way to instruct Photoshop what portions of the active document you want to change and which you want to protect from change.

The Marquee tools are considered Photoshop's "good old" selection tools. In fact they've been a part of Photoshop since the early days. Where the marquee tools let you select areas of an image in a structured way (using squares, circles, lines), the lasso tools add a bit of freeform selection to the mix. Lasso tools require a certain amount of hand/eye coordination. For example, you can use the lasso tool to create a customized selection area around just about any object in a document, be it an animal, vegetable, or mineral. It just requires a good eye, a steady hand, and a really big mouse pad (I hate it when I run out of mouse pad).

Creating a selection lets you influence a specific area of the image. For example, If you are changing the color of a car from red to blue, this is where making a selection really shines. When you select an area of a Photoshop document, the selection becomes the work area—filters, adjustments, and brushes will only work within the selection boundary. Since selection is such an important aspect of controlling what happens in a document, Photoshop gives you many ways to create your desired selection. Mastering the art of selection gives you control over not just what you do, but where you do it.

What You'll Do

Use the Rectangular Marquee Tool

Use the Elliptical Marquee Tool

Use the Single Row and Single Column Marquee Tools

Use the Lasso Marquee Tool

Use the Magnetic Lasso Tool

Use the Polygonal Lasso Tool

Use the Quick Selection Tool

Use the Magic Wand Tool

Select by Color Range

Refine a Selection Edge

Modify an Existing Selection

Add, Subtract and Crop a Selection

Use Channels to Create and Store Selections

Use Free Transform and Transform

Use Content-Aware Scaling

Using the Rectangular Marquee Tool

 PS 3.1

The Rectangular Marquee tool lets you create rectangular and square selection marquees. The Rectangular Marquee tool is excellent for a quick crop, or selecting and moving blocks of image information. Select the Rectangular Marquee tool on the toolbox from the available Marquee options, and then drag the tool using the mouse (or drawing tablet) to control your movements. To further control a selection, hold down the Shift key to produce a perfect square, and hold down the Alt (Win) or Option (Mac) key to create a selection marquee that starts from the center and moves outwards. Releasing the mouse instructs the Rectangular Marquee tool to create the selection.

Use the Rectangular Marquee Tool

1. Select the **Rectangular Marquee** tool on the toolbox.

2. Click the **Tool Preset** list arrow, and then select from the available tool presets.

3. Use the selection options on the Options bar to create a new selection, or add to, subtract from, or intersect with an existing selection.

4. Enter a numerical value (0 to 250) in the Feather box to create a feathered selection edge or click the Refine Edge box to visually fine-tune your feather size.

5. Click the **Style** list arrow, and then select from the available styles:

   ◆ **Normal.** Lets you create freeform rectangular, or square marquee selections.

   ◆ **Fixed Ratio.** Lets you create selections using a specific ratio, such as a 2 to 1 ratio. Enter the Fixed Ratio values in the Width and Height boxes.

   ◆ **Fixed Size.** Lets you create selections based on an absolute size such as 30 pixels by 90 pixels. Enter the Fixed Size values in the Width and Height boxes.

6. Drag the selection area you want.

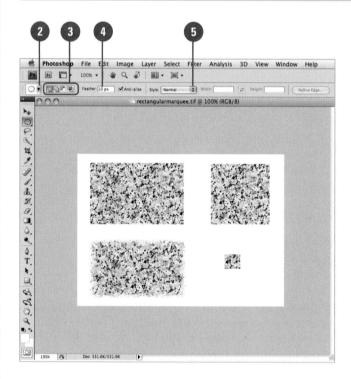

For Your Information

Selecting Areas for a Standard Monitor

If you are selecting areas of an image and plan to display them on a standard monitor (not DVD), then click the Fixed Aspect Ratio option on the Options bar, and then enter a width value of 4, and a height value of 3. Since a normal computer monitor (regardless of resolution) has a 4 by 3 ratio, then selection you make will fit a computer monitor perfectly.

Using the Elliptical Marquee Tool

 PS 3.1

The Elliptical Marquee tool lets you create oval or circular selection marquees. When used with the Layer Mask option, and a couple of creative filters, you can create some awesome vignettes. Select the Elliptical Marquee tool on the toolbox from the available Marquee options, move into the document, and then drag with the tool using the mouse to control your movements. To further control a selection, hold down the Shift key to produce a perfect circle, and hold down the Alt (Win) or Option (Mac) key to create a selection marquee that starts from the center and moves outwards. Releasing the mouse instructs the Elliptical Marquee tool to create the selection.

Use the Elliptical Marquee Tool

1. Select the **Elliptical Marquee** tool on the toolbox.

2. Click the **Tool Preset** list arrow, and then select from the available tool presets.

3. Use the selection options on the Options bar to create a new selection, or add to, subtract from, or intersect with an existing selection.

4. Enter a numerical value (0 to 250) in the Feather option to create a feathered selection edge or click the Refine Edge box to visually fine-tune your feather size.

5. Select the **Anti-alias** check box to create a softer selection.

6. Click the **Style** list arrow, and then select from the available styles:

   ◆ **Normal.** Lets you create freeform elliptical or circular marquee selections.

   ◆ **Fixed Ratio.** Lets you create selections using a specific ratio. Enter the Fixed Ratio values in the Width and Height boxes.

   ◆ **Fixed Size.** Lets you create selections based on an absolute size. Enter the Fixed Size values in the Width and Height boxes.

7. Drag the selection area you want.

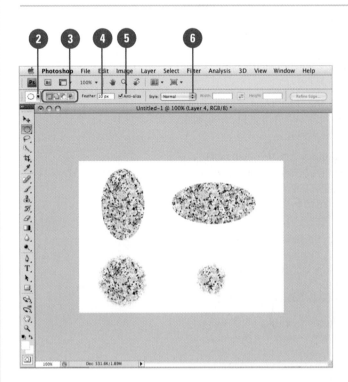

Using the Single Row and Single Column Marquee Tools

 PS 3.1

The Single Row/Single Column Marquee tools let you create a 1-pixel wide horizontal or vertical selection. Select the Single Row or Single Column Marquee tool on the toolbox from the available Marquee options, and then click the tool within the active document to create a single-pixel horizontal or vertical selection. To move the selection, place your cursor on the selection; when you see the cursor change to an arrow, then click and drag. Release the mouse when you have the selection correctly positioned. For precise positioning, press the arrow keys to move the selection 1 pixel at a time.

Use the Single Row and Column Marquee Tool

1. Select the **Single Row Marquee** or **Single Column Marquee** tool on the toolbox.

2. Click the **Tool Preset** list arrow, and then select from the available tool presets.

3. Use the selection options on the Options bar to create a new selection, or add to, subtract from, or intersect with an existing selection.

4. Drag the selection area you want.

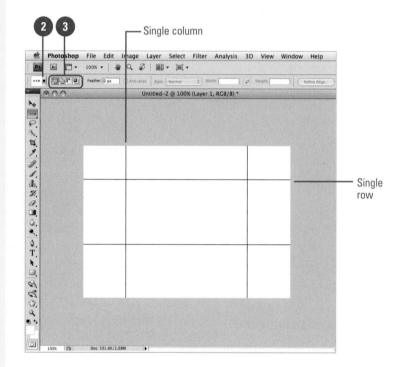

Single column

Single row

Did You Know?

The Column Marquee tools don't have an Anti-Alias option. The reason is that a monitor displays digital information using pixels. Since the pixels fit together just like bricks in a wall, and the Column Marquee tools can only draw vertical or horizontal lines, there is no need to make them look smoother because they're following the horizontal and vertical lines of the pixels.

For Your Information

Creating Customized Guides

Have you ever needed a 45-degree angled guideline? Create a new layer, select the single row (or column) marquee tool, and then click to create a selection in the active document. Now, select black (or any other color) and press Alt+Backspace (Win) or Option+Delete (Mac) to fill the 1-pixel selection with the default color. Click the Edit menu, point to Transform, and then click Rotate. Enter a value of 45 in the Angle option on the Options bar and then you'll have an instant 45-degree guide. Since the guide is in a separate layer, you can use the Move tool to reposition it anywhere it's needed.

Using the Lasso Marquee Tool

 PS 3.1

The Lasso Marquee is a freeform tool that requires a bit of hand-to-eye coordination. Select the Lasso tool on the toolbox from the available Lasso options, move into the active document, and then drag the tool, using the mouse (or drawing tablet) to control your movements. Hold down the Alt (Win) or Option (Mac) key, and then drag to draw straight-line segments. Releasing the mouse instructs the Lasso tool to close the selection shape. That's all there is to it. I did mention that it requires good hand-to-eye coordination, didn't I? When you use this tool, don't drink too much coffee, and have a really big mouse pad.

Use the Lasso Marquee Tool

1. Select the **Lasso** tool on the toolbox.

2. Click the **Tool Preset** list arrow, and then select from the available tool presets.

3. Use the selection options on the Options bar to create a new selection, or add to, subtract from, or intersect with an existing selection.

4. Enter a numerical value (0 to 250) in the Feather box to create a feathered selection edge or click the Refine Edge box to visually fine-tune your feather size.

5. Select the **Anti-alias** check box to create a softer selection (useful with intensely rounded or curved selections).

6. Drag the selection area you want.

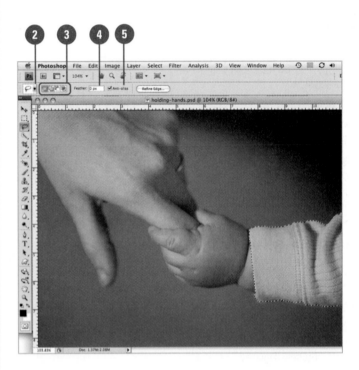

Did You Know?

You can temporarily convert the Lasso tool into a straight-line drawing tool (called the Polygonal Lasso tool). Hold down the Alt (Win) or Option (Mac) key, then release the mouse, move to a different area of the document window and click to draw a straight line between the two points.

Using the Magnetic Lasso Tool

 PS 3.1

The Magnetic Lasso creates a selection by following along the edge of a visible object. For example, it will follow around the edge of a building set against a bright blue sky. In reality there are no edges in a photographic document, so the tool follows along the shifts of brightness created when one tonal value is next to another. Select the Magnetic Lasso tool in the toolbox from the available Lasso options. Click on the visible edge of an object within your image, and then move (don't drag) around the object. The Magnetic Lasso will follow the visible edge of the object, occasionally adding anchor points to the line as you move. Double-clicking the mouse instructs the Magnetic Lasso tool to close the selection shape.

Use the Magnetic Lasso Tool

1. Select the **Magnetic Lasso** tool on the toolbox.

2. Click the **Preset Tool** list arrow, and then select from the available tool presets.

3. Use the selection options on the Options bar to create a new selection, or add to, subtract from, or intersect with an existing selection.

4. Enter a numerical value (0 to 250) in the Feather box to create a feathered selection edge or click the Refine Edge box to visually fine-tune your feather size.

5. Select the **Anti-alias** check box to create a softer selection (useful with intensely rounded or curved selections).

6. Enter a Width value (0 to 256) to instruct the Magnetic Lasso tool how many pixels to consider for the edge.

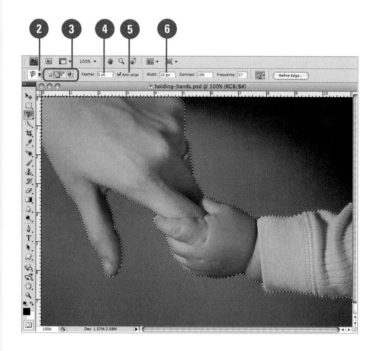

7 Enter an Edge Contrast value (0% to 100%) to instruct the Magnetic Lasso how much of a shift in the brightness values to use in determining the edge.

8 Enter a Frequency value (0 to 100) to instruct the Magnetic Lasso where points are added to the selection line.

9 Click once to create an anchor point, and then move the pointer along the edge you want to trace.

10 If the border doesn't snap to the desired edge, click once to add a anchor point manually. Continue to trace the edge, and add anchor points as needed.

11 Double-click or click the starting point to complete the selection.

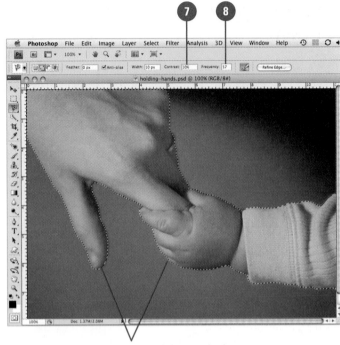

Magnetic Lasso selection

Did You Know?

You can remove anchor points. When you're using the Magnetic Lasso tool and you want to reverse the selection, simply backtrack the mouse all the way back to the last anchor point. To move even farther backwards, press the Backspace (Win) or Delete (Mac) key to remove the last anchor.

You can temporarily use the Magnetic Lasso tool as a freeform Lasso tool. Hold down the Alt (Win) or Option (Mac) key, and then drag to draw. Release the mouse to return to the Magnetic Lasso tool.

Using the Polygonal Lasso Tool

 PS 3.1

The Polygonal Lasso creates straight-line selections, perfect for creating a selection around a windowpane or the roofline of a house. Select the Polygonal Lasso tool in the toolbox from the available Lasso options, and click to create a point; then, move and click to create straight lines between the two points. Keep clicking and moving your mouse until the desired selection shape appears. Double-clicking the mouse instructs the Polygonal Lasso tool to close the selection shape.

Use the Polygonal Lasso Tool

1. Select the **Polygonal Lasso** tool on the toolbox.

2. Click the **Tool Preset** list arrow, and then select from the available tool presets.

3. Use the selection options on the Options bar to create a new selection, or add to, subtract from, or intersect with an existing selection.

4. Enter a numerical value (0 to 250) in the Feather box to create a feathered selection edge or click the Refine Edge box to visually fine-tune your feather size.

5. Select the **Anti-alias** check box to create a softer selection (useful with intensely rounded or curved selections).

6. Click to create anchor points, and then double-click or click the starting point to complete the selection.

Did You Know?

You can temporarily use the Polygonal Lasso tool as a freeform Lasso tool. Hold down the Alt (Win) or Option (Mac) key, and then drag to draw. Release the mouse to return to the Polygonal Lasso tools.

Using the Quick Selection Tool

PS 3.1

The Quick Selection tool makes it easier to select the areas of an image you want. Simply paint a loose selection using an adjustable round brush tip to select the area you want. As you paint with the Quick Selection tool, the selection expands outward and automatically finds and follows defined edges in the image. You can also enable the Auto-Enhance option to reduce roughness and pixelation in the selection edge.

Use the Quick Selection Tool

1. Select the **Quick Selection** tool on the toolbox.

2. Click the **Tool Preset** list arrow, and then select from the available tool presets.

3. Use the selection options on the Options bar to create a new selection, or add to/subtract from an existing selection.

4. Click the **Brush** list arrow, and then select the brush options you want: Diameter, Hardness, Spacing, Angle, Roundness, and Size.

5. Select the **Sample All Layers** check box to create a selection based on all layers, not just the currently selected one.

6. Select the **Auto-Enhance** check box to reduce roughness and pixelation in the selection edge.

7. Paint with the Quick Selection tool to create the selection you want.

   TIMESAVER *Press the right bracket (]) or left bracket ([) to increase or decrease the Quick Selection tool brush size.*

Using the Magic Wand Tool

 PS 3.1

The Magic Wand tool (so named since it looks like a magic wand) is unique in the fact that you do not drag and select with this tool; you simply click. The Magic Wand tool creates a selection based on the shift in brightness ranges within an image. If there is a definable shift in the brightness of the pixels, it can be a very powerful tool for the selection of odd-shaped areas. For example, a brightly colored sunflower contrasted with a bright blue sky would be a snap for the Magic Wand tool. To use the Magic Wand, click on the Magic Wand Tool button in the toolbox. Sometimes it's easier to select what you don't want. In this example, the blue sky was selected and removed. However, you might have wanted to select the sunflower, and move it into another image. If that's the case, it is still easier to select the sky using the Magic Wand, click the Select menu, and then click Inverse to reverse the selection.

Use the Magic Wand Tool

1. Select the **Magic Wand** tool on the toolbox.

2. Use the **Preset Tool** list arrow, and then select from the available tool presets.

3. Use the selection options on the Options bar to create a new selection, or add to, subtract from, or intersect with an existing selection.

4. Enter a Tolerance value (0 to 255). The higher the value, the more information the Magic Wand tool selects.

5. Select the **Anti-alias** check box to create a softer selection (useful with intensely rounded or curved selections).

6. Select the **Contiguous** check box to select adjacent pixels within the active document.

7. Select the **Sample All Layers** check box to sample image information from all layers.

8. Click an area to make a selection.

Results of the Magic Wand tool

86

Selecting by Color Range

 PS 3.1

Photoshop makes selection easy by giving you ways to draw selection borders in any shape, size, or form. However, selection is more than dragging your mouse across the screen to create a selection. In addition to standard drawing tools, Photoshop lets you select image information based on channel color information. Maybe it's that bright red car in your background, or the white stucco finish adorning an adobe house. It doesn't matter, because Photoshop lets you choose the color and the maximum range to select. When you work with the Color Range option, the image displayed in the dialog box becomes a mix of black and white. The white areas represent the selected portions of the image, while the black areas represent the masked portions of the image.

Selection by Color Range

1. Click the **Select** menu, click **Color Range**, and then select an option:

   - **Select.** Lets you choose Sampled Colors, a specific color, or Out-of-Gamut colors.

   - **Localized Color Clusters. (New!)** Select when you want to constrain your color selection to a specific area. Use the Range slider to fix the distance to use with the localized color selection.

   - **Selection or Image.** Lets you view the Selection Mask or the Image.

   - **Selection Preview.** Changes the view of the image in the document window. Select None, Grayscale, Black Matte, White Matte, or Quick Mask.

2. Click the **eyedroppers** to add to or subtract from colors from the selection, and then click within the image.

3. Click the **Fuzziness** slider to increase or decrease the color values selected (0 to 200).

4. Select the **Invert** check box to reverse the Selection Mask.

5. Click **OK** to turn the color range information into a selection.

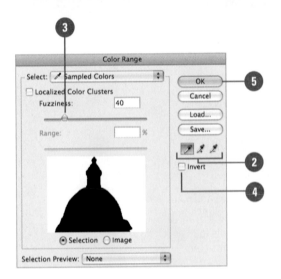

Refining a Selection Edge

 PS 3.4

After you make the initial selection, you can use the Refine Edge tool to fine-tune the selection to your exact specifications. The Refine Edge tool allows you to adjust the selection using the following options: Radius, Contrast, Smooth, Feather, and Contract/Expand. You can also change the view mode to preview the selection against different backgrounds.

Use the Refine Edge Tool

1. Use one of the selection tools to make a selection.

2. Click **Refine Edge** on the Options bar, or click the **Select** menu, and then click **Refine Edge**.

3. Select the **Preview** check box to preview changes.

4. Drag the sliders to adjust the selection.

   ◆ **Radius.** Specifies the size of the selection. Increase to create a more exact selection.

   ◆ **Contrast.** Sharpens the selection edges and removes fuzziness.

   ◆ **Smooth.** Smooths out the rough edges of the selection (from 0 to 100).

   ◆ **Feather.** Creates a soft edge around the selection boundary (from 0 to 250 pixels).

   ◆ **Contract/Expand.** Decreases or increases the selection edge.

5. To change the view modes, click a Selection View icon.

   A description appears below the view mode. Click the **Description** button, if necessary.

   ◆ Double-click the Quick Mask view to change the color mask.

6. Use the **Zoom** or **Hand** tools to change the view size or position.

7. Click **OK**.

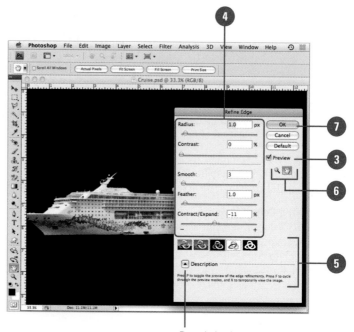

Description button

Modifying an Existing Selection

PS 3.3

Selections can be as simple as dragging a circle or square with one of the marquee tools or as complicated as a freeform selection. Whatever the case, Photoshop allows you to enhance any selection with its useful modification tools. After creating a selection, you can modify it with the various options that Photoshop offers in order to make complex selections easier to use. With selection being an important part of the Photoshop workflow, practice is the key to success.

Selection

Modify an Existing Selection

1 After creating a selection, click the **Select** menu, and then select an option:

◆ **All.** Selects all pixels within the active document.

◆ **Deselect or Reselect.** Removes the active selection or recreates the last active selection.

◆ **Inverse.** Lets you reverse the previous selection.

◆ **All Layers.** Lets you select all the layers in the Layers panel (excluding the Background).

◆ **Deselect Layers.** Deselects all layers in the Layers panel.

◆ **Similar Layers.** Selects similar layers such as: all type layers, or all shape layers.

◆ **Color Range.** Creates a selection based on a range of colors within the active document.

◆ **Feather.** Creates a visually softer selection edge.

◆ **Modify.** Lets you modify the border, Expand, Contract, or Smooth the selection in the active document.

◆ **Grow.** Lets you increase a selection by adding pixels.

◆ **Similar.** Lets you increase a selection by adding non-contiguous pixels.

◆ **Transform Selection.** Creates a bounding box around the active selection that you can modify.

◆ **Edit in Quick Mask Mode.** (**New!**) View your selection in Quick Mask Mode.

◆ **Load or Save Selection.** Lets you load or save a previously saved channel mask selection.

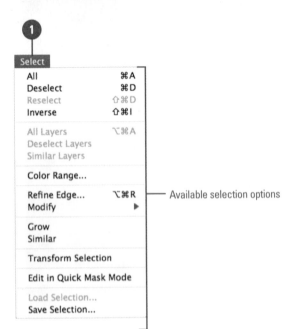

Available selection options

Adding, Subtracting, and Cropping a Selection

PS 3.3, 5.5

To say that Photoshop helps you make selections easily would be an understatement. Not only can you modify selections in any number of ways, Photoshop gives you the option to change your mind by adding and subtracting to an existing selection or even using the selection tools to crop the image. Since most selections are not perfect the first time around, knowing how to modify a selection marquee gives you the control you need to make perfect selections. Adding to and subtracting from an image is accomplished by simple keyboard shortcuts, or by making choices from the Options bar. Either way, you can create complex selections with ease.

Add to an Existing Selection

1. Create a selection using any of Photoshop's selection tools.

2. Add to the selection by holding down the Shift key, and then use a selection tool to add to the existing selection (the selected areas do not need to be contiguous).

3. Release the mouse and the Shift key to complete the addition.

Two separate selections

Subtract from an Existing Selection

1. Create a selection using any of Photoshop's selection tools.

2. Subtract from the selection by holding down the Alt (Win) or Option (Mac) key.

3. Create a selection that intersects with the existing selection.

4. Release the mouse and the keys to complete the subtraction.

Crop an Image

① Create a selection using any of Photoshop's selection tools.

The selection area does not have to be a rectangle.

② Click the **Image** menu, and then click **Crop** to crop the image.

Image cropped

Using Channels to Create and Store Selections

PS 5.3, 5.6

Photoshop's primary method of creating selections is through the use of tools from the toolbox, such as the Marquee, Lasso, and Magic Wand, and while they create impressive and complex selections, Photoshop has other ways to capture that tricky selection using the Channels panel. The Channels panel primarily holds color information, but that's not all it can hold. You can use the Channels panel to create and store complex selections. Photoshop holds selection information using black (masked), white (selected), and shades of gray (percentages of selection). In addition, channels can be saved with the image file.

Create Selections with Channels

1. Select the **Channels** panel.

2. Click the individual color channels.

3. Look for a channel that represents a brightness difference between what you want to select and what you want to mask.

4. Make a copy of the channel by dragging it down over the New Channel button on the Channels panel.

5. Select the new channel.

6. Click the **Image** menu, point to **Adjustments**, and then click **Threshold**.

7. Drag the **Threshold** slider left or right until the visible image represents a black and white mask of your selection.

8. Click **OK**.

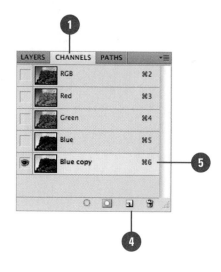

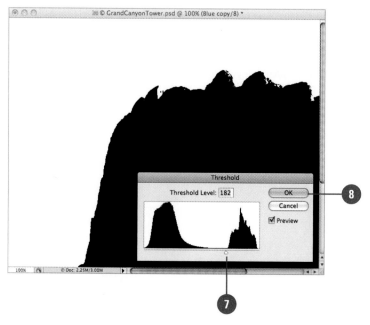

Did You Know?

Selection masks created from color channels will not always be perfect. For example, you may see unwanted spots of white or black. When that happens, do the best you can using the Threshold command, and then paint with white or black to clean up the mask.

Apply Selection Masks to an Image

1. Click the **Select** menu, and then click **Load Selection**.

2. Click the **Channel** list arrow, and then select the newly created channel.

3. Click **OK**.

See Also

See "Creating Channel Masks from Selections" on page 243 for more information on using channel masks as selections.

Selection

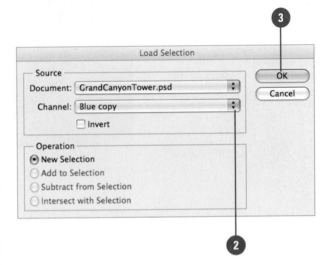

Using Free Transform and Transform

PS 1.4, 3.3

Once a selection is made, the next step is to get to work. Selections are not just useful for correcting color or for image enhancement. It's possible you may need to use some of Photoshop's transform commands on your selections before making further modifications. The Transform commands let you move, modify, or resize the area enclosed within the selection area. Unlike the Free Transform command, Transform gives you several options, such as Scale, Distort, Perspective, and Warp, which you can use to modify an existing selection. The selection area is visually defined by a bounding box with nodes, or anchor points, in the four corners and the center of each axis.

Use the Free Transform Command

1. Select an area of an image using any of Photoshop's selection tools.

2. Click the **Edit** menu, and then click **Free Transform**.

3. Move to any of the four corners, and then drag to expand or contract the size of the selection.

   Move outside the bounding box selection until your cursor resembles a curved arrow, and then drag to rotate the selection.

   You can also drag the horizontal or vertical nodes to expand the image.

4. Press Enter (Win) or Return (Mac), or double-click inside the bounding box to apply the transformation.

Selection enlarged and rotated

andy-Vail.psd @ 33.3% (Layer 1, RGB/8)

3

Did You Know?

You can create proportional transform boundaries. Holding down the Shift key while dragging a corner handle maintains the proportions of the original image.

You can use the Free Transform command to create distorted images. Hold down the Ctrl (Win) or ⌘ (Mac) key, while dragging a corner handle to create a distorted selection.

Use the Transform Command

① Select an area of an image using any of Photoshop's selection tools.

② Click the **Edit** menu, point to **Transform**, and then select an option:

◆ **Again.** Lets you repeat the previous Transform command.

◆ **Scale.** Lets you increase or decrease the size of the selected area.

◆ **Rotate.** Lets you rotate the selection area 0 to 360 degrees.

◆ **Skew.** Lets you select a node and drag it in a vertical or horizontal direction without affecting the other nodes.

◆ **Distort.** Lets you select a node and drag it in any direction desired without affecting the other nodes.

◆ **Perspective.** Lets you change the perspective of a selection.

◆ **Warp.** Lets you wrap an image around any shape using a modifiable grid. To warp an image using a specific shape, click the Warp Style list arrow on the Options bar, and then select a shape, such as Twist, Flag, Fisheye, or Inflate.

TIMESAVER *To show or hide the warp grid and anchor points, click the View menu, and then click Extras.*

③ Select any settings you want on the Options bar and modify the transformed image as desired using the anchor points, a segment of the bounding box or grid, or an area within the grid.

Additional transform commands

Warp   Grid

Using Content-Aware Scaling

The Content-Aware Scale command (**New!**) allows you to resize an image without affecting important parts of the image, such as people, buildings, etc. When you normally scale an image, all the pixels in the image are affected. With Content-Aware scaling, only the pixels in non-important areas are affected. You can upscale or downscale images to fit them on a page or change the orientation. If you want to preserve specific areas of an image, you can use an alpha channel to protect the selected area.

Use Content-Aware Scaling

1. Open a document with the image that you want to scale.

2. To protect content when scaling, select the area that you want to protect using any selection tool.

3. If you're scaling a Background layer, click the **Select** menu, and then click **All**.

4. Click the **Edit** menu, and then click **Content-Aware Scale**.

5. Use any of the following:

   - **Reference Point Location.** Click a square to select a scale point.

   - **Relative Positioning for Reference Point.** Click to specify a new position in relation to its current position.

   - **Image Size.** Enter specific sizes.

   - **Scaling Percentage.** Enter specific percentages for scaling.

   - **Amount.** Specify a ratio of content-aware scaling to normal scaling.

   - **Protect.** Select an alpha channel that specifies an area to protect.

   - **Protect Skin Tones.** Click to preserve areas with skin tones.

6. Drag a handle on the bounding box to scale the image. Use the Shift key to scale proportionately.

7. Click the **Commit Transform** button to keep the change or **Cancel Transform** button to cancel it.

Background layer

Working with Layers

5

Introduction

To be successful with Adobe Photoshop, you need to be in control. You need to control color, to control elements of the design, and you even need to control the order of design elements. If control is what you crave, then Layers, more than any other feature, helps you achieve that control. Layers give you the ability to separate individual elements of your design, and then control how those elements appear. You can think of Layers as a group of transparent sheets stacked on top of each other. Through the creative use of these electronic sheets, you can blend the elements of two or more layers, and create layers to adjust and control contrast, brightness, and color balance. You can even group layers together to help organize and manage your design.

Layers are a digital designer's canvas, and they are just as real as a stretched canvas is to a natural media designer. The strokes you apply to a real canvas, using a brush, are equivalent to strokes in a Photoshop layer when you use any of the painting tools. The natural artist may use oils or watercolor in the design while the Photoshop artist uses electronic ink. The Layers panel allows you to view the image almost as if you were actually painting or designing with natural media. However, our canvas—the Layers panel—goes far beyond anything possible in the "real" world.

In Photoshop, using multiple layers is the way to control the information within a document. There are times when you will create several layers; each layer will contain a separate aspect of the total design. Having multiple layers allows you to adjust and move each element independently. Eventually, multiple layers may no longer be necessary. However, you might not want to link them together, or even place them within the same folder. Instead, you might want to combine them into a single unit. Once again, Photoshop comes to the rescue by giving you several options for combining layers without flattening the entire document.

What You'll Do

Understand the Layers Panel

Define Layer Designations and Attributes

Create a New Layer

Select Layers

Create a Layer Group

Create a Selection from a Layer

Create a Layer from a Selection

Convert a Background into a Layer

Control Image Information Using the Layers Panel

Move Layers Between Documents

Use Merge Layer Options

Link and Unlink Layers

Work with Layer Blending Modes

Duplicate and Delete Layers

Change Layer Properties

Work with Layer Comps Panel

Export Layers as Files

Set Layers Panel Options

Use Smart Guides

Understanding the Layers Panel

With the Layers panel, you can control elements of a Photoshop design by assigning separate layers to each individual object. In addition, Layer effects control the application of everything from drop shadows to gradient overlays, and adjustment layers let you control color overlays and image corrections. To access the Layers panel, select the Layers panel or, if the Layers panel is not visible, click the Window menu, and then click Layers.

Blending Modes. Select this option to change how two or more layers interact or "blend" together.

Opacity. Select a value from 0% to 100% to change the opacity of the active layer.

Fill. Select a value from 0% to 100% to change the opacity of the active layer without changing the opacity of any applied layer styles.

Lock options. Click the Lock Transparent Pixels, Lock Image Pixels, Lock Position, or Lock All button.

Link Layers. Hold down the Shift key and click to select two or more layers, and then click this button to link the layers.

Add Layer Style. Click this button, and then select from the available layer styles.

Add Layer Mask. Click this button to apply a layer mask to the active layer. Click this a second time to add a vector mask to the active layer.

Create New Fill or Adjustment Layer. Click this button, and then select from the available fill or adjustment layers.

Create New Group. Click this button to create a new group. A group is a folder where you can drag, store, and organize layers.

Create New Layer. Click this button to create a new layer in the active document.

Delete Layer. Click this button to delete the active layer.

Layers Options. Click this button to access a menu of layer-specific commands.

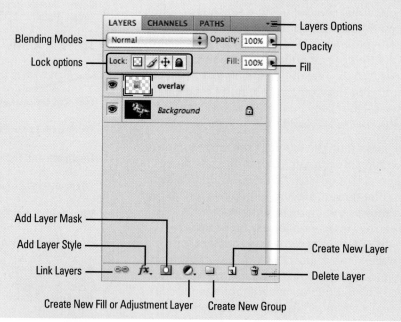

98

Defining Layer Designations and Attributes

Not only does Photoshop give you the ability to generate layers, it allows you to generate layers with different designations. The **designation** of a layer determines the type of information the layer contains. For example, a type layer holds editable text, and a mask layer holds image masks. The ability to control the designation of a layer helps to organize the different elements that typically make up a Photoshop image.

Background. The Background is a unique type of layer element (technically, it's not called the Background layer, just the Background). Backgrounds are always positioned at the bottom of the layer stack and they cannot be moved. In addition, the Background does not support transparency.

Layer. Clicking the Create New Layer button creates Photoshop layers. New layers are always inserted directly above the active layer. All of Photoshop's drawing and shape tools, as well as opacity and fill and blending mode options, are available to use on layers created with this method, except for type. These "traditional" layers can be moved up and down in the layer stack by dragging them where you want them.

Type. To create a Type layer, select one of Photoshop's Type tools, click in the active document and begin typing. Photoshop automatically creates the Type layer directly above the active layer in the Layers panel.

Mask. Masks are applied to a layer by clicking the Add Layer Mask button on the Layers panel. Masks serve a function; they create transparent areas in the visible image. Use masks to remove elements of an image without physically erasing them.

Shape. Shape layers control vector data by the use of a vector mask. You can create a shape layer in one of several ways: select the Pen tool from the toolbox, click the Shape Layer button (located on the Options bar) and begin drawing, or select any of Photoshop's shape tools using the Shape layer option.

Adjustment. Adjustment layers let you control everything from contrast to color. To create an Adjustment layer, click the Create New Fill or Adjustment Layer button, and then select from the available options. The adjustment layer is placed directly above the active layer and controls the information in all the underlying layers. You can also choose from one of the 15 icons in the Adjustments panel (**New!**).

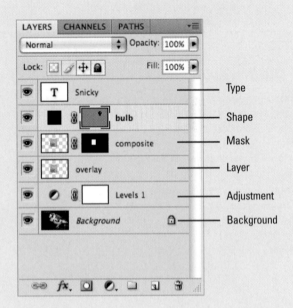

Creating a New Layer

PS 4.1, 5.5

Layers give you control over the design elements of your document, so Adobe Photoshop makes sure you have plenty of layers available to you (up to 8,000). While that may be more layers than you would ever use in a single document, that flexibility guarantees that you have the creative options to carry your designs to any level you desire. To create a new layer, you must first have an open document. A new image in Photoshop has a single layer. If you have more than one document open, make sure the active image is the one to which you want to add a layer. You can quickly add a layer using a menu or button, or add a layer and select options using a dialog box. You can select options to name the layer, designate it as a clipping group, or even change its color Blending mode, and Opacity.

Add Layers to an Active Document

1. Select the **Layers** panel.

2. Click the **Layers Options** button, and then click **New Layer**.

   TIMESAVER *Click the Create New Layer button on the Layers panel to quickly add a layer.*

   The new layer is inserted directly above the active layer.

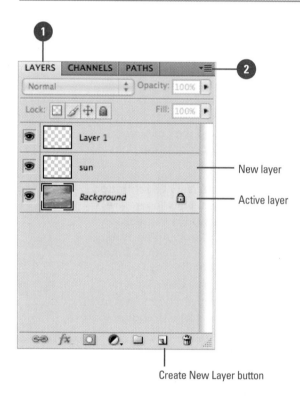

New layer

Active layer

Create New Layer button

Did You Know?

You can move a layer in the stacking order. Press the Ctrl (Win) or ⌘ (Mac) key, and then use the Left/Right Bracket keys ([ ]). The Left Bracket key moves the layer down and the Right Bracket moves the layer up.

You can hide all layers except the clipping mask layer and the layer to which it is clipped. Press the Alt (Win) or Option (Mac) key, and then click the layer's visibility icon.

Add Layers and Select Options

1 Select the **Layers** panel.

2 Hold down the Alt (Win) or Option (Mac) key, and then click the **Create New Layer** button to open the New Layer dialog box.

3 Select the layer options you want:

◆ **Name.** Enter the name of the layer into the Name box.

◆ **Use Previous Layer to Create Clipping Mask.** Select this check box to use the image information in the previous layer to mask the elements of the new layer.

◆ **Color.** This option lets you color-code your layers. Click the Color list arrow, and then select from the available colors.

◆ **Mode.** Click the Mode list arrow, and then select from the available blending modes.

◆ **Opacity.** This option controls the visibility of the new layer. Select a value from 0% to 100%.

4 Click **OK**.

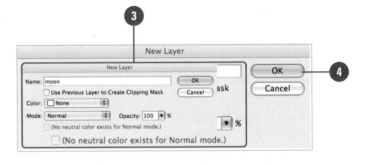

Did You Know?

You can control to which layers the adjustment is applied. To confine the effects of an adjustment layer to the layer immediately below, hold down the Alt (Win) or Option (Mac) key, and then click on the visible line separating the adjustment layer from the next lower layer.

For Your Information

Selecting Layer Options

When you create a new blank layer in Photoshop, the size of the file does not increase. It's only when you begin painting, or adding information to the layer that the size of the Photoshop document will begin to grow. For example, creating a blank layer in a document with a file size of 10 MB does nothing to increase the size of the file. However, opening a 10 MB file, and creating a copy of the original document layer, will create a file size of 20 MB. Layers are great creative tools, but you only want to use them when you need them. Remember, performance is directly related to the size of the active document file, and the bigger the file size, the slower Photoshop performs.

Selecting Layers

 PS 4.1, 4.2

Photoshop lets you select multiple layers either in the Layers panel, or directly in the document window, using the Move tool. Say, for example, you want to quickly move two or more layers but you don't want to spend the time linking, and then unlinking them. You just want to quickly select the layers, and then perform the move. Or, perhaps you want to delete several layers but don't want to delete them one at a time. The ability to select multiple layers allows you to exert even more control over Photoshop, and that control provides more fuel for your creative energy. A single selected layer is called the **active layer**.

Select Layers

1. Open a multi-layered document.

2. Select multiple layers in the Layers panel using the following options:

   ◆ **Contiguous Layers.** Click on the first layer, and then Shift+click the last layer to select first, last, and all layers in-between.

   ◆ **Non-Contiguous Layers.** Click on a layer, hold down the Ctrl (Win) or ⌘ (Mac) key, and then click on another layer.

3. Select layers in the document window using the following options:

   ◆ **Single and Multiple Layers.** Select the Move tool, choose the Auto-Select Layer or Auto-Select Group in the Options bar, and then click on an object in the document window. The layer holding that object is selected. To add to or subtract layers from the selection, Shift+click (or drag).

   TIMESAVER *Select the Move tool, hold down the Ctrl (Win) or ⌘ (Mac) key, and then click on an object. Hold down the Shift+Ctrl (Win) or Shift+⌘ (Mac), and click on another object to add that object's layer to the selection.*

4. To deselect all layers, click the **Select** menu, and then click **Deselect Layers**.

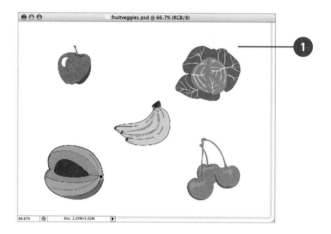

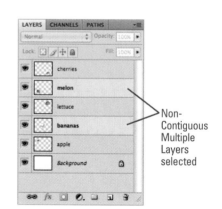

Contiguous Multiple Layers selected

Non-Contiguous Multiple Layers selected

Creating a Layer Group

PS 4.1, 4.3

Layer groups help to bring organization to large, multi-layered documents. Photoshop layer groups give you control over all the layers within the group at one time. For example, multiple layers within a group can all be hidden or locked with one click of a button. In addition, if you click on the Group name, you can transform or move all the layer objects within the group as one unit. To further help organize your Layers panel, Photoshop lets you create nested groups. Nested groups are groups that are located within other groups. When you nest groups, you control all of the groups by clicking on the main group's name, or you can control the individual groups by selecting the nested group name.

Create a Layer Group or Nested Layer Group

1 Open a document.

2 Select the **Layers** panel.

3 If the document contains a layer group, click the **triangle** to expand the group, and then select one of the layers within the group to create a nested group.

4 Click the **Create New Group** button on the Layers panel, or press Ctrl+G (Win) or ⌘+G (Mac).

Photoshop creates a layer group.

TIMESAVER *To quickly create a Layer Group, hold down the Shift key and click the layers you want in the group, click the Layers Options button, and then click New Group from Layers.*

5 To add layers to the group, drag layers from the Layers panel onto the folder icon of the group.

6 To remove layers from the group, drag them from the group back into the Layers panel.

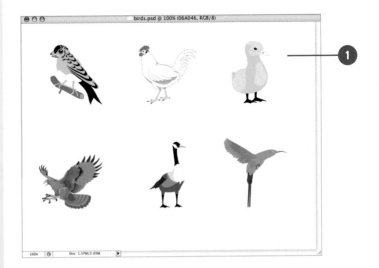

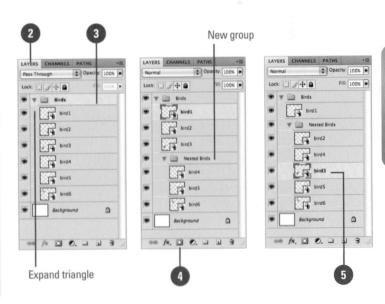

New group

Expand triangle

Creating a Selection from a Layer

Photoshop's traditional layers basically function like sheets of transparent acetate or clear plastic. Once created, they support all of Photoshop's painting tools, as well as shape and gradient tools. While traditional layers may start out transparent, they don't remain that way for long. In fact, a layer can, over time, become a complicated mix of non-transparent (the image), and transparent areas. It's also possible you might want to make a selection out of that complicated image. Photoshop knows this and gives you an easy way to convert a layer into a selection.

Create a Selection from a Layer

1. Select the **Layers** panel.

2. Hold down the Ctrl (Win) or ⌘ (Mac) key, and then click on the image thumbnail of the layer you want converted into a selection. Be sure you click on the image thumbnail, not the layer name as you would have in previous versions.

   The visible portions of the image on the layer are converted into a selection.

   IMPORTANT *Since Photoshop creates the selection based on the image information, there must be transparent and non-transparent areas within the image or the command selects the entire layer as if you had clicked the Select menu, and then clicked All.*

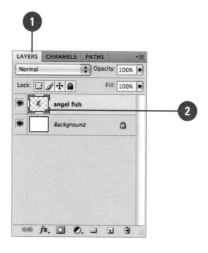

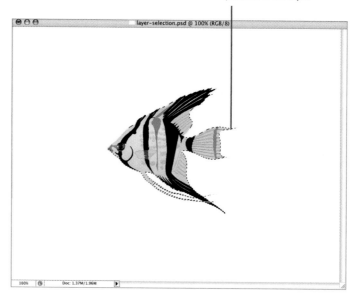

Selection based on the visible portions of the layer.

Creating a Layer from a Selection

On the previous page, you learned how to create a selection based on the image information within a layer. In addition to creating a selection from a layer, Photoshop gives you the ability to instantly create a layer from a selection. Creating layers from selections opens up all kinds of opportunities for generating special effects. For example, you could select an object from one layer, and then make a layer with that selection, or you could make a selection of just that portion of an image and then apply a layer style to the new layer copy. The possibilities are endless, and part of the fun of using Photoshop lies in exploring those possibilities.

Create a Layer from a Selection

1. Select the **Layers** panel.

2. Click on the layer containing the information you want to convert into a layer.

3. Select an area of the image using any of Photoshop's selection tools.

4. Press Ctrl+J (Win) or press ⌘+J (Mac) to make a copy.

   Photoshop converts the selected area into a new layer, and places that layer directly above the active layer.

Did You Know?

You can make a copy of all elements within a layer. Select the layer in the Layers panel, and then click Ctrl+J (Win), ⌘+J (Mac). Since there are no selections, Photoshop creates a copy of the entire layer.

You can make copies of layer objects without a selection. To make a copy of a layer that contains an object, select the layer in the Layers panel, select the Move tool, hold down the Alt (Win) or Option (Mac) key, and then click and drag (in the document window).

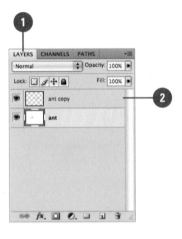

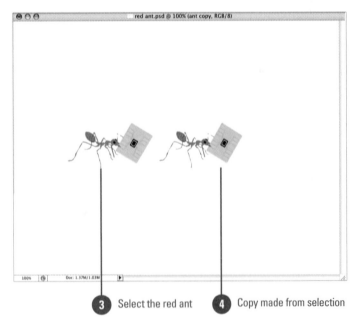

3 Select the red ant   4 Copy made from selection

Converting a Background into a Layer

The Background layer serves a unique function in Photoshop. Since some layout programs do not support Photoshop's multiple layer and transparency capabilities, a final image must sometimes be converted into a background layer by a process called **flattening**. When an image is flattened, all of the document's layers are compressed into a single layer in the Layers panel, named Background. That means no more layers, no more transparency, and no more control. Background layers are a necessary evil because Photoshop does not stand alone, and it's sometimes necessary to move images from Photoshop into other applications. However, there are times you may start with an image that only contains a Background layer (for example, when working with original images from a digital camera, scanned images, or images from a photo CD or DVD) and you want to apply transparency, blending modes, or other adjustments to it that cannot be applied to a Background layer. In that case, you will need to convert the Background into a traditional Photoshop layer.

Convert a Background

① Select the **Layers** panel.

② Double-click on the Background to open the New Layer dialog box.

③ Rename the layer in the Name box (leave the other options at their default values).

④ Click **OK**.

The Background is converted into a traditional layer.

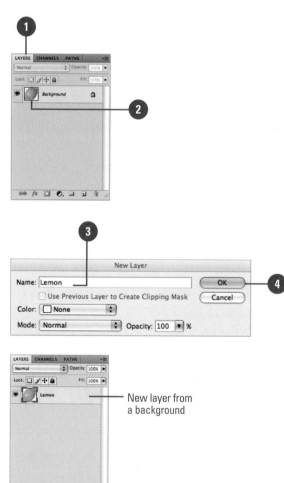

New layer from a background

Convert a Multi-Layered Document into a Background

1 Select the **Layers** panel.

2 Click the **Layers Options** button, and then click **Flatten Image**.

The multi-layered document is compressed into a single-layer Background.

Did You Know?

You can create a composite image of a multi-layered document without flattening the image. Create and select a new layer, and then hold down the Alt (Win) or Option (Mac) key. Now, go to the Layers panel, click the Layers Options button, and then click Merge Visible. Photoshop creates a composite of all the visible layers in the new layer. You now have the control and flexibility of a multi-layered document, along with a separate composite layer. Control gives you the confidence to be more creative.

See Also

See "Using Merge Layer Options" on page 110 for more information on how to merge two or more layers without flattening all the layers.

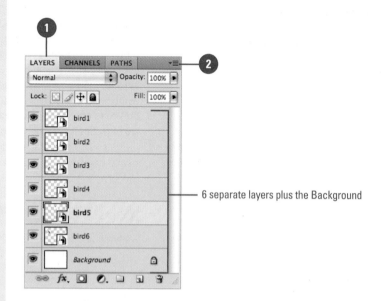

6 separate layers plus the Background

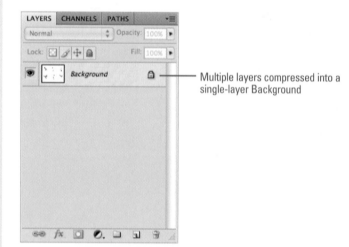

Multiple layers compressed into a single-layer Background

Controlling Image Information Using the Layers Panel

PS 4.2

When you work on multi-layered documents, it's important to understand the options Photoshop gives you to control image information. For example, working on a document that contains 20 layers is a difficult proposition. Fortunately, Photoshop gives you complete control over the document; everything from layer names to locking pixel information is available in Photoshop's bag of image-control tricks. For example, when linking two layers together, you can move or resize the layers at the same time, thus saving valuable time. Let's explore some of the ways you can control image information with the Layers panel.

Control Image Information

1 Select the **Layers** panel, and then use one of the following options:

- **Layer Name.** To name a layer, double-click on the current layer name, type a new name, and then press Enter (Win) or Return (Mac).

- **Show/Hide.** To temporarily hide or show a layer (make its contents invisible or visible in the document window), click the Eyeball button, located in the Show/Hide box.

- **Linking.** To link two or more layers, hold the Shift key and click the layers you want to link, and then click the **Link Layers** button (located at the bottom left of the Layers panel). The link icon indicates the layers are linked. Linking lets you move or resize the layers as a unit.

- **Locking.** The four available locking options are: Lock Transparent Pixels, Lock Image Pixels, Lock Position, and Lock All.

- **Stacking Order.** To change the position of a layer in the stack, drag the layer up or down. A dark line appears as a visual cue to indicate the new layer location.

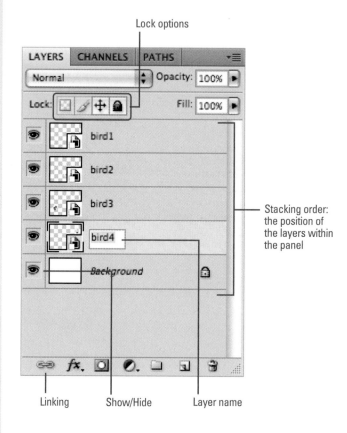

Moving Layers Between Documents

 PS 4.2

Photoshop documents typically contain multiple layers. One web survey concluded that Photoshop designers tend to create documents with an average of 14 layers. Controlling layers is an important aspect of design, because the more control you maintain, the more organized you are, and the better your design will be. But what about controlling layers across multiple documents? For example, you're working on a design, and you need access to some additional image information. The only problem is that the additional information is located in another Photoshop document. Photoshop gives you the ability to move layers between open documents.

Move Layers Between Documents

1 Open the documents in which you want to move layers.

2 To have more than one document in view, click the **Window** menu, point to **Arrange**, and then click **Cascade** or **Tile**.

3 Click on the document containing the layer you want to move.

4 Drag the layer from the Layers panel into the window of the receiving document.

Photoshop creates a new layer with a copy of the image information from the other document.

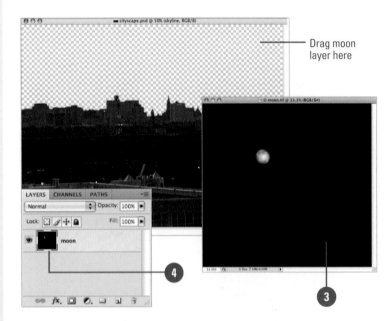

Drag moon layer here

Did You Know?

You can control the position of the moved layer. Hold down the Shift key while dragging the layer into the other document. Photoshop aligns the new layer to the center of the receiving document.

You can move selected portions of a layer. Select the area you want to move, click the Move tool, and then drag the selected area directly from the document window into the window of the receiving document.

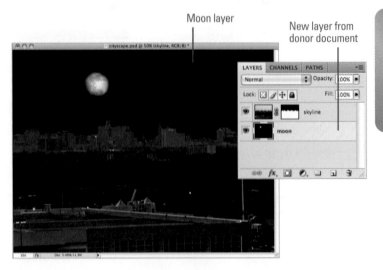

Moon layer

New layer from donor document

Using Merge Layer Options

PS 4.2

The Merge Down option lets you merge one selected layer into the layer directly below it in the layer stacking order. Merged layers take on the characteristics of the layer into which they are being merged. For example, if you merge one layer into another that uses the Darken blending mode, the two merged layers will both use Darken. Or, if you merge a layer into the Background layer, the merged layer becomes a part of the Background. The Merge Visible option enables you to merge all of the layers that have the Show option enabled with just one click.

Merge Down

① Select the **Layers** panel.

② Select the layers you want to merge.

③ Click the **Layers Options** button, and then click **Merge Down** (for single selection) or **Merge Layers** (for multiple selection).

The selected layers merge into the next layer down. When you use the Merge Down command, the top layer will take on the name and characteristics of the bottom layer.

TIMESAVER *Press Ctrl+E (Win) or ⌘+E (Mac) to merge layers down.*

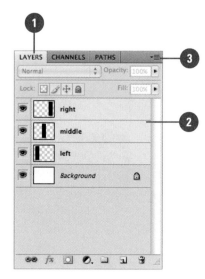

Merge Visible

① Select the **Layers** panel.

② Click the **Show** option for all layers you want to merge.

③ Click the **Layers Options** button, and then click **Merge Visible**.

All layers with the Show option enabled are merged together.

TIMESAVER *Press Alt (Win) or Option (Mac), click the Layer menu, and then click Merge Visible to merge all visible layers into a new layer.*

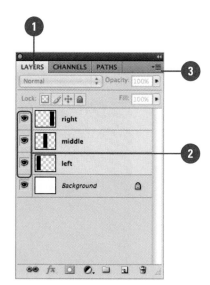

Linking and Unlinking Layers

If you're currently looking at the Layers panel, and wondering where the linking button is, don't worry. It's not missing; it's just been moved. Linking multiple layers is a snap. Simply select one or more layers and then click the Link Layers button at the bottom of the Layers panel. You can link two or more layers or groups. Unlike selected multiple layers, linked layers retain their relationship (stay together) until you unlink them, which allows you to move or resize the layers as a unit.

Link Layers

1. Open a multi-layered document.

2. Select the **Layers** panel.

3. Select two or more layers.

4. Click the **Link Layers** button, located at the bottom of the Layers panel.

   The selected layers are now linked. A link icon appears next to the linked layers.

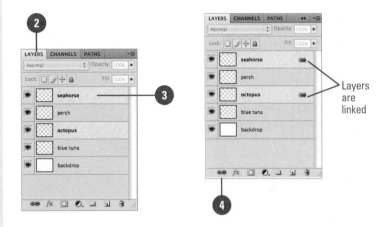

Unlink Layers

1. Open a multi-layered document that contains links.

2. Select the **Layers** panel.

3. Select a layer that contains the link icon.

   TIMESAVER *To unlink several linked layers, select them before continuing.*

4. Click the **Link Layers** button, located at the bottom of the Layers panel.

   TIMESAVER *To temporarily disable a linked layer, Shift+click the link icon. A red X appears. Shift+click the link icon again to enable it.*

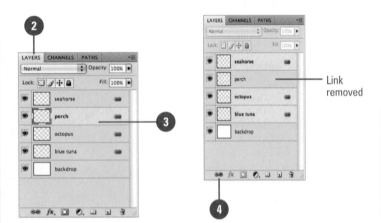

Working with Layer Blending Modes

 PS 4.4

Mix Layer Information with Blending Modes

1. Open a multi-layered document.

2. Select the **Layers** panel.

3. Select a layer.

   Since blending modes affect all layers below the one to which the blending mode is applied, select the layer directly above the layer you want to blend.

4. Click the **Blending Mode** list arrow, and then select a blending mode.

   Photoshop uses the selected blending mode to visually blend the image through all the layers below the blending mode layer.

Did You Know?

You can control the number of layers to which a blending mode is applied. Hold down the Alt (Win) or Option (Mac) key, and then click on the visible line separating the adjustment layer from the next lower layer.

Layer Blending Modes are one of the most creative areas within the Layers panel. With blending modes, you can instruct Photoshop to mix the image information between two or more layers. For example, using the Multiply blending mode instructs Photoshop to multiply the color of one layer with that of another layer, resulting in a darker color. Blending modes give you control over Photoshop images above and beyond what you would expect to find in the "analog" world.

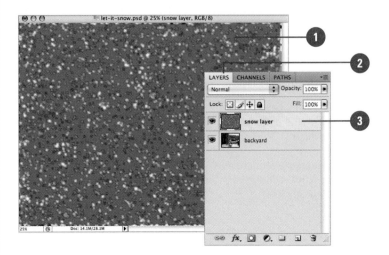

The snow layer blended with the backyard layer.

Duplicating a Layer

There are times when you will need a copy of a Photoshop layer. Duplicating a layer is a simple process that creates a pixel-to-pixel copy of the selected layer. Once the copied layer is created, it becomes a separate image within the document. You can then begin to make changes to the new layer. Duplicating a layer gives you the ability to control each layer separately and to apply nondestructive effects to your image by making them on a copy of the image instead of the original.

Duplicate a Layer

1. Select the **Layers** panel.

2. Select the layer you want to duplicate.

3. Click the **Layers Options** button, and then click **Duplicate Layer**.

4. Enter a name for the new layer.

5. To place the layer in another open document, click the **Document** list arrow, and then select a document.

6. Click **OK**.

Did You Know?

You can duplicate a layer with the Create New Layer button. Drag the layer over the Create New Layer button and Photoshop creates an exact copy of the layer and appends the word *copy* at the end of the original layer name.

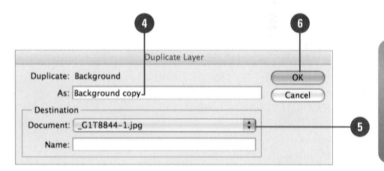

Deleting Layers

PS 4.2

While Photoshop lets you add layers to a document (up to 8,000), it also lets you delete layers. Remember that once you've deleted a layer and saved the document, there is no way to recover the deleted layer. However, while the document is open, there is always the chance of recovering the deleted layer through the History panel.

Delete Layers

1. Select the **Layers** panel, and then select the layer you want to delete.

2. Hold down the Alt (Win) or Option (Mac) key, and then click the **Delete Layer** button.

Did You Know?

You can delete a layer from the layers panel by dragging. Click the layer you want to delete, and then drag it to the Delete Layer button.

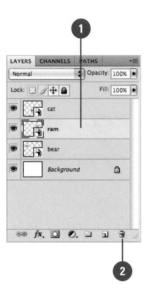

The selected layer has been removed from the Layers panel.

Delete Linked Layers

1. Select the **Layers** panel, and then hold down the Shift key and click on the layers you want to delete.

2. Hold down the Alt (Win) or Option (Mac) key, and then click the **Delete Layer** button.

    Photoshop deletes all the linked layers.

Did You Know?

You can delete hidden layers from the Layers panel. Click the Layers Options button, and then click Delete Hidden Layers.

Selected layers are removed from the Layers panel.

Changing Layer Properties

The Layer Properties dialog box gives you control over two very important characteristics of a layer: the layer's name and its identifying color. For example, if you're working on a document with 20 layers and you're not naming the layers, after a while you'll lose track of each layer's contents. When you name your layers, you have a visual identifier of the information contained within that specific layer (assuming you name the layer correctly). In addition, you can use the Colorize option to apply a color to a specific group of layers—coloring all the type layers red, for example. Layer properties may not seem that important, but they go a long way towards helping you organize a complex, multi-layered document.

Change Layer Properties

1. Select the **Layers** panel.

2. Click the **Layers Options** button, and then click **Layer Properties**.

   TIMESAVER *Hold down the Alt (Win) or Option (Mac) key and double-click a layer name to open Layer Properties.*

3. Change the name of the layer.

4. Click the **Color** list arrow, and then click a layer color.

5. Click **OK**.

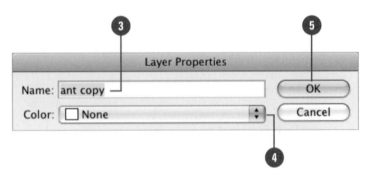

Working with the Layer Comps Panel

 PS 4.3

Layer Comps are an image or snapshot of the current state of the Layers panel. When you create a Layer Comp, you're recording layer visibility, a layer's position within the document, and any layer styles applied to the image. Making changes to the layers in your document and then updating the Layer Comps panel creates a new Layer Comp. Any time you want to view a particular Layer Comp, just select it from the Layer Comps panel. Layer Comps create different versions of your document and saves them all in one file, giving you different creative options for the same document. In addition, they give you the option of printing the same document with different variations, by choosing different Layer Comps during printing.

Work with the Layer Comps Panel

1. Open a document.

2. Click the **Window** menu, and then click **Layer Comps** to open the Layer Comps panel.

3. Click the **Create New Layer Comp** button to create a snapshot of the current state of the image.

4. Select check boxes to adjust a layer's visibility, position, or appearance (layer style).

5. Click **OK**.

6. Click the **Create New Layer Comp** button to create another snapshot of the current state of the image.

7. Repeat steps 4 and 5 to create as many layer comps as you need.

8. Click the left and right arrows to cycle through the current layer comps.

9. Click the **Update Layer Comp** button to update the selected layer comp to the current state of the image.

10. Click the **Layer Comp** icon to change the active image to the selected layer comp state.

11. To remove a layer comp, click the **Delete Layer Comp** button.

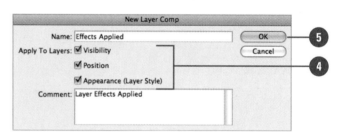

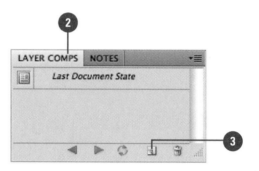

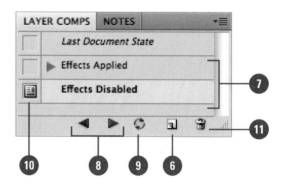

Exporting Layers as Files

Photoshop gives you the option of exporting and saving layers as individual files using a variety of formats including PSD, BMP, JPEG, PDF, Targa, and TIFF. When exporting layers to files, one format is applied to all exported layers. The Export Layers to Files script command gives you the ability to create individual files from the individual layers and select options specific to the file format you want.

Export Layers to Files

1. Open a document.

2. Click the **File** menu, point to **Scripts**, and then click **Export Layers to Files**.

3. To specify a destination for the files, click **Browse**, and then select a folder location.

4. Enter the name you want at the beginning of the files.

5. To export only visible layers, click the **Visible Layers Only** check box.

6. Click the **File Type** list arrow, and then select an output option: PSD, BMP, JPEG, PDF, Targa, TIFF, PNG-8, or PNG-24.

7. To embed a color profile, select the **Include ICC Profile** check box.

8. Specify the options you want that relate to the selected file format.

9. Click **Run**.

10. Upon completion, click **OK**.

   The files are named with the prefix you specified and numbered in sequential order.

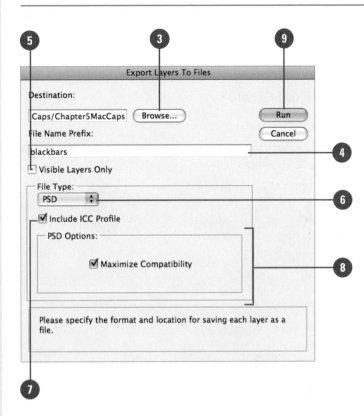

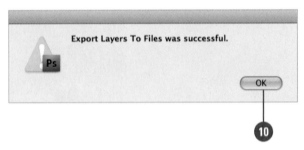

Setting Layers Panel Options

Photoshop doesn't have a lot of options for controlling the Layers panel itself; in fact, there is only one—changing the size of the layer thumbnail and how it fits within the thumbnail box. You can choose to view the layer thumbnail in a small, medium, or large size, or you can select to have no thumbnail shown at all. When you change the size of the thumbnail, you're instructing Photoshop to spend either more, or less, processing time on the display of the image. The larger the thumbnail, the easier it is to see, but the longer it takes for Photoshop to draw the image in the Layers panel. If you're experiencing performance issues with Photoshop, and you're using the large thumbnail size option, you might consider choosing a smaller thumbnail size.

Set Layers Panel Options

1. Select the **Layers** panel.

2. Click the **Layers Options** button, and then click **Panel Options**.

3. Click a thumbnail size or the **None** option.

4. Click the **Layer Bounds** or **Entire Document** option.

5. Select the **Use Default Masks on Fill Layers** check box to automatically insert a mask when creating a new Adjustment layer.

   Select **Expand New Effects** if you would like to view Smart Filters or Layer Styles in the Layers panel. You can also click the triangle next to the Smart Filter or Layer Style icon in the Layers panel.

6. Click **OK**.

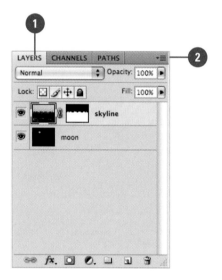

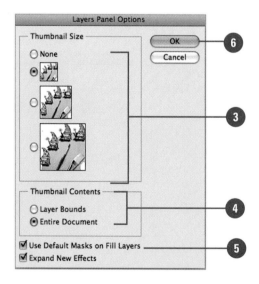

Using Smart Guides

Photoshop gives you the ability to use Smart Guides to help align shapes, slices, and selections as you draw. They appear automatically as you draw a shape or create a selection or slice, and then disappear after the shape is drawn. They enable you to visually align one object to another with a minimum of effort. Smart Guides are automatically turned on by default.

Use Smart Guides

1 Open or create a multi-layered document.

2 Select a layer that contains an object.

3 Select the **Move** tool, and drag the object.

As you move the object, Smart Guides appear to help you align the objects.

4 Release the mouse and the guides disappear.

Did You Know?

You can turn Smart Guides on and off. Click the View menu, point to Show, and then click Smart Guides.

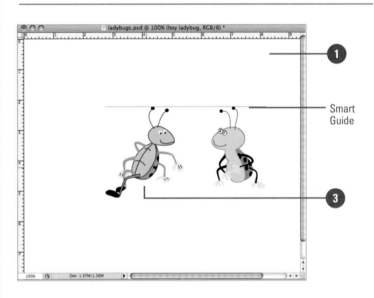

Smart Guide

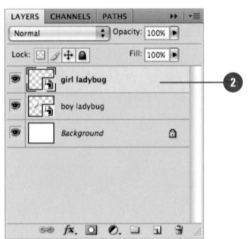

Working with the History Panel

6

Introduction

Adobe introduced the History panel in Photoshop 5, and the graphic design world hasn't been the same since. On an elementary level, the History panel gives you the ability to perform multiple undos. Think of History as a magical mistake correction tool that never wears out. However, the History panel does much more than give you the ability to go back in time and correct your mistakes. The History panel is simply a tool, but when you combine the power of the History panel with the History brush and the Art History brush, you have a trio of tools that can take your creative designs to the next level and beyond.

Adobe Photoshop gives you two ways to use the History panel—linear and non-linear. The **linear** mode helps you keep track of your recent steps, and erases any steps that interfere with a linear flow to the panel. The **non-linear** mode preserves all the steps (linear or non-linear), and is useful when you need to think outside the linear box.

Photoshop raises the bar with the History panel by giving you the ability to record and save the commands performed to a document in a text file. Now, you can finally know exactly what you did to an image. And since the document can be printed, you can create History text documents of your favorite restoration and manipulation techniques, and save them.

In addition, when you combine the History brush with the History panel, you have an awesome creative tool that can't be beat. In fact, it's even possible to convert the Eraser tool into a History brush.

What You'll Do

Set History Panel Options

Work with Linear and Non-Linear History

Control the Creative Process with Snapshots

Duplicate a History State in Another Document

Save the History State of a Document

Review the History State Text File

Combine the History Brush with a History State

Use the Art History Brush

Change the Eraser Tool into the History Brush

Control History States

Setting History Panel Options

Working with the History panel requires a firm understanding of how the panel functions, and what you can and cannot do with History. The History panel records your steps as you work through a document. A step is defined as a specific action, such as creating a layer or adding a brush stroke. Every time you perform an action, a step is recorded in the History panel. The History panel gives you the ability to go back to a previous history state, which is the same as performing an undo command. You can perform multiple undo commands up to the number you set in Photoshop preferences for the History States. In addition, the History panel creates snapshots of the document. **Snapshots** are images of the current state of the document. Snapshots are used in conjunction with the History and Art History Brushes to create special effects.

Set Number of History States

1. Click the **Edit** (Win), or **Photoshop** (Mac) menu, point to **Preferences**, and then click **Performance**.

2. Enter a value from 0 to 1000 for the number of steps recorded in the History States box.

3. Click **OK**.

Did You Know?

You can duplicate a History State. Hold down the Alt (Win) or Option (Mac) key, and then click the History State you want to duplicate.

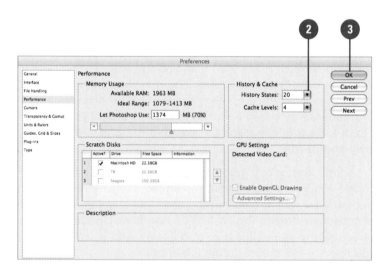

For Your Information

Performing Multiple Undos

The History panel represents the ability to perform multiple undo commands (as many History States as you originally chose in the Performance/History & Cache section of Preferences. However when you press Ctrl+Z (Win), or ⌘+ Z (Mac) you only move back and forth between the last two commands, just like a normal undo. To perform multiple undo commands, press Ctrl+Shift+Z (Win) or ⌘+Shift+Z (Mac) to move forward through all your History steps, or press Alt+Shift+Z (Win) or Option+Shift+Z (Mac) to move backwards through the available History steps.

Set History Options

① Select the **History** panel.

② Click the **History Options** button, and then click **History Options**.

③ Select the check boxes for the History Options you want to use:

◆ **Automatically Create First Snapshot.** Creates a snapshot (image) when the document first opens.

◆ **Automatically Create New Snapshot When Saving.** Creates a snapshot every time you save the document.

This is useful for keeping track of the changes made to a document.

◆ **Allow Non-Linear History.** Allows you to operate History in a non-linear state.

◆ **Show New Snapshot Dialog By Default.** Opens a dialog box with options each time you create a new snapshot.

◆ **Make Layer Visibility Changes Undoable.** Instructs Photoshop to make any changes made to a layer's visibility undoable.

④ Click **OK**.

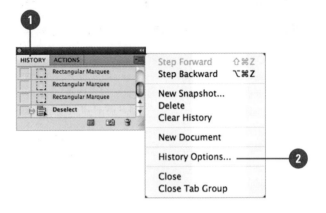

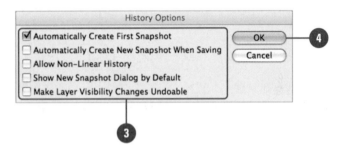

Working with Linear and Non-Linear History

The History panel records each step performed on a Photoshop document in a linear fashion from top to bottom. However, the purpose of the History panel is not to simply record your progress through a document; it's there to help you make changes and go back in time to correct mistakes. Photoshop gives you two History panel modes—linear and non-linear. When you work in a linear History panel, clicking on a previous step causes all steps underneath to become grayed out (unavailable). If you then add a step, the grayed-out steps are removed and the new step is added to the bottom of the list. A linear panel is organized and very RAM efficient; however, once a History Step is removed, it cannot be retrieved. When you work in a non-linear History panel, clicking on a previous step does not cause the steps underneath to become grayed out. If you then add a step, the new step is added to the bottom of the History panel. The new step represents the characteristics of the step you selected, plus any added actions. A non-linear panel is not organized and consumes more RAM. Its advantage lies in the fact that History steps are not deleted, they are simply reorganized.

Work with Linear History

1. Select the **History** panel.

2. Click the **History Options** button, and then click **History Options**.

3. Clear the **Allow Non-Linear History** check box, and then click **OK**.

4. Work in the document until you have generated 10 or 15 steps in the History panel.

5. Move halfway up the History panel, and then click on a step.

   The steps below the selected step turn gray.

6. Perform another action to the image.

   The grayed steps are removed, replaced by the latest action applied to the image.

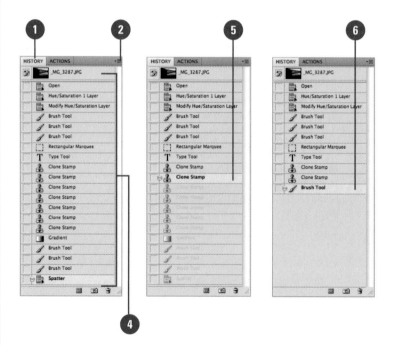

Work with Non-Linear History

1 Select the **History** panel.

2 Click the **History Options** button, and then click **History Options**.

3 Select the **Allow Non-Linear History** check box.

4 Click **OK**.

5 Work in the document until you have generated 10 or 15 steps in the History panel.

6 Move halfway up the History panel, and then click on a step.

The steps below the selected step do not change.

7 Perform another action to the image.

The new step is added to the bottom of the History steps.

Did You Know?

You can quickly purge the History States, and therefore recoup additional RAM. Hold down the Alt (Win) or Option (Mac) key, click the History Options button, and then click Clear History. But be warned; there is no undo available. You are stuck with your decision.

You can reduce memory usage by using linear history. Non-linear History requires more RAM to maintain. If you don't require a non-linear history and want to decrease RAM usage, then you can turn it off. In the History panel, click the History Options button, click History Options, clear the Allow Non-Linear History check box, and then click OK.

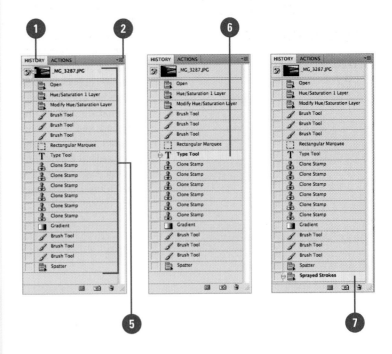

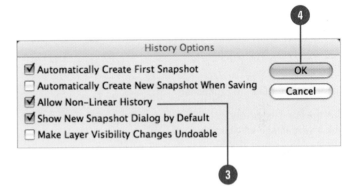

Controlling the Creative Process with Snapshots

The History panel contains more than just steps; it also holds Snapshots. A Snapshot is an image of the document as it exists at the time the snapshot was taken. The History panel can hold as many snapshots as needed, and they are not subject to the number of History States you chose in Preferences. That means they stay with the document throughout the creative process. By default, Photoshop takes a snapshot of the image when it first opens. This snapshot represents the original state of the image, before any adjustments or modifications are applied, and is identified with the file name of the image. It's a good idea to create a snapshot every time you make a major change to the image. That way, if you want to start all over, all you have to do is click on the snapshot, and Photoshop returns you to the moment in time in which the snapshot was created. It's like having your own personal time machine.

Create Snapshots

1. Select the **History** panel.

2. Click the **History Options** button, and then click **History Options**.

3. Select the **Show New Snapshot Dialog by Default** check box, and then click **OK**.

4. Perform several actions to the image.

5. Click the **Create New Snapshot** button.

6. Type a name for the new snapshot.

7. Click the **From** list arrow, and then click a save image information option:

   ◆ **Full Document.** Saves the entire visible image and all layers.

   ◆ **Merged Layers.** Saves only the merged layers.

   ◆ **Current Layer.** Saves only the active layer.

8. Click **OK**.

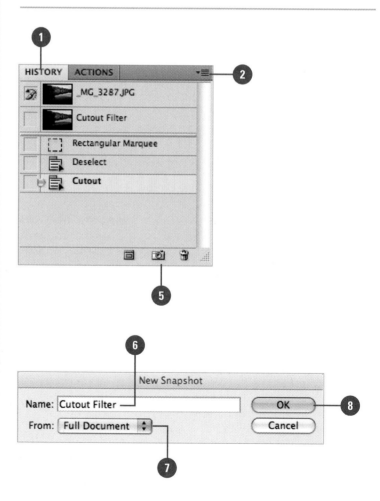

Duplicating a History State in Another Document

Here's a tool to help you gain control over the creative process, and save you a lot of time and effort as well. The History panel lets you create new documents based on a specific History step or snapshot. For example, you're working on a complicated image, and you want to isolate a portion of the image in another document. This will not only help you reduce the clutter, but working on a portion of the image in a separate document creates a document with a much smaller file size, and that will help Photoshop work faster.

Create Another Document

1. Select the **History** panel.

2. Click on the snapshot or History State you want to use for the new document.

3. Click the **Create New Document From Current State** button.

Photoshop creates a new document based on the selected snapshot or state. The new document's History panel contains one snapshot or one state.

IMPORTANT *Snapshots are not saved with the Photoshop document. When you reopen a document, the History panel will display one snapshot of the current state of the image or one History state.*

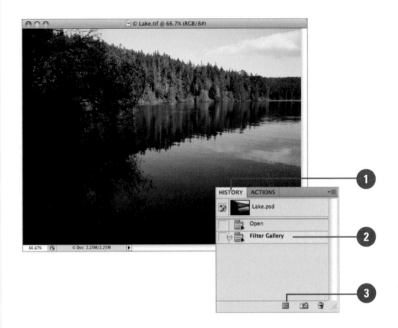

Did You Know?

You can save RAM by using the History panel. When you create a new document using the History panel, it's very RAM efficient, as opposed to the traditional copy and paste method.

New document based on the selected snapshot or state.

Saving the History State of a Document

Photoshop gives you the ability to save the History states of a document as a separate text document, or as embedded metadata. Saving History is an excellent way to retrace the steps you took to produce a particular design. Not only does the saved data record the steps you took, it also records the date and time each step was performed. This gives you a running record of the time spent on a document, which is useful for client billing purposes. Photoshop saves the history files as a standard text document, which can be opened in any text-editing program you choose.

Set Up to Save History

1. Click the **Edit** (Win) or **Photoshop** (Mac) menu, point to **Preferences**, and then click **General**.

2. Select the **History Log** check box.

3. Select the file type option you want to use in saving history information:

    ◆ **Metadata.** Records the data as embedded metadata.

    ◆ **Text File.** Records the data to a text file.

    ◆ **Both.** Records the information as both metadata and text.

4. Click **Choose**, and then select a location where you want to store the files.

5. Click the **Edit Log Items** list arrow, and then select the type of data you want to save:

    ◆ **Sessions Only.** Only records basic information, such as when the file was opened or closed.

    ◆ **Concise.** More information on actions taken.

    ◆ **Detailed.** The most data, including dates and times for actions, and each individual state.

6. Click **OK**.

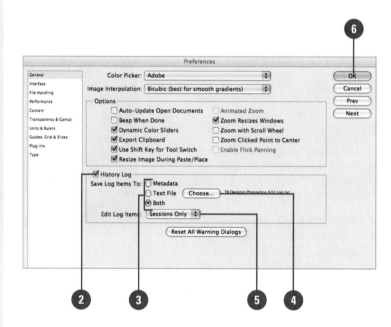

Reviewing the History State Text File

Photoshop creates the History State file on the fly; as you work, each step is precisely recorded. Photoshop does not create a separate data file for each working session; instead, it creates a single file recording all work sessions. If you delete the original history data file, Photoshop will create a new file, and place it in the same location with the same name. Have you ever worked on a document, performing command after command and suddenly you step back, and really like the end result? Then you immediately grab a notepad and attempt to jot down all the steps—it's always the most important step that you forget. That won't happen if you use the History text file. The text document faithfully records each and every step. Later, after the project is finished, you can access the file and all your commands and steps will be listed.

Open the History State Text File

1. Close Photoshop.

2. Open the folder where the History text file is saved.

   The default name is Photoshop Edit Log.txt, and the default location is the desktop.

3. Double-click to open the document with your default text editor.

   Use NotePad (Win), TextEdit (Mac), or a word processing program, such as Microsoft Word.

   ◆ The date and time the file was opened is recorded at the top of the document.

   ◆ The steps performed are listed, one at a time.

   ◆ The date and time the file was closed is recorded at the bottom of the document.

4. Close your text editor program.

Date and time file was opened

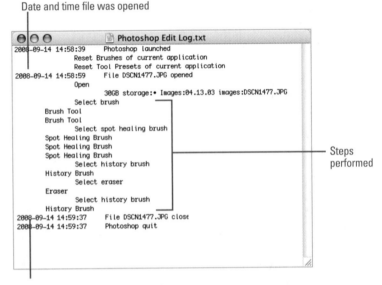

Steps performed

Date and time the file was closed

Combining the History Brush with a History State

When Adobe created History, they advertised the fact that Photoshop now had more than one undo. Multiple undos are a great thing; however, if all you use the History panel for is to correct your mistakes, you're missing a key benefit. The History panel is linked to the History brush, which receives its information from a selected state or snapshot. For example, the History panel holds a snapshot of the way the image looked when it was first opened, and by default the History brush is linked to that snapshot. Think of the History brush as a photo restoration tool that always remembers the original state of the image. As you work on a document you will make changes. If during the current work session, you wish to restore the document back to its original (first opened) state, the History brush is your tool. The History brush is not just for correcting mistakes, but also for creating awesome special effects. All you need is a bit of imagination and a couple of additional snapshots.

Correct Mistakes with the History Brush

1. Select the **History Brush** tool on the toolbox.

2. Click the **Brushes** panel, and then select a size brush.

3. Drag the History brush across the image.

   The areas you drag are restored to their original (first opened) state.

Did You Know?

When you use the History brush on an image layer, you're changing the information based on the chosen History state or snapshot. However, you will gain more control if you use the History brush in a separate layer. Just create and select a new layer, and when you use the History brush, paint in the layer. Not only does the separate layer isolate the original image from damage, but you can utilize blending modes and opacity settings for even greater creative control.

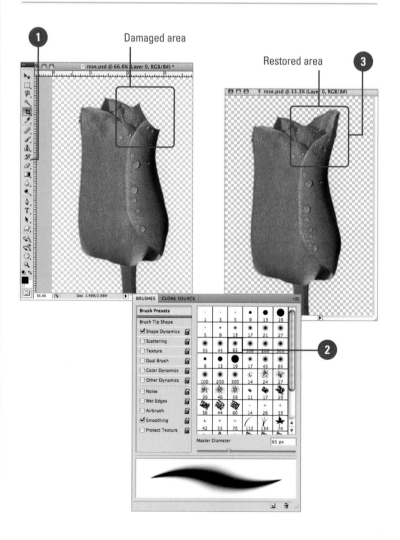

Damaged area

Restored area

130

Get Fancy with the History Brush

1. Apply a major change to a document (possibility a Brush Stroke filter).

2. Select the **History** panel.

3. Click the **Create New Snapshot** button to take a snapshot of the image in its current state.

4. Click on the original snapshot to return it back to its first-opened state.

5. Click in the History source box for the snapshot you created in step 3 to change the designation of the History brush.

   This instructs the History brush to paint using the version of the image with the filter applied.

6. Drag your mouse over the image to replace the original image with the image information contained in the selected snapshot.

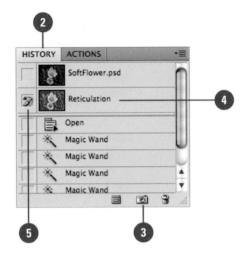

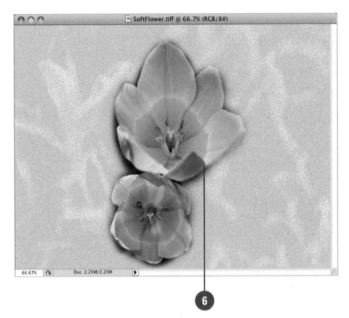

Using the Art History Brush

Photoshop comes equipped with two History brushes—the History and Art History brushes. The History brush paints the image back to whatever state or snapshot is selected. The Art History brush gives you the ability to create some painted effects, using information from one or more snapshots or History states. In effect, the Art History brush gives you the power to combine image information (based on the active snapshot or history state) with artistic brush strokes.

Use the Art History Brush

1. Click and hold the **History Brush** tool on the toolbox, and then click the **Art History Brush** tool.

2. Select from the following options on the Options bar:

   ◆ **Brush.** Select a brush tip and style.

   ◆ **Mode.** Select a blending mode from the list. The blending modes, when applied to a brush, control how the colors blend with the colors in the document.

   ◆ **Opacity.** Enter or select a value from 1% to 100%.

   ◆ **Style.** Select a style for the Art History brush.

   ◆ **Area.** Enter a value from 0 to 500 pixels to define the painting area.

   ◆ **Tolerance.** Select a value from 0% to 100%. Choosing higher values limits paint strokes to areas in the image that differ from the color used by the Art History brush. Choosing lower values lets the Art History brush use unlimited strokes, regardless of the color values in the image.

3. Drag your mouse over the image, using small, controlled strokes.

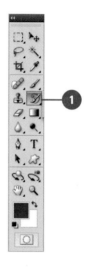

Original image

Effect applied with the Art History Brush

Changing the Eraser Tool into the History Brush

Photoshop has one more tool that works with the History panel—the Eraser tool. By changing a preference on the Options bar, you can turn the Eraser tool into a History brush. Using the Eraser tool to restore the image is just another way to get the same result as the History brush. And if you know anything about Adobe, they give you at least three ways to do everything. Consider multiple ways to perform the same function as a control advantage. No two Photoshop users will create the same design, and no two Photoshop users will ever tackle a problem in the same way. Adobe gives you choices, so choose the best way to accomplish a task based on the available options. And remember, if you change the color mode, resolution, or canvas size of the active image, the History brush tools will not work.

Change the Eraser Tool into the History Brush

1. Select the **Eraser** tool on the toolbox.

2. Select the **Erase to History** check box on the Options bar.

3. Select a history state or snapshot from the History panel.

4. Drag the Eraser tool in the image.

   The eraser tool does not erase the image; instead, it paints the image based on the current History selection.

Did You Know?

You can use multiple layers with the History brush. When you use any of the History brush tools, it's a smart idea to create a new layer, and do your History painting in the new layer. That way, if you don't like what you see, you can always delete the layer. In addition, placing the History information in a separate layer gives you the creative control of using layer transparency and blending mode settings to achieve greater creative results.

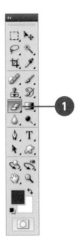

Controlling History States

The History panel is a fantastic tool! It can help you go back in time and correct errors, and even take snapshots of the image, which you can use to create new documents. But all great tools come with a price. The History panel's price is consumption of RAM. The more you use the History panel, the more RAM it needs. If you find Photoshop slowing down on you, or if you get a warning message stating that Photoshop is running low on RAM, you might want to try a few things to help gain back some of that lost efficiency. Photoshop lets you choose between 0 and 1,000 History states. That's 1,000 undos, and while that might seem like a great thing to have, History states take up memory. You can also check on your History settings. Non-linear History requires more RAM to maintain. If you don't require a non-linear history, then you can turn it off. Since Photoshop uses a lot of RAM (64 MB just to open the program), Adobe gives you a way to purge, or clear, your memory.

Purge RAM

1. Click the **Edit** (Win) or **Photoshop** (Mac) menu, point to **Purge**, and then select from the following options:

   ◆ **Undo.** Select this option to remove the Undo states from History.

   ◆ **Clipboard.** If you have used the Copy and Paste commands, that information is still contained in RAM. Use this option to purge the Clipboard memory.

   ◆ **Histories.** Select this option to purge all the states from the History panel.

   ◆ **All.** Select this option to clear all operations from memory used by Undo commands, the History panel, or the Clipboard.

   IMPORTANT *The purge option has no undo. If you select any of the purge options, there is no going back, so make sure you want to purge memory.*

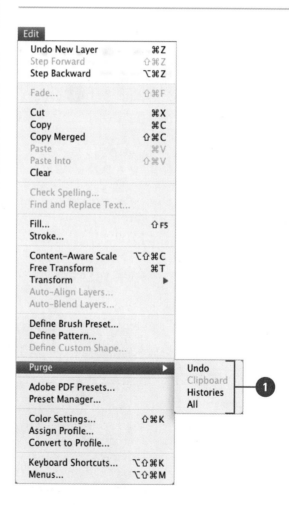

Working with Adjustment Layers, Filters, and Tools

7

Introduction

If you want to visually control an Adobe Photoshop document, then adjustment layers are the ultimate tool. The purpose of an adjustment layer is to show how a specific adjustment, such as Hue & Saturation, changes the appearance of the image. Since the adjustment is contained within a separate layer, the original image never changes. This gives you the ability to experiment with different settings. Since adjustment layers can be saved with the document, you can close the document, then return at a later time to make further adjustments.

Another advantage of adjustment layers is size. Adjustment layers do not increase the size of a Photoshop document. Most Photoshop layers are composed of pixels, so adding traditional layers to a document increases the size of the file. Since adjustment layers are simply a set of mathematical data, they do not increase the size of the file.

Photoshop has two ways to apply adjustments to an image. You could go to the Image menu, and choose Adjustments; however, when you apply an adjustment using this method, it's permanent. The other way is to use an adjustment layer—the very definition of control over time. When working with adjustment layers, you can modify, merge, or even create a temporary composite image, all while your original image stays intact. With all of their advantages, you may never perform adjustments using the Image menu again.

In addition to letting you apply adjustments to an image without changing the original data, adjustment layers, because they are separate layers, give you the ability to apply standard layer controls, such as blending modes, opacity, and fill. Adjustment layers come with their own built-in masks, and allow you to control how and where the adjustment is applied to the image.

What You'll Do

Create an Adjustment Layer

Modify an Adjustment Layer

Merge Adjustment Layers

Create a Temporary Composite Image

Control Adjustment Layers through Clipping Groups

Delete an Adjustment Layer

Use Blending Modes and Opacity with Layers

Use Masks with Adjustment Layers

Create Masks with Selection

Retouch Images with Filters

Keep Proper Perspective with Vanishing Point

Work with the Lens Correction Filter

Retouch Images with Tools and Filters

Control Tonal Range

Work with the Histogram Panel

Creating an Adjustment Layer

Adjustment layers are applied within the Layers panel and use the Adjustment panel (**New!**). By default, all layers beneath the adjustment layer are changed. In addition, adjustment layers will work on any type of Photoshop layer, including the Background. You can have as many adjustment layers as you need. For example, you might create a Levels adjustment layer to control the contrast of an image, and add a Curves adjustment layer to correct image color. When you create more than one adjustment layer, each adjustment is applied to the image based on its stacking order in the Layers panel.

Create an Adjustment Layer

1. Select the **Layers** panel.

2. Click the layer you want to adjust.

3. Click the **Create New Fill or Adjustment Layer** button, and then select from the available types of adjustment layers.

   You can also open the Adjustments panel to set adjustment settings. You can choose from 15 icons (**New!**) representing most of the adjustment layer options. Below the icons are a listing of presets available for some adjustments. When you click one of the icons, controls for that type of adjustment appear on the panel for you to adjust as you wish.

4. Adjust the controls for the specific adjustment in the Adjustment panel.

5. At the bottom of the Adjustments panel, you can use buttons that allow you to go back to the list of adjustment types, switch the panel from Expanded to Standard view, clip the adjustment to the layer below, make the layer visible or invisible, revert to the image state before adjustment was made, reset adjustment defaults, or delete the adjustment.

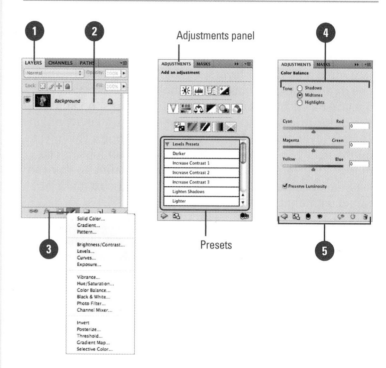

Adjustments panel

Presets

For Your Information

Applying Adjustment Layers

When you apply an adjustment layer to an image, you are no longer required to save the document in the PSD (Photoshop Document) format. Photoshop supports saving files with multiple layers, including adjustment layers, in the TIFF (Tagged-Image File Format) file type. The files can be opened just like ordinary TIFF files in standard layout applications. However, when the file is opened in applications that support multiple layers, such as Corel Painter or Adobe InDesign, the adjustment layers are preserved.

Modifying an Adjustment Layer

The beauty of adjustment layers is in the control they offer to the Photoshop user. When you use the Image menu, and click Adjustments, any changes made to the image are permanent as soon as you click OK. But that's not true of adjustment layers. Adjustment layers keep the changes isolated in a separate layer, and this allows you to modify the adjustment minutes, or even days later. With this type of creative control at your fingertips, you can experiment with different settings until the image looks exactly the way you want.

Modify an Adjustment Layer

① Select the **Layers** panel.

② Double-click on the thumbnail of the Adjustment layer you want to modify.

The options for that specific adjustment reopens in the Adjustments panel. If you didn't already have the Adjustments panel open, clicking on the layer you want to modify will open it automatically. Options for each type of adjustment dialog box varies.

③ Make the changes you want for the specific adjustment.

④ Click **OK**.

Did You Know?

You can move adjustment layers up and down in the layer stack. Since each adjustment layer interacts with other adjustment layers, changing the order of the layers creates a totally different image.

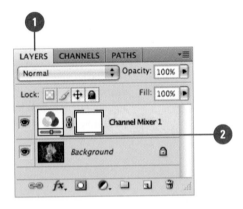

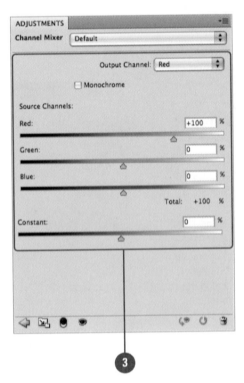

Merging Adjustment Layers

Photoshop lets you create as many adjustment layers as you need. For example, you might create a Levels adjustment layer to balance image contrast, a Curves adjustment layer to correct color, and a Photo Filter adjustment layer to create an overall warming effect to the image. Each adjustment layer works with the other adjustment layers to produce the final image. It's not unusual to have three, four, or even five adjustment layers controlling a single image. At some point in the design, you might decide to save space by merging some or all of the adjustment layers. However, when you merge the adjustment layers, the adjustment effects are lost, as a result of how Photoshop deals with adjustment layers. Each adjustment layer controls one specific part of the adjustment, such as Curves or Levels. The layers themselves do not hold an image; they hold mathematical data on how to change an image. A single adjustment layer cannot hold more than one set of adjustments. That's why you have multiple adjustment layers. Merging two or more adjustment layers together forces Photoshop to discard all of the adjustment data and the merged adjustment layers turn into one plain old transparent layer. To solve the problem, try merging the adjustment layers and the image layer into one single layer.

Merge Adjustments with Images

1 Open a document containing an image layer, and two or more adjustment layers.

2 Select the **Layers** panel.

3 Click the **Layers Options** button, and then select from the following merge options:

◆ **Merge Layers.** Merges only the layers selected in the Layers panel into a single layer.

◆ **Merge Visible.** Merges only the layers that are visible, leaving the hidden layers untouched.

◆ **Flatten Image.** Merges all layers into a flattened background. If you have one or more layers hidden, Photoshop will open a warning dialog box and ask if you want to discard the hidden layers.

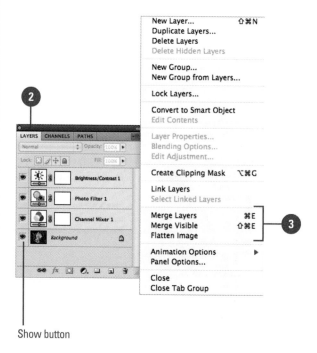

Show button

Creating a Temporary Composite Image

When you merge adjustment layers into the image, you wind up with a single layer that contains all of the adjustments. By merging the adjustment layers, you do lose control over the individual adjustment layers. It's basically a trade-off of smaller file sizes and less layers to contend with, but also less control over the image. Let's say you want the best of both worlds—a single layer that contains the image, all of the adjustments, and the original image with separate adjustment layers. It's possible; all you have to do is create a composite layer.

Create a Temporary Composite Image

1. Open a document that contains an image, and two or more visible adjustment layers.

2. Select the **Layers** panel, create a new layer at the top of the layer stack, and then select it.

3. Hold down the Alt (Win) or Option (Mac) key, click the **Layers Options** button, and then click **Merge Visible**.

   Photoshop combines all of the visible layers into a new layer, while leaving the original layers untouched.

Did You Know?

You can use the composite layer option on any multi-layered Photoshop document. Once you've created the composite layer, you can perform other adjustments without impacting the original image, or even drag and move the composite into another Photoshop document.

You can use the link option to control the composite image. Create a new layer, and then link the layers you want included in the composite. Follow the steps for creating a composite, except click Merge Linked.

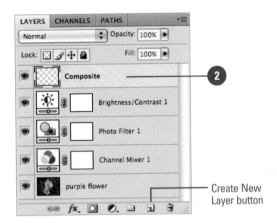

Create New Layer button

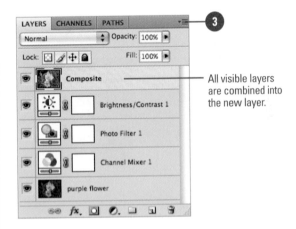

All visible layers are combined into the new layer.

Controlling Adjustment Layers with Clipping Groups

When you work with adjustment layers, the adjustments are applied to all the layers below the adjustment layer, including any additional adjustment layers. However, there are times when you only want the adjustment applied to a specific layer. For example, you're working on a multi-layered document and you create a Curves Adjustment layer for the purpose of adjusting the color in the next layer down. Unfortunately, the Curves adjustment is applied to all the layers. The answer is simple; just create a clipping group to combine the adjustment layer with the one layer you want to be affected.

Control Adjustment Layers with the Clipping Group Option

① Select the **Layers** panel, and then click the layer you want to adjust.

② Move your cursor down until the fingertip of the hand pointer touches the line separating the adjustment layer from the next layer down.

③ Hold down the Alt (Win) or Option (Mac) key.

The cursor changes from a hand pointer to a double-circle button (the clipping group button).

④ Click your mouse to group the two layers together.

The thumbnail of the adjustment layer indents to indicate the two layers are grouped. The effect of the adjustment layer impacts the layer below and no others.

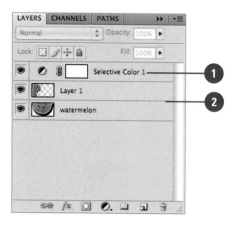

Layers linked as a clipping group

Did You Know?

You can group more than one layer together. Hold down the Alt (Win) or Option (Mac) key, and then click on the line separating the next layer to add a layer to the group. To remove a layer from the group, hold down the Alt (Win) or Option (Mac) key, and then click on the line separating two grouped items.

Deleting an Adjustment Layer

When you delete an adjustment layer you are simply deleting the adjustment, not the image. Adjustment layers do not contain pixels; they only manipulate the information contained within the image layer. Deleting an adjustment layer is as easy as deleting any other layer type. The effect is the same; the function of the layer is removed from the document. For example, if you delete a Curves adjustment layer, the effects are removed and the image returns to its original state. When you delete an adjustment layer, the change to the image created by the adjustment layer is removed, and the image returns to its original state.

Delete an Adjustment Layer

1. Select the **Layers** panel.

2. Click the adjustment layer you want to delete.

3. Drag the adjustment layer onto the Delete Layer button.

Did You Know?

You can convert an adjustment layer into a regular layer. By default, adjustment layers come with a built-in mask. To remove the mask while preserving the adjustment layer, select the adjustment layer in the Layers panel, hold down the Alt (Win) or Option (Mac) key, and then click the Delete Layer button.

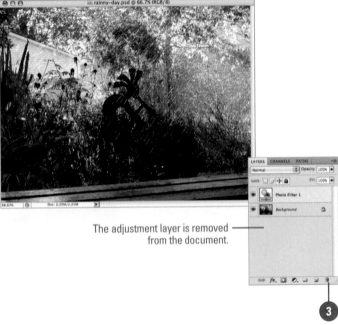

The adjustment layer is removed from the document.

Using Blending Modes and Opacity with Layers

 PS 4.4

Adjustment layers perform two functions—they adjust the image and they give you control. Since an adjustment is held in a separate layer, you have the advantage of isolating the adjustment and keeping your original image information intact. Combine that with an adjustment layer's ability to manipulate pixel information and you have a very powerful image-editing tool. Blending Modes change how two or more layers interact. For example, the Multiply blending mode instructs Photoshop to mix the pixels of two or more layers, thus creating an entirely new image from the mix. With that in mind, the five modes that produce the most stunning results are Multiply, Screen, Hard Mix, Difference, and Exclusion. The opacity of an adjustment layer controls the intensity of the selected adjustment. You can reduce the opacity of the Hue & Saturation adjustment to 50% and it would reduce its effect on the image. Since each adjustment layer has its own opacity settings, multiple adjustment layers can be fine-tuned to create a custom effect on the image.

Use Blending Modes with Adjustment Layers

1. Select the **Layers** panel.

2. Click the layer you want to adjust.

3. Click the **Blending Mode** list arrow, and then select from the available options.

   The results of the blend are visible in the document window.

Blending Mode change applied to image

142

Control Through Opacity

1. Select the **Layers** panel.

2. Click the layer you want to adjust.

3. Click the **Opacity** list arrow, and then drag the slider to lower the opacity of the layer.

   The results of the change appear in the document window.

   TIMESAVER *Click inside the Opacity box, and then use the Up and Down Arrow keys to increase or decrease the opacity 1 percentage point at a time. Hold the Shift key, and then use the Up and Down Arrow keys to increase or decrease the opacity 10 percentage points at a time. You can also select the percentage in the box and enter a value.*

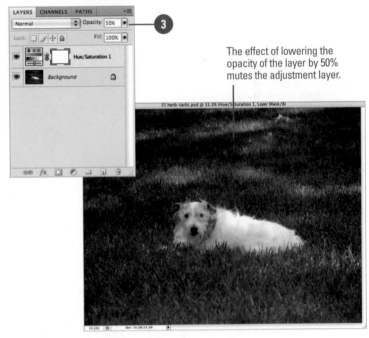

The effect of lowering the opacity of the layer by 50% mutes the adjustment layer.

Using Masks with Adjustment Layers

PS 5.1, 5.2, 5.4

When you create an adjustment layer, the effects of the adjustment are applied to the entire image. For example, if you use the Curves adjustment, the resulting changes are applied to the entire image. It's true you can modify the adjustment with the use of layer blending modes and opacity settings but the effects are applied equally to the entire image. The problem is that many times you don't want the adjustment applied to the entire image. For example, you may want to color-correct just a portion of the image, or lighten the shadows of an image without applying the same lightening adjustment to the highlights. Photoshop handles this problem with the use of masks. When you create an adjustment layer, Photoshop automatically creates a mask with the image. The mask controls how the adjustment is applied to the image, and you control the effect by painting in the mask with black, white, or a shade of gray. When you paint in the mask with black, it will totally mask the adjustment; painting with white fully applies the adjustment. If you paint with 50% gray, then the adjustment is applied to the image at 50% strength.

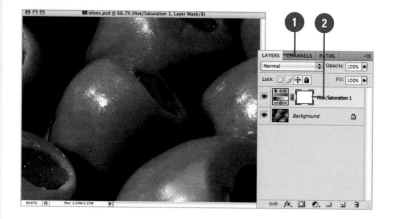

Paint on an Adjustment Mask

1. Select the **Layers** panel.

2. Click the layer mask thumbnail in which you want to paint a mask.

3. Select a **Paintbrush** tool.

4. Select a brush size on the Options bar.

5. Select the **Masks** panel (**New!**) to display details about both pixel and vector masks and select from options to change the opacity (density) of the mask, as well as feather options. You can also access the Color Range command from here and invert the mask.

6. Set the **Foreground Color** box on the toolbox to black as the paint color.

7. Paint the areas of the image that you want to mask. The adjustment layer must be selected. The areas painted black mask the adjustment, returning the image to normal.

8. To restore the masked areas, switch to white and drag across the image in the areas previously painted black.

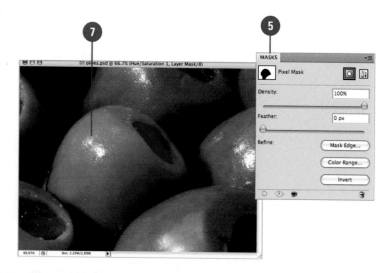

Creating Masks with Selections

You can create an instant mask using traditional selection techniques. Before creating the adjustment layer, select the area of the image to which you want the adjustment applied. Use any of Photoshop's selection tools for this purpose. When you create the adjustment layer, Photoshop converts the selection into a mask, and only the selected areas of the image are changed.

Create Masks with Selections

1. Use any of Photoshop's selection tools to create a selection around the area of the image to which you want the adjustment applied.

2. Select the **Layers** panel.

3. Click the **Create New Fill or Adjustment Layer** button, and then select from the available adjustments or use the new Adjustments panel to choose one of the adjustment icons.

   Photoshop creates a mask based on your selection with the selected areas being adjusted and the non-selected areas masked.

Did You Know?

You can use any of Photoshop's filters on an adjustment layer mask.
For example, you could use the Gaussian Blur filter to soften the edge between adjustment and mask. Experiment with different filters for different creative effects.

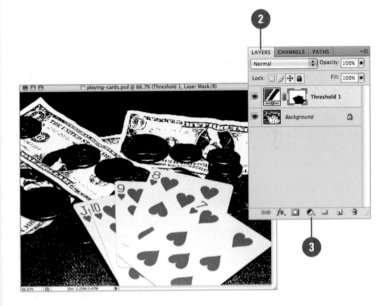

Using the Add Noise Filter

The Add Noise filter applies random pixels to an image. When you want to simulate a film grain effect, you can apply the Add Noise filter. For example, you could use the Add Noise filter to make an image look like it was taken using high-speed film. In addition, the Add Noise filter can be used to reduce banding in feathered selections or graduated fills or even give a more realistic look to heavily retouched areas. Experiment with the Add Noise filter in combination with other filters, such as Motion Blur filters, to create eye-catching special effects.

Use the Add Noise Filter

1. Select the **Layers** panel.

2. Select the layer to which you want to apply the Add Noise filter.

3. Click the **Filter** menu, point to **Noise**, and then click **Add Noise**.

4. Select from the following options:

   ◆ **Amount.** Drag the slider, or enter a value (0.10 to 400) to increase or decrease the amount of noise added to the image.

   ◆ **Distribution.** Click the Uniform option to create a more ordered appearance, or click the Gaussian option to create a more random noise pattern.

   ◆ **Monochromatic.** Select this check box to apply the filter to the tonal elements in the image without changing the colors.

   TIMESAVER *The plus and minus signs, located directly under the image preview, let you increase or decrease the viewable area of the image.*

5. Click **OK**.

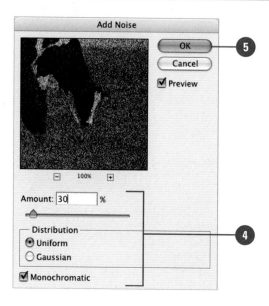

For Your Information

Using Filters to Retouch an Image

One of Photoshop's most powerful features is its ability to recreate a photographic image. Photographers use the term **photographic restoration** to describe image retouching. Photo restoration describes the process of returning an image to its original state. For example, you could remove dust and scratches from an old image using the Dust and Scratches filter, or repair other problems associated with old or damaged images using Photoshop filters. Since the same tools and filters can be used to restore an image as you have been using to apply effects to your images, you can experiment with various filters to find out which ones will help you with your image restoration.

Using the Reduce Noise Filter

The Reduce Noise filter helps to remove the random noise that crops up in digital images. It's called noise, but in reality it is a pattern of distracting color or grayscale information on top of the original image information. Noise can be generated by the Add Noise filter, but it typically comes from scanners and even digital cameras. Since there is a mathematical pattern to most noise, the Reduce Noise filter is designed to seek out and reduce the amount of noise in an image. The Reduce Noise filter works on individual layers, not the entire document. After applying the filter, you can use other restoration tools, such as the Healing Brush and Patch tool, to further clean up problem areas in your image.

Use the Reduce Noise Filter

1. Click the **Filter** menu, point to **Noise**, and then click **Reduce Noise**.

2. Select the **Preview** check box to view the changes to the image.

3. Select the **Basic** or **Advanced** option. Advanced allows you to adjust the noise on individual channels.

4. Select from the following options:

   - **Settings.** Click the setting arrow and select a user-defined preset.

   - **Strength.** Drag the slider to determine how strong to apply the Reduce Noise filter.

   - **Preserve Details.** Drag the slider to determine a balance between blurring the noise and preserving details.

   - **Reduce Color Noise.** Drag the slider to convert noise composed of colors into shades of gray (this may desaturate other areas of the image).

   - **Sharpen Details.** Drag the slider to determine where the details of the image exist, in terms of shifts in brightness.

   - **Remove JPEG Artifact.** Check to help remove artifacts (typically noise within shadows) from severely compressed JPEG images.

5. Click **OK**.

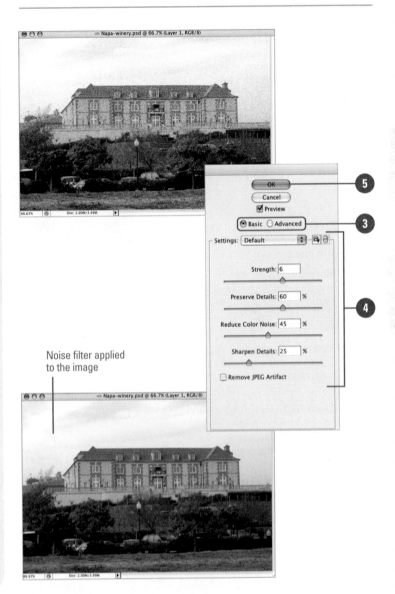

Noise filter applied to the image

Keeping Proper Perspective with Vanishing Point

PS 10.3

Vanishing Point gives you the ability to move and/or copy objects and still maintain the same visual perspective of the original. Let's say that you shoot an image of a roadway disappearing into the distance, and along the road there's a billboard. You want the billboard to appear as if it's farther away, but to retain its proper perspective within the image. With Vanishing Point, you simply create a framework, or plane, that identifies the depth of the image, and then move the billboard (using the Move or Clone Stamp tools). Wherever you move the sign, it will appear within the proper perspective. If you have Photoshop Extended, you can adjust the angle of the plane for greater flexibility or take measurements. When you finish working in Vanishing Point, you can use the Vanishing Point menu to render grids to Photoshop. With Photoshop Extended, you can also export 3D information and measurements to DXF or 3DS formats.

Use the Vanishing Point Tool

1. Open an image.

2. Click the **Filter** menu, and then click **Vanishing Point**.

3. The following tools are available:

   - **Edit Plane.** Adjusts the grid to match the perspective of the image.

   - **Create Plane.** First tool to use; it creates the initial perspective grid plane.

   - **Marquee Tool.** Makes selections in the grid and then changes their perspective as you move them to match the perspective of the grid.

   - **Stamp Tool.** Lets you make copies of areas and then stamp them onto other areas using the perspective of the grid.

   - **Brush Tool.** Lets you paint with color within the grid. If you click the Heal button and then click Luminance, Vanishing Point adapts the color to the shadows or textures of the areas being painted.

   - **Transform Tool.** Lets you rotate, resize or flip a selection created with the Marquee tool.

   - **Eyedropper Tool.** Click to select a specific color from the image.

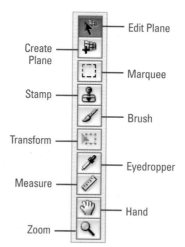

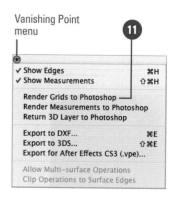

- ◆ **Measure Tool.** Lets you draw a measurement line over an object in a perspective plane (Extended).

- ◆ **Hand Tool.** Click to move the image within the Vanishing Point window.

- ◆ **Zoom Tool.** Click to Zoom in, or Alt+click (Win) or Option+click (Mac) to zoom out.

4. Select the **Create Plane** tool.

5. Click on the image to create the first point of the grid, and then click three more times to create the box shape of the grid.

- ◆ **Angle.** Lets you adjust the plane angle (Extended).

6. Use the **Edit Plane** tool to change the perspective of the plane, and to extend the plane over the area you want fixed.

The grid should be blue; however, if the grid turns red or yellow, that means Vanishing Point believes you have a bad grid.

7. Select the **Zoom** tool, and zoom in on the working areas of the image.

8. Select the **Stamp** tool.

9. Position the Stamp tool directly over the image area you want to use to fix the offending portions of the image, and then Alt+click (Win) or Option+click (Mac) to confirm the selection.

10. Move to the area you want to fix and then click and drag with the Stamp tool, which replaces the original information; the perspective changes to match the grid.

11. To show the grid in Photoshop, click the **Vanishing Point** menu, and then click **Render Grids To Photoshop**.

12. Click **OK**.

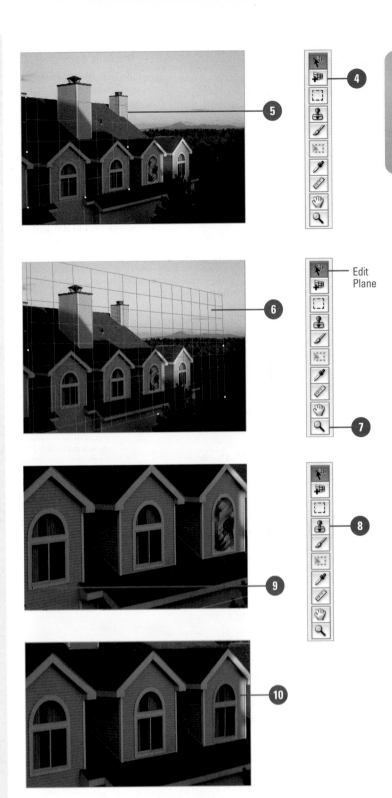

Edit Plane

Working with the Lens Correction Filter

The Lens Correction filter fixes flaws that occur during the shooting of images, such as barrel and pincushion distortion, vignetting, and even chromatic aberration. **Barrel** distortion causes straight lines to bow out toward the edges of the image. On the other hand, **Pincushion** distortion has the opposite effect (straight lines bend inward). **Vignetting** is a defect where edges of an image are darker than the center. **Chromatic** aberration appears as a fringe of color along the edges of objects caused by the lens focusing on different colors of light in different planes. In addition, you can use the Lens Correction filter to rotate an image or fix perspective caused by tilting the camera. Although some of these corrections can be made with the Transform command, the image grid in the Lens Correction filter makes adjustments easier.

Use the Lens Correction Filter

1. Open an image.

2. Click the **Filter** menu, point to **Distort**, and then click **Lens Correction**.

3. Select from the following tools:

   - **Remove Distortion Tool.** Click in the grid and then drag left or right to remove barrel or pincushion distortion.

   - **Straighten Tool.** Click in the grid and drag to draw a new horizon line (image will shift to the new horizon).

   - **Move Grid Tool.** Drag to reposition the visible grid.

   - **Hand Tool.** Select the tool, then click and drag to move the image within the view window.

   - **Zoom Tool.** Select the tool, and then click in the view window to zoom in, or Alt+click (Win) or Option+click (Mac) to zoom out.

4. Select from the following tools:

   - **Settings.** Click and choose from user-defined settings, or to apply the previous settings to the current image.

   - **Remove Distortion.** Drag the slider left or right to precisely remove pincushion or barrel distortion.

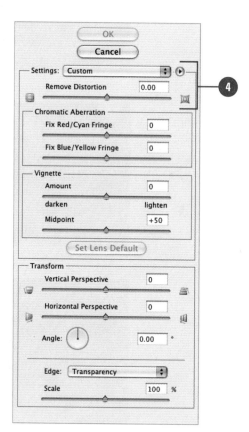

5 Select from the following Chromatic Aberration options:

 ◆ **Fix Red/Cyan Fringe.** Drag left or right to remove a red or cyan fringe from the image.

 ◆ **Fix Blue/Yellow Fringe.** Drag left or right to remove a blue or yellow fringe from the image.

6 Select from the following Vignette options:

 ◆ **Amount.** Drag left or right to create a light or dark vignette around the image.

 ◆ **Midpoint.** Drag left or right to select the midpoint for the vignette.

7 Click **Set Lens Default** to change the setting to default values.

8 Select from the following Transform options:

 ◆ **Vertical Perspective.** Drag left or right to change the image's vertical perspective.

 ◆ **Horizontal Perspective.** Drag left or right to change the image's horizontal perspective.

 ◆ **Angle.** Drag the angle option to rotate the image clockwise or counter clockwise.

 ◆ **Edge.** Click and select to fill in transparent areas of the image with the background color, Edge Extension, or Transparent.

 ◆ **Scale.** Drag left or right to change the scale (size) of the image.

9 Select the **Preview** check box to view changes as they are made.

10 Select the **Show Grid** check box to view or hide the visible grid.

11 Click the **Size** list arrow to change the size of the grid boxes.

12 Click the **Color** box to change the color of the grid.

13 Click **OK**.

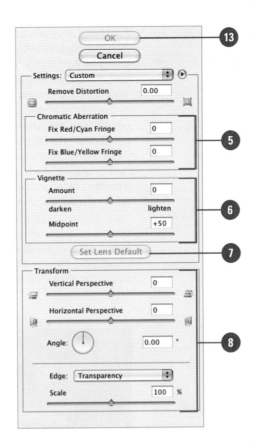

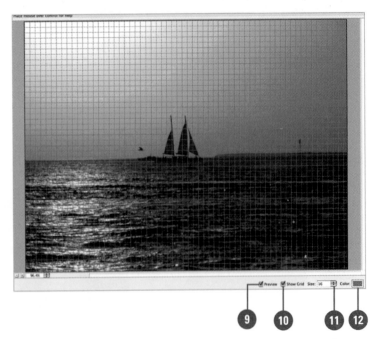

Using the Box, Surface, and Shape Blur Filters

Photoshop provides a variety of filters to blur the look of an image, including Box, Surface, and Shape. The Box Blur filter blurs an image based on the average color value of neighboring pixels. Its primary function is the creation of special effects. You can adjust the size of the area used to calculate the average value for a given pixel; a larger radius results in more blurring. The Surface Blur filter blurs an image while saving the visible edges; this filter is useful for creating special effects or removing that pesky noise or grain. The Radius option specifies the size of the area sampled for the blur. The Threshold option controls how much the tonal values of neighboring pixels must diverge from the center pixel value before being part of the blur. Pixels with tonal value differences less than the Threshold value are excluded from the blur. The Shape Blur filter uses a specified shape to create the blur. Choose a kernel from the list of custom shape presets, and use the radius slider to adjust its size. You can load different shape libraries by clicking the triangle and choosing from the list. Radius determines the size of the shape; the larger the shape, the greater the blur.

Use the Box Blur Filter

1. Open an image.

2. Click the **Filter** menu, point to **Blur**, and then click **Box Blur**.

3. Drag the **Radius** slider left or right to decrease or increase the amount of blur applied to the image.

4. Click **OK**.

Results of Box Blur

Use the Surface Blur Filter

1 Open an image.

2 Click the **Filter** menu, point to **Blur**, and then click **Surface Blur**.

3 Drag the **Radius** slider left or right to decrease or increase the amount of blur applied to the image.

4 Drag the **Threshold** slider left or right to decrease or increase the acceptance of the shift in brightness of the image information (the edges).

5 Click **OK**.

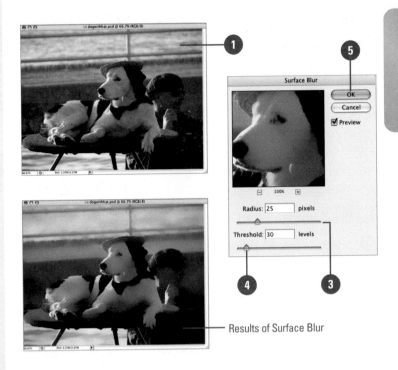

Results of Surface Blur

Use the Shape Blur Filter

1 Open an image.

2 Click the **Filter** menu, point to **Blur**, and then click **Shape Blur**.

3 Select a shape (called a kernel) from the available options.

4 Drag the **Radius** slider left or right to decrease or increase the amount of blur applied to the image.

5 Click **OK**.

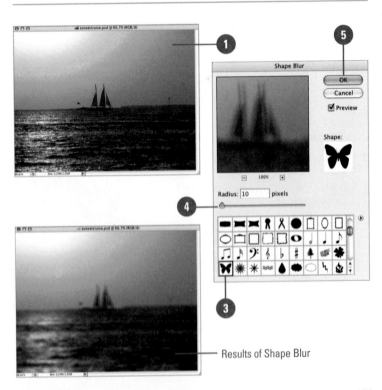

Results of Shape Blur

Using the Gaussian Blur and Despeckle Filters

You can also apply the Gaussian Blur filter that blurs an image or a selection by a controllable amount. While not strictly a restoration tool, the Gaussian Blur filter can be used to add a sense of depth to the image. For example, you could select and blur the background of an image while leaving the foreground in focus. The outcome of the filter is to create a hazy, out-of-focus effect on the image or selection. Another filter, the Despeckle filter, detects the edges in an image and blurs the entire image except those edges. Of course, there are no real edges in a Photoshop document—the Despeckle filter works along areas where there is a significant shift in the brightness of the pixels. Since a shift in brightness usually signifies an edge, the Despeckle filter performs a very accurate blurring of the image while preserving detail.

Use the Gaussian Blur Filter

1. Select the portions of the image you want to blur or leave the image unselected to apply the filter to the entire image.

2. Click the **Filter** menu, point to **Blur**, and then click **Gaussian Blur**.

3. Select the **Preview** check box to view the results.

4. Drag the **Radius** slider or enter a pixel value to increase or decrease the amount of Gaussian blur applied to the image.

5. Click **OK**.

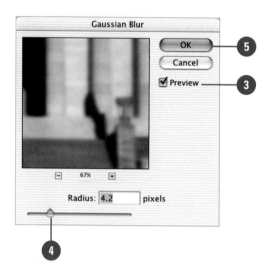

Use the Despeckle Filter

1. Select the **Layers** panel.

2. Select the layer to which you want to apply the Despeckle filter.

3. Click the **Filter** menu, point to **Noise**, and then click **Despeckle**.

Photoshop applies the Despeckle filter to the image.

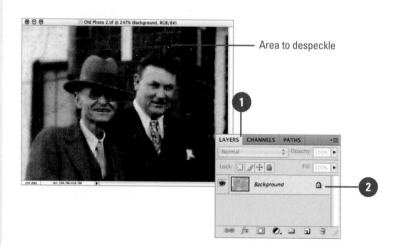

Area to despeckle

Using the Unsharp Mask Filter

The Unsharp Mask filter creates a visually sharper image by locating pixels that differ in value from surrounding pixels. When the filter is applied to the image, the bordering pixels specified by the threshold option get lighter and the darker pixels get darker. It's important to understand that the Unsharp Mask does not actually sharpen the image; it only attempts to create the illusion of sharpness. Be careful; an over-application of this filter creates harsh images with ragged edges and shadows. Also, the effects of the Unsharp Mask filter appear more severe when viewed with the low resolution of a computer than when the document is output to a printer.

Use the Unsharp Mask Filter

1 Select the **Layers** panel.

2 Select the layer you want to sharpen.

3 Click the **Filter** menu, point to **Sharpen**, and then click **Unsharp Mask**.

4 Select from the following options:

- ◆ **Preview.** Select the option to view changes to the image directly in the active document window.

- ◆ **Amount.** Drag the slider or enter a value to determine how much to increase the contrast of pixels.

- ◆ **Radius.** Drag the slider or enter a value to determine the number of pixels surrounding the edge pixels that affect the sharpening.

- ◆ **Threshold.** Drag the slider or enter a value to determine how different the sharpened pixels must be from the surrounding area before they are considered edge pixels and sharpened by the filter.

5 Click **OK**.

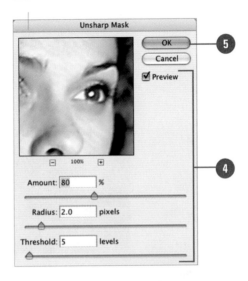

The Unsharp Mask filter applied to the image.

Using the Smart Sharpen Filter

The Smart Sharpen filter attempts to sharpen the pixels of an out-of-focus image in much the same way as the Unsharp Mask filter. The major difference is the ability of Smart Sharpen to remove previously applied Gaussian, Lens, and Motion Blur filters. For example, you've applied the Lens Blur filter to an image, but later decide to reduce the effect. The problem is that Unsharp Mask will attempt to sharpen what it assumes to be an out-of-focus image. Unfortunately, an image taken with an out-of-focus lens, and a Lens blur are two different things, and that's where the Smart Sharpen filter comes to the rescue.

Use the Smart Sharpen Filter

1. Select the **Layers** panel.

2. Select the layer you want to sharpen.

3. Click the **Filter** menu, point to **Sharpen**, and then click **Smart Sharpen**.

4. Select the **Preview** check box to view the results.

5. Select the **Basic** or **Advanced** option.

6. Click the **Settings** list arrow, and then select from a list of user-defined settings.

7. Select from the following Sharpen options:

   ◆ **Amount.** Drag the slider to determine the amount of sharpness applied to the image.

   ◆ **Radius.** Drag the slider to determine the width of the sharpening effect.

   ◆ **Remove.** Click the list arrow and then select what type of blur effect you are removing from the image.

   ◆ **Angle.** Enter the angle of the Motion Blur filter to remove.

   ◆ **More Accurate.** Select for a more accurate (slower) sharpening effect.

Original image

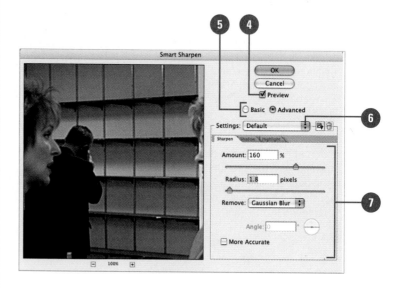

8 Select the **Shadow** panel and then select from the following Shadow options:

◆ **Fade Amount.** Drag the slider to determine the amount of shadow correction applied to the image.

◆ **Tonal Width.** Drag the slider to set the width of the tonal values in the image shadows.

◆ **Radius.** Drag the slider to choose the scale size for the shadows.

9 Select the **Highlight** panel, and then select from the following Highlight options:

◆ **Fade Amount.** Drag the slider to determine the amount of highlight correction applied to the image.

◆ **Tonal Width.** Drag the slider to set the width of the tonal values in the image highlights.

◆ **Radius.** Drag the slider to choose the scale size for the highlights.

10 To save a copy of the current Smart Sharpen settings, click the **Save** button.

11 To delete the active saved Smart Sharpen settings, click the **Delete** button.

12 Click **OK**.

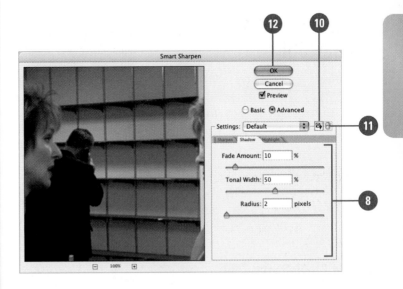

Image using Smart Sharpen

Using the Clone Stamp Tool

PS 2.4

One of Photoshop's most powerful features is its ability to retouch a photographic image. When you want to manipulate an image, you can apply the Clone Stamp tool. The Clone Stamp tool allows you to sample the image, and then apply that sample somewhere else on the same image, or on another open document. When you use the Clone Stamp tool, by selecting Aligned in the Options bar, you can reuse the most current sampling point no matter how many times you start and stop painting. When Aligned is deselected, you'll reuse the same sampled pixels each time you paint. For example, you could use the Clone Stamp tool to repair damage to an image, remove a tree, or even remove or add someone from an image. If you want to take multiple samples, the Clone Source panel allows you to set up to five different sample sources for the Clone Stamp or the Healing Brush tools. Select Show Overlay and the Clipped (**New!**) option to see the clone source inside your brush cursor as you paint.

Use the Clone Stamp Tool

1. Select the **Clone Stamp** tool on the toolbox.

2. Select a brush tip, and then select brush options, such as blending mode, opacity, and flow, on the Options bar.

3. Select the **Aligned** check box on the Options bar to sample pixels continuously without losing the current sampling point. Clear the check box to continue using pixels from the initial sampling point each time you stop and resume painting.

4. Click the **Sample** list arrow on the Options bar, and then select the layer option you want to use to obtain sample data: Current Layer, Current & Below, or All Layers.

5. Hold down the Alt (Win) or Option (Mac) key, and then click an area to sample the portion of the image you want to use for your sample.

6. Drag over the area of the image you want to restore or modify.

7. To select more samples, click the **Window** menu, click **Clone Source**, click a clone button, and then repeat steps 5 & 6.

Clone Stamp tool

Joshua tree removed using the Clone Stamp tool

Using the Dodge and Burn Tools

You can also use the Dodge and Burn tools to lighten or darken specific areas of an image. If you wanted to lighten the shadow areas of an image, you would use the Dodge tool, and conversely, if you wanted to darken the highlight areas of an image, you would select the Burn tool. While there are other ways to control the highlights and shadows of an image, such as a Levels adjustment, the Dodge and Burn tools are controlled by using a brush and painting in the image. That kind of control gives you the option to choose exactly what you want to modify.

Use the Dodge and Burn Tools

1. Select the **Dodge** or **Burn** tool on the toolbox.

2. Select a brush tip, and then select brush options on the Options bar.

3. Click the **Range** list arrow on the Options bar, and then click **Midtones** (middle range of grays), **Shadows** (dark areas), or **Highlights** (light areas).

4. Specify the Exposure value for the stroke.

5. To use the brush as an airbrush, click the **Airbrush** button. Alternately, select the Airbrush option in the Brushes panel.

6. Select the **Protect Tones** (**New!**) check box to minimize clipping and reduce hue shifting within the image.

7. Drag over the part of the image you want to lighten or darken.

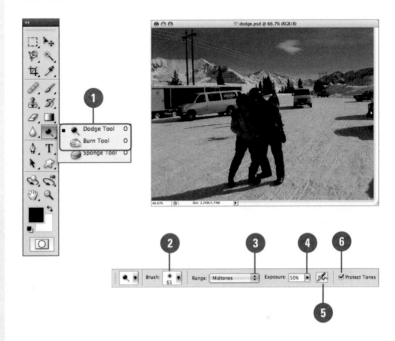

Did You Know?

The Sponge tool does not lighten or darken an image. It saturates or desaturates color values as you drag over parts of the image. Since overexposed or underexposed images have a tendency to lose some tonal values and appear flat, you can use the Sponge tool (with Saturate) to return some of the color values back to the image.

Dark areas restored using the Burn tool

Using the Healing Brush and Patch Tools

PS 2.4

These tools have become my favorite tools for working with digital images and correcting problems. The Healing Brush tool allows you to correct small imperfections, making them disappear into the surrounding image. This tool works from a sample of the original image, and then matches the texture, lighting, transparency, and shading of the sampled pixels into the source pixels. If an image contains a lot of random noise, before working with the Healing Brush, try lowering the amount of noise with the Reduce Noise filter. After you've applied the Reduce Noise filter, you can use the Healing Brush to clean up the rest of the problem areas. The Patch tool takes a sample and matches the texture, lighting, transparency, and shading of the sample to the source, creating an almost seamless repair of the image. You can also use the Patch tool to clone isolated areas of an image. When you use healing operations in a separate layer, you gain control over the process; you can even use the opacity and blending mode settings to further control the healing process. Always use the Healing Brush in a separate layer…always.

Use the Healing Brush Tool

① Select the **Healing Brush** tool.

② Select a soft round brush on the Options bar.

③ Create a new layer above the layer you want to modify.

④ Click the **Sample** list arrow, and then select the layer option you want to use to obtain sample data: Current Layer, Current & Below, or All Layers.

⑤ Hold the Alt (Win) or Option (Mac) key, and then click on the area of the image for a sample.

This area should represent the texture (not color) of the areas you want to heal.

⑥ Use small short strokes and carefully drag over the areas you want to change, then release your mouse and move to the next area.

The Healing brush works to match the sample to the source.

⑦ If the texture of the area you are healing changes, repeat step 4, and sample a different area.

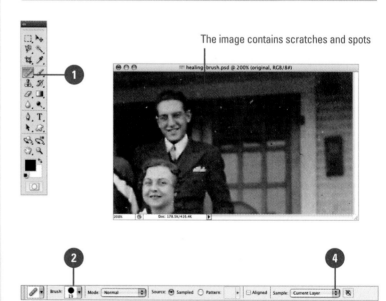

The image contains scratches and spots

The Healing Brush makes short work of correcting damaged images.

Use the Patch Tool

① Select the **Patch** tool.

② Select the layer you want to modify.

③ Using the Patch tool, select the damaged area of the image you want to repair (the Patch tool functions just like the Lasso selection tool).

④ Click the **Source** option on the Options bar.

⑤ Move into the middle of the selection marquee, and drag the selection over the area you want to repair and release. As you drag, you will see a copy of the area you are moving over appear in the original selection.

⑥ Release your mouse when you see the best match.

The Patch tool corrects the damaged area of the image.

⑦ Repeat steps 2 through 6 to patch any other damaged areas of the image.

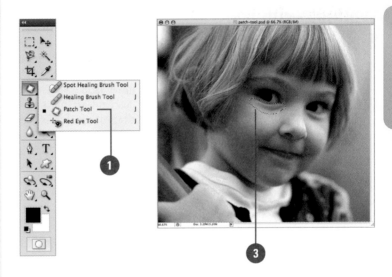

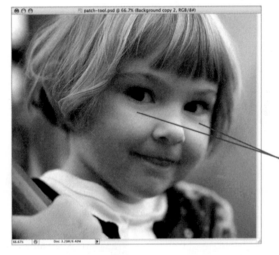

The Patch tool removed the rings under the model's eyes

Did You Know?

The Patch tool options on the Options bar provide power. On the Options bar, use the Source option with the Patch tool if you are selecting the damaged area and dragging it over the good area, and use the Destination option if you would rather select a good area to drag over the damaged area. The Transparent option preserves transparent areas during the patching process.

Working with the Spot Healing Brush

A powerful tool in Photoshop's formidable arsenal of restoration and correction tools is the Spot Healing Brush. With a name similar to the Healing Brush, you might expect that the tools have similar features, and you would be correct. The main difference between the two tools is that the Spot Healing Brush does not require you to take a sample of the area to heal. The Spot Healing Brush tool takes the area sample as you work by sampling the surrounding pixels. The Spot Healing Brush, as its name implies, works best on small spots and imperfections. To heal larger areas, the standard Healing Brush, Patch tool, and even the good old Clone Stamp tool are your best bets.

Use the Spot Healing Brush

1. Select the **Spot Healing Brush** tool.

2. Select a soft round brush on the Options bar.

3. Create a new layer above the layer you want to modify.

4. Select the **Sample All Layers** option.

5. Using small short strokes, carefully drag over the areas you want to change, then release your mouse and move to the next area.

   The Spot Healing brush works to match the sample to the source.

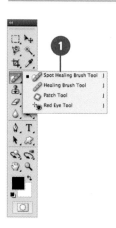

The Spot Healing Brush smoothed out some of the wrinkles

Did You Know?

You can use the Clone Source panel to set different sampling points. The Clone Source panel allows you to set up to five different sampling source points for the Clone Stamp tools or Healing Brush tools. Click a clone source button in the Clone Source panel, and then click a sampling point. To open the Clone Source panel, click the Window menu, and then click Clone Source. You can also scale or rotate the clone source, or show an overlay of the clone source.

Working with the Red Eye Tool

The Red Eye tool not only gives the digital restorer an excellent tool for removing pesky red eye, it will also remove the green and white reflections in pet's eyes. The biggest generator of red eye is the onboard flash on your camera. Actually, if they would simply rename a camera's built-in flash, "red eye generator," it might help amateur photographers pay more attention. However, until that day comes, designers will still have to deal with images that contain red eye. The Red Eye tool performs two operations: it desaturates the red values, and darkens the pupil.

Use the Red Eye Tool

1. Select the **Red Eye** tool.

2. Select from the following options on the Options bar:

   ◆ **Pupil Size.** Select the size of the pupil in relation to the amount of red eye.

   ◆ **Darken Amount.** Select how much you want to darken the pupil area of the eye.

3. Click in the middle of the red portion of the eye, and release.

   The red is removed, and the pupil is darkened.

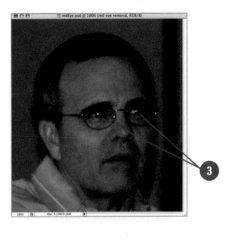

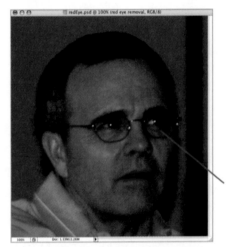

The red eye is removed with the click of your mouse.

Controlling Tonal Range

PS 2.1

The Levels adjustment lets you adjust the tonal range of an image by giving you three sliders—one for shadows, midtones, and highlights. Dragging the sliders precisely adjusts the tonal ranges of an image. In addition, the Output sliders let you adjust the ink percentages used to print during output. By adjusting the output ink levels, you avoid the overly black images that sometimes plague images printed with high dot-gain papers.

Control Tonal Range

1. Open a document in which you want to change the tonal range.

2. Select the **Layers** panel, and then select the layer to which you want to apply the Levels adjustment.

3. Click the **Create New Fill or Adjustment Layer** button, and then click **Levels** or use the icon for Levels from the Adjustments panel (**New!**).

4. To use common Levels settings, click the **Levels** popup, and then select a preset. If you select Auto, Photoshop will make a Levels adjustment for you.

5. Click the **Channel** list arrow to select whether to work on the entire image, or just one of the image's default color channels (useful for color correction).

6. Drag the **Shadow** input slider to the right to adjust the balance of black in the image.

7. Drag the **Midtone** input slider left or right to lighten or darken the midtones of the image.

8. Drag the **Highlight** input slider to the left to adjust the balance of white in the image.

9. Drag the **Black** and **White Output Levels** sliders left and right to adjust the percentage of ink used in printing the image.

10 To load a previously saved Levels adjustment, click **Load Levels Preset** from the Levels options menu, and then select and load the file.

11 Click **Save Levels Preset** from the Levels options menu to save the current Levels adjustment.

12 Use the eyedropper tools to select black, white, and midtone points directly within the active image.

13 Use the available buttons to fine-tune the adjustment and navigate through the Adjustments panel (**New!**).

◆ Left-pointing arrow moves you back to the list of available adjustment layer types.

◆ Folder icon with arrow toggles the panel from Expanded view to Standard view.

◆ The double circle icon creates a clipping group.

◆ The eye icon toggles visibility of the adjustment layer.

◆ The eye icon with an arrow allows you to see the previous state before the adjustment was made.

◆ The circular arrow returns the image to the default adjustments.

◆ The trash can icon deletes the adjustment layer.

Did You Know?

You can view the Levels Histogram anytime. Click the Window menu, and then click Histogram. Photoshop opens a Histogram panel that lets you view tonal changes to the image as you make them.

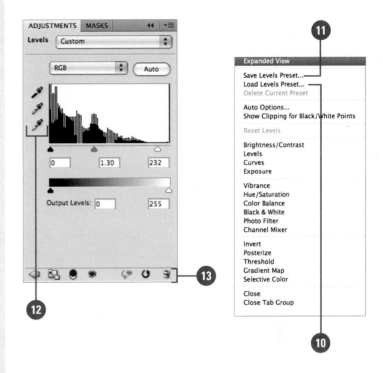

Tonal changes applied

Working with the Histogram Panel

Photoshop's Histogram panel gives you many options for viewing tonal and color information about the active image. The Histogram's default display is the tonal range of the entire image. However, you can use any of Photoshop's selection tools, select a portion of the active document, and display a histogram for just that portion of the image. You can also view a specific color channel or view all the channels at once. The tonal range and color values for an image are vitally important to generating great graphics, and the Histogram panel is a great resource for instant up-to-date information.

Work with the Histogram Panel

① Select the **Histogram** panel.

TROUBLE? *Click the Window menu, and then click Histogram.*

② Click the **Histogram Options** button, and then select from the following options:

◆ **Uncached Refresh.** Click to refresh the image cache (rescans the image).

◆ **Compact View.** Click to create a small, panel-size view of the Histogram panel.

◆ **Expanded View.** Click to create an expanded view of the Histogram panel. Includes options to view specific channels, luminosity settings or color.

◆ **All Channels View.** Click to view all the color channels.

◆ **Show Statistics.** Click to show history statistics.

◆ **Show Channels In Color.** Click to show the channels using specific colors, such as red, green, and blue.

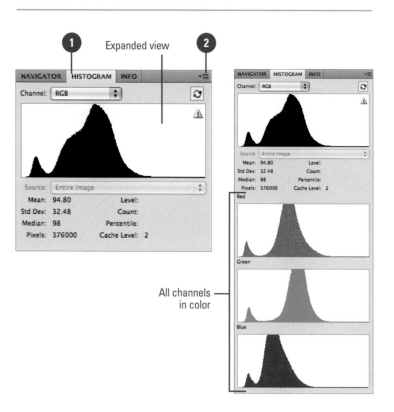

Expanded view

All channels in color

Understanding Colors and Channels

8

Introduction

In the world of design, color is one of the most important elements. When you're creating a brochure, advertisement, or banner using Adobe Photoshop, good use of color attracts the attention of the viewer. It also helps draw the elements of your design into one cohesive unit. Color is a strong motivator and is used in all aspects of our daily life.

Since color is so important to design, Photoshop lets you use industry-standard color sets, or you can create and save your own customized color panels. You can also color-correct a photograph by removing the color entirely or selectively remove colors from portions of the image. In addition, Photoshop gives you ways to select areas based on color, and then fill those areas with any color you choose.

Not only is it important to understand how color is used, it's also important to understand how Photoshop manages color information and that's where the Channels panel comes into the picture. **Channels** are where color information is stored. The number of channels in an image is based on its **color mode**, or color model, such as RGB (Red, Green, and Blue) or CMYK (Cyan, Magenta, Yellow, and Black). A firm understanding of channels and color modes, and their function in Photoshop, will go a long way in helping you control and manage color.

When adjusting your image, you can use various commands—Auto Contrast and Color, Curves, Color Balance, Brightness/Contrast, and Desaturate, just to name a few. You can also use the Match Color and Selective Color adjustments to further fine-tune your image. Photoshop also provides a Photo Filter adjustment, as well as a Shadows and Highlights adjustment to correct those overexposed or underexposed images. With all of the commands and adjustments available, the real dilemma will be, where do you begin?

What You'll Do

Work with 8-, 16-, and 32-Bit Images

Work with the Channels Panel

Work with Color Modes

Understand the Various Color Modes

Use the Replace Color Adjustment

Work with the Color Panel

Work with the Swatches Panel

Use the Stroke and Fill Commands

Create Spot Color Channels

Use the Variations Adjustment

Use Levels Adjustment Commands

Use Auto Contrast and Auto Color

Use Curves and Color Adjustments

Use Hue/Saturation and Desaturate

Use Match and Selective Color

Use Channel Mixer and Gradient Map

Use Photo Filter and Shadows/ Highlights

Use the Exposure Adjustment

Use the Invert and Equalize Commands

Use the Threshold and Posterize Adjustments

Use the Black & White Adjustment

Working with 8-, 16-, and 32-Bit Images

PS 1.6, 10.5

It's all about the numbers, and that's a fact. The number of colors available for displaying or printing each pixel in an image is called **bit depth**—also known as pixel depth or color depth. A higher bit depth means more available colors and more accurate color representation in an image. A bit depth setting of 2 bits displays 4 colors, 4 bits displays 16 colors, 8 bits displays 256 colors, 16 bits displays 32,768 colors, and 24 bits and 32 bits both display 16.7 million colors. Most digital images currently use 8 bits of data per channel. For example, an RGB image with 8 bits per channel is capable of producing 16.7 million (a 24-bit RGB image: 8 bits x 3 channels) possible colors per pixel. While that may seem like a lot of color information, when it comes to color correction and adjustment, it isn't.

In response to Photoshop users needing more control, Photoshop supports 16-bit and now 32-bit—known as **High Dynamic Range**

(HDR)—images. High Dynamic Range images with 32 bits per channel have a more extended dynamic range than lower bit depth images. **Dynamic Range** describes the ability of a channel to capture maximum information from the black to white and dark and bright areas of an image. An 8-bit channel image has a dynamic range of 250:1 (per channel), similar to the dynamic range of printed paper or a computer display. A 16-bit channel image has a dynamic range of 65,000:1, and a 32-bit channel image has a dynamic range of over 200,000:1. The greater dynamic range translates into better control over an image when making fine color and contrast adjustments using Levels and Curves (shown below). Working with HDR images is very similar to using raw files and applying exposure changes after the fact. Photographers can capture the full dynamic range of a scene with multiple exposures and merge the files into a single image.

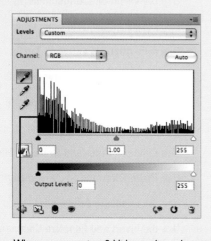

When you correct an 8-bit image, it can lose tonal values.

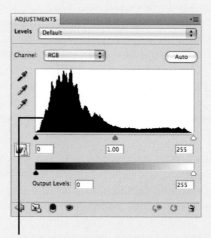

16- and 32-bit images hold more image data and therefore provide more to work with during correction operations.

Changing Bits Per Channel

The ability to work with 32-bit images is relatively new in Photoshop, and initially you had a limited use of adjustments and filters. However, in Photoshop many more adjustments and filters have become available for 32-bit images, such as Hue/Saturation, Levels, Gaussian Blur, Add Noise, Smart Sharpen, Vibrance (**New!**), and more.

When adjusting the color or contrast of an image, first convert a standard 8-bit image to 16 bits, and then make your corrections. This helps prevent loss of color information, and banding between light and dark shades. Once all the color/contrast adjustments have been made, you can (if necessary) convert the image back to 8 bits. It's that simple. You can change an image's bit depth by displaying the image, clicking the Image menu, pointing to Mode, and then clicking 8 Bits/Channel, 16 Bits/Channel, or 32 Bits/Channel.

When you convert a 32-bit image to 8 or 16 bits per channel, if you choose to merge your layers before changing the bit depth, Photoshop opens the HDR Conversion dialog box to let you make exposure and contrast corrections so the image retains the dynamic range you want. The Exposure and Gamma option lets you manually adjust brightness and contrast. Drag the Exposure slider to adjust the gain and drag the Gamma slider to adjust the contrast. The Highlight

Compression option automatically adjusts highlight values to fit within the range for 8- or 16-bit images. The Equalize Histogram option automatically preserves image contrast. The Local Adaptation option adjusts the tonality (local brightness regions) in the image. Drag the Radius slider to specify the size of the local brightness regions and then drag the Threshold slider to specify the distance between tonal values before they are included in the brightness region. If you want to reuse these settings in the future, you can save them, and then load them again as needed.

Viewing 32-Bit Images

The dynamic range of HDR images exceeds the display capabilities of standard monitors. When you view a 32-bit HDR image, the highlights and shadows may look dark or washed out. To correct the problem, Photoshop allows you to adjust 32-bit preview options so 32-bit images display properly on your monitor. The preview options are stored in the image file, so each file retains its own settings. To set preview options, open a 32-bit HDR image, click the View menu, and then click 32-Bit Preview Options. In the 32-bit Preview Options dialog box, select the preview settings you want (described earlier in this topic), and then click OK.

Working with the Channels Panel

PS 5.1, 5.3

The Channels panel is Photoshop's storage locker for color and selection information. For example, when you open an RGB image, the Channels panel displays color channels of red, green, and blue. When you open a CMYK image, the color channels are cyan, magenta, yellow, and black. These primary color channels are defined as the native color channels of the image. The Channels panel can also contain spot color channels and selection masks. In addition to color information and selection masks, the Channels panel contains a composite channel. The composite, when selected, lets you view the full-color image in the document window. Selecting any of the individual native color channels changes the active view of the image to display the selected color channel. The Channels panel stores color information using shades of gray, and each color channel is capable of displaying 256 gradations from black to white. A zero-value pixel displays as black, and a 255-value pixel displays as white. The darker the shade of gray, the less of the selected ink color is used to create the visible colors within the image.

Work with the Channels Panel

1. Open a color document.

2. Select the **Channels** panel.

3. Click on the individual channels to view the native color channels of the active document.

4. Click the composite channel to view the full-color image.

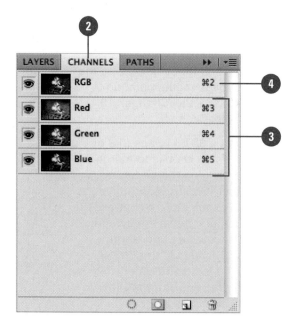

See Also

See "Creating Spot Color Channels" on page 188 for more information on using the Channels panel.

See "Using Channels to Create and Store Selections" on page 92 for more information on using Channels.

Working with Color Modes

Color modes define the colors represented in the active document. Although you can change the color mode of a document, it is best to select the correct color mode at the start of the project. Photoshop's color modes are Bitmap, Grayscale, Duotone, Indexed Color, RGB (Red, Green, and Blue), CMYK (Cyan, Magenta, Yellow, and Black), Lab, and Multichannel. See "Selecting Color Modes and Resolution" on page 13 for information on the best use for each color mode. The number of channels in an image depends on its color mode. For example, a CMYK image contains at least four channels, one for each color.

Color modes determine the number of colors, the number of channels, and the file size of an image. For example, an RGB image has at least three channels (like a printing plate), one for red, green, and blue color information. Color modes not only define the working color space of the active document, they also represent the color space of the output document. It's the document output (print, press, or monitor) that ultimately determines the document color mode. Color modes do not just determine what colors the eye sees; they represent how the colors are mixed, and that's very important because different output devices use different color mixes.

Therefore, when selecting a color mode, know the file format of the document and where it will be used. An image taken with a digital camera and then opened in Photoshop would most likely be in the RGB color mode. An image displayed on a monitor would be RGB, or possibly Indexed Color. A photograph scanned on a high-end drum scanner would most likely be in the CMYK color mode. An image being sent to a 4-color press would be CMYK, too. If you were creating a Photoshop document from scratch, the color mode you choose should represent the eventual output destination of the document, such as on a web page, to an inkjet printer, or a 4-color press.

Switching Between Color Modes

Unfortunately, images do not always arrive in the correct format. For example, you take several photographs with your digital (RGB) camera, but the images are being printed on a 4-color (CMYK) press, or you want to colorize a grayscale image. Changing color modes is a snap, but changing the color mode of an image isn't the problem. The problem is what happens to the digital color information when you change color modes. For example, if you open an RGB image with the intent of sending it out to a 4-color press (CMYK), the smartest course of action is to remain in the RGB color mode through the processing of the image, and then convert the image into the CMYK mode at the end. The reason has to do with how Photoshop moves between those two color spaces. For example, if you move a color-corrected CMYK image into the RGB color mode, and then back to CMYK, the colors shift because Photoshop rounds color values during the change process. On top of that, a CMYK image is 25% larger than an RGB image, and the RGB color mode represents the color space of your monitor, not a printing press. It is impossible to view subtractive CMYK color on an RGB device. If, however, the image originally came to you as a color-corrected CMYK image, then stay in and work inside that color mode.

Understanding the RGB Color Mode

The RGB color mode is probably the most widely used of all the color modes. RGB generates color using three 8-bit channels: 1 red, 1 green, and 1 blue. Since each channel is capable of generating 256 steps of color, mathematically, that translates into 16,777,216 possible colors per image pixel. The RGB color mode (sometimes referred to as Additive RGB) is the color space of computer monitors, televisions, and any electronic display. This also includes PDAs (Personal Digital Assistants), and cellular phones. RGB is considered a device-dependent color mode. Device-dependent means that the colors in images created in the RGB color mode will appear differently on various devices. In the world of computer monitors and the Web, what you see is very seldom what someone else sees; however, understanding how Photoshop manages color information goes a long way to gaining consistency over color.

Convert an Image to RGB Color

1. Open an image.

2. Click the **Image** menu, point to **Mode**, and then click **RGB Color**.

   Photoshop converts the image into the RGB color mode.

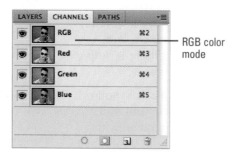

RGB color mode

Understanding the CMYK Color Mode

The CMYK color mode is the color mode of paper and press. Printing presses (sometimes referred to as a 4-color press) convert an image's colors into percentages of CMYK (Cyan, Magenta, Yellow, and Black), which eventually become the color plates on the press. One at a time, the plates apply color to a sheet of paper, and when all 4 colors have been applied, the paper contains an image similar to the CMYK image created in Photoshop. The CMYK color mode can take an image from a computer monitor to a printed document. Before converting an image into the CMYK mode, however, it's important to understand that you will lose some color saturation during the conversion. The colors that will not print are defined as being **out of gamut**. To view the areas of an RGB image that will lose saturation values, click the View menu, and then click Gamut Warning. Photoshop will mask all the areas of the image that are out of gamut.

Convert an Image to CMYK Color

1. Open an image.

2. Click the **Image** menu, point to **Mode**, and then click **CMYK Color**.

   Photoshop converts the image into the CMYK color mode.

See Also

See "Using Curves and Color Adjustments" on page 192 for more information on adjusting the color of an image.

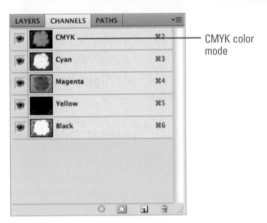

CMYK color mode

Understanding the Grayscale Color Mode

The Grayscale color mode utilizes an 8-bit pixel (8 on/off light switches) to generate 1 black, 1 white, and 254 shades of gray. Although scanning and working on old black and white images might seem the obvious reason to use the Grayscale color mode, the speed and power of Photoshop, combined with faster computer systems, has prompted most photo restorers to switch to the RGB color space because of its greater versatility and ability to generate millions of colors (or shades of gray). Yet despite the move to RGB, the Grayscale color mode is still used extensively with black and white images, where file size is a consideration (grayscale images are two-thirds smaller than RGB images), and when output to rag-style papers, such as newsprint, fail to produce the detailed information available with RGB.

Convert an Image to Grayscale

1. Open an image.

2. Click the **Image** menu, point to **Mode**, and then click **Grayscale**.

   The image is automatically converted into the Grayscale color mode.

Grayscale color mode

Did You Know?

You can colorize a grayscale image. Convert the image into the RGB mode, and then select a color, brush, and brush size on the Options bar. The trick is to change the blending mode of the brush on the Options bar to Color. Then, as you paint on the image, the selected color will replace the original grays.

For Your Information

Colorizing a Grayscale Image

If you're planning on colorizing a grayscale image, you can increase your control of the image by creating a layer directly above the image layer, and painting in the new layer. Leave the blending mode of the brush at Normal and change the blending mode of the new layer to Color. When you paint, the color is applied and controlled in the new layer, and you have the additional option of using layer opacity to control the intensity of the effect.

Understanding the Bitmap Color Mode

Bitmap images consist of two colors: black and white. Bitmap images are sometimes referred to as 1-bit images. Think of a bitmap as a light switch with two positions, on and off. Each pixel in a bitmap image is either on or off, black or white. Because they are only 1 bit, the file size of a bitmap image is typically very small. Bitmap images have limited use, but often are employed for black and white ink drawings, line art, sketches, and for creating halftone screens.

Convert an Image to Bitmap

① Open an image.

② Click the **Image** menu, point to **Mode**, and then click **Bitmap**.

> **IMPORTANT** *Before converting an image into a bitmap, it must first be in the Grayscale color mode.*

③ Enter a value for Output Resolution.

④ Click the **Use** list arrow, and then select from the available options:

  ◆ **50% Threshold.** Converts pixels with gray values above the middle gray level (128) to white and below to black. The result is a high-contrast, black-and-white image.

  ◆ **Pattern Dither.** Converts an image by organizing the gray levels into geometric patterns of black and white dots.

  ◆ **Diffusion Dither.** Converts pixels with gray values above the middle gray level (128) to white and below to black using an error-diffusion process. The result is a grainy, film-like texture.

  ◆ **Halftone Screen.** Simulates the effect of printing a grayscale image through a halftone screen.

  ◆ **Custom Pattern.** Simulates the effect of printing a grayscale image through a custom halftone screen. This method lets you apply a screen texture, such as a wood grain, to an image.

⑤ Click **OK**.

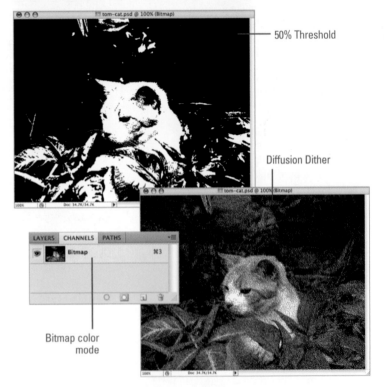

50% Threshold

Diffusion Dither

Bitmap color mode

Understanding the Indexed Color Mode

The Indexed Color mode gives you two advantages. You can create images as small as grayscale (8-bit pixels), and you get color instead of shades of gray. Its small file size and ability to generate color make it a winning color mode for images displayed on web pages, as well as graphics used in computer-generated presentations. Its one drawback is the number of colors generated; Indexed Color images generate a maximum of 256 colors (the same number as the steps of gray in a grayscale image). The good news is that you get to choose the colors. When you convert an image into the Indexed Color mode, Photoshop creates a color lookup table (CLUT) to store the image's color information. When a color in the image cannot be found in the lookup table, Photoshop substitutes the closest available color.

Convert an Image to Indexed Color

1. Open an image.

2. Click the **Image** menu, point to **Mode**, and then click **Indexed Color**.

3. Select from the following Indexed Color Mode options:

   ◆ **Palette.** Click the list arrow to choose from the available color panels, or click Custom and create your own palette.

   ◆ **Colors.** Select the number of colors for the lookup table (9 to 256).

   ◆ **Forced.** Force the lookup table to hold specific colors. Black and White adds a pure black and a pure white to the color table; Primaries adds red, green, blue, cyan, magenta, yellow, black, and white; Web adds the 216 web-safe colors; and Custom allows you to specify your own colors.

   ◆ **Transparency.** Select the check box to preserve transparent areas of the image (if there are no transparent areas, this option is disabled).

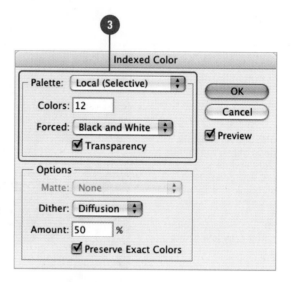

4 Select from the following options:

◆ **Matte.** Click the list arrow to fill transparent areas of the original image with a specific color.

◆ **Dither.** Click the list arrow, and then select a pixel-mixing (dither) scheme. Dithering helps transitional areas of the image (shadows, light to dark) appear more natural.

◆ **Amount.** If the Dither option is selected, the Amount instructs Photoshop how much color information to use in the dithering process (0% to 100%).

◆ **Preserve Exact Colors.** Select the check box to hold exact color measurements in the lookup table.

5 Click **OK**.

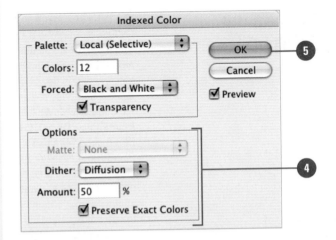

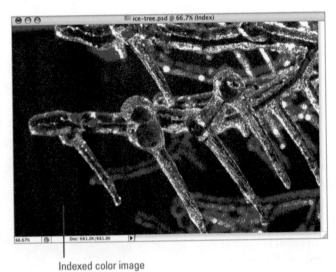

Indexed color image

Indexed color mode

Understanding the Lab Color Mode

The Lab color mode is an old color measuring system. Created in France, its purpose was to measure color based on visual perception. Since personal computers had not been created at that time, the Lab mode is not based on a particular computer or operating system, and so Lab color is device independent. The Lab mode measures color using a lightness channel, an "a" channel (red to green), and a "b" channel (blue to yellow). Lab Color works well for editing images obtained from Photo CDs or DVDs, moving images between operating systems (Photoshop Mac to Photoshop Win), and for printing color images to PostScript Level 2 or 3 devices. Because of its ability to separate the gray tones of an image into an individual channel (lightness), the Lab color mode is excellent for sharpening, or increasing the contrast of an image without changing its colors. Just convert the original RGB image to Lab color, select the Lightness channel, and perform sharpening or Levels and Curves adjustments directly to the channel.

Convert an Image to Lab Color

1. Open an image.

2. Click the **Image** menu, point to **Mode**, and then click **Lab Color**.

   Photoshop converts the image into the Lab color mode.

Did You Know?

You can use the Lab color mode to archive RGB color images. Since the Lab color space is device-independent, and RGB is device-dependent, archiving RGB images in the Lab color mode stabilizes the image's color information and insures color accuracy, no matter what editing application is used.

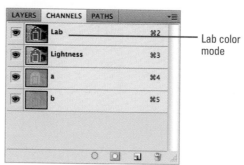

Lab color mode

Understanding the Duotone Color Mode

The Duotone Color mode converts a grayscale image into a monotone (1-color), duotone (2-color), tritone (3-color), or quadtone (4-color) image using 1 to 4 custom inks. Duotones are frequently used to increase the tonal depth of a grayscale image. For example, most printing presses produce 50 levels of gray per color. By converting an image into a duotone, and using black and a mid-gray value, the press can produce a grayscale image with more dynamic range. A more common method for employing the Duotone color mode is to create an image with an overall color cast, for example, by converting the grays in the image to a sepia tone. If you're uncertain how to create the proper color mix for a duotone image, Photoshop comes equipped with dozens of sample duotone, tritone, and quadtone color presets.

Convert an Image to Duotone

1. Open an image. Click the **Image** menu, point to **Mode**, and then click **Duotone**.

   IMPORTANT *Before converting an image into a duotone, it must first be in the Grayscale color mode.*

2. Choose from duotone presets available in the Preset drop-down menu. Choose to save or load a preset by clicking on the menu options triangle to the right of the preset menu.

3. Click the **Type** list arrow, and then select from the following options:

   ◆ **Monotone.** Uses one color to generate image tone (limited dynamic range).

   ◆ **Duotone.** Uses two colors to generate image tone (better dynamic range for B&W images).

   ◆ **Tritone.** Uses three colors to generate image tone.

   ◆ **Quadtone.** Uses four colors to generate image tone.

4. Click the **Overprint Colors** button to adjust how the colors will display when the inks are printed.

5. Click **OK**.

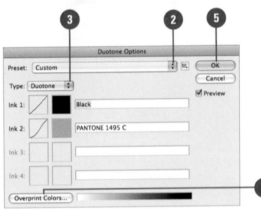

Duotone color mode

Using Multichannel Color Mode

The Multichannel color mode is a specialized mode that converts the original color channels into shades of gray, with the grays based on the luminosity values of the original image. The original channels are converted into spot colors. Since Multichannel mode is used almost exclusively by the printing industry, converting a CMYK image into Multichannel color mode produces Cyan, Magenta, Yellow, and Black spot channels, and converting an RGB image into Multichannel mode produces Cyan, Magenta, and Yellow spot channels, minus the Black channel. In both instances, converting to Multichannel Color mode causes the loss of the Composite channel.

Use the Multichannel Color Mode

① Open an image.

② Click the **Image** menu, point to **Mode**, and then click **Multichannel**.

Photoshop converts the image into the Multichannel mode.

IMPORTANT *Images converted to the Multichannel mode must be saved in the DCS 2.0 format (Desktop Color Separations). The DCS 2.0 format generates a separate file for each of the image's spot colors.*

See Also

See "Preparing an Image for the Press" on page 392 for more information on saving an image in the DCS 2.0 format.

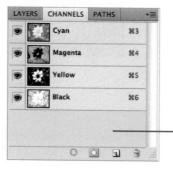

The Multichannel panel minus the Composite channel

Using the Replace Color Adjustment

Photoshop's Replace Color command lets you create a selection based on image color, and replace that color selection with any other color. The Replace Color adjustment accomplishes this by giving you access to the three components of color: Hue, Saturation, and Brightness. Hue gives you the ability to change the image's actual color, Saturation controls the amount of color, and Brightness determines how bright the color is based on its Hue and Saturation.

Use the Replace Color Adjustment

1. Open a color document.

2. Click the **Image** menu, point to **Adjustments**, and then click **Replace Color**.

3. Select the **Localized Color Clusters** (**New!**) check box if you want to limit your color selection to a specific area on the active document, using the Selection eyedroppers to select, add, or subtract colors.

4. Click the **Color** box to select a specific color for the selection.

5. Drag the **Fuzziness** slider to increase or decrease the sensitivity of the eyedropper tools.

6. Click the **Selection** or **Image** option to toggle between a view of the selection mask and the active image (white areas of the mask represent selected areas).

7. Drag the **Hue**, **Saturation**, and **Lightness** sliders to change the selected areas.

8. Select the **Preview** check box to view the changes in the active document.

9. Click **OK**.

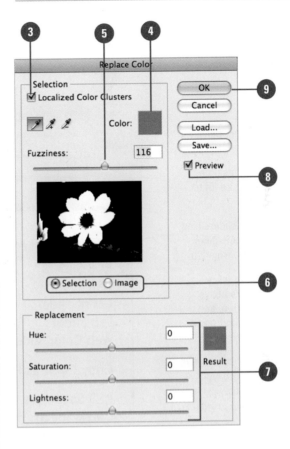

Working with the Color Panel

Photoshop not only lets you select virtually any colors you desire, it also lets you store those colors for future use. For example, you create a color scheme for a recurring brochure and you want a way to save those colors, or you're working on an Internet graphic and you need a web-safe color panel. Whatever your color needs, Photoshop stands ready to meet them. The Color panel gives you access to Photoshop's color-generation tools. This single panel lets you create colors using 6 different sliders, 2 spectrum color selectors, a grayscale ramp, and an option that lets you create a color ramp for the current foreground and background colors.

Work with the Color Panel

1. Select the **Color** panel.

2. Click the **Color Options** button.

3. Select from the following Color Sliders:

   ◆ **Grayscale.** Creates a single slider going from white (0) to black (100).

   ◆ **RGB.** Creates three sliders (red, green, and blue). Each slider has a possible value from 0 to 255.

   ◆ **HSB.** Creates three additive sliders (hue, saturation, and brightness). Each slider has a possible value from 0 to 255.

   ◆ **CMYK.** Creates four subtractive sliders (cyan, magenta, yellow, and black). Each slider has a possible value from 0 to 100.

   ◆ **Lab.** Creates three sliders (L, a, and b). The L slider has a possible value from 0 to 120, and the a, b sliders have a possible value from -120 to 100.

   ◆ **Web Color.** Creates three sliders (red, green, and blue). Each slider has a possible hexadecimal value from 00 to FF.

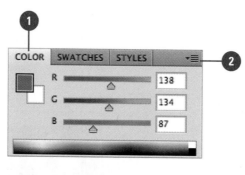

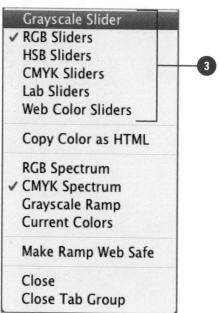

④ Click the **Color Options** button, and then select from the following Spectrums or Ramps:

◆ **RGB.** Converts the lower portion of the Color panel to the RGB spectrum. Clicking anywhere in the spectrum changes the active color.

◆ **CMYK.** Converts the lower portion of the Color panel to the CMYK spectrum. Clicking anywhere in the spectrum changes the active color.

◆ **Grayscale.** Converts the lower portion of the Color panel to a grayscale ramp. Clicking anywhere in the ramp changes the active color.

◆ **Current Colors.** Converts the lower portion of the Color panel to a color ramp, using the current foreground and background colors. Clicking anywhere in the ramp changes the active color.

⑤ To restrict the color ramp to only web-safe colors, click the **Color Options** button, and then click **Make Ramp Web Safe**.

⑥ To change a color using the Adobe Color Picker, double-click a color box, select a color using the color range or color mode options, and then click **OK**.

You can choose colors using four color models: HSB, RGB, Lab, and CMYK.

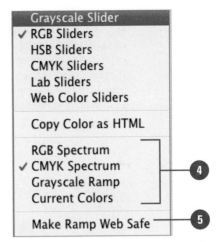

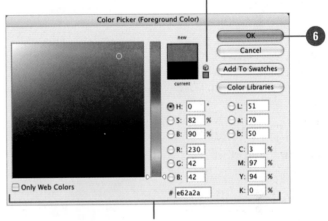

Cube indicates the color is not web-safe; click to select the closest web color. An alert triangle indicates the color is out of gamut (non-printable).

Select options or click the color range to select a color.

For Your Information

Understanding Spectrums and Ramps

Spectrums and Ramps are located at the bottom of the Color panel, and represent the entire spectrum for the chosen color space. For example, the CMYK spectrum displays a rainbow of colors in the CMYK color gamut. Moving the eyedropper into the spectrum box and clicking lets you select any color and gives you a visual representation of the relationships between various colors. The Grayscale Ramp gives you linear access to the 256 available grayscale values.

Working with the Swatches Panel

Photoshop not only lets you select virtually any colors you desire, it also lets you store those colors for future use in a library of color swatches, the Swatches Panel. Where the Color panel lets you select virtually any color you need, the Swatches panel lets you save and use specific colors that you use often. By default, the Swatches panel holds over 30 predefined color swatches, and has the ability to save as many user-defined swatches as you desire.

Add a Color Swatch to the Swatches Panel

1. Select the **Swatches** panel.

2. Click the **Swatches Options** button, and then choose from the predefined color swatches.

3. Click the **Append** button to add the selected color swatch to the panel.

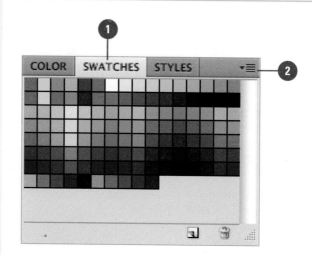

Change and Delete Colors on the Swatches Panel

1. Select the **Swatches** panel.

2. Select a color, and then change the following:

   ◆ **Foreground.** Change the color by clicking on any color in the Swatches panel.

   ◆ **Background.** Change the color by holding down the Ctrl (Win) or ⌘ (Mac) key, and then clicking on any color in the Swatches panel.

   ◆ **Delete.** Hold down the Alt (Win) or Option (Mac) key (your cursor will turn into a pair of scissors), and then click the color in the Swatches panel.

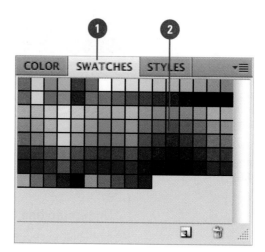

Add Colors to the Swatches Panel

1. Select the **Color** panel, and then drag the sliders or enter values to create a new color swatch.

2. Select the **Swatches** panel, and then drag the lower right corner to expand its size beyond the range of the available colors.

3. Move the cursor just below the last swatch color until it resembles a paint bucket.

4. Click once, name the color, and then click **OK**.

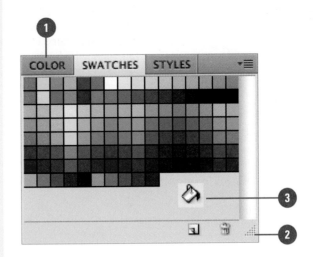

Save Customized Swatch Panels

1. Select the **Swatches** panel.

2. Create a customized swatch panel by adding and/or deleting colors from an existing panel.

3. Click the **Swatches Options** button, and then click **Save Swatches**.

4. Enter a name in the Save As box.

5. Click the **Save In** (Win) or **Where** (Mac) list arrow, and then select a location to store the swatch.

6. Click **Save**.

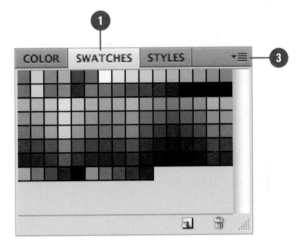

Did You Know?

You can access your customized swatches from the Swatches Options button. When you save swatchs in the Color Swatches folder (default location), your customized swatches appear at the bottom of the Swatches Options menu.

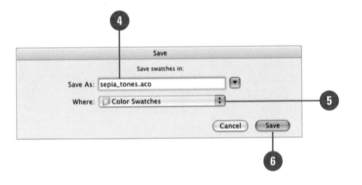

Using the Stroke and Fill Commands

Photoshop gives you many choices when it comes time to add or modify the colors of a document—paintbrushes, airbrushes, and drawing tools, just to name a few. Two little-used but powerful tools are the Stroke and Fill Commands. Both the Stroke and Fill commands work with selection tools. For example, you may want to create a unique stroke around an object, or fill a specific area of a document with a color or pattern. If that's the case, then the Stroke and Fill commands are the best and fastest ways to perform those operations.

Create a Stroke

1. Create a selection using any of Photoshop's selection tools, or really get fancy and make a selection from one of Photoshop's Shape drawing tools.

   TIMESAVER *To further control the process, perform the stroke (or fill) operations within a new layer.*

2. Click the **Edit** menu, and then click **Stroke**.

3. Enter a Width value (1 to 250) for the stroke.

4. Click the **Color** box, and then select a color (the color box defaults to the foreground color).

5. Select a location option (Inside, Center, or Outside) for the stroke of the selection marquee.

6. Click the **Mode** list arrow, and then select a blending mode.

7. Enter an Opacity percentage value (0% to 100%) for the stroke.

8. Select the **Preserve Transparency** check box to protect any transparent image areas (if there are no transparent areas, this option is disabled).

9. Click **OK**.

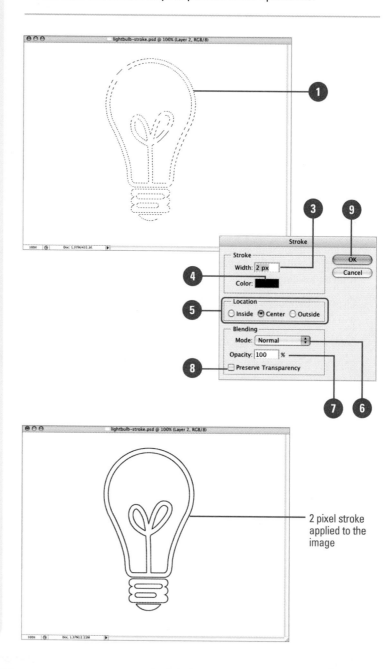

2 pixel stroke applied to the image

Create a Fill

1. Create a selection using any of Photoshop's selection tools.

2. Click the **Edit** menu, and then click **Fill**.

3. Click the **Use** list arrow, and then select a fill option:

   ◆ Foreground Color

   ◆ Background Color

   ◆ Color

   ◆ Pattern

   ◆ History

   ◆ Black

   ◆ 50% Gray

   ◆ White

4. Click the **Mode** list arrow, and then select a blending mode.

5. Enter an Opacity value (0% to 100%) for the stroke.

6. Select the **Preserve Transparency** check box to protect any transparent image areas (if there are no transparent areas, this option is disabled).

7. Click **OK**.

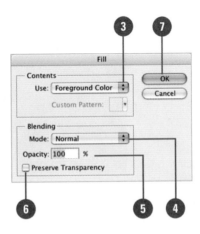

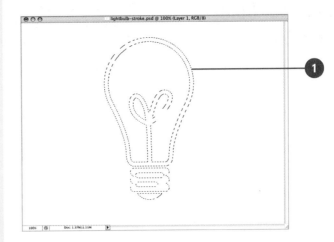

Did You Know?

You can use the Fill command for more than filling an area with a solid color or unique pattern. For example, selecting a sepia color, and changing the Fill Blending mode to Color, tints the selected area with sepia, creating an old-style, sepia-toned image. Experiment with the Fill blending modes to create unique image effects.

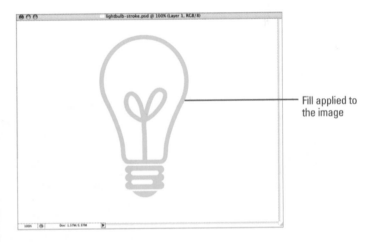

Fill applied to the image

Creating Spot Color Channels

When you work in the world of service bureaus and printing presses, there are certain things you must do to create an accurate printed document. The color mode of the image will be CMYK, and the output of the document will most likely be in a format designed to create color plates such as DCS 2.0 (Desktop Color Separations). In addition, you may want to apply a spot color to the image. **Spot colors** instruct a printer to apply a specific color to a specific portion of a document. For example, you may want to create a book cover jacket, and you want the author's name in a specific Pantone Blue, or you may want to apply a varnish to a portion of a brochure. Whatever the case, you will need to create a spot color channel.

Create a Spot Color Channel

1. Open a document.

2. If the document is not in the CMYK format, click the **Image** menu, point to **Mode**, and then click **CMYK** to convert it.

3. Create a selection, defining the area for the spot color. Use any of Photoshop's selection tools, including the Type Mask tool.

4. Select the **Channels** panel.

5. Click the **Channels Options** button, and then click **New Spot Channel**.

6. Click the **Color** box, and then select a color.

   If you need a specific press color, such as one from the Pantone Matching System, click the **Color Libraries** button in the Color Picker, select from the available color sets, and then click **OK**.

   The Name box displays the name of the selected color.

7. Enter a Solidity value (0 %to 100%) to view the spot color at a specific opacity (Solidity does not affect press output).

8. Click **OK**.

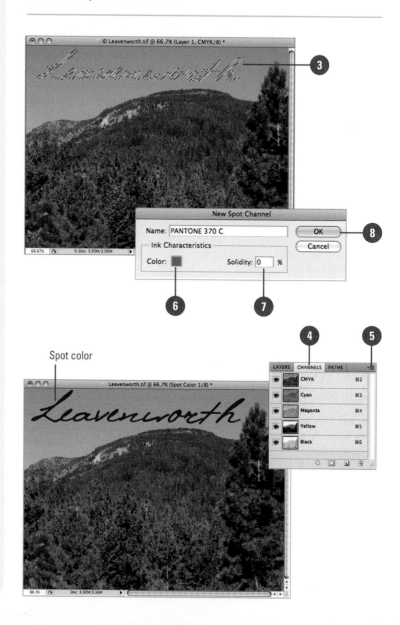

Spot color

Using the Variations Adjustment

Photoshop's Variations adjustment gives you a look at how working with analogous and complementary colors impacts the color in a Photoshop document. For example, if an image has an overall green cast, it needs additional magenta to reduce the green. Understanding how colors interact and work to produce different colors helps you decide on the correct course of action, and the Variations adjustment is an excellent teacher.

Use the Variations Adjustment

1. Open a document.

2. Click the **Image** menu, point to **Adjustments**, and then click **Variations**.

   The Original and Current Pick are displayed in the upper left portions of the Variations dialog box.

3. To restore the image, click **Original** any time during the adjustment process.

4. Click the **Shadows**, **Midtones**, **Highlights**, or **Saturation** options to apply a color shift.

5. Drag the **Fine/Coarse** slider to determine how much change occurs with each adjustment.

6. Select the **Show Clipping** check box to display a mask over areas of the image outside of the CMYK printable color space.

7. Click the color thumbnails surrounding the image to add specific colors to the Current Pick.

8. Click Lighter or Darker to change the brightness of the image.

9. Click **OK**.

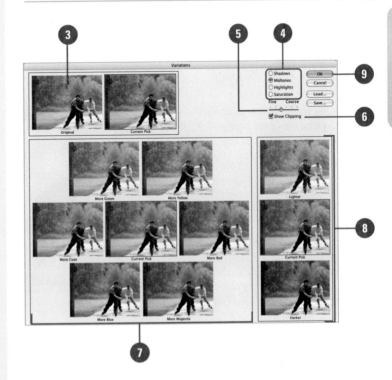

Using Levels Adjustment Commands

Through interactive feedback using a Histogram, the Levels adjustment gives you live information about the tonal values in the active image. It's an excellent tool to perform overall tonal adjustments and some color correction. Auto Levels is considered a quick-fix color adjustment which, in some cases, works just as well as manually correcting color. However, the average photo usually has more than one simple problem, so it's usually best to manually adjust an image. Since the Auto Levels command relies soley on information contained within the actual image—information that is sometimes inaccurate—it's usually best to correct the image manually using the Levels Adjustment command.

Adjust Levels Manually

1. Open an image.
2. Click the **Image** menu, point to **Adjustments**, and then click **Levels**.
3. Click the **Channel** list arrow, and then select the composite channel.
4. Drag the **Input Levels** sliders to adjust the brightness level.
5. Drag the **Output Levels** sliders to adjust the level of ink sent to the output device (printer).
6. Click **OK**.

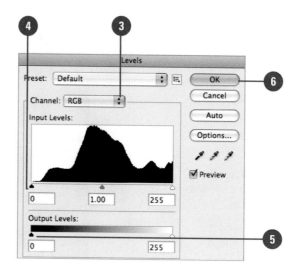

Adjusts Levels Automatically

1. Open an image.
2. Click the **Image** menu, point to **Adjustments**, and then click **Levels**.

Did You Know?

You can use the Preset drop-down menu to choose from predefined Levels presets (New!). For example, you can make the midtones brighter or darker, or increase the contrast. You can also tweak any of the presets and save it as a new preset by clicking on the Levels Options menu button to the right of the Preset drop-down menu.

190

Using the Auto Contrast and Auto Color Commands

 PS 2.1

The Auto Contrast command adjusts the tonality of the image without impacting color. The Auto Color command adjusts the tonality and color of the image by ignoring channels and looking directly at the composite image. The automatic color commands receive their adjustment cues from information within the active image, including any erroneous color information. For example, if the image contains a large border (typically white), the auto commands will factor that information into the correction of the image. It's best to correct any dust or scratch problems and crop out any borders before applying the Auto Contrast and Auto Color commands.

Use the Auto Contrast Command

1. Open an image.

2. Click the **Image** menu, and then click **Auto Contrast**.

> **IMPORTANT** *Use the Auto buttons (Levels, Contrast, Color) only if you do not understand how to manually control the image using powerful adjustments, such as Levels and Curves.*

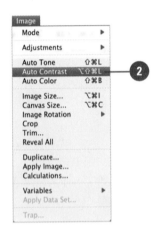

Use the Auto Color Command

1. Open an image.

2. Click the **Image** menu, and then click **Auto Color**.

Did You Know?

You can use a selection to define how the Auto Contrast and Auto Color commands work. If the image contains a border, and you don't want the Auto command using the border to influence the correction, simply select the Rectangular marquee and draw a border around the image. When the Auto command is applied, only the selected areas will be adjusted.

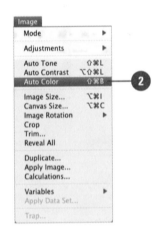

Using Curves and Color Adjustments

PS 2.1

The Curves adjustment lets you adjust tonal ranges in the image without changing image exposure. Curves is an excellent adjustment method for lightening the dark shadows of an image to bring out detail, or for creating special effects like solarization. To make it easy to use, Photoshop provides presets to use and save. The Color Balance adjustment lets you change the highlight, shadows, and midtones of an image separately. The Color Balance dialog box performs linear adjustments to color; therefore, it's a good tool for correcting common tonal problems, such as those caused by using film balanced for daylight indoors and getting a green cast to the image. The Brightness/Contrast adjustment changes an image by an overall lightening or darkening of the image pixels. While good for special effects, its linear way of changing an image's brightness and contrast do not lend themselves well to photo restoration. Curves and Levels are much better for this type of work.

Use the Curves Adjustment

1. Open an image.

2. Click the **Image** menu, point to **Adjustments**, and then click **Curves**.

3. To select preset mix levels, click the **Preset** list arrow, and then select the preset you want.

4. Click the **Channel** list arrow, and then select the composite channel.

5. Drag the **Black** and **White** sliders to adjust tonal values.

6. Click on the diagonal line to add an edit point, and then drag up or down to increase or decrease the tonal values of the active image.

7. Use the Eyedropper tools to select tonal values directly in the active image window.

8. Select the **Preview** check box to view changes to the image.

9. Click the curve option to adjust the curve by adding points or click the pencil option to draw a curve.

10. To save settings, click the **Preset Options** button, click **Save Preset**, type a name, and then click **Save**.

11. Click **OK**.

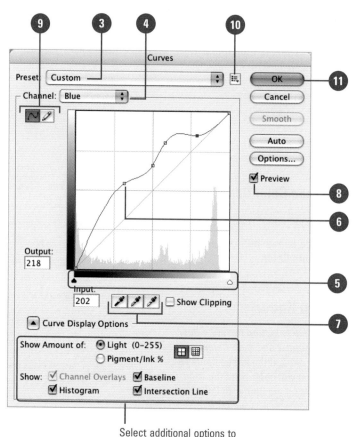

Select additional options to show different looks.

Use the Color Balance Adjustment

① Open an image.

② Click the **Image** menu, point to **Adjustments**, and then click **Color Balance**.

③ Drag the **CMYK** to **RGB** sliders to adjust the color.

④ Click a Tone Balance option.

⑤ Click **OK**.

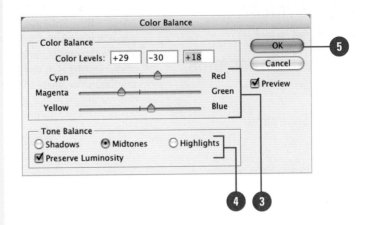

Use the Brightness/Contrast Adjustment

① Open an image.

② Click the **Image** menu, point to **Adjustments**, and then click **Brightness/Contrast**.

③ Drag the **Brightness** slider left to decrease the brightness values or right to increase the values of the colors in the active image.

④ Drag the **Contrast** slider to the left to decrease the color steps or right to increase the steps in the image.

⑤ If you prefer the CS2 method for Brightness/Contrast, select the **Use Legacy** check box.

⑥ Click **OK**.

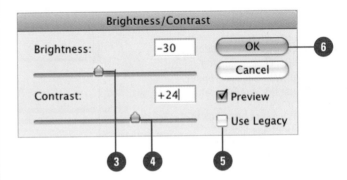

Did You Know?

You can use a selection to control the Brightness/Contrast adjustment. Use any of Photoshop's selection tools to isolate a portion of the image before using the Brightness/Contrast adjustment, and then only the selected areas will be adjusted.

For Your Information

Understanding Brightness and Contrast

The Brightness/Contrast adjustment performs linear adjustments to an image. For example, moving the brightness slider to the right will increase the brightness values of all the pixels in the image equally. Since photographs are not linear in nature, the Brightness/Contrast adjustment is not recommended for use on images. Instead, use a Levels, or a Curves (non-linear) adjustment for photographs, and a Brightness/Contrast adjustment for clip art, text, and non-photographic images.

Using the Hue/Saturation and Desaturate Commands

The Hue/Saturation adjustment gives you individual control over an image's Hue, Saturation, and Brightness, and its Colorize option lets you apply an overall color cast to an image, similar to a duotone effect. The Desaturate command removes all the color from an image, which preserves the Hue and Brightness values of the pixels, and changes the Saturation value to zero. The result is a grayscale image.

Adjust Hue/Saturation

1. Open an image.

2. Click the **Image** menu, point to **Adjustments**, and then click **Hue/Saturation**.

3. Click the **Preset** list arrow, and then select a preset, such as Cyanotype, Sepia, or Red Boost.

4. Drag the **Hue**, **Saturation**, and **Lightness** sliders to adjust levels.

5. Click the **Edit** list arrow, select a color, and then click inside the active image with the eyedropper tools to adjust the Hue/Saturation.

6. Select the **Preview** check box to see how your image looks.

7. Select the **Colorize** check box to tint with the foreground color.

8. Click **OK**.

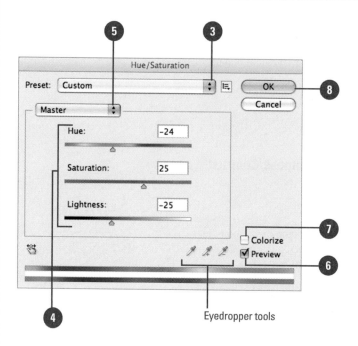

Eyedropper tools

Desaturate an Image

1. Open an image.

2. Click the **Image** menu, point to **Adjustments**, and then click **Desaturate**.

Did You Know?

You can Desaturate selected areas of an image using the Sponge tool. Click the Sponge tool, click Desaturate on the Options bar, and then drag to slowly remove color from the image.

Using the Match Color Adjustment

 PS 2.1

The Match Color adjustment lets you select colors in the image, and then match and change them—using Luminance, Color Intensity, and Fade sliders—to another image. The Match Color adjustment will only work on images in the RGB Color mode. Match Color is a great tool to help you get that consistent look you'll need when you need to match colors between images.

Use the Match Color Adjustment

1. Open an image.

2. Click the **Image** menu, point to **Adjustments**, and then click **Match Color**.

3. Drag the various sliders (Luminance, Color Intensity, and Fade) to adjust the image.

4. Select the **Neutralize** check box to automatically remove any color cast in the active image.

5. Click the **Image Statistics Source** list arrow, and then select another image or layer for matching the color in the Destination Image.

   If you select a portion of an image before entering the Match Color dialog box, you can choose whether to use the selection in the source or the target document to calculate the color match.

6. Click **Save Statistics** to save the current adjustment, or click **Load Statistics** to load adjustments made to other images.

7. Select the **Preview** check box to view changes to the active image.

8. Click **OK**.

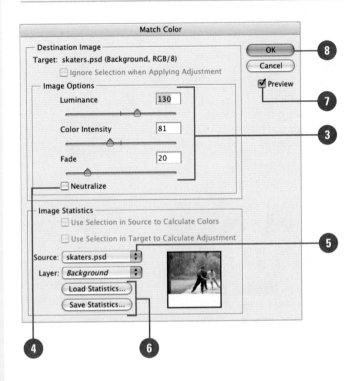

Using the Selective Color Adjustment

 PS 2.1

The Selective Color adjustment is designed to give you the ability to add or subtract specific amounts of cyan, magenta, yellow, and black inks. This is an excellent tool for making adjustments to an image based on a color proof, or for adding/subtracting certain primary colors based on information supplied by your printer. You can adjust color values for CMYK (Cyan, Magenta, Yellow, and Black), specify a color using a percentage of the color's total ink, and change an existing color using an absolute value of 1% to 100%.

Use the Selective Color Adjustment

1. Open an image.

2. Click the **Image** menu, point to **Adjustments**, and then click **Selective Color**.

3. Click the **Colors** list arrow, and then click the specific color to adjust.

   You can save your settings as a preset by choosing **Save Preset** in the Options menu to the right of the Preset drop-down menu.

4. Drag the **Cyan**, **Magenta**, **Yellow**, and **Black** sliders to the right or left to decrease or increase the color values.

5. Click the **Relative** option to change the selected color using a percentage of the color's total ink.

6. Click the **Absolute** option to change the existing color using an absolute value of 1% to 100%.

7. Select the **Preview** check box to view changes to the active image.

8. Click **OK**.

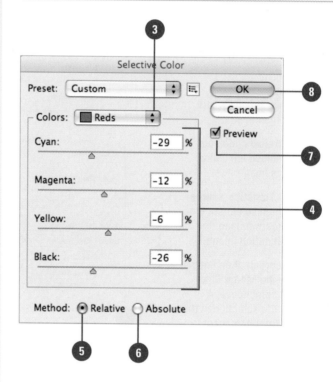

Using the Channel Mixer Adjustment

 PS 2.1

The Channel Mixer adjustment is a great way to adjust individual color channels, or for making an image conversion to black and white. The Channel Mixer adjustment modifies the selected output channel by blending it with a mix of the existing image color channels. Since color channels record information using shades of gray, you're essentially adding or subtracting grayscale information, not color information like when you use the Selective Color adjustment. That's what makes the Channel Mixer adjustment ideal for converting images into grayscale. To the make it easy to use, Photoshop provides presets to use and save.

Use the Channel Mixer Adjustment

1. Open an image.

2. Click the **Image** menu, point to **Adjustments**, and then click **Channel Mixer**.

3. To select a set of preset mix levels, click the **Preset** list arrow, and then select the preset you want.

4. Click the **Output Channel** list arrow, and then select from the available output channels.

5. Drag the **Source Channels** sliders right or left to increase or decrease the colors in the active image.

6. Drag the **Constant** slider left or right to adjust the grayscale output of the active image.

   Dragging to the left adds more black to the image; dragging to the right adds more white.

7. Select the **Monochrome** check box to convert the colors of the image into shades of gray.

8. Select the **Preview** check box to view changes to the active image.

9. To save settings, click the **Preset Options** button, click **Save Preset**, type a name, and then click **Save**.

10. Click **OK**.

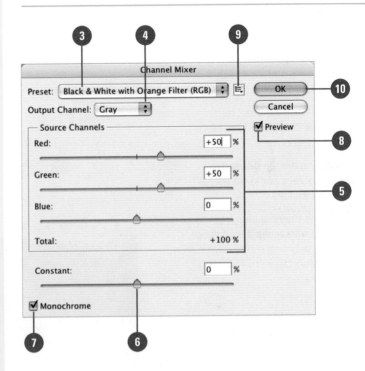

Using the Gradient Map Adjustment

The Gradient Map adjustment replaces the tonal values of the image with the colors supplied by a gradient. It's a great tool for generating special color effects. In addition, the Gradient Map adjusts the active image's colors to the colors of the selected gradient, taking the shadows of the image and mapping them to one end point of the gradient, and the highlights to the other point. You can also specify options to dither or reverse the color gradient. Select the Preview check box to preview your changes in the document window.

Use the Gradient Map Adjustment

1. Open an image.

2. Click the **Image** menu, point to **Adjustments**, and then click **Gradient Map**.

3. Click the **Gradient Used for Grayscale Mapping** list arrow to adjust the gradient.

4. Select or clear the **Dither** or **Reverse** check boxes for the Gradient Options.

5. Select the **Preview** check box to view changes to the active image.

6. Click **OK**.

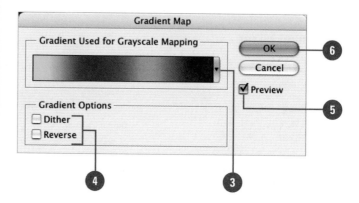

Gradient map applied to the image

Using the Photo Filter Adjustment

 PS 2.1

The Photo Filter adjustment lets you apply a specific filter or color to an image. Applying the Photo Filter adjustment to an image is similar to placing a colored filter in front of a camera lens. Photographers use filters to help correct color problems associated with unique lighting conditions like early morning sunlight or indoor fluorescent lighting. You can use Photoshop's Photo Filter adjustments to get the same results using color, density, and luminosity options.

Use the Photo Filter Adjustment

1. Open an image.

2. Click the **Image** menu, point to **Adjustments**, and then click **Photo Filter**.

3. Click the **Filter** option, click the **Filter** list arrow, and then select from the available color filter options.

4. Click the **Color** option to select a user-defined color filter.

5. Drag the **Density** slider left or right to adjust the intensity of the filter effect on the active image.

   The higher the value, the greater the effect.

6. Select the **Preserve Luminosity** check box to preserve the color of the image highlights.

7. Select the **Preview** check box to view changes to the active image.

8. Click **OK**.

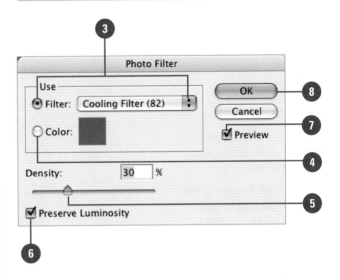

Cooling Photo Filter applied to the image

Using the Shadows/Highlights Adjustment

The Shadows/Highlights adjustment lets you quickly correct the problems associated with the underexposed and overexposed areas of an image such as deep shadows or bright highlights. In addition, the Shadows/ Highlights adjustment makes quick work out of images that have really dark shadows or overexposed areas by adjusting the problem areas without changing the midtones in the image. However, this type of adjustment will not work on images in the CMYK color mode.

Use the Shadows/Highlights Adjustment

1. Open an image.

2. Click the **Image** menu, point to **Adjustments**, and then click **Shadows/Highlights**.

3. If necessary, select the **Show More Options** check box to display Adjustments options.

4. Drag the **Shadows Amount**, **Tonal Width**, and **Radius** sliders right or left to adjust the shadow areas of the active image.

5. Drag the **Highlights Amount**, **Tonal Width**, and **Radius** sliders right or left to adjust the highlight areas of the active image.

6. Drag the **Adjustments Color Correction** and **Midtone Contrast** sliders left or right to decrease or increase the color saturation values of the adjusted areas of the image.

7. Enter values from 0% to 50% in the Black Clip and White Clip boxes to indicate how much of the shadow and highlight values will be clipped in the new image. Greater values produce images with more contrast.

8. Select the **Preview** check box to view changes to the active image.

9. Click **OK**.

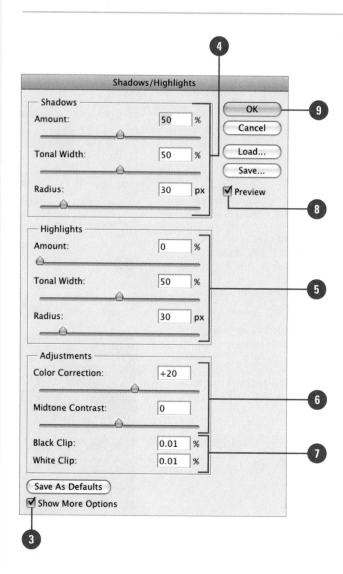

Using the Exposure Adjustment

 PS 10.5

Photoshop's Exposure adjustment is primarily designed for performing tonal adjustments to 32-bit High Dynamic Range (HDR) images, but it works with 8-bit and 16-bit images as well. The Exposure adjustment changes an image using a linear color space (gamma 1.0), not the image's current color space. When used with HDR images, it gives you the ability to draw out details of the image that otherwise might be completely lost within the shadows and highlights.

Use the Exposure Adjustment

1. Click the **Image** menu, point to **Adjustments**, and then click **Exposure**.

2. To select from preset exposure amounts, click the **Preset** list arrow, and then select the preset you want, or select from the following options.

   ◆ **Exposure.** Adjusts the highlight end of the image's tonal scale with little effect in the extreme shadows.

   ◆ **Offset.** Darkens the shadows and midtones with little effect on the highlights.

   ◆ **Gamma Correction.** Adjusts the image gamma, using a simple power function. Similar to adjusting the midpoints in an image's brightness.

3. Use the eyedroppers to adjust only the image's luminance values, not all the color channels, as you would with Levels or Curves.

   ◆ **Black.** Sets the Offset, shifting the point you click to pure black.

   ◆ **White.** Sets the Exposure, shifting the point you click to pure white.

   ◆ **Midtone.** Sets the Gamma, shifting the point you click to middle gray.

4. Select the **Preview** check box to view changes to the active image.

5. Click **OK**.

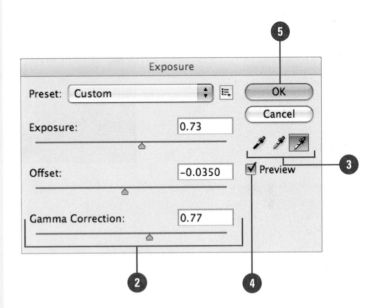

Using the Invert and Equalize Commands

The Invert command reverses the colors and tonal values to their opposite values, in effect, creating a negative. The Equalize command exaggerates contrast between similar color values. It's useful in finding stray pixels in a seemingly solid color, or to produce a special color effect.

Use the Invert Command

① Open an image.

② Click the **Image** menu, point to **Adjustments**, and then click **Invert**.

The brightness values of each image channel are reversed, creating a negative color or grayscale image.

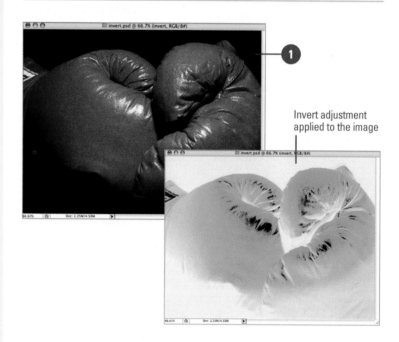

Invert adjustment applied to the image

Use the Equalize Command

① Open an image.

② Click the **Image** menu, point to **Adjustments**, and then click **Equalize**.

The brightness values of the image pixels are distributed in a way that more accurately represents the entire range of brightness levels from white to black.

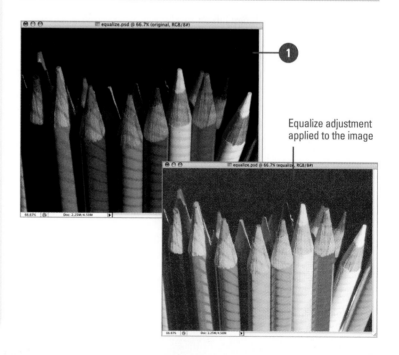

Equalize adjustment applied to the image

Using the Threshold and Posterize Adjustments

The Threshold adjustment reduces an image into only black and white pixels, based on their original brightness levels. It's useful for locating the darkest and lightest pixels in an image, or for creating some great-looking black and white special effects. The Posterize adjustment creates a simpler image by reducing the number of colors. It's useful for creating an image with a clip art look, or for reducing the number of colors in preparation for output to the Web.

Use the Threshold Adjustment

1. Open an image.

2. Click the **Image** menu, point to **Adjustments**, and then click **Threshold**.

3. Drag the **Threshold** slider to the right or left to change the point at which black and white are defined.

   For example, setting the threshold slider to a value of 75 creates an image where all pixels with a brightness value of 75 or less are black, and all pixels with a value of 76 or higher are white.

4. Click **OK**.

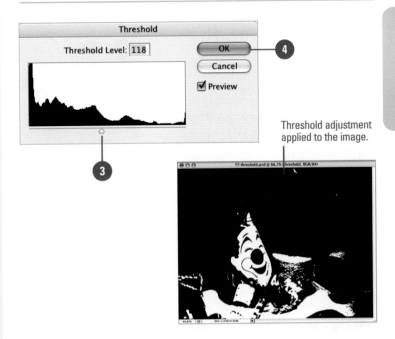

Threshold adjustment applied to the image.

Use the Posterize Adjustment

1. Open an image.

2. Click the **Image** menu, point to **Adjustments**, and then click **Posterize**.

3. Drag the slider to select a Levels value (2 to 255) to define the number of colors used.

   Lower values produce less colors and more visual contrast.

4. Click **OK**.

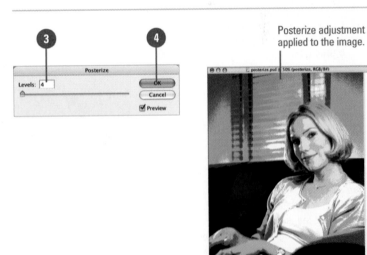

Posterize adjustment applied to the image.

Using the Black & White Adjustment

PS 2.1, 4.7

The Black & White adjustment allows you to convert a color image to grayscale. During the adjustment process you can control how individual colors (Reds, Yellows, Greens, Cyans, Blues, and Magentas) are converted. You can also apply a tint to the grayscale image by adjusting the hue and saturation, in a similar way to using the Channel Mixer. If you're not sure how or where to start, you can use the Auto button to set grayscale values based on maximizing the distribution of gray values.

Use the Black & White Adjustment

1. Open an image.

2. Click the **Image** menu, point to **Adjustments**, and then click **Black & White.**

3. To select a set of preset mix levels, click the **Preset** list arrow, and then select the preset you want.

4. To set auto adjustments, click **Auto**. Select the **On-Image control** icon and drag in image to control adjustment (**New!**).

5. Drag the **Reds**, **Yellows**, **Greens**, **Cyans**, **Blues**, and **Magentas** sliders to the desired levels.

   ◆ Alt+click (Win) or Option+click (Mac) a color box to reset a slider to its initial setting.

6. To adjust the tint, select the **Tint** check box.

7. If you selected the Tint check box, adjust the Hue and Saturation.

8. Click **OK**.

Did You Know?

You can save Black & White mix levels. In the Black and White dialog box, adjust the levels you want, click the Preset Options button, click Save Preset, type a name, and then click Save.

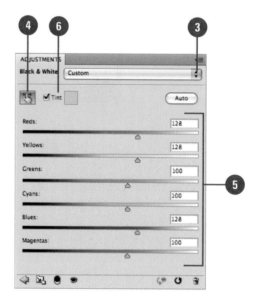

Black & White adjustment applied to the image

Using the Paint, Shape Drawing, and Eraser Tools

9

Introduction

Adobe Photoshop supplies you with all types of adjustment and manipulation tools. In addition to image enhancement, Photoshop can also be a powerful application for designing from scratch. With the vast array of supplied brushes, tips, and shape drawing tools, Photoshop helps you produce any images, either enhanced or developed from scratch, that you might need for virtually any conceivable project.

Brushes come in all sizes and shapes, and can be controlled with a mouse or drawing tablet. Since the shape of the tip controls brush strokes, Photoshop gives you access to several sets of predefined brush tip shapes, or you can create your own customized sets. As for shape drawing tools, Photoshop doesn't limit your creativity to just drawing circles and squares; it gives you instant access to dozens of predefined shapes. You can even create and save your own custom shapes. When it comes to Photoshop's paint and drawing tools, your choices are limitless, based only on your knowledge of the available tools, and a creative imagination—the more you know, the more you can do with Photoshop.

And, when all the drawing is said and done, there will be a need for cleaning up. With the various Eraser tools that Photoshop provides, you can make quick work of touching up those small problem areas. Photoshop provides regular eraser tools, eraser tools that erase to a definable edge, and even eraser tools that target specific color values.

When enhancing an image, you might want to apply a gradient. Gradients can be something as simple as black and white, or as complex as one that contains the colors of the rainbow. Gradients can be applied to an image by completely covering the original image information, or they can be controlled through targeted selection, and creative uses of blending modes.

What You'll Do

Understand Foreground and Background Colors

Use the Brushes Panel

Modify the Brushes Panel

Select Brush Tip Sets

Create and Save Customized Brush Tips

Work with Brush Presets

Work with the Brush, Airbrush and Pencil Tools

Work with Auto Erase

Work with the Line and Standard Shape Tools

Work with the Custom Shapes Tool

Create and Save Custom Shape Sets

Use the Paint Bucket Tool

Work with the Eraser Tools

Work with the Magic Eraser Tool

Create and Apply Gradients

Create and Save Customized Gradients

Use the Color Replacement Tool

Understanding Foreground and Background Colors

 PS 9.1

The Foreground and Background colors, located near the bottom of the toolbox, are Photoshop's way of identifying your primary painting color, as well as the color Photoshop uses in conjunction with the Background layer. When you select any of Photoshop's painting or drawing tools, the color applied to the document will be the foreground color—that's its purpose. Hence, it's sometimes referred to as Photoshop's active color. The Background color serves several functions—its primary purpose is to instruct Photoshop how to handle erasing on the Background layer. When you use an eraser tool on a Photoshop layer, by default, the pixels are converted to transparency. However, when you use an eraser tool on the Background, something different happens. Since the Background does not support transparency, it replaces the erased pixels with the current background color.

Change the Active Foreground and Background Colors

Use any of the following methods to change the active foreground or background colors:

◆ Select the **Eyedropper** tool on the toolbox, and then click anywhere in the active document to change the foreground color.

Hold down the Alt (Win) or Option (Mac) key, and then click to change the background color.

◆ Click on a color swatch in the Swatches panel to change the foreground color.

Hold down the Ctrl (Win) or ⌘ (Mac) key, and then click to change the background color.

◆ Click the **Foreground** or **Background** thumbnail to choose the color's destination. Create a color in the Color panel.

◆ Click the **Foreground** or **Background** Color box to open the Color Picker dialog box, select a color or enter color values, and then click **OK**.

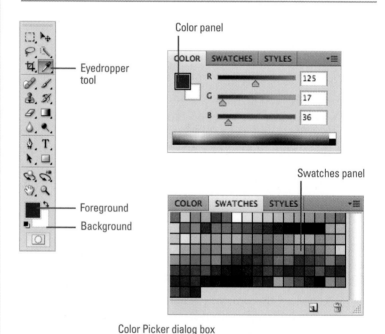

Color panel

Eyedropper tool

Swatches panel

Foreground

Background

Color Picker dialog box

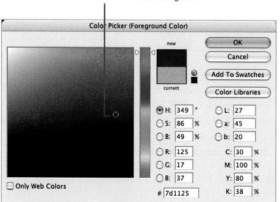

Use Default and Switch the Foreground and Background Colors

1. Click the **Default Foreground and Background Colors** button to revert the foreground and background colors to their default values of black and white.

2. Click the **Switch Foreground and Background Colors** button to switch current colors.

   TIMESAVER *Press D to change the foreground and background colors to their default values of black and white, and press X to switch the current colors.*

Did You Know?

You can add colors from the Color Picker to the Swatches panel. Open the Color Picker dialog box, select the color you want to add to the Swatches panel, click Add To Swatches, type a name for the color, and then click OK.

For Your Information

Selecting Colors

In Windows, you can use the Color dialog box, which displays basic and custom color squares and a color matrix with the full range of colors in the color spectrum, to help you select a color. You can enter RGB values for hue, saturation, and luminosity (also known as brightness) to specify a color. **Hue** is a pure color (one without tint or shade); the name of the color (red, green, etc.) is measured by its location on the color wheel. **Saturation** is a measure of how much white is mixed in with the color. A fully saturated color has vivid tones; a less saturated color is more of a washed-out pastel. **Luminosity** is a measure of how much black is mixed with the color. A very bright color contains little or no black. You can also change the hue by moving the pointer in the color matrix box horizontally; you can change the saturation by moving the pointer vertically, and the luminosity by adjusting the slider to the right of the color matrix box. On the Macintosh, you click one of the color modes and select a color, using its controls. You can select RGB values by selecting the color sliders at the top of the dialog box, then choosing RGB Sliders from the pop-up menu, and dragging the Red, Green, and Blue sliders. Or, you can enter values (color numbers) to select a color. You can select hue, saturation, and brightness (or luminosity) values by selecting Color Sliders, choosing HSB Sliders, then dragging the sliders or entering your own values.

Using the Brushes Panel

 PS 2.2

Photoshop's Brushes Panel (released in version 7) changed forever how Photoshop designers use brushes. Previously, Photoshop gave you the ability to create a brush in any size and shape, and then use the brush in a traditional manner. However, with the exception of changing the brush's spacing, it wasn't much more than a glorified paintbrush. The current painting engine configuration, with options such as Shape Dynamics, Scattering, Texture, Dual Brush, and Color Dynamics, gives you control over brushes in ways that once were only available in programs like Corel Painter and Adobe Illustrator.

An Overview of the Brushes Panel

Photoshop's Brushes panel is, by default, located in the Dock on the Options bar. To access this panel, you will first need to have a brush tool, or a tool that requires the use of a brush, such as the Eraser tool, chosen from the toolbox, and then click the Brushes panel icon. You can also go to the Window menu, and choose Brushes to make the panel appear. In this version of Photoshop, the brush engine has been improved for quicker response (**New!**), especially with a graphics tablet.

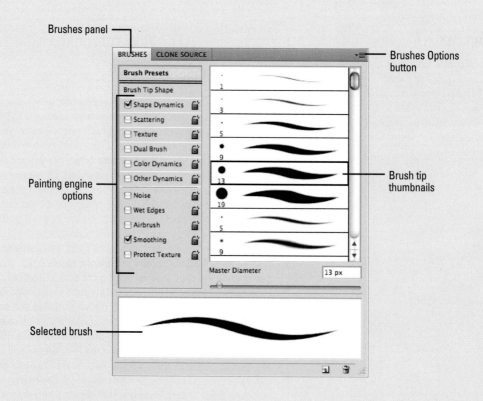

Modifying the Brushes Panel

The Brushes panel comes in many forms; you can view brushes as strokes, or you can choose thumbnails, or even text descriptions. The form of the Brushes panel does not impact its performance, only how you view the available brush tips. Choose the version that best suits your current design needs, and then change the view as needed. When you select a brush, it becomes the default for that tool only. This gives you the ability to choose a default brush for each of the brush-specific tools.

Change the Brushes Panel View

1. Select a Brush tool on the toolbox, and then select the **Brushes** panel.

2. Click the **Brushes Options** button, and then select from the available View options:

   ◆ **Expanded View.** Click Expanded View to gain access to painting engine options: Brush Tips, Shape Dynamics, Scattering, Texture, Dual Brush, Color Dynamics, and Other Dynamics.

   ◆ **Text Only.** Select this option to display all brush tips by their names.

   ◆ **Small Thumbnail.** Select this option to display all brush tips using a small thumbnail.

   ◆ **Large Thumbnail.** Select this option to display all brush tips using a large thumbnail.

   ◆ **Small List.** Select this option to display all brush tips by their names and small thumbnail.

   ◆ **Large List.** Select this option to display all brush tips by their names and large thumbnail.

   ◆ **Stroke Thumbnail.** Select this option to display all brush tips with a stroke. (This is useful in determining how the brush will look when applied in the document).

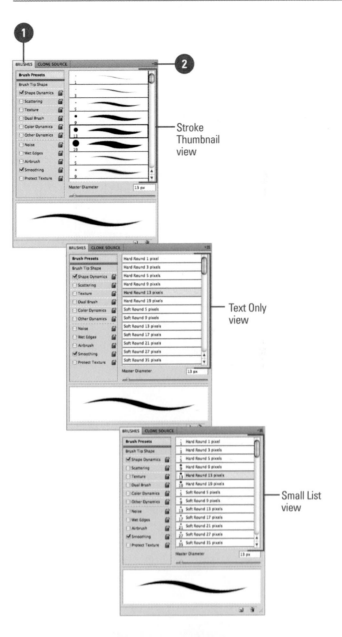

Stroke Thumbnail view

Text Only view

Small List view

Selecting Brush Tip Sets

 PS 2.2

The Brushes panel comes with 12 predefined brush tip sets. Each set organizes specific brush tips by name. Since other Photoshop tools also use brush tips, it's important to have the right tool (brush tip) for the right job. Using or making do with the wrong brush tip is akin to digging a swimming pool with a teaspoon. You wouldn't paint a portrait with a house-painting brush, so don't settle for anything less than the exact brush tip you need to get the job done.

Select Brush Tip Sets

1 Select a **Brush** tool on the toolbox, and then select the **Brushes** panel.

2 Click the **Brushes Options** button.

3 Click any of the predefined brush sets.

4 Click **OK**.

This replaces the current brush tips with the selected set, or you can click Append to add them to the current set.

Did You Know?

You can draw straight lines using Photoshop's brush tools. Holding the Shift key while dragging constrains the brush to a 90-degree line. To draw a straight line between two points, click once in the document window, move the mouse to another position, hold down the Shift key, and then click a second time. A straight line will be drawn between the first and second mouse clicks.

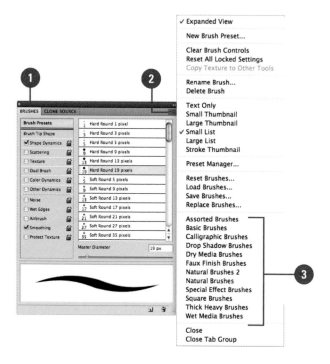

Creating Customized Brush Tips

 PS 2.3

Although Photoshop's Brushes panel gives you many choices for brush tips, any good designer will tell you that no matter how many brush tips you have, you'll always want more. For example, you're working on a 100-year-old photograph, and you need a specific brush to add hair details to the blown-out areas of the image. You'll want to find a special type of brush that literally creates the illusion of wavy hair and add it to your collection of brush tips. Photoshop, in an effort to help keep you organized, gives you the ability to create your very own customized brush tips, and then save them later in organized sets.

Create a New Brush Tip

1. Open an image, scan an item, or select any of Photoshop's painting tools and create a shape for a new brush tip.

   IMPORTANT *Since the color of a brush is determined when the brush tip is selected, create the brush tip using black or shades of gray.*

2. Select the brush tip using any of Photoshop's selection tools.

   IMPORTANT *Photoshop picks up any pixel information in the underlying layers, even white. If you want the brush to have a transparent background, make sure the areas surrounding the image are transparent.*

3. Click the **Edit** menu, and then click **Define Brush Preset.**

4. Enter a name for the new brush preset.

5. Click **OK**.

   Open the Brushes panel, and then scroll to the bottom of the list to access your newly created brush tip.

   Since the Define Brush Preset button picks up any background colors within the selection area, it always creates the brush tip in a blank layer.

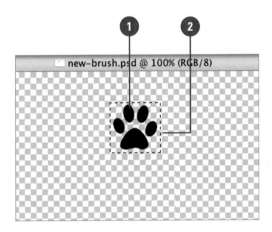

Layer with new brush tip

Saving Customized Brush Tips

PS 2.3

Once a brush tip is created, it becomes part of the current set. However, the brush has not yet been permanently saved in Photoshop. Although the new brush tip will reappear every time you access the Brushes panel, if you choose the option to reset the panel, the new brush will be lost. To keep brushes you must save them into customized sets.

Save a Customized Brush Tip

1. Select a **Brush** tool on the toolbox, and then select the **Brushes** panel.

2. Create a set of customized brushes.

3. Click the **Brushes Options** button, and then click **Save Brushes**.

4. Type the name of the set (with a .abr extension).

5. Click the **Save In** (Win) or **Where** (Mac) list arrow, and then select where you want to save the brush set.

6. Click **New Folder** or **Add To Favorites** to add your customized brush set.

7. Click **Save**.

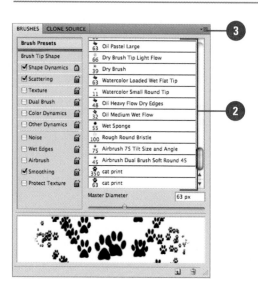

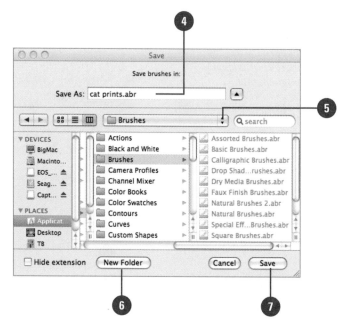

Did You Know?

You can access your customized sets directly from the Brushes Options menu. When you save your customized brush set, put them in the Brushes folder, located in the Adobe Photoshop CS4/Presets folder. Brush sets saved here appear in the Brushes Options menu along with the other Photoshop presets.

Working with Brush Presets

The Brush Presets area of the Brushes panel provides a series of controls that let you define how a brush tip is applied to the active image. Features such as Scattering and Color Dynamics let you further customize your brush tips so you can create that specialized brush for all your image enhancement needs.

Work with Brush Presets

1. Select a **Brush** tool on the toolbox, and then select the **Brushes** panel.

2. Click the **Brushes Options** button, and then click **Expanded View**.

3. Click to select a specific brush tip.

4. Select from the various Painting Engine options:

   ◆ **Brush Tip Shape.** Lets you modify the angle, roundness, and spacing of the brush tip. In addition, you can flip the brush shape along its x (left to right), or y (top to bottom) axis.

   ◆ **Shape Dynamics.** Lets you randomly (jitter) generate different sizes, angles, and roundness for the brush tip.

   ◆ **Scattering.** Lets you randomly scatter the shape. Options include the ability to distribute (Scatter) the shape, as you draw, choose how many to use (Count), and randomly change the number (Count Jitter), as you draw.

   ◆ **Texture.** Lets you select a predefined or custom texture, in place of a solid color.

   ◆ **Dual Brush.** Lets you select a second brush.

   ◆ **Color Dynamics.** Lets you key off of the active foreground and background colors.

   ◆ **Other Dynamics.** See Table.

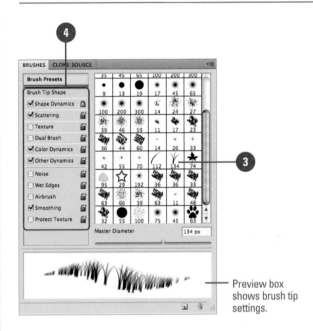

Preview box shows brush tip settings.

Other Dynamics

Dynamic	Purpose
Noise	Generates random noise in the brush tip as you draw.
Wet Edges	Fades the edges of the drawn shape, similar to running a watercolor brush over a wet canvas.
Airbrush	Changes the Brush tool into an Airbrush.
Smoothing	Applies anti-aliasing to the drawn shapes, creating a smoother shape.
Protect Texture	Preserves texture pattern when applying brush presets.

Working with the Brush and Airbrush Tools

PS 2.2

Photoshop's Brush and Airbrush tools were designed to reproduce the visual effect of applying paint to a canvas. You have full control over the brush tip, color, size, opacity, and even the brush's blending mode. Control over the image is achieved by using additional layers to hold the brush strokes—but remember, adding additional layers increases the file size of a Photoshop document. Since layers have their own individual options, such as opacity, fill, and blending modes, you achieve even greater control over the final design by giving brush strokes their own layers. Once the brush stroke is to your liking, you can always merge the brush-stroke layer into the image to conserve file size.

Work with the Brush and Airbrush Tools

1. Select the **Brush** tool on the toolbox.

2. Select a brush tip on the Options bar or from the Brushes panel.

3. Specify Paint Engine options for the brush from the Brushes panel.

4. Select from the following Brush options on the Options bar:

   ◆ **Mode.** Click the list arrow to choose from the available blending modes. The blending modes controls how the active brush color blends with the colors in the active image.

   ◆ **Opacity.** Enter an opacity percent (1% to 100%), or click the list arrow, and then drag the slider left or right.

   ◆ **Flow.** Enter a flow percentage (1% to 100%), or click the list arrow, and then drag the slider left or right. When you apply the brush, Flow controls the amount of ink supplied to the brush.

   ◆ **Airbrush.** Click the button to change the Brush into an Airbrush.

5. Drag within the image to paint.

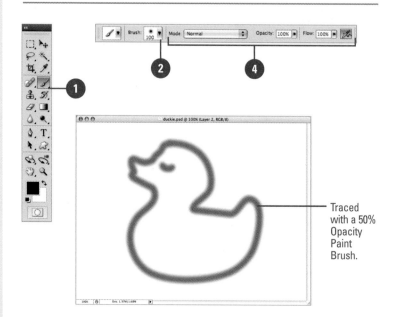

Traced with a 50% Opacity Paint Brush.

For Your Information

Using the Brush and Airbrush Tools

The Brush and Airbrush tools look the same, but they perform quite differently. The Brush tool maintains a specific opacity; for example, if you choose 50% opacity, the Brush maintains that opacity no matter how many times you pick up your pen and start again. However, if you release and drag again over the same area, the Brush adds another 50% application of ink to the image, producing a more saturated result. The Airbrush tool works by accumulation—dragging the image produces a brush stroke based on the opacity of the brush and the speed with which you move the tool across the image. If you hold the Airbrush tool in one position, the ink color will slowly increase until it reaches 100%, just like a real airbrush.

Working with the Pencil Tool

The Pencil tool is exactly what its name implies…a pencil. The Pencil tool is limited to hard brush tips of any size or shape, and creates freeform lines using the current foreground color. In fact, the major difference between the Pencil and Brush tools is the Pencil tool's inability to draw anything *but* a hard-edged line. A unique feature of the Pencil tool is its ability to switch between the current foreground and background colors using the Auto Erase feature.

Work with the Pencil Tool

1. Select the **Pencil** tool on the toolbox.

2. Click the **Brush Preset Picker** list arrow, and then click a brush tip.

3. Click the **Mode** list arrow, and then select a blending mode.

4. Enter an Opacity percentage value (1% to 100%).

5. Drag the **Pencil** tool across the active document.

Did You Know?

You can use the Pencil tool to create calligraphy lettering. Select the Pencil tool, click black as your painting color, and then click one of the oblong brush tips on the Options bar. If you own a drawing tablet, use the tablet with the Pencil tool to create beautifully formed calligraphy letters.

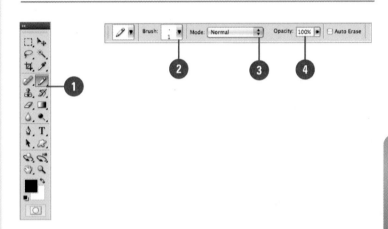

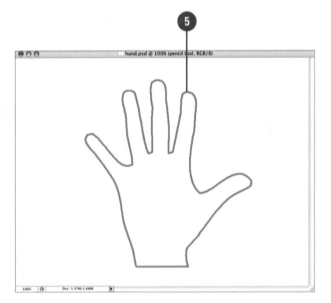

Working with Auto Erase

PS 2.2

The Auto Erase feature lets you automatically switch the Pencil tool's painting color using the current foreground and background color swatches. The trick is where you start drawing the line. If you start dragging the brush tip from a new location in the document, the Pencil tool creates a line in the active foreground color. If you then place the brush tip on a previously drawn line and drag, the Pencil tool creates a new line in the active background color. Since the Auto Erase feature doesn't really erase anything, it will perform exactly the same way on a transparent layer as it does on the background layer.

Work with Auto Erase

1. Select the **Pencil** tool on the toolbox.

2. Select the **Auto Erase** check box on the Options bar.

3. Drag the **Pencil** tool across the active document to create a line in the active foreground color.

4. Click anywhere in the background and the Pencil tool will use the foreground color.

5. Move the brush tip over one of the previous lines, and then drag to create a line in the active background color.

Did You Know?

You can draw straight lines with the Pencil tool. Click once in the document to create a black dot, move to another position, hold down the Shift key, and then click again. When you hold down the Shift key, the Pencil tool creates a straight line between the two mouse clicks.

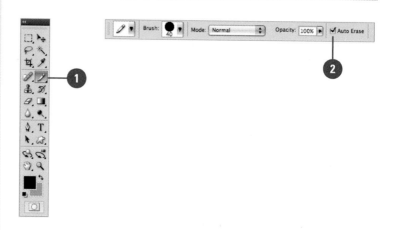

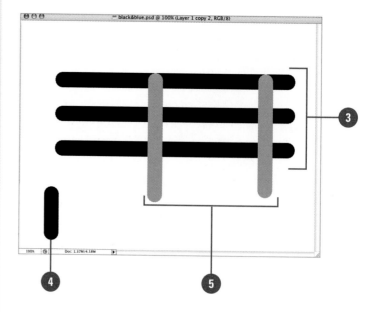

Working with the Line Tool

The Line tool lets you draw lines by dragging from one point in the active document and releasing in another. You can draw lines at precise 45- or 90-degree angles by holding down the Shift key as you drag. Select the Line tool, or if you already have another drawing tool selected, you can choose the Line tool from the toolbox. Then configure the Line tool using the Options bar. It's also a good idea to create the lines in a separate layer. That way, once the lines have been drawn, it's as easy as selecting the Move tool and repositioning them where you want them.

Work with the Line Tool

1. Select the **Line** tool on the toolbox.

2. Click the **Fill Pixels** button to create raster shapes in the active foreground color.

3. Click the **Geometry** options list arrow, and then select from the following options:

   ◆ **Arrowheads.** Select the Start and/or End check boxes to create arrowheads on the line.

   ◆ **Width.** Enter a percentage (10 to 1,000), to determine the width of the arrowhead in relation to the width of the line.

   ◆ **Length.** Enter a percentage (10 to 5,000), to determine the length of the arrowhead.

   ◆ **Concavity.** Enter a percentage (-50 to +50) to determine the concavity of the arrowhead.

4. Enter a value (1 to 1,000 pixels) to determine the weight of the line.

5. Click the **Mode** list arrow, and then select a blending mode.

6. Enter an Opacity percentage value (1% to 100%).

7. Select the **Anti-alias** check box to create a visually smoother line.

8. Drag in the document window to create the line.

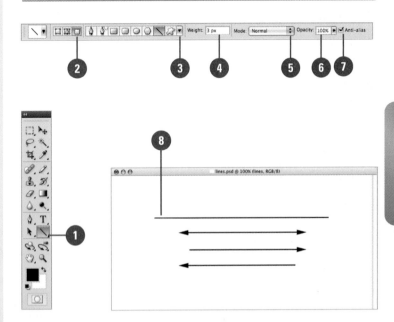

For Your Information

Using the Line Tool

The Line tool can be used to create customized guidelines for those projects that require something other than vertical or horizontal guidelines. Just create a new layer, and then select the Line tool. Choose a line weight (width) of one or two pixels, select a drawing color that contrasts with the image, and then draw the required guides. When you're finished, lock the layer, and use the visual guides to complete your project. Hide the layer when it's not needed, and finally, delete the layer when you're done with the job. One more thing—remember to turn off the Arrowheads option.

Using the Standard Shape Tool

PS 4.5

Creating standard shapes, such as polygons or rectangles with rounded corners, used to be a hassle. That is, until Photoshop released its Standard Shape drawing tools. Now, it's a simple matter of selecting the correct tool, choosing a color, and then drawing the shape. As with any of Photoshop's drawing functions, control is maintained with the use of additional layers. Photoshop's standard shapes include rectangles, rounded rectangles, ellipses, and polygons. Each one of the shape tools comes with additional options to control exactly how the shape appears when drawn.

Work with the Standard Shape Tool

1. Select the **Rectangle** tool on the toolbox.

2. Click the **Fill Pixels** button to create raster shapes in the active foreground color.

3. Click the **Rectangle**, **Rounded Rectangle**, **Ellipse**, or **Polygon** tool buttons.

4. Click the **Geometry** options list arrow, and then select from the following drawing options or check boxes:

   ◆ **Unconstrained.** (Rectangle, Rounded Rectangle, Ellipse)

   ◆ **Square.** (Rectangle, Rounded Rectangle)

   ◆ **Circle.** (Ellipse)

   ◆ **Fixed Size.** (Rectangle, Rounded Rectangle, Ellipse)

   ◆ **Proportional.** (Rectangle, Rounded Rectangle, Ellipse)

   ◆ **From Center.** (Rectangle, Rounded Rectangle, Ellipse)

   ◆ **Snap to Pixels.** (Rectangle, Rounded Rectangle)

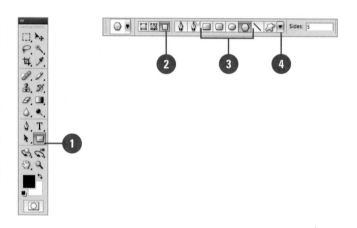

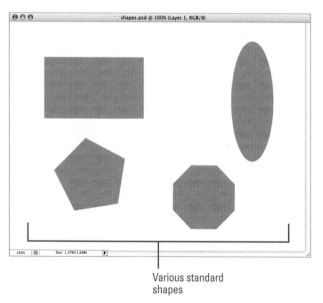

Various standard shapes

- ◆ **Radius.** (Polygon)
- ◆ **Smooth Corners.** (Polygon)
- ◆ **Star.** (Polygon)
- ◆ **Indent Sides By.** (Polygon)
- ◆ **Smooth Indents.** (Polygon)

5 Click the **Mode** list arrow, and then select a blending mode.

6 Enter an Opacity percentage value (1% to 100%).

7 Select the **Anti-alias** check box to create a visually smoother image.

Useful when drawing shapes with curved edges.

8 Drag in the document window to create the shape.

IMPORTANT *Maintain control over your design by drawing shapes in separate layers.*

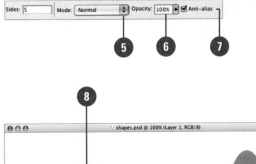

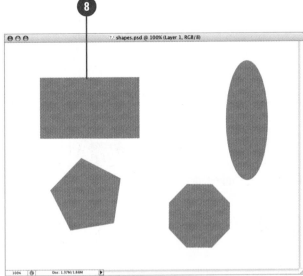

For Your Information

Using the Standard Shape Tool

Once a shape has been created, you can use Photoshop's extensive layer effects options to colorize the shape, add a drop shadow or bevel, or even apply a gradient or pattern to the shape. Remember that in order to apply layer effects to the shape it must be isolated on its own layer.

Working with the Custom Shape Tool

Having the ability to draw a perfect polygon or rounded-corner rectangle is nice; however, Photoshop went way beyond standard shapes when it introduced the Custom Shape tool. Photoshop now comes packaged with dozens of predesigned shapes, or you can even create your own. User-defined shapes can be made from literally any vector object. For example, a company logo can be converted to a custom shape. Custom shapes have many time-saving applications. As previously mentioned, a company logo, if used frequently, is only a mouse click away. Any vector form, outline, or shape used on a recurring basis, can be converted to a custom shape and saved for future use. Select the Custom Shape tool or, if you have any shape drawing tool selected, click the Custom Shape button from the Options bar, and then configure the shape using choices from the Options bar.

Work with the Custom Shape Tool

1. Select the **Custom Shape** tool on the toolbox.

2. Click the **Fill Pixels** button to create raster shapes, using the active foreground color.

3. Click the **Geometry** options list arrow, and then select from the available options: Unconstrained, Defined Proportions, Defined Size, Fixed Size, or From Center.

4. Click the **Shape** list arrow, and then select a shape from the available options.

5. Click the **Mode** list arrow, and then select a blending mode.

6. Enter an Opacity percentage value (1% to 100%).

7. Select the **Anti-alias** check box to create a visually smoother line.

8. Drag in the document window to create the customized shape.

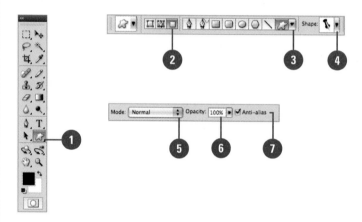

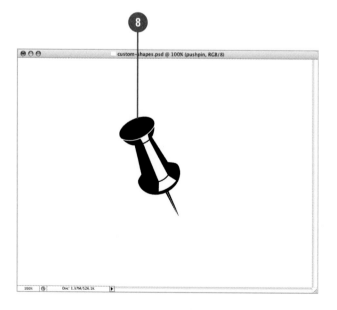

Creating a Custom Shape

Custom shapes can be created from anything you choose, and the process is quick and simple. You just create the shape, select the shape, and name the shape. That's it. Since shapes are vector images, they're resolution-independent, which means you can draw them at any size without impacting image quality. Once custom shapes are saved, they can be accessed by opening a document, selecting the Shape tool, and choosing your new shape from the Custom Shapes panel.

Create a Custom Shape

1. Open a document that contains the vector image you want to convert into a shape, or create a shape using any of Photoshop's vector drawing tools.

2. Click the **Edit** menu, and then click **Define Custom Shape**.

3. Enter a name for the new shape.

4. Click **OK**.

   The shape appears as a thumbnail at the bottom of the active Custom Shapes panel.

Did You Know?

You can move Photoshop shapes into other vector programs, such as Illustrator, FreeHand, and even Flash. Click the File menu, point to Export, and then click Paths To Illustrator. Name the new document, and then click Save.

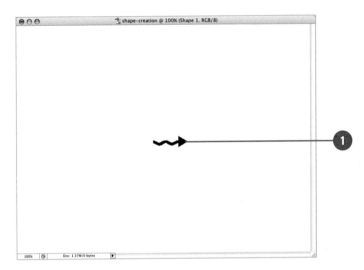

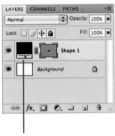

Shape designed
in a Shape layer

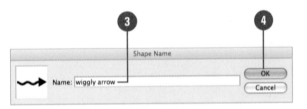

Saving Custom Shape Sets

Creating customized sets of shapes is an excellent way to get organized. The next time you need a specific shape all you have to do is select the shape from your organized sets. Organization can save you time, but it also lends a sense of consistency to designs. Using the same customized shapes repeatedly helps to tie the elements of a design together, and Photoshop gives you the perfect way to maintain that consistency with customized shape sets.

Save Custom Shape Sets

1. Select the **Custom Shape** tool on the toolbox.

2. Click the **Shape** list arrow to see a list of the current shapes.

3. Create new shapes, and then add them to the current list.

   IMPORTANT *As you create new shapes, if there are some you don't like, delete them. Right-click the shape, and then click Delete Shape.*

4. To add preexisting shapes, click the **Options** button, and then click **Load Shapes**, or choose from the available predefined shape lists.

5. Click the **Options** button, and then click **Save Shapes**.

6. Enter a descriptive name for the new set in the **File Name** (Win) or the **Save As** (Mac) box.

7. Click the **Save In** (Win) or **Where** (Mac) list arrow, and then select a location to save the new set.

   IMPORTANT *If you save the new set in the Custom Shapes folder, located in the Adobe Photoshop CS4 application folder, the new set will appear as a predefined set when you click the Shapes Options button.*

8. Click **Save**.

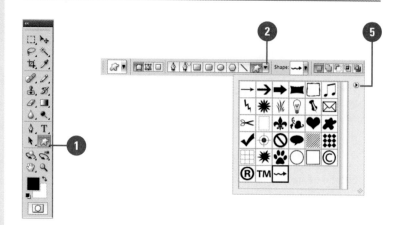

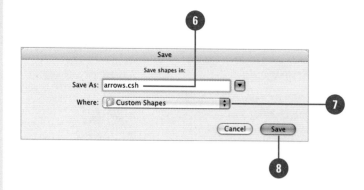

Using the Paint Bucket Tool

Adobe Certified Expert PS 2.2

The Paint Bucket tool is not new; in fact, it's been around almost as long as Photoshop. The Paint Bucket's primary function is to fill an area with the active foreground color, but that's not all it's capable of doing. The Paint Bucket tool can fill areas with a selected pattern and, much the same way that the Magic Wand tool selects image information, the fill area can be controlled by the shift in brightness of image pixels. Combine those features with the ability to change the Paint Bucket's blending mode or opacity, and you have a tool with a lot of horsepower.

Use the Paint Bucket Tool

1. Select the **Paint Bucket** tool on the toolbox.

2. Click the **Fill** list arrow, and then select an option:

   ◆ **Foreground.** Fills a selected area with the current foreground color.

   ◆ **Pattern.** Fills a selected area with a pattern.

3. Click the **Pattern** list arrow, and then select a predefined fill pattern. This option is available if you select Pattern as a fill option.

4. Click the **Mode** list arrow, and then select a blending mode.

5. Enter an Opacity percentage value (1% to 100%).

6. Select a Tolerance value (0 to 255). The Tolerance value influences the range that the Paint Bucket uses to fill a given area.

7. Select the **Anti-alias** check box to create a visually smoother line.

8. Select the **Contiguous** check box to restrict the fill to the selected area.

9. Select the **All Layers** check box to fill the color range information from all the image's layers.

10. Click the **Paint Bucket** tool cursor on the area to be changed.

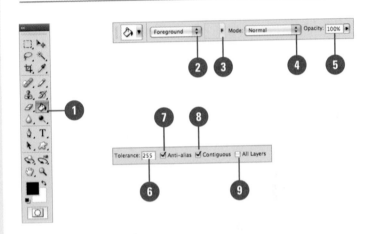

Working with the Eraser Tools

Photoshop's basic Eraser tool converts image pixels in a layer to transparent pixels. While the primary function of the Eraser tool has not changed, the tool itself has been greatly improved. For example, you can use the Eraser tool to remove a specific color or to erase around the edge of an object. You can instruct the Eraser tool to remove a specific color while protecting another color and at the same time, increase or decrease the tool's tolerance (the range of selection). If you use the Eraser tool on a layered document, the tool will erase to transparency. If the Eraser tool is used on a flattened document (flattened documents do not support transparency), the Eraser tool will use the active background color to perform the erasure. As you can see, the eraser tools do more than blindly erase image information. As you master the eraser tools, you just may find those complicated eraser jobs becoming easier and easier. The Background Eraser tool lets you select specific colors within an image and erase just those colors.

Use the Basic Eraser Tool

1. Select the **Eraser** tool on the toolbox.

2. Click the **Brush** list arrow, and then select a brush tip.

3. Click the **Mode** list arrow, and then select a blending mode.

4. Enter an Opacity percentage value (1% to 100%) to determine how much the eraser removes from the image.

5. Enter a Flow percentage value (1% to 100%) to determine the length of the eraser stroke.

6. Click the **Airbrush** button to change the solid eraser stroke of the eraser to that of an airbrush.

7. Select the **Erase To History** check box to temporarily turn the Eraser into a History Brush.

8. Drag the Eraser over an image layer to convert the image pixels to transparency.

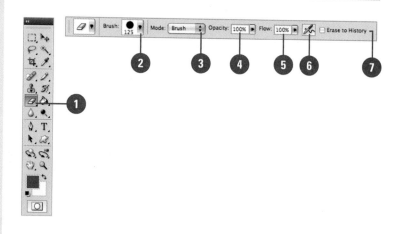

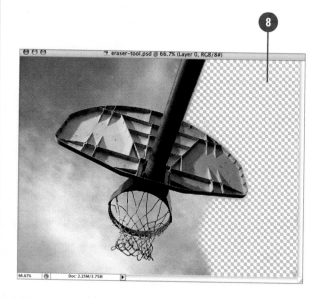

Use the Background Eraser Tool

1. Select the **Background Eraser** tool on the toolbox.

2. Click the **Brush** list arrow, and then select a brush tip.

3. Click one of the Sampling buttons (determines how the Background Eraser selects the color range):

    ◆ **Continuous.** Continually selects a color range as you drag the Eraser tool across the image.

    ◆ **Once.** Samples a color range when you first click your mouse.

    ◆ **Background Swatch.** Only erases the active background color.

4. Click the **Limits** list arrow, and then click how far you want the erasing to spread:

    ◆ **Discontiguous.** Lets the Eraser tool work with all similar color range pixels throughout the image.

    ◆ **Contiguous.** Restricts the Eraser tool to the selected color range, without moving outside the originally sampled area.

    ◆ **Find Edges.** Looks for a shift in color range and attempts to erase to the visual edge of the image.

5. Select a Tolerance percentage value (1% to 100%). The higher the tolerance, the greater the range.

6. Select the **Protect Foreground Color** check box to prevent that color from being erased.

7. Drag in the image to erase.

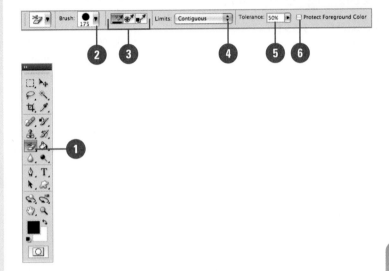

For Your Information

Using the Background Eraser Tool

The Background Eraser tool erases an image by converting the image pixels to transparency. If you attempt to use the Background Eraser tool on a flattened image, the tool will automatically convert the flattened background into a normal layer. Photoshop is actually making an assumption that if you're using the Background Eraser tool, you obviously need the image to be on a layer that supports transparency, not a background layer.

Working with the Magic Eraser Tool

 PS 2.2

The Magic Eraser tool functions the same way as the Magic Wand selection tool, except that instead of selecting an area, it erases it. The Magic Eraser tool works on any traditional Photoshop layer, as well as the Background layer. Clicking with the Magic Eraser tool converts image pixels into transparent pixels. Since the Background layer does not support transparency, using the Magic Eraser tool causes Photoshop to convert the Background into a traditional layer.

Work with the Magic Eraser Tool

1 Select the **Magic Eraser** tool on the toolbox.

2 Enter a Tolerance value (0 to 255). The higher the value, the greater the range the Magic Eraser erases.

3 Select the **Anti-alias** check box to create a visually softer eraser (useful when dealing with intensely rounded or curved selections).

4 Select the **Contiguous** check box to select adjacent pixels within the active document.

5 Select the **Sample All Layers** check box to sample image information from all layers (Photoshop then treats the visual image as a composite).

6 Click within the active document.

The Magic Eraser tool, depending on the options you choose, samples the pixels directly under the tool and uses that data to create a range for erasing image information.

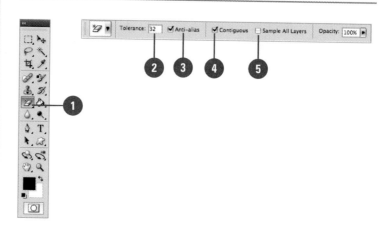

Creating and Applying Gradients

While most of Photoshop's painting and drawing tools let you select and paint with a single color, the Gradient tool lets you paint with a veritable rainbow of colors. The Gradient tool comes packaged with several sets of predesigned gradients, or you can create and save your own customized gradient sets. The process of creating a gradient is simple; you select a gradient along with a specific type (Linear, Radial, etc.), and then drag in the document window. The length and angle of the drag determines how the gradient is applied. Since gradients, by default, overwrite image pixels, it's a good idea to create gradients in separate layers.

Create a Standard Gradient

① Select the **Gradient** tool on the toolbox.

② Click the **Gradient** list arrow, and then select from the available gradients.

③ Select one of the following gradient types from the five icons:

   ◆ Linear, Radial, Angle, Reflected or Diamond.

④ Click the **Mode** list arrow, and then select a blending mode.

⑤ Enter an Opacity percentage value (1% to 100%).

⑥ Select the **Reverse** check box to reverse the color order of the selected gradient.

⑦ Select the **Dither** check box to visually create a smoother transition between gradient colors.

⑧ Select the **Transparency** check box to create gradients using a gradient mask (allows for transparency in the gradient).

⑨ Drag in the image to create a gradient.

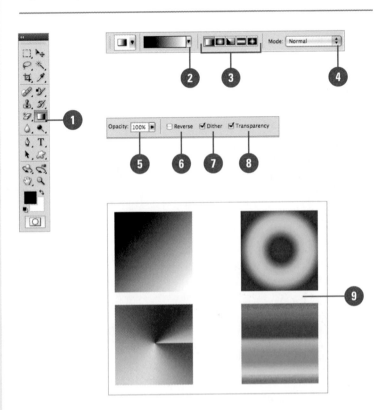

For Your Information

Adding Predefined Gradients

To add a predefined gradient, you must first select the Gradient tool. Click the Gradient Picker button, located on the Options bar, to use one of the available gradient sets. Choose to append the new gradients to the existing list, or click OK to replace the existing gradients with the new ones.

Creating and Saving Customized Gradients

PS 2.5

Customized gradients are easy to create and essential when you just can't find what you want in Photoshop's predefined sets. It doesn't matter how many gradients Photoshop provides for you, there will always be that one instance where they just don't do the required job. With just a few clicks of your mouse, you can create your own customized gradients. You can start with one of Photoshop's gradients and modify it to your needs. You can also start completely from scratch; the choice is yours, and so are the rewards of creating that one-of-a-kind stunning gradient you can use for your current and future projects.

Create and Save a Customized Gradient

1. Select the **Gradient** tool on the toolbox.

2. Click the thumbnail of the active gradient on the Options bar to open the Gradient dialog box.

3. Select a gradient from the available options that is close to what you want to create.

4. Enter a name for the new gradient.

5. Click **New**.

   A thumbnail (copy of the selected gradient) appears at the bottom of the list.

6. Click the **Gradient Type** list arrow, and then select one of the following:

   ◆ **Solid.** Uses solid colors for the gradient.

   ◆ **Noise.** Uses noise to distribute the colors.

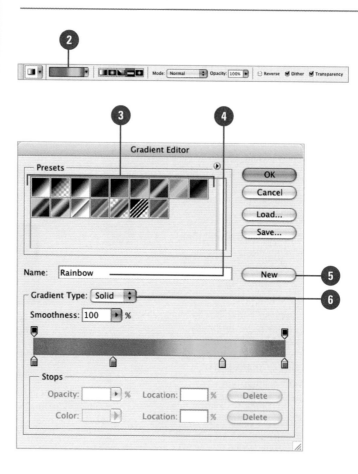

7 Click the **Smoothness** list arrow, and then select one of the following:

- ◆ **Smoothness.** A percentage value (0% to 100%) that determines how smoothly the colors of the gradient blend together (available when the Solid option is selected).

- ◆ **Roughness.** A percentage value (0% to 100%) that determines how much noise to introduce into the gradient colors (available when the Noise option is selected).

8 To add Opacity Stops, click above the gradient line; to remove Opacity Stops, drag the stop away from the line.

9 To add Color Stops, click below the gradient line; to remove Color Stops, drag the stop away from the line.

10 Click on an Opacity Stop, and then enter an Opacity percentage (0% to 100%), and a Location percentage (0% to 100%) for the stop to place it on the line.

11 Click on a Color stop, and then select a color, and a Location percentage (0% to 100%) for the stop to place it on the line.

12 Click **Delete** to delete the selected opacity or color stop.

13 Click **Save** to save the new gradient set.

The set will include the new gradients, and all the gradients that appear in the Presets panel.

14 Click **OK**.

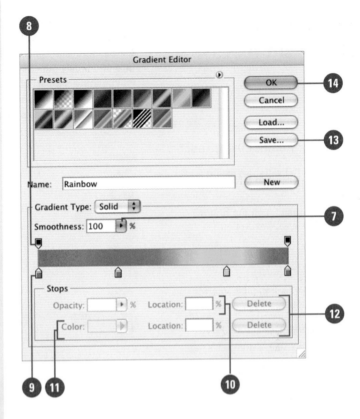

For Your Information

Creating a Customized Gradient

Gradients serve many purposes. They can be used to jazz up a shape drawn with Photoshop's drawing tools or they can be applied to an entire document and used as a background on a web page, brochure or newsletter. Whatever you use gradients for, remember that they are powerful image elements. Use gradients to attract attention to a document, but don't use them if they draw people's eyes away from the main elements of the image. It will be a small consolation to know that your fantastic marketing graphic attracted attention, but everyone was so focused on your special effects and gradients, they forgot to buy what you were selling. Remember, it's always about the message. An image is worth a thousand words…let the image tell its story.

Using the Color Replacement Tool

The Color Replacement tool lets you replace a specific color in your image. For best results use soft brushes with this tool to help blend the colors into the original image. Have you ever captured that perfect picture of a family member or friend, only to find they have red eyes? Or maybe there's a part of your image where the color draws attention away from the focal point. Either way, the Color Replacement tool is a great feature that allows you to take control of the final image.

Use the Color Replacement Tool

1. Select the **Color Replacement** tool on the toolbox.

2. Select a Brush tip on the Options bar.

3. Select from the available Sampling options:

   ◆ **Continuous.** Samples colors continuously as you drag.

   ◆ **Once.** Replaces the targeted color only where you click.

   ◆ **Background Swatch.** Erases areas matching the background.

4. Select from the available Limits options:

   ◆ **Discontiguous.** Replaces the sampled color under the pointer.

   ◆ **Contiguous.** Replaces connected areas containing the sampled color and preserves the sharpness of shape edges.

   ◆ **Find edges.** Limits painting of the replacement color within an object as defined by its edges.

5. Enter a Tolerance percentage value (0% to 255%).

6. Select the **Anti-alias** check box for a smoother edge on areas you correct.

7. Select a foreground color to use to replace the unwanted color.

8. Drag in the image over the color you want to replace.

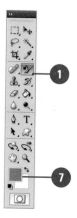

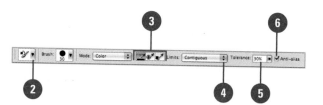

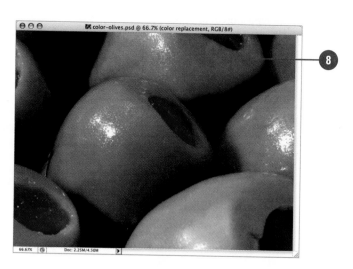

230

Creating Layer and Channel Masks

10

Introduction

When you work on documents in Adobe Photoshop, the application does its best to make the experience as similar to the real world as possible. When you select the Brush tool and drag within the document, you expect to see a swath of color using the preselected size and brush tip. That's what you expect to see when you drag a brush on a canvas, and that's what you see in Photoshop. Creating a realistic experience is what Photoshop is all about. Yet, as realistic as the Photoshop experience is, there are elements of digital design that go way beyond the real world. For example, Photoshop has an undo button; the real world does not. Layer masks, for example, give you the ability to remove elements of a layer without actually erasing the image pixels. Layer masks give you ultimate control over your Photoshop design by deciding what elements of an image are visible, and making changes to the image without destroying any pixels. In addition, layer masks are editable, which means you can change your mind at any time during the creative process.

Imagine creating a complicated selection in Photoshop. Selections are temporary; they last only as long as your document is open. But what if you want to save this selection for use later in the design? What you need is a channel mask. Channel masks hold simple, or complicated selections, and can be saved with the document. Channel masks are created from preexisting selections, or can be created from scratch by painting the mask with black, white, or shades of gray. The process of creating a Channel mask is simple, but the results are powerful.

Understanding the Role of Layer Masks

 PS 5.1, 5.4

Layer masks are not new; however, Photoshop designers find new ways to use them every day. A layer mask is an attachment to a layer that defines the visible elements of the layer. Each layer type in Photoshop, with the exception of the Background, has the ability to hold a layer mask. Imagine a layer mask as a piece of paper on top of the image. Then take a trimming blade and cut holes in the paper. The holes in the paper represent the visible area of the image underneath the mask, while the rest of the paper (layer mask) hides the rest of the image. Each layer in a multi-layered document can have its own mask; the mask only influences the image elements of the layer to which it's attached. Once a mask is created, it can be modified using any of Photoshop's painting or drawing tools. Black represents transparent (invisible) elements, and white represents visible elements. Painting with a shade of gray introduces a variable level of transparency. For example, painting with 50% gray makes the image pixels appear 50% transparent.

Creating a Layer Mask

The creation of a layer mask requires two things: an open document and any type of Photoshop layer with the exception of the Background. When you add a layer mask, you will be working with two layer elements—the image and the mask. It's important to know which element you're working on or you might wind up painting on the image instead of the mask. When that occurs, it's good to remember the Undo button. Once the mask is created, you can selectively control, without erasing, the visible portions of the image.

Create a Layer Mask

1. Open a document.

2. Click the **Layers** panel.

3. Click the layer that will contain the mask.

4. Click the **Add Layer Mask** button.

5. Click on the image thumbnail to modify or adjust the image.

   The active pointer resembles a hand with a pointing finger.

6. Click on the mask thumbnail to modify or paint on the mask.

7. Click the **link** button to separate the mask from the image. Control the opacity (density) of the mask and adjust the edge by using the sliders on the Masks panel (**New!**). You can also access the Color Range command from this panel, delete/invert the mask or load a mask selection.

8. Click the **link** button again to reestablish the connection between the mask and the image.

9. Shift+click on the mask thumbnail to disable or enable the mask, or click on the Disable/Enable Mask button in the Masks panel (**New!**).

10. Alt+click (Win) or Option+click (Mac) on the mask thumbnail to view or hide the mask in the document window.

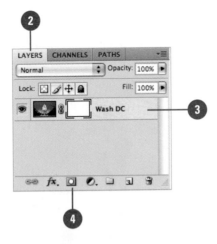

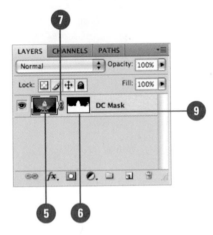

Working with the Paint Tools

PS 5.2

Unless a mask is created using a selection, layer masks begin their lives as completely white. The reason a newly created layer mask does not appear to have any visible effect on the image is that the color white indicates visible areas of the image. It's only when you begin painting on the mask that the image changes. You create transparency in the image by painting in shades of gray. The deeper the shade of gray, the more transparent the image. Painting the mask with pure black produces 100% image transparency. Any of Photoshop's drawing or painting tools can be used to create a mask. In fact, you could even use the Custom Shape drawing tools and create a mask in the shape of a rubber duck. The trick is to use the right tools to create the right effect. For example, using a hard-edged brush creates an image with sharp edges and using a soft-edged brush creates an image where the visible edges of the image blend smoothly with transparent elements.

Work with the Paint Tools

1. Open a document.

2. Create a layer mask on one of the active image layers.

3. Click the layer mask thumbnail.

4. Select the **Brush** tool and brush tip.

5. Move into the document window and paint with black to create transparency.

6. Use white to touch up the image.

7. Use shades of gray to create partial transparency.

See Also

See "Working with the Brush and Airbrush Tools" on page 214 for more information on using the Brush tool.

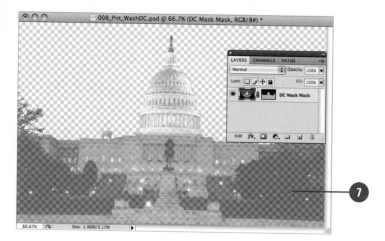

Using Selections to Generate Complex Layer Masks

 PS 5.2, 5.6

Layer masks are easy to create; you select a layer and then click the Add Layer Mask button. Unfortunately, when you create a mask this way, it's up to you to define the transparent areas, using drawing or painting tools. There is another way to generate a mask, and that's by making a selection first. When you click the Add Layer Mask button, Photoshop searches the document for any selected areas. If it doesn't find any, it creates a blank (all white) mask. However, if you first select an area of the image, Photoshop interprets the selection as the area you want to remain visible.

Use Selections to Generate Masks

1. Open a document.

2. Select the areas of the image you want to preserve.

3. Click the **Add Layer Mask** button.

   Photoshop generates a layer mask based entirely on your selection.

Did You Know?

You can apply layer styles to a masked image. Create the mask, and then click the Add Layer Style button, located at the bottom of the Layers panel. Then use any of Photoshop's layer styles, such as Drop Shadow, or Bevel and Emboss. The layer style will only be applied to the visible portion of the image.

See Also

See Chapter 4, "Mastering the Art of Selection," on page 77 for information on selecting areas of an image using different tools.

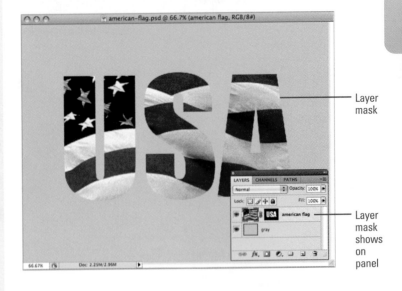

Layer mask

Layer mask shows on panel

Using Layer Masks to Generate Soft Transparency

PS 5.2

Use Layer Masks for Transparency

1. Open a document.

2. Create a selection around the area you want to preserve.

3. Click the **Select** menu, and then click **Refine Edge**.

4. Drag the slider to select a Feather Radius value (1 to 250). The greater the value, the greater the feathering effect.

5. Click **OK**.

6. Click the **Add Layer Mask** button.

   The layer mask uses the Feather option to soften the visual effect of the mask.

Did You Know?

You can also use Gaussian Blur to create a soft transparency. Another way to create a soft edge is to create a hard-edged mask from a selection, and then visually create a softer mask using a filter named Gaussian Blur.

See Also

See Chapter 14, "Manipulating Images with Filters," on page 319 for more information on using filters.

When you create a layer mask using Photoshop's selection tools, the edges of the image where transparency occurs appear as if cut out with a knife. This occurs because selection tools create hard-edged selections, and then, when you create the layer mask, the edges appear as ragged as the mask. To soften the edge of the selection boundary, you can use the Feather option in the Refine Edge dialog box, which can also be accessed from the Masks panel by clicking on the Mask Edge button (**New!**). As you adjust the Feather value, the feather effect appears in the Document window with a preview of the image. When you create the layer mask, the edges appear soft and feathered.

Feather effect

Blending Images with Layer Masks

PS 5.2

You can use layer masks to make areas of an image appear transparent by painting with black. Then just as quickly, you can make those areas reappear by painting with white. There are obvious applications to the use of layer masks—changing a sky, removing a tree, or even removing a person from the photo. For example, you have a line art image and you want to change it to a normal photograph. To accomplish this, you'll need a copy of the image in a separate layer, a layer mask, and the linear gradient tool.

Blend Images with Layer Masks

1. Open a document.

2. Select the layer you want to use for the effect in the Layers panel. If this is a multi-layered document, this layer should be at the top of the layer stack.

3. Drag the layer over the **Create New Layer** button to make a copy.

    TIMESAVER *If making a copy of a layer is a common practice, press Ctrl+J (Win) or ⌘+J (Mac).*

4. Click the **Add Layer Mask** button, and then add a layer mask to the layer copy.

5. Use any of Photoshop's adjustment or filter effects to make changes to the layer copy.

6. Select black and white for the default foreground and background colors.

7. Select the **Gradient** tool, and then select a linear gradient using the foreground to background gradient option.

8. Click the layer mask thumbnail in the copy layer.

9. Drag the **Gradient** tool across the document, left to right.

    The image slowly becomes transparent from left to right, exposing the original image.

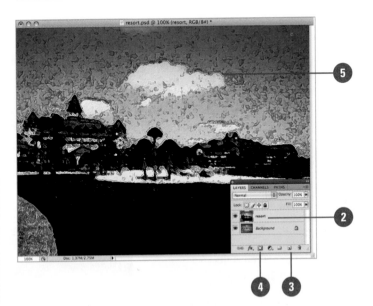

Using a Layer Mask to Create a Vignette

When you open a document in Photoshop, the image is displayed in a standard bounding-box format—a square or rectangle with 90-degree corners. Bounding boxes serve a purpose, and many times a nice square or rectangle box is exactly what you want. But let's face it, bounding boxes can be a bit boring, especially when you want to spice up that image with a nice soft vignette. To create a soft vignette, you need four things—an image, a selection, a layer mask, and the Gaussian Blur filter.

Create a Vignette

1 Open a document.

2 Select the **Elliptical Marquee** tool, and then create an oval selection in the document. The Ellipse should contain the area you want to preserve.

3 Click the **Add Layer Mask** button in the Layers panel.

4 Click the layer mask thumbnail.

5 Click the **Filter** menu, point to **Blur**, and then click **Gaussian Blur**.

6 Drag the Radius slider right or left to increase or decrease the amount of blur applied to the mask.

7 Select the **Preview** check box, and then watch the live preview until you are satisfied with the amount of blurring applied to the layer mask.

8 Click **OK**.

Soft vignette applied to the image

238

Creating Unique Layer Mask Borders

PS 5.2

Layer masks can create more than simple vignettes around an image. In fact, with the right filters you can create some very interesting and fun-looking borders. For example, when you create a selection using one of Photoshop's standard selection tools—rectangle, ellipse, or lasso—the selection has a sharp, definable border. The secret to creating unique borders is to create a general selection around a portion of the image you want to preserve, create the layer mask, and then use some of Photoshop's creative filter effects, such as the Artistic or Distort filters on the mask. Using filters on the image mask creates eye-catching borders and it's only a filter away.

Create a Layer Mask Border

1. Open a document.

2. Click the layer in the Layers panel to which you want to apply a unique border.

3. Create a rectangular selection around a portion of the image.

4. Click the **Add Layer Mask** button.

5. Click the layer mask thumbnail.

6. Click the **Filter** menu, point to **Brush Strokes**, and then click the **Sprayed Strokes** filter.

7. Adjust the filter options to change the edge of the layer mask.

8. Click **OK**.

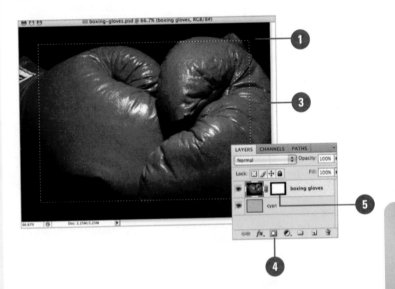

Did You Know?

You can apply more than one filter to a layer mask border. For example, using the Spatter filter creates a ragged edge to the layer mask. Applying a small amount of Gaussian Blur to the mask softens the effect and creates a more pleasing visual transition between the mask and the background.

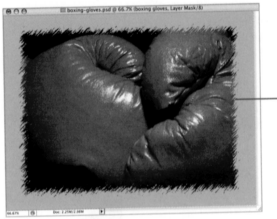

The Sprayed Strokes filter applied to the layer mask.

Understanding Channel Masks

The Channels panel serves three purposes—to hold color information, to hold spot color information, and to hold selections (channel masks). Creating channel masks can be as easy as clicking the Create New Channel button and then using any painting or drawing tools to create the mask, or by making a selection and converting the selection into a mask by clicking the Save Selection As Channel button. When you paint the channel mask, the defaults are—black for masked areas, white for selected areas, and shades of gray for percentages of selection.

Use Channel Masks

1. Open an image and create a selection.

2. Select the **Channels** panel.

3. Click the **Create New Channel** button.

4. Select the new channel.

5. Select the **Brush** tool on the toolbox, and then select a brush tip on the Options bar.

6. Paint areas of the mask white to create a selection.

7. Paint areas of the mask black to mask the image.

Did You Know?

You can quickly convert a channel mask into a selection. To view a channel mask as a selection, open the Channels panel, and then Ctrl+click (Win) or ⌘+click (Mac) on the channel. Photoshop instantly translates the black, white, and gray areas of the mask into a visible selection in the document window.

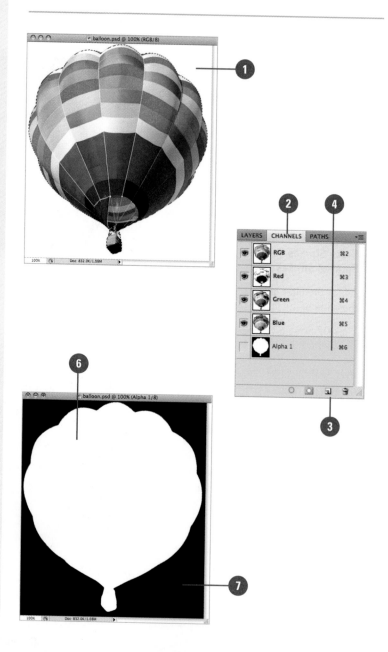

Creating Channel Masks from Scratch

 PS 5.3

Channel masks are easy to create and once created, are just as easy to modify. All you need is an open document, and access to the Channels panel. After selecting a painting or drawing tool, you paint on the mask to define the selection area. The problem is you can't see the image; you can only see the mask. What you need is the ability to view the mask and the image at the same time, as if you were using tracing paper, and then use the drawing tools to paint (trace) the portions of the image you want to select. The secret to viewing the image as you create the mask is to temporarily enable or show, the composite channel. In fact, the composite channel acts like a toggle switch—when it's visible, you see the image and the mask (tracing paper); when it's hidden, you only see the mask.

Create Channel Masks

1. Open an image.

2. Select the **Channels** panel.

3. Click the **Create New Channel** button.

4. Click the **Show/Hide** button on the composite channel. The image is revealed in the document window (the new Alpha channel should still be selected). You will use the image to guide the creation of the mask.

5. Select the **Brush** tool on the toolbox.

6. Paint areas of the image using white to create a selection (painting with white exposes the original image).

7. Paint areas of the image black to mask the image (painting with black masks the image with the default color of red).

8. Click the **Show/Hide** button on the composite channel. The image is hidden, revealing just the mask.

9. Repeat steps 6-8 until the mask is complete.

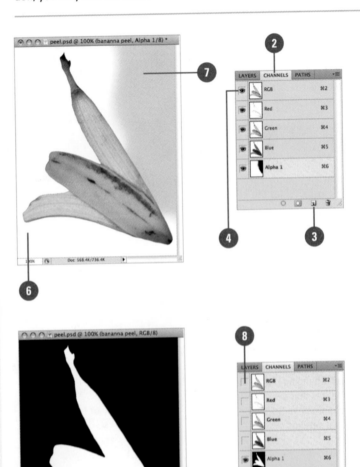

Modifying Channel Mask Options

Channel masks have default options that control how the mask looks and functions. Photoshop gives you the ability to change the default options of a channel mask. For example, you could change the default color from red to blue, or you could change the function of the channel mask from Selection to Spot Color. Knowing you can change the mask options gives you more control over the final results.

Modify Channel Mask Options

1. Open a document.

2. Select the **Channels** panel.

3. Click the **Channels Options** button, and then click **New Channel**.

4. Enter a name for the new channel.

5. Click the option to define the mask color as the Masked Areas, Selected Areas, or Spot Color.

6. Click the **Color** box, and then select a color from the Color Picker.

7. Enter an Opacity percentage value (1% to 100%) for the color.

8. Click **OK**.

Did You Know?

You can change the Channel options for a preexisting channel. Double-click on the channel, and Photoshop will open the Channel options dialog box.

You can set Channel options for each channel. Changing the Channel options only impacts that specific channel. Each channel can have its own individual settings.

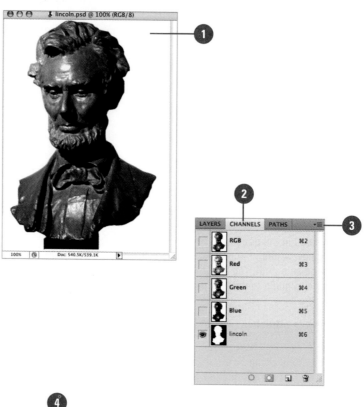

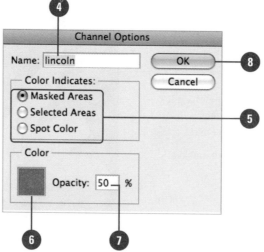

Creating Channel Masks from Selections

Adobe Certified Expert

PS 3.2, 5.3, 5.6

Creating channel masks from scratch (using brush and drawing tools) is a useful feature, and gives you the ability to create a mask in any desired size or shape. However, there are times when it would be easier to first define the areas you want to protect, and then create the mask. When you create a channel mask from an existing selection, Photoshop uses the selected areas to create the mask. For example, you have an image of a woman wearing a red dress, and you want to change the color of the dress to green. The first step would be to select the red dress. Rather than create a new mask, and paint out the area representing the dress, it would be easier to first use a tool like the Magic Wand, select the dress, and then convert the selected area (the dress) into a channel mask. Once the mask is created, you could fine-tune the mask using Photoshop's painting tools, and then change the dress color. Whether you create a mask from scratch or choose to create one through a predefined selection depends on the image and what you're trying to accomplish.

Create Channel Masks from Selections

1. Open a document.

2. Create a selection using any of Photoshop's traditional selection tools.

3. Select the **Channels** panel.

4. Click the **Save Selection As Channel** button.

Photoshop creates a new channel mask based on the selected areas of the document.

The selection is converted into an Alpha mask.

Making Channel Masks from Native Color Channels

Creating a channel mask from a native color channel takes a few steps; however, if you're successful, the effort spent making the selection is well worth it. The trick to creating a mask with a native color channel is to use the shifts of gray in one specific color channel to create the black and white areas characteristic of a typical channel mask. For example, you have an image of a model, and you want to remove the model from the background. Unfortunately, that requires selecting around the model's hair, a difficult thing to accomplish, even in the best of circumstances. To make the channel mask, open the Channels panel and examine the native color channels, one at a time. You're looking for a color channel that displays a significant shift of gray (amount of contrast) between the model's hair and the background. For example, you click on the red channel of an RGB image and the model's hair appears dark gray, while the background appears light gray. The difference is so pronounced you can actually see individual strands of hair standing out against the background. If you can find such a contrast, you can quickly make a channel mask.

Make Channel Masks from Native Color Channels

1. Open a document.

2. Click the **Channels** panel.

3. Click and view the individual native color channels one at a time.

4. Click the channel that best represents a visual difference between what you want to select and what you want to mask.

5. Drag the selected channel over the **Create New Channel** button.

   Photoshop makes a copy of the selected native color channel.

6. Click the native color channel copy.

244

7 Click the **Image** menu, point to **Adjustments**, and then click **Threshold**.

8 Move the **Threshold** slider left or right until you see a sharp black and white image with the black and white representing the selected and masked areas of the image.

9 Click **OK**.

10 Use Photoshop's painting tools with black and white to touch up the new mask.

Did You Know?

You can use native color channel masks to perform image correction. Channel masks created from native color channels can be used for more than creating a mask. For example, you have a photo where the shadow portions of the image are too dark. Correct the problem by creating a channel mask that selects just the darker portions of the image, and then use the mask to control the Levels or Curves adjustments to lighten the overexposed areas of the image.

Loading Channel Masks

PS 3.2, 5.3

Once you create a channel mask (and you can have up to 28 separate masks in one document), the next step is to use the masks. To save the channel mask all you have to do is save the document in a format that supports channels, such as Photoshop's native PSD format, or even the TIFF format. The next time you open the document, your channel masks will be there. Deleting a channel mask is simple; just drag the channel mask over the Delete button located at the bottom of the Channels panel, or select the channel mask you want to delete, and click the Delete button. However, sooner or later, you're going to want to do more than just save or delete—you're going to want to use a channel mask. Using a channel mask involves a process of converting the mask back into a selection. It's an easy step, but necessary to complete the process from mask to selection.

Load Channel Masks

1. Open a document that contains a channel mask, or create a new channel mask.

2. Click the **Select** menu, and then click **Load Selection**.

3. If more than one document is open, click the **Document** list arrow, and then select the document you want to use.

4. Click the **Channel** list arrow, and then click the channel you want to convert into a selection (native color channels do not appear in this list).

5. Select the **Invert** check box to instruct Photoshop to use the black areas of the mask (instead of the white areas) for the selection.

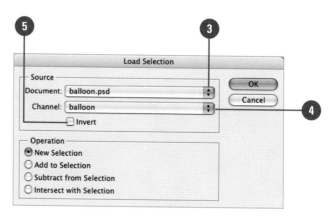

6. Select the Operation option you want to perform:

- ◆ **New Selection.** Creates a new selection.

- ◆ **Add To Selection.** Adds the channel mask to an existing selection.

- ◆ **Subtract From Selection.** Uses the channel mask to subtract from an existing selection.

- ◆ **Intersect With Selection.** Uses the channel mask to intersect with an existing selection.

7. Click **OK**.

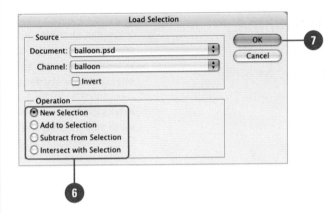

For Your Information

Working with Channel Masks

Channel masks provide control over the selected areas of an image. By default, the white areas of the mask represent the selected areas, and the black areas represent the masked areas. When a mask is applied to an image, the black and white areas of the mask create a very sharp-edged selection. To soften the effect of the mask, click the Filter menu, point to Blur, and then click Gaussian Blur. Apply a small amount of blur (one or two pixels) to the mask. Now, when the mask is applied to the image, the Gaussian blur will soften the effects of the selection and create a visually softer transition.

Moving Channel Masks Between Documents

PS 5.3

Once you create a channel mask in one document, it is possible to move that channel mask to another document. While most channel masks are so specific to a particular document it wouldn't be practical to move them—a channel mask defining a selection of a specific tree against a blue sky, for example—many channel masks can be used over and over again. For example, you might have a series of channel masks creating unique selection borders around an image. You spent a lot of time creating the borders, and you would like to apply those same border selections to other images. If that's the case, then increase your efficiency by saving them as channel masks and moving them between documents. Not only will it save you a lot of time, but using selections more than once can add a sense of cohesiveness to a design.

Move Channel Masks Between Documents

1. Open a document that contains a channel mask.

2. Open a second document (this is the document you will move the mask into).

3. Position the two document windows side by side.

4. Click the document containing the channel mask.

5. Select the **Channels** panel.

6. Drag the channel mask from the Channels panel into the open document window of the second document.

Combining Channel Masks

Channel masks are simply selections defined by black, white, and shades of gray. Once a channel mask is placed in the Channels panel, you can use Photoshop's vast array of drawing and painting tools or filters. The Gaussian Blur filter can make a great enhancement to a channel mask. It's even possible to combine the selection elements of two or more channels together, and in doing so, create an even more complicated mask.

Combine Channel Masks

1 Open a document that contains two or more channel masks.

2 Click the **Channels** panel.

3 Press Ctrl+click (Win) or ⌃⌘+click (Mac) on one of the channel masks.

The white areas of the channel become a selection.

4 Press Shift+Ctrl+click (Win) or Shift+⌃⌘+click (Mac) on the second channel mask.

The white areas of the second channel mask are added to the previous selection.

5 Click the **Save Selection As Channel** button.

Photoshop takes the combined areas of the two channels and creates a new channel mask.

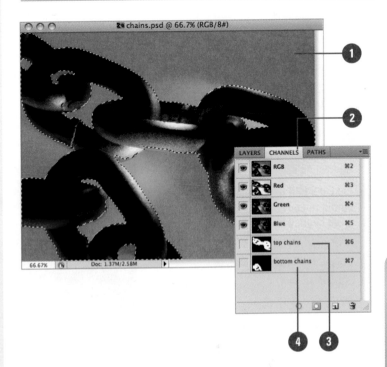

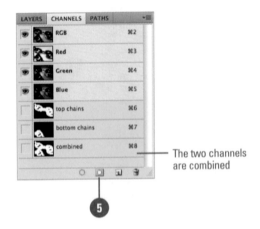

The two channels are combined

Using the Quick Mask Mode

PS 5.6

Quick Mask mode gives you the ability to create a selection using painting and drawing tools without creating a channel mask. For example, you're creating a selection using traditional selection tools and there's a portion of the image you're having difficulty selecting. Since this is a one-time selection, you don't want to go to the trouble of creating a channel mask. The solution is to move into the Quick Mask mode. Quick Mask mode toggles between a normal (Standard) selection view and a Quick Mask view. When you enter Quick Mask mode, any preexisting selections are converted into a red mask, and changes to the mask are performed using painting tools. When you return to Standard mode, the masked (painted) areas are converted into a selection. While Quick Masks are created the same way as channel masks, they're temporary. It's a quick way to create a one-time selection.

Use the Quick Mask Mode

1. Open a document.

2. Create a selection using any of Photoshop's selection tools.

3. Click the **Edit in Quick Mask Mode** button to convert the selection into a red overlay mask (the button toggles to Standard mode).

4. Select the **Brush** tool.

5. Paint with white to open up more selection areas.

6. Paint with black to mask the image; the mask, by default, is red.

7. Click the **Edit in Standard Mode** button again to return to a standard selection (the button toggles to Quick Mask mode).

8. Toggle between Quick Mask and Standard modes until you create the perfect selection.

Did You Know?

You can convert a Quick Mask into a permanent Channel mask. Create the Quick Mask, return to Standard Mode, select the Channels panel, and then click the Create Channel From Selection button.

Working with Quick Mask Options

When you work in the Quick Mask mode, the color for the mask is red, the opacity of the mask is 50%, and the red mask represents the masked areas of the document. Photoshop uses these Quick Mask options as the default, but they can be modified. For example, it would be very difficult to view a red mask if you were working on a primarily red image, or you might want to increase or decrease the opacity of the mask. Photoshop lets you do this through Quick Mask options.

Work with Quick Mask Options

1. Click the **Edit in Quick Mask Mode** or **Edit in Standard Mode** button (the button toggles between Quick Mask mode and Standard mode).

2. Click the **Masked Areas** or **Selected Areas** option to instruct Photoshop whether to create a mask or a selection from the color areas of the mask.

3. Click the **Color** box, and then select a color from the Color Picker.

4. Enter an Opacity percentage value (0% to 100%).

5. Click **OK**.

   IMPORTANT *Quick Mask options are program specific, not document specific. The changes made to the Quick Mask options remain set until you change them.*

Did You Know?

Once you've created a Quick Mask selection, you can save it as a permanent Channel mask. Just return the screen to Standard mode, open the Channels panel, and then click the Save Selection As Channel button.

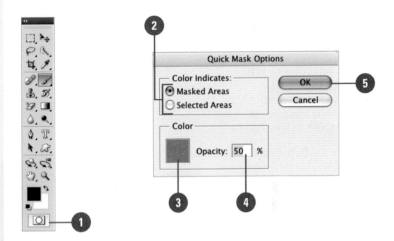

For Your Information

Using Quick Masks

One of the powerful features of a Quick Mask is that you can use filters directly on the mask. Create a selection in the Quick Mask mode, and then click the Filter menu and choose from Photoshop's many filters, such as Brush Strokes, Blur, or Distort. When you click OK, the filter is applied directly to the Quick Mask. Then, when you return to Standard mode, the effect of the filter is applied to the selection. Working with filters and Quick Masks gives you the option of creating highly complicated masks without ever using the Channels panel.

Modifying Selections with Quick Mask Mode

Photoshop represents an active selection using an animated, single-pixel wide marquee, sometimes referred to as a "marching ant" marquee. Typically, the enclosed or "marquee" area represents the working area of the document. Unfortunately, when selections become complicated, you could wind up with ants marching all over the screen. While complicated selections are a part of the Photoshop designer's life, they shouldn't have to be hard to visualize or modify. Photoshop knows this and created the Quick Mask option. When you're using Quick Mask, Photoshop displays the selected areas with a user-defined color and opacity. Then, by using your painting tools, you can make quick work of modifying the selection.

Modify Selections with Quick Mask Mode

1. Create a selection using any of Photoshop's selection tools.

2. Click the **Default Colors** button to default your foreground and background painting colors to black and white.

3. Click the **Edit in Quick Mask** button to enter Quick Mask mode.

    By default the selected area remains clear and the unselected area becomes masked with a 50% red.

4. Select the **Brush** tool on the toolbox.

5. Refine the selection by painting on the Quick Mask with white and/or black. In Quick Mask mode, painting with black masks the image using a 50% opacity red, and painting with white reveals the original image.

6. Click the **Edit in Standard Mode** button to revert the image back to a normal selection marquee.

7. Continue to toggle back and forth between **Edit in Quick Mask** and **Edit in Standard Mode** until you achieve the desired selection.

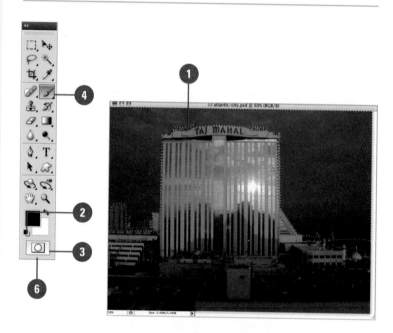

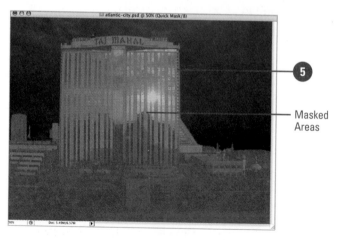

Masked Areas

Using the Paths Panel

11

Introduction

Adobe Photoshop can not handle raster information (pixels), it can also work with vector information (paths). Photoshop stores raster information in the Layers panel, and stores vector information in the Paths panel. When you use Photoshop's vector drawing, or pen tools, Photoshop creates a path in the Paths panel to store that information. In addition, it is possible to create a selection with Photoshop's traditional selection tools, and convert that selection into a path. Paths are defined mathematically using anchor points and segments. Once created, they can be precisely modified to fit any design situation. In many ways, paths serve a function similar to channel masks—they can define selections, but because they're vector and not raster, they are much more precise. When paths are saved, they take up far less room than channels.

Working with the various Pen tools, it's possible to create precise paths, and even create complicated selections around virtually any shape. Once the path is created, it's a simple matter to subtract anchor points, and add new or modify existing anchor points to produce complex paths. It's even possible to convert straight segments (the visible line that connects two anchor points together) into elegantly curved segments, or you can remove the curve from a segment with a single click of the Convert Point tool. Paths can be used to precisely guide a brush stroke, or the interior of a path can be filled with any color, pattern, or gradient available in Photoshop using the Stroke and Fill Commands. Paths can even be used to create a clipping path around an image. When moving an image into a layout program such as Adobe InDesign, a clipping path lets you define certain areas of an image as transparent. In addition, you can create paths in Photoshop, then export and open them in Adobe Illustrator. Photoshop paths give you precise, mathematical control over the creation of complex shapes, selections, and even transparency.

What You'll Do

Understand Vector and Raster Images

Convert a Selection into a Path

Work with Pen Tools

Create Paths Using the Freeform Pen Tool

Use the Magnetic Option with the Freeform Pen Tool

Add and Delete Anchor Points

Modify Anchor Points

Modify Existing Direction Lines

Convert Straight Points and Curved Points

Work with Clipping Paths

Fill an Area of an Image Using Paths

Stroke an Area of an Image Using Paths

Create Shapes as Paths

Export Paths to Adobe Illustrator

Export Paths Using the Export Method

Understanding Vector and Raster Images

 PS 6.2

Photoshop is a hybrid application that gives you great control over photographic (raster) images, and seamlessly combines pixel data with the elegance and form of artistic (vector) shapes. When you work on the raster side of Photoshop, you're dealing with an image that is a like a brick wall with each brick (or pixel) identifying one piece of color information. The reason raster images are considered resolution-dependent is that once the image is created or scanned, any enlargement of the image forces Photoshop to enlarge and average the existing color information in the document.

This process, called **interpolation**, is what causes enlarged raster images to become blurred, or pixelated. Vector images are created using mathematical shapes, not pixels, and that's why vector shapes are considered resolution-independent. For example, if you enlarge a vector image to 100 times its original size, Photoshop merely changes the mathematical formulas to reflect the new size, and since vector shapes are constructed of mathematical data instead of pixels, file sizes are extremely small.

Raster Image

Close up shows pixels

Vector Image

Close up shows lines

Converting a Selection into a Path

PS 6.3

Selection marquees are Photoshop's way of identifying the work areas within the active document. Since selections are created using pixels, the accuracy of the selection is based on the resolution of the active image. This can be a problem when you're working with low-resolution images such as web and presentation graphics. However, when you convert a selection into a path, you can precisely reshape it using Photoshop's vector tools, and this gives you more control over the final results.

Convert a Selection into a Path

1. Open a document.

2. Select an area of the image, using any of Photoshop's traditional selection tools.

3. Select the **Paths** panel.

4. Hold down the Alt (Win) or Option (Mac) key, and then click the **Make Work Path** button.

5. Enter a Tolerance value (0.5 to 10).

   Using low tolerance values creates a path with many anchor points, and the path conforms precisely to the selection marquee, but low tolerances can cause printing errors (too much information). Using higher tolerance values creates a path with fewer anchor points, and the path will be smoother.

6. Click **OK**.

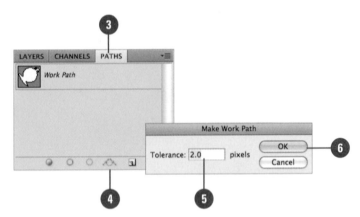

Working with Pen Tools

When you work with Photoshop's Pen tools, you're creating a path without needing to convert from a pixel selection (raster) to a path (vector). Vector paths are mathematical and are therefore not hampered by image resolution issues. For example, a path created in a low resolution image (72 ppi) would function the same as a path created in a high-resolution (300 ppi) image. An added benefit of paths is that they take up less disk space than selections saved as channel masks. When you create a path using the Pen tools, Photoshop automatically creates a path in the Paths panel. If you have an existing path selected, Photoshop adds the new path to the selected path.

Work with Pen Tools

1. Open a document.

2. Select the **Standard Pen** tool on the toolbox.

3. Click the **Paths** button on the Options bar.

> **IMPORTANT** *To view the segments as you draw, click the Geometry Options list arrow on the Pen Options bar, and then select the Rubber Band check box.*

4. Create an anchor point (or node) by clicking once in the open document.

5. To create a straight segment (two anchor points connected by a line), move and click again.

6. To create a curved segment (two anchor points connected by a curved line), move and drag.

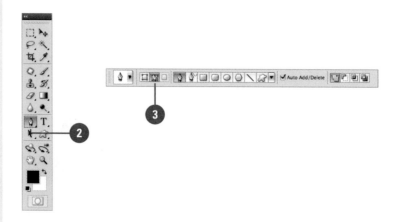

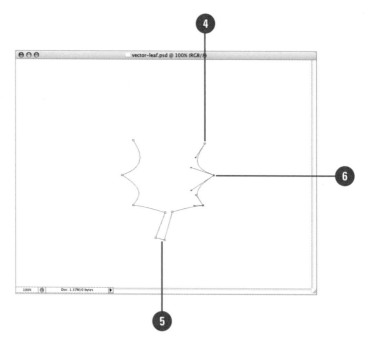

7 Continue to move through the document, clicking or dragging until the shape is complete.

8 Create a closed shape by moving the Pen tool over the original anchor point and clicking when you see a small circle appear underneath the Pen tool.

IMPORTANT *As with any tool, control is gained through practice. Work with the Pen tool until you can make a path around any shape. The more time you spend practicing, the better your paths will be, and the better your designs.*

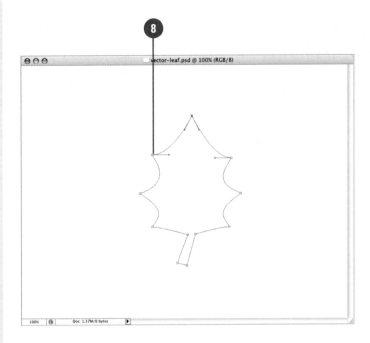

Did You Know?

You can create an open shape. Move away from the last anchor point created, and then press Ctrl+click (Win) or ⌘+click (Mac).

Creating Paths Using the Freeform Pen Tool

PS 6.1, 6.3

While the Pen tool requires you to click and move your mouse, the Freeform Pen tool lets you drag on the screen to create any desired path. When you create a path with the Freeform Pen, Photoshop adds anchor points to the line at predefined intervals. The distance between anchor points is determined by a value called Curve Fit. The more complicated the design, the more anchor points the Freeform Pen tool must create to support the path. Once created, you can always modify the path or even add or subtract anchor points.

Use the Freeform Pen Tool

1. Open a document.

2. Select the **Freeform Pen** tool on the toolbox.

3. Click the **Paths** button on the Options bar.

4. Drag in the document window using your mouse or drawing tablet pen to create a unique shape.

5. Close the shape by dragging the Freeform Pen tool over the shape's starting point, and then releasing when you see a small circle appear underneath the tool.

6. Create an open shape by dragging and releasing anywhere except over the starting point.

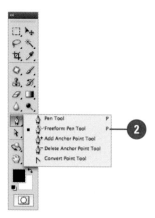

Did You Know?

You can control the complexity of a path. Click the Geometry Options button on the Options bar, and then enter a Curved Fit value from 0.5 to 10. The higher the value, the less complex the path (less anchor points), and the lower the value, the more precise, but more complex the path.

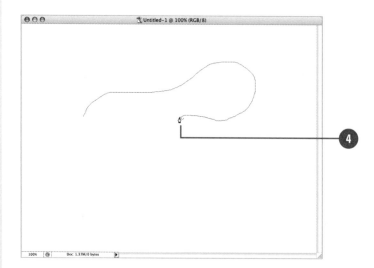

Using the Magnetic Option with the Freeform Pen Tool

PS 6.1

The Magnetic option changes the Freeform Pen tool into a magnetic vector drawing tool. For example, selecting the Magnetic option forces the tool to follow the visible edge of an object in the document window. The Magnetic option instructs the Freeform Pen tool to identify the shifts in brightness between an object and its background. It's a great way to make a difficult path. Once you click to define the starting point, it's not necessary to hold down the mouse; just move the mouse while closely following the visible edge of the image. If you get to a tricky point where the Freeform Pen doesn't know what to do, just click your mouse to add a user-defined anchor point.

Use the Magnetic Option with the Freeform Pen Tool

1. Open a document.

2. Select the **Freeform Pen** tool on the toolbox.

3. Select the **Magnetic** check box on the Options bar.

   IMPORTANT *When using the Magnetic option with the Freeform Pen tool, you cannot create an open shape.*

4. Click the **Shape Layers** or **Paths** button.

5. Position the **Freeform Pen** tool over the edge of a shape, and then click and release the mouse.

6. Drag in the document window using your mouse or drawing tablet pen to follow the visible edge.

   The magnetic option helps you follow the edge more precisely.

7. Close the shape by dragging the Freeform (magnetic) Pen tool over the shape's starting point, and then releasing when you see a small circle appear underneath the tool, or by double-clicking.

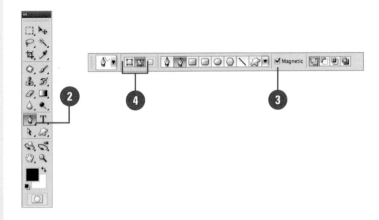

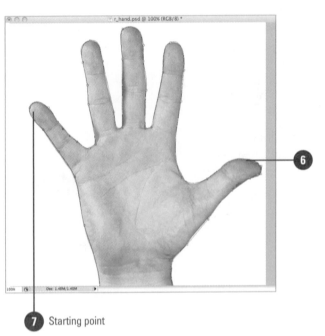

7 Starting point

Adding and Deleting Anchor Points

Creating a path is not necessarily the end of the job; in fact, there are many ways you can modify a path once it's been created. For example, you can add, subtract, or delete anchor points on an existing path. You can also modify those points to conform to any desired shape. In addition, existing anchor points can be modified to change the segments connecting the points. Just like anything else in Photoshop, paths are flexible. They can be modified to meet whatever design considerations are needed to make the job successful.

Add Anchor Points

1. Open a document that contains an existing path, or create a new path.

2. Select the **Paths** panel.

3. Select a path.

4. Select the **Add Anchor Point** tool on the toolbox.

5. Click once on the path to add, not modify, a new anchor point.

6. Click and drag on the path to add, and modify the segment.

Did You Know?

You can move anchor points using your arrow tools. Select the Direct Selection tool, and then click on an anchor point. Click your arrow keys to move the anchor point up, down, left or right one pixel at a time. To move 10 pixels at a time, hold down the Shift key while using the arrow keys.

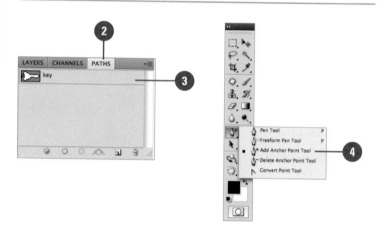

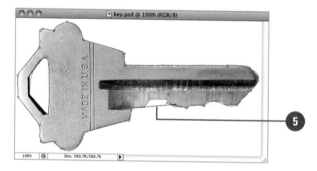

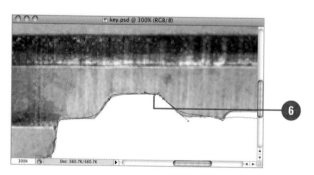

Delete Anchor Points

1 Open a document that contains an existing path, or create a new path.

2 Select the **Paths** panel.

3 Select a path.

4 Select the **Delete Anchor Point** tool on the toolbox.

There are no additional options for the Delete Anchor Point tool.

5 Click once on an existing anchor point to remove it from the path.

The anchor points on either side of the deleted point are now used to define the segment.

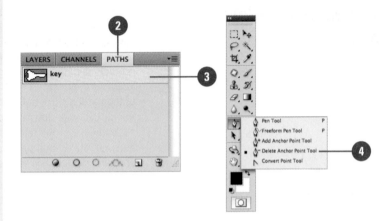

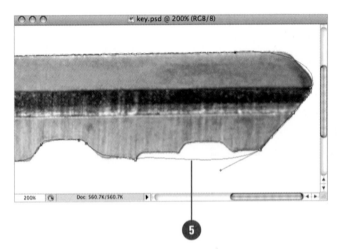

Modifying Anchor Points

Anchor points can be added or deleted, and existing anchor points can be modified. In reality, the anchor points are used to define the length and curve of the segments, or lines that connect the anchor points together. Just think of a farmer who strings up a line of barbed wire to protect his cattle by placing posts in the ground and stringing the wire between the posts. The more posts he uses, the more complex the path of the barbed wire. In Photoshop, the posts are the anchor points, and the barbed wire corresponds to the segments. However, we have one advantage over the farmer; we can cause a segment line to curve between the anchor points, while the farmer must stretch the barbed wire in a straight line between posts.

Modify Anchor Points

1. Open a document that contains an existing path, or create a new path.

2. Select the **Paths** panel.

3. Select the path you want to modify.

4. Select the **Path Selection** tool on the toolbox.

5. Click on the path to move, without modifying, the entire path.

Did You Know?

You can move a path using the keyboard. Click the path and then use the arrows on the keyboard to move it.

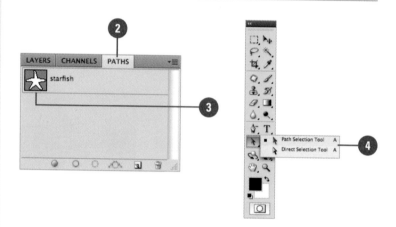

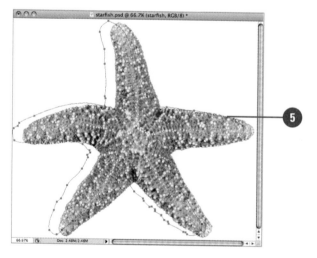

6 Select the **Direct Selection** tool on the toolbox.

7 Drag an individual anchor point to move the anchor to another location.

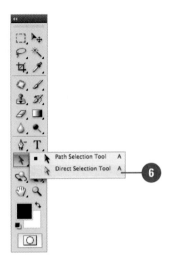

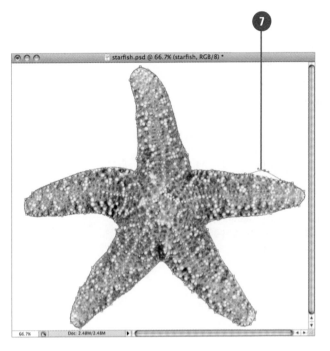

Modifying Existing Direction Lines

 PS 6.1, 6.3

Anchor points are composed of two elements—the anchor point and direction lines. The anchor point is the fence post that connects segments together. The direction lines influence the amount of curve applied to the segment. The farther away a direction point is from the anchor, the more aggressive the curve. Conversely, the closer the direction lines are to the anchor point, the more gradual the curve. If an anchor point does not have any direction lines, it is said to be a straight anchor point.

Modify Existing Direction Lines

1. Open a document that contains a path, or create a new path.

2. Select the **Paths** panel, and then select the path you want to modify.

3. Select the **Direct Selection** tool on the toolbox.

    There are no additional options for the Direct Selection tool.

4. Click the very end of the direction line, and then drag to change the curve of the segment.

5. Hold down the Alt (Win) or Option (Mac) key, and then click at the very end of the direction line to break the line at the anchor point.

    This lets you independently control each end of the direction line as it extends out from the anchor point.

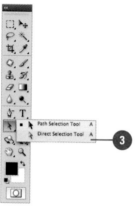

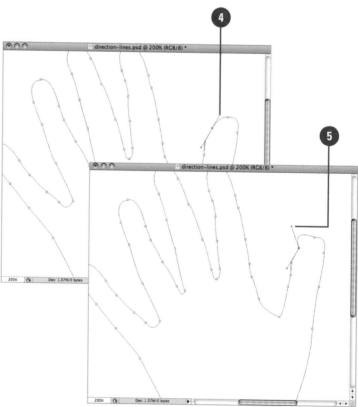

Converting Straight Points and Curved Points

PS 6.1, 6.3

Sooner or later you'll encounter a situation where you want to convert an anchor point from curved to straight or straight to curved. Rather than try to collapse the direction lines into the anchor point (a difficult task), or try to drag nonexistent direction lines from a straight anchor point, Photoshop gives you a useful conversion tool called the Convert Point tool. The Convert Point tool lets you convert existing points on a path. For example, to convert a curved point into a straight point, click once on the curved anchor point, and it's instantly converted into a straight point. To convert a straight point to a curved point, simply drag on the anchor point and the line changes from straight to curved.

Convert Points

1. Open a document that contains a path, or create a new path.

2. Select the **Paths** panel, and then select the path you want to modify.

3. Select the **Convert Point** tool on the toolbox.

4. Click on a curved anchor point to convert it into a straight point.

5. Click and drag a straight anchor point to convert it into a curved point.

Did You Know?

You can change the curve of a segment line with a click and drag. Click the Direct Selection tool, and then drag directly on the line, not the anchor point.

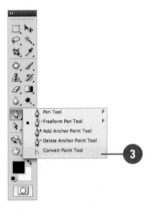

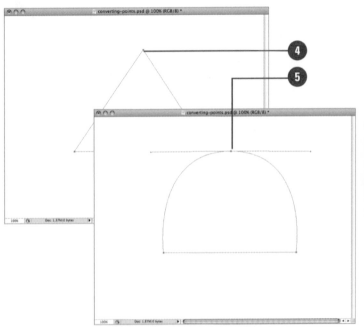

Working with Clipping Paths

Image clipping paths allow you to isolate part of an image and make everything else, such as a white background, transparent when the image is printed or placed in another application, such as QuarkXPress or Adobe Illustrator. You can place a Photoshop PSD file directly in Adobe InDesign and retain transparency; otherwise, you can create an image clipping path. To create an image clipping path, create a well defined path around the part of the image you want, convert the path to a clipping path on a transparent background, and then save and use it in other applications. Clipping paths work to create a transparent area without the sacrifice of the actual image. Therefore, it is not necessary to delete any of the image when creating the clipping path.

Work with Clipping Paths

1. Open a document.

2. Select the **Pen** or **Freeform Pen** tool on the toolbox.

3. Click the **Paths** button on the Options bar.

4. Create a path around the portion of the image you want to keep.

   IMPORTANT *The edges of clipping paths are vector-based (having hard edges), so they appear as if they were cut out with a pair of scissors, which makes it difficult to select objects with soft edges.*

5. Select the **Paths** panel.

6. Double-click on the new Work Path, enter a Name for the path, and then click **OK**.

7. Click the **Paths Options** button, and then click **Clipping Path**.

Did You Know?

You can restore the original image with transparency. Just open the Paths panel, and then delete the clipping path.

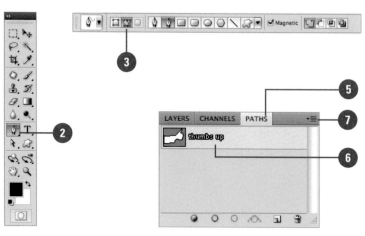

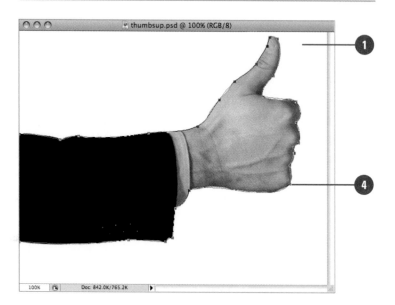

8 Click the **Path** list arrow, and then select the new path.

9 Enter a Flatness value (0 to 100) or leave it blank to use the printer's default settings (recommended).

For high-resolution printing (1,200 dpi to 2,400 dpi) use 8 to 10, and for low-resolution printing (300 dpi to 600 dpi) use 1 to 3. The lower the flatness value, the greater the number of straight lines used to draw the curve and the more accurate the curve.

10 Click **OK**.

11 If you're going to print the file using process colors, convert the file to CMYK mode.

12 Click the **File** menu, and then click **Save As**.

13 Click the **Format** list arrow, and then select the **Photoshop EPS** format.

To export in Adobe InDesign or Adobe PageMaker 5.0 or later, save in TIFF format.

14 Click **Save**.

15 In the EPS or TIFF Options dialog box, leave the default options and change the following:

◆ For TIFF. Set **Image Compression** to None.

◆ For EPS. Set **Preview** to TIFF (8/ bits/pixel) (Win) or Preview to Mac (8/bits/pixel) (Mac) and **Encoding** to ASCII85.

The image, when placed in a layout program, appears with a transparent background.

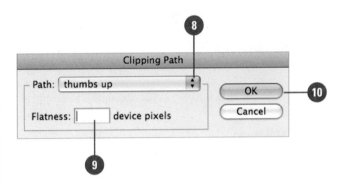

For Your Information

Exporting a Clipping Path to Adobe Illustrator

Draw and save a path. Click the File menu, point to Export, and then click Paths To Illustrator. Choose a file location, then enter a file name. Make sure to select Work Path in the Write menu to export the path, click Save, then open the file in Adobe Illustrator.

Filling an Area of an Image Using Paths

Paths are easy to create and versatile. Once you create a path, it has many applications—you can convert a path into a clipping path, or you can even convert a path into a standard selection, and use it to define a work area. In addition to some of the more common applications, paths can be used to define an area to be filled, or you can use the Stroke command to control any of Photoshop's drawing tools.

Fill an Area of an Image Using Paths

1. Open a document that contains a path, or create a new path.

2. Select the **Paths** panel, and then select one of the paths.

   IMPORTANT *When you select a path from the Paths panel, the path becomes visible in the document window.*

3. Select the **Paths Options** button, and then click **Fill Path**.

4. Click the **Use** list arrow, and then select from the available fill options.

5. Click the **Mode** list arrow, and then select a blending mode.

6. Select an Opacity percentage value (0% to 100%) for the blending mode.

7. Select the **Preserve Transparency** check box to protect any transparent areas in the active image.

8. Enter a Feather Radius value (0 to 250) to feather the edge of the fill.

9. Select the **Anti-alias** check box to visually soften the fill.

10. Click **OK**.

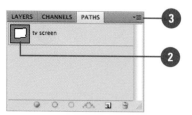

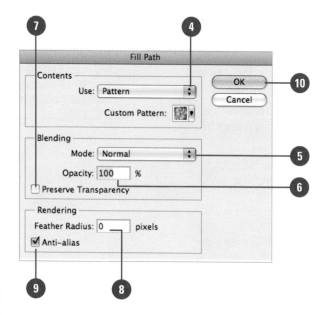

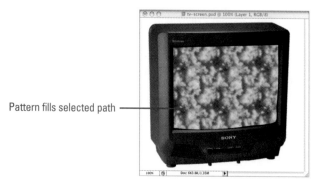

Pattern fills selected path

Stroking an Area of an Image Using Paths

 PS 6.3

The Stroke Path option is an excellent way to add a design element to any of Photoshop's drawing or image-editing tools. When you select the Stroke Path options, you're essentially using a preexisting path to control the shape of the stroke. The important thing to remember is that the tool selected for the Stroke Path option will perform the way it was last used. For example, if the last time you used the Paintbrush tool you selected a star-shaped, 40-pixel brush, selecting the Paintbrush as the Stroke tool will cause it to stroke the path using a star-shaped, 40-pixel brush.

Stroke an Area of an Image Using Paths

1. Open a document that contains a path, or create a new path.

2. Select the **Paths** panel, and then select one of the paths.

3. Click the **Paths Options** button, and then click **Stroke Path**.

4. Click the **Tool** list arrow, and then select from the available tools.

5. Select the **Simulate Pressure** check box to mimic the pressure variables experienced when using a drawing tablet.

6. Click **OK**.

   The Stroke Path command applies the stroke using the original path to guide the brush.

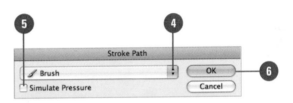

Stroke applied using the original path to guide the brush.

Creating Shapes as Paths

PS 6.3

Paths can be created using any of Photoshop's traditional Pen tools, or you can use shape tools to create a unique path. For example, you want to create a unique stroke border around an image, and you find the perfect shape in Photoshop's Custom Shapes panel. Rather than create the shape, select it, and then convert it into a path, Photoshop lets you draw any shape and place it directly into the Paths panel. Once the shape is placed in the Paths panel, you can modify or change it, just like any other path.

Create Shapes as Paths

1. Open a document.

2. Select the **Custom Shape** tool (or any of Photoshop's drawing tools) on the toolbox.

3. Click the **Shape Layers** button.

4. Click the **Shape** list arrow, and then select a predefined shape.

5. Select the **Paths** panel.

6. Draw the shape in the document window.

   Photoshop creates a Work Path containing the custom shape.

See Also

See "Modifying Anchor Points" on page 262 for information on reshaping a path.

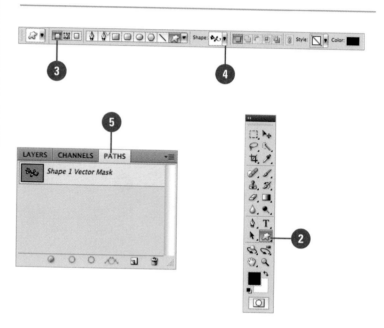

Exporting Paths to Adobe Illustrator

Paths are vector shapes, and programs such as Adobe Illustrator support paths created in Photoshop. Say you want to create a unique path in Photoshop, and then use Illustrator's creative vector controls to further enhance the image. If that's the case, Photoshop gives you several ways to move the image out of Photoshop and into Illustrator. Remember, when you export a path into Adobe Illustrator, you're not moving an image; you're moving vector data with specific stroke and fill information.

Export Photoshop Paths Using the Save As Method

① Open a document that contains a path, or create a new path.

② Click the **File** menu, and then click **Save As**.

③ Enter a file name.

④ Click the **Format** list arrow, and then select the **Photoshop EPS** format.

⑤ Click the **Save In** (Win) or **Where** (Mac) list arrow, and then select a location for the file.

⑥ Click **Save** to open the EPS Options dialog box.

⑦ Click **OK**.

⑧ Open the image in Adobe Illustrator.

Illustrator gives you full access to the path, including the ability to manipulate, add, and delete anchor points.

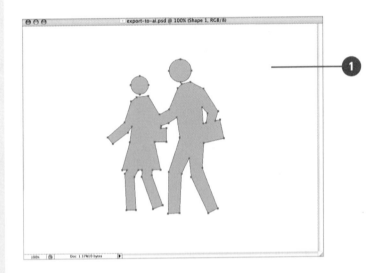

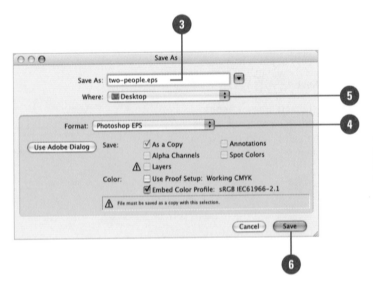

Exporting Paths Using the Export Method

The Paths to Illustrator command lets you quickly export a Photoshop path into a format acceptable to Adobe Illustrator. This makes the process of working with Photoshop and Illustrator artwork much more efficient. For example, you could create a path in Photoshop, and then export the path to Illustrator for use in other artwork. In addition, exported Photoshop paths can be used to help align elements of an Illustrator document to that of its Photoshop counterpart. Later, the two documents can be combined to produce one piece of art. You get two pieces of art, created in separate applications, precisely combined with the use of an exported path. In other words, paths give you control, which you can use to your advantage.

Export Photoshop Paths Using the Export Method

1. Open a document that contains a path, or create a new path.

2. Click the **File** menu, point to **Export**, and then click **Paths to Illustrator**.

3. Enter a file name.

   The file extension is .ai (Adobe Illustrator).

4. Click the **Save In** (Win) or **Where** (Mac) list arrow, and then select a location for the file.

5. Click the **Paths** (Win) or **Write** (Mac) list arrow, and then select which path or paths to export.

6. Click **Save**.

   Photoshop creates an Adobe Illustrator document containing only the paths (not pixels) in the document.

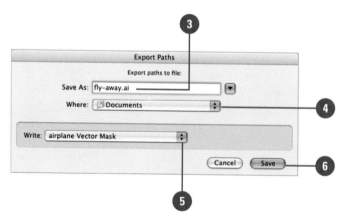

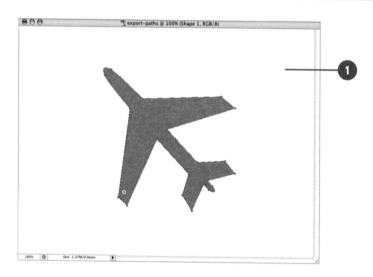

Working with Layer Styles

12

Introduction

Layer styles are the very definition of creativity and control when using Adobe Photoshop. Using styles such as Bevel and Emboss or Drop Shadow, you can move from two-dimensional images into the world of three-dimensional. You can effortlessly change the look of a document with Gradient Overlay, Color Overlay, and Pattern Overlay, and you can do it all without ever changing the original image. That means you can apply a style to an image, and at any time in the creative process, change your mind. This level of control gives you the power you need to take your designs to the creative edge and beyond.

When you create a customized layer style, you can move that style to another layer, save the style in the Styles panel, or even move the style between two open documents. That kind of flexibility gives you consistency in your designs with a minimum of effort, and since layer styles do not change the original image, you can modify or remove the style at any time during the creative process. Not only do layer styles let you create special effects, but they give you the control you need over the image to experiment until you see exactly what you want.

Understanding Layer Styles

Adobe Certified Expert

PS 4.5, 4.6

Layer styles are applied to the layers in the active document. When you add a style to a layer, the results of the style are only displayed in that layer. Each layer can have its own style, and you can apply more than one style to a single layer. Layer styles can be applied to any layer except the Background.

Two of Photoshop's layer styles require both transparent and non-transparent layer elements (Drop Shadow and Outer Glow). For example, to apply a Drop Shadow to a layer, it would require a transparent area within the image to hold the shadow.

Layer Styles

Drop Shadow

Satin

Inner Shadow

Color Overlay

Outer Glow

Gradient Overlay

Inner Glow

Pattern Overlay

Bevel & Emboss

Stroke

Adding a Layer Style

PS 4.5, 4.6

To add a layer style to the active layer, select the layer, and apply one or more of the styles by clicking the Add a Layer Style button. Once selected, the layer style appears as a sub-element of the active layer. Once applied, layer styles are easy to modify. Each of Photoshop's layer styles has options to control exactly how the style appears in the active document. To modify a style, just reopen the Layer Style dialog box, and make your changes. In addition, each layer style has its own Show/Hide button. The Show/Hide button is a toggle that lets you temporarily hide the layer styles in the document.

Add a Layer Style

1. Select the **Layers** panel.

2. Select a layer.

3. Click the **Add Layer Style** button, and then select from the available style options.

4. Make changes to the layer style in the dialog box using the options; options vary depending on the layer style.

5. Click **OK**.

   The selected layer style appears as a sub-element of the active layer.

Modify an Existing Layer Style

1. Select the **Layers** panel.

2. Double-click on the attached name of the layer style.

3. Make changes to the layer style in the dialog box using the options; options vary depending on the layer style.

4. Click **OK**.

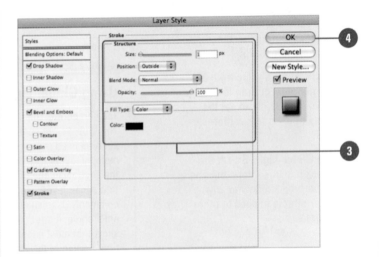

Creating and Modifying a Drop Shadow

 PS 4.5, 4.6

The Drop Shadow style is probably the most common layer style used (next to Bevel and Emboss). Since Photoshop needs somewhere to apply the drop shadow, you will need a layer that contains an object surrounded by a transparent background. For example, you could create a type layer or use the shape drawing tools to create a unique object, add a drop shadow with a click of the mouse, and then use the layer style options to control the color, shape, and direction of the shadow. Once the shadow is created, it can be transferred to other objects in other layers—not only making the process easy, but consistent.

Work with a Drop Shadow

1. Select the **Layers** panel.

2. Click the layer to which you want to apply the Drop Shadow style.

3. Click the **Add Layer Style** button, and then click **Drop Shadow**.

4. Select from the following Drop Shadow options:

   ◆ **Blend Mode.** Click the list arrow, and then select how you want the color of the shadow to blend with underlying layers (default: Multiply).

   ◆ **Color.** Click the Color Swatch, and then select a color for the shadow (default: Black).

   ◆ **Opacity.** Specify an Opacity percentage value for the shadow, or drag the slider left or right (default: 75%).

   ◆ **Angle.** Enter a value from 0 to 360 degrees, or drag the radius slider left or right to set the angle of the shadow (default: 30).

   ◆ **Use Global Light.** Select the check box to conform the angle of the drop shadow to any other effects applied to other layers.

For Your Information

Using Global Light and Shadow Angles

You can control the direction of a light source across multiple layers. The Global Light option is very important because it ties the light sources used in multiple layers together. For example, if you create multiple layers with drop shadows, and you change the direction of the shadow in one of the layers, the Global Light option will ensure that all the layers maintain the same light source direction. The most commonly used shadow angle is 125 degrees; called the "comfortable" angle, it directs the shadow down and to the right. Studies show that most people expect the light source to be in the upper right portion of the image.

- **Distance.** Enter a value from 0 to 30,000 pixels, or drag the slider left or right. Distance determines the amount the shadow is offset from the original image (default: 5).

- **Spread.** Enter a value from 0% to 100%, or drag the slider left or right. Spread determines the amount of image used for the spread of the shadow (default: 0%).

- **Size.** Enter a value from 0 to 250 pixels, or drag the slider left or right. Size determines the amount of blur applied to the shadow (default: 5).

- **Contour.** Click the list arrow, and then select from the available options. Contours are mathematical curves that determine the brightness of the shadow at different levels (default: Linear).

- **Anti-aliased.** Select the check box to create a visually smooth drop shadow.

- **Noise.** Enter a value from 0% to 100%, or drag the slider left or right. The noise option introduces a random shift to the colors of the Drop Shadow.

- **Layer Knocks Out Drop Shadow.** Select the check box to create a knockout in the underlying layers.

5 Click **OK**.

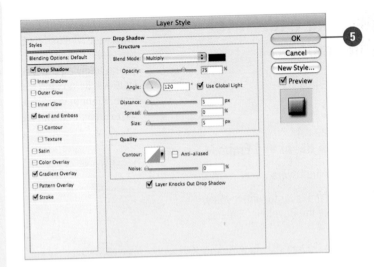

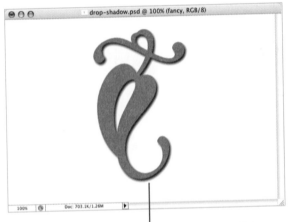

Drop Shadow style applied

Working with Bevel and Emboss

PS 4.5, 4.6

The Bevel and Emboss style, second only to Drop Shadow in popularity, creates a 3D illusion of roundness to a flat surface. You can apply the Bevel layer style to text to get the impression of 3D text. If the layer you're applying the Bevel and Emboss to has no transparent areas, the style will be applied to the outer edge of the image, and if you want to experiment beyond the standard rounded bevel, you can use a Chisel Hard Technique that makes text appear as if it's carved out of stone.

Work with Bevel and Emboss

1. Select the **Layers** panel.

2. Select the layer to which you want to apply the Bevel and Emboss style.

3. Click the **Add Layer Style** button, and then click **Bevel And Emboss**.

4. Select from the available Bevel and Emboss options:

   ◆ **Style.** Click the list arrow, and then select from Outer Bevel, Inner Bevel (default), Emboss, Pillow Emboss, and Stroke Emboss.

   ◆ **Technique.** Click the list arrow, and then select from Smooth (default), Chisel Hard, and Chisel Soft.

   ◆ **Depth.** Enter 0% to 1,000%. Higher Depth values increase the intensity of the bevel or emboss.

   ◆ **Direction.** Click the Up or Down option to reverse the highlights and shadows of the bevel or emboss.

   ◆ **Size.** Enter 0 to 250 pixels, or drag the slider left or right. Size determines how much of the image is used to create the Bevel/Emboss style.

   ◆ **Soften.** Enter 0 to 16 pixels. The higher the value, the softer the edge of the bevel (default: 0).

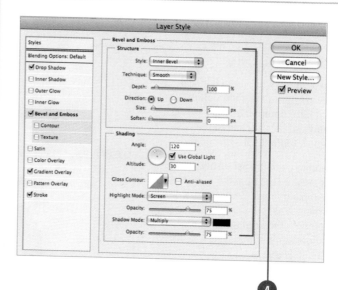

- **Angle.** Enter 0 to 360 degrees. Angle determines the angle of the light source in relation to the bevel/emboss (default: 30).

- **Use Global Light.** Select the check box to conform the angle of the bevel and emboss to any other styles applied to other layers.

- **Altitude.** Enter a value from 0 to 90 degrees. Altitude determines the height of the light source in relationship to the image.

- **Gloss Contour.** Click the list arrow, and then select from the available options. Gloss Contours are mathematical curves that determine the brightness of the bevel/emboss at different levels.

- **Highlight Mode.** Click the list arrow and Color box, and then select a blending mode and color for the highlights (default: Screen, White).

- **Opacity for Highlight Mode.** Enter a value from 0% to 100%. Opacity determines the overall transparency of the highlights. Higher values equate to more aggressive highlights.

- **Shadow Mode.** Click the list arrow and Color box, and then select a blending mode and color for the shadows (default: Multiply, Black).

- **Opacity for Shadow Mode.** Enter a value from 0% to 100%. Opacity determines the overall transparency of the shadows. Higher values equate to more aggressive shadows.

5 Click **OK**.

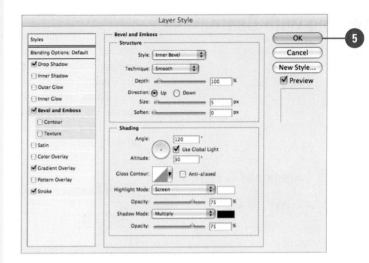

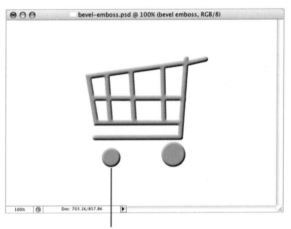

Bevel and Emboss style applied

For Your Information

Understanding the Contour Option

The Contour option redistributes the brightness levels of the shadow and highlight portions of the Bevel and Emboss layer style. By experimenting with alternate contours, you can enhance the realism of a bevel or create a surrealistic emboss.

Working with Contour and Texture

 Adobe Certified Expert PS 4.5, 4.6

The Bevel and Emboss layer styles have two powerful options: the ability to add a contour or a texture to the active bevel or emboss. This lets you give your creative elements more of a realistic texture. When you apply the Contour and Texture options, the image takes on a three dimensional texture, based on a selected pattern. Once applied, the relative depth and intensity of the texture can be precisely controlled to create rough rock-like surfaces, as well as brushed metal. In addition, the Contour option lets you shape the appearance of the shadow areas of the texture style, creating even more realistic surfaces.

Work with Contour and Texture

1. Select the **Layers** panel.

2. Select the layer to which you want to apply the Bevel and Emboss style.

3. Click the **Add Layer Style** button, and then click **Bevel and Emboss**.

4. Select the appropriate bevel or emboss.

5. Click **Contour**, and then select from the available options:

   ◆ **Contour.** Click the list arrow, and then select from the available options. Contours are mathematical curves that determine the brightness of the bevel or emboss at different levels (default: Linear).

   ◆ **Anti-aliased.** Select the check box to create a visually smooth bevel or emboss.

   ◆ **Range.** Enter a value from 1% to 100%, or drag the slider left or right. Range determines the range of the contour as it is applied to the image (default: 50%).

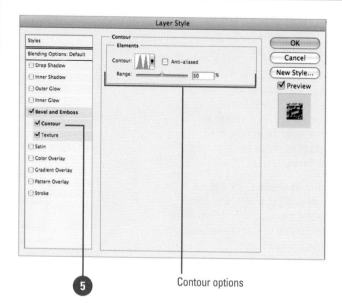

Contour options

See Also

See "Working with Bevel and Emboss" on page 278 for more information on using the Contour option.

6 Click **Texture**, and then select from the available options:

◆ **Pattern.** Click the list arrow, and then select from the available patterns. To add additional patterns from the Photoshop pattern library, click the Pattern Options button, located in the upper right of the Pattern dialog box, and then select from the available pattern options.

◆ **Add To Presets.** Click the button to add the current pattern to Photoshop's list of presets.

◆ **Snap To Origin.** Click the button to begin the pattern tiling from the upper left corner of the document layer.

◆ **Scale.** Enter a value from 1% to 1,000%. Scale determines the size of the pattern as it applies to the active image (default: 100%).

◆ **Depth.** Enter a value from -1000% to 1000%. Depth determines the intensity of the highlight and shadow areas in the texture. Negative numbers reverse the highlights and shadows (default: 100%).

◆ **Invert.** Select the check box to reverse the color set of the pattern.

◆ **Link With Layer.** Select the check box to physically link the active pattern with the active layer (default: checked).

7 Click **OK**.

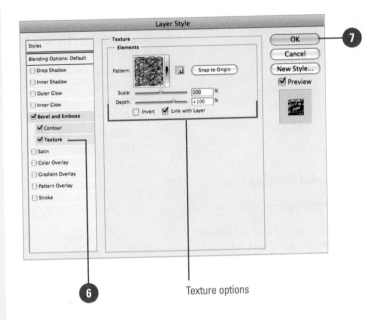

6

Texture options

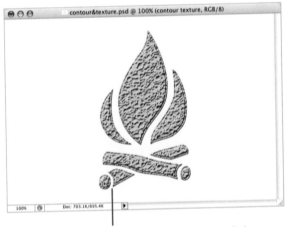

Contour and Texture style applied

Applying a Color Overlay

PS 4.5, 4.6

The Color Overlay style covers the elements of a layer with any color you choose. For example, you create some black text and you want to experiment with other colors, without changing the original color values of the text. Or, possibly you want to change the Blend Mode option, so you can see how a specific color blends into the image. Whatever the case, Color Overlay temporarily masks the image with whatever color you choose. In addition, you can use the Color Overlay style with other layer styles to produce hundreds, if not thousands, of style combinations.

Apply a Color Overlay

1. Select the **Layers** panel.

2. Click the layer to which you want to apply the Color Overlay style.

3. Click the **Add Layer Style** button, and then click **Color Overlay**.

4. Select from the available Color Overlay options:

   ◆ **Blend Mode.** Click the list arrow, and then select from the available options. The Blend Mode option instructs Photoshop how to blend the selected Color Overlay with the colors of the active image (default: Normal).

   ◆ **Color.** Click the Color swatch box, and then select any color from the Color Picker (default: red).

   ◆ **Opacity.** Enter a value from 0% to 100%. Opacity determines how much of the Color Overlay masks the original image pixels (default: 100%).

5. Click **OK**.

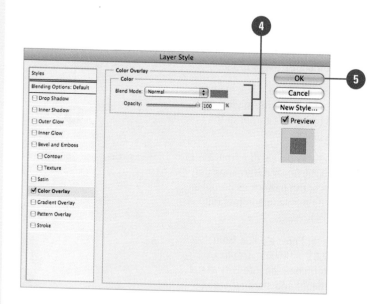

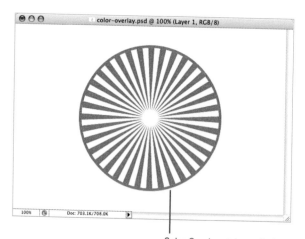

Color Overlay style applied

Using the Stroke Layer Style

The Stroke Layer style lets you apply a stroke around any layer object. Since the stroke will be applied to the edge of the object, it must be surrounded by transparent pixels. For example, you could use the stroke feature to apply a solid color around text outlines, or apply a stroke around an image. Strokes are not limited to solid colors; you can also use gradients and even patterns as a stroke. The Stroke Layer style can provide you with many interesting styles.

Use the Stroke Layer Style

1. Select the **Layers** panel.

2. Select the layer to which you want to apply the Stroke Layer style.

3. Click the **Add Layer Style** button, and then click **Stroke**.

4. Select from the Stroke options:

   ◆ **Size.** Enter 1 to 250 pixels to define the width of the stroke.

   ◆ **Position.** Click the list arrow, and then select to place the stroke on the Outside, Inside, or Center of the layer object.

   ◆ **Blend Mode.** Click the list arrow, and then select from the available options. The Blend Mode option instructs Photoshop how to blend the selected Stroke color with the colors of the active image.

   ◆ **Opacity.** Enter a value from 0% to 100%, or drag the slider left or right. Opacity determines how much of the Stroke masks the original image pixels (default: 100%).

   ◆ **Fill Type.** Click the list arrow, and then select to create a stroke from a solid color, gradient, or pattern.

   ◆ **Color.** Click the color box, and then select a color.

5. Click **OK**.

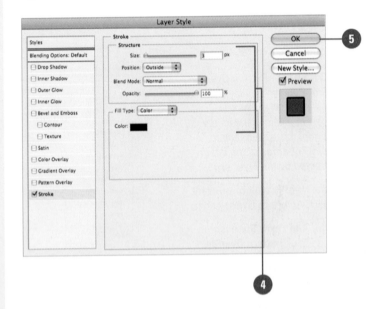

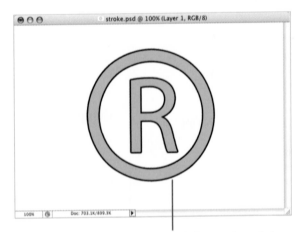

Stroke Layer style applied

Using Pattern Overlays

 PS 4.5, 4.6

Pattern Overlays replace the pixels in the active layer with a specific pattern. Photoshop comes equipped with dozens of preexisting patterns, or you can create and save your own. Patterns can be used to spice up an otherwise dull area of an image—like covering a completely white wall in your house with decorative wallpaper. When you apply a pattern, the original image is overlaid with the selected pattern, and once that's accomplished you can use blending modes and opacity to control the effect the pattern has on the original image.

Use Pattern Overlay

1 Select the **Layers** panel.

> **IMPORTANT** *Pattern Overlays, like all of Photoshop's layer styles, are applied to all the non-transparent pixels in the image. You cannot use a selection to control what areas of the image are affected by the layer style.*

2 Click the layer to which you want to apply the Pattern Overlay style.

3 Click the **Add Layer Style** button, and then click **Pattern Overlay**.

4 Select from the available Pattern Overlay options:

◆ **Blend Mode.** Click the list arrow, and then select from the available options. The Blend Mode option instructs Photoshop how to blend the selected Pattern Overlay with the colors of the active image (default: Normal).

◆ **Opacity.** Enter a value from 0% to 100%. Opacity determines how much of the Pattern Overlay masks the original image pixels (default: 100%). For example, 50% opacity would let 50% of the original colors blend with the Pattern Overlay.

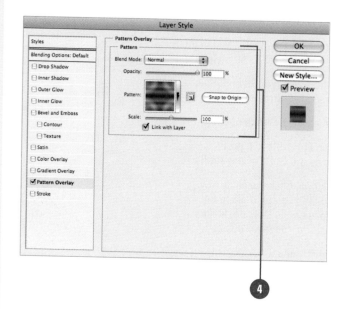

For Your Information

Using Pattern Overlays

You can use a pattern overlay on a photograph. Normally, a pattern completely covers the original image information; however, if you use different Blending Mode options when you apply the pattern, you can achieve some interesting results. Experiment with photographs and patterns using the Multiply, Screen, and Overlay blending modes to start. The style is a combination of the pattern blending with the photograph.

- ◆ **Pattern.** Click the list arrow, and then select from the available patterns. To add additional patterns from the Photoshop pattern library, click the Pattern Options button, located in the upper right of the pattern dialog box, and then choose from the available pattern options.

- ◆ **Add To Presets.** Click the button to add the current pattern to Photoshop's list of presets.

- ◆ **Snap To Origin.** Click the button to begin the pattern tiling from the upper left corner of the document layer.

- ◆ **Scale.** Enter a value from 1% to 1,000%. Scale determines the size of the pattern as it applies to the active image (default: 100%).

- ◆ **Link With Layer.** Select the check box to physically link the active pattern with the active layer (default: checked).

5 Click **OK**.

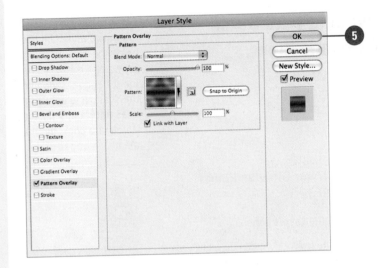

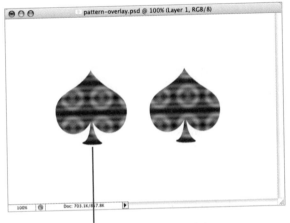

Pattern Overlay style applied

Did You Know?

You can reposition any Pattern Overlay. Open the Layer Style dialog box and click any pattern from the Pattern library. However, before you click OK, move into the document window and drag. The pattern is repositioned as you drag. Click the Snap To Origin button to return the pattern to its default position.

Working with Outer Glow and Inner Shadow

PS 4.5, 4.6

Outer Glow applies a glow in any color you choose to all objects within the active layer. Since the Outer Glow style needs an area in which to work, the objects must be surrounded by transparent pixels. The Outer Glow style is an excellent way to create a neon effect on text. The Inner Shadow style applies a shadow to the inside of an object. Since the shadow is applied directly to the image, the Inner Shadow style does not require an image object surrounded by transparent pixels. When you apply the Inner Shadow style, the shadow effect appears on the inside edges of the image—like a reverse drop shadow.

Apply an Outer Glow and Inner Shadow Style

1. Select the **Layers** panel.

2. Click the layer to which you want to apply the Outer Glow style.

3. Click the **Add Layer Style** button, and then click **Outer Glow**.

4. Select from the available Outer Glow options:

   ◆ **Structure.** Allows you to change Blending Mode and Opacity (determines how much of the Outer Glow masks the original image pixels), plus you can add a bit of Noise (introduces a random shift to the colors of the Outer Glow), and even change the Color or use a Gradient on the Outer Glow.

   For example, 50% opacity would let 50% of the original colors blend with the Outer Glow.

   ◆ **Elements.** Allows you to change the Technique used (softer or more precise glow), as well as change the Spread and Size of the glow. The precise option creates a realistic, but more complex Outer Glow. Spread determines the amount of image that is used for the spread of the glow.

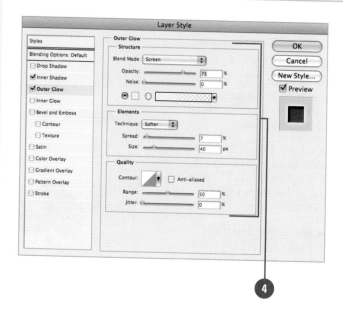

For Your Information

Creating Neon

You can create realistic neon using the Outer Glow layer style and some text. Just create a text layer using a rounded font, such as Arial Rounded, and then choose a typical neon color for the font, such as red or yellow. Don't forget; text must be rasterized before you can apply an effect, so be sure you have the text the way you want it first. Apply an Outer Glow using a light yellow for the glow color. Place the text against a black Background layer (for effect), and then tweak the glow options until you see a realistic glow appear around the text. Add a Bevel and Emboss style to the text to complete the effect of a glowing neon sign.

◆ **Quality.** Allows you to access the Contour of the glow to create interesting special effects. Select the Anti-aliased check box to visibly smooth the glow (or drop shadow), as well as change the Range of the contour and Jitter (random value of gradients) of the glow.

Contours are mathematical curves that determine the brightness of the glow at different levels.

5 Click **Inner Shadow** from the available styles.

6 Select from the available Inner Shadow options:

◆ **Structure.** Allows you to change Blending Mode and Opacity, as well as the Angle of the shadow. In addition, you can control the shadow's Distance, Choke and Size.

◆ **Quality.** Allows you to access the Contour of the shadow to create interesting special effects. Select the Anti-aliased check box to visibly smooth the glow (or drop shadow), as well as add a bit of Noise to the final product.

7 Click **OK**.

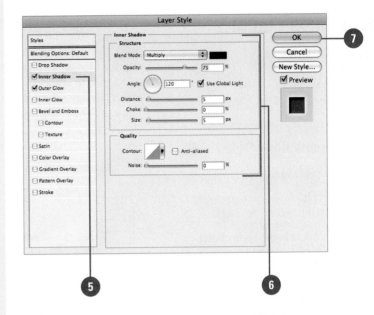

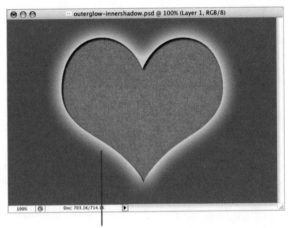

Outer Glow and Inner Shadow style applied

Applying an Inner Glow Style

PS 4.5, 4.6

The Inner Glow style creates the appearance of a glow on the inside of an object. For example, creating black text and applying an Inner Glow style changes the object by lightening the edges of the text. Once you apply an Inner Glow, you can control the color size and intensity of the glow style to create the exact special effect you're after. You can also apply the Outer Glow style to the image, and the glow effect spreads out into the surrounding transparent areas of the layer.

Apply an Inner Glow Style

1. Select the **Layers** panel.

2. Click the layer to which you want to apply the Inner Glow style.

3. Click the **Add Layer Style** button, and then click **Inner Glow**.

4. Select from the available Inner Glow options:

   ◆ **Blend Mode.** Click the list arrow, and then select from the available options. The Blend Mode option instructs Photoshop how to blend the selected Inner Glow with the colors of the active image (default: Screen).

   ◆ **Opacity.** Enter a value from 0% to 100%, or drag the slider left or right. Opacity determines how much of the Inner Glow masks the original image pixels (default: 75%).

   ◆ **Noise.** Enter a value from 0% to 100%, or drag the slider left or right. The noise option introduces a random shift to the colors of the Inner Glow (default: 0%).

   ◆ **Solid Color.** Click the Solid Color swatch box, and then select a color from the Color Picker dialog box (default: light yellow).

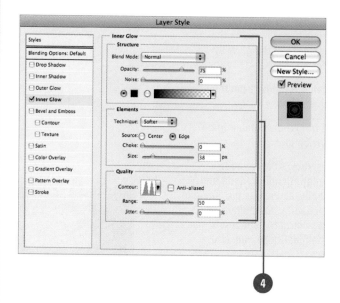

Creating Chiseled Text with Inner Glow

You can create realistic chiseled text using the Inner Glow style. Just create some white text and apply an Inner Glow using a dark gray color. Put the text on a dark background layer, and the text appears as if it's chiseled into the background.

- **Gradient.** Click the Gradient list arrow, and then select a gradient (as opposed to a solid color) for the Inner Glow.

- **Technique.** Click the list arrow, and then select between a Softer, and a Precise glow. The precise option creates a realistic, but more complex Inner Glow.

- **Source.** Click the Center option to have the glow illuminate from the center, or the Edge option to have the glow illuminate from the edge.

- **Choke.** Enter a value from 0% to 100%, or drag the slider left or right. Choke reduces the layer mask prior to blurring (default: 0%).

- **Size.** Enter a value from 0 to 250 pixels, or drag the slider left or right. Size determines the size of the glow (default: 5)

- **Contour.** Click the list arrow, and then select from the available options.

- **Anti-aliased.** Select the check box to create a visually smooth Inner Glow.

- **Range.** Enter a value from 1% to 100%, or drag the slider left or right. Range determines the range of the contour as it is applied to the image (default: 50%).

- **Jitter.** Enter a value from 1% to 100%, or drag the slider left or right. Jitter increases or decreases the random value of gradients applied to the Inner Glow (default: 0%).

5 Click **OK**.

Gradient list arrow

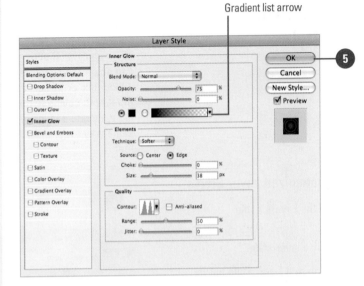

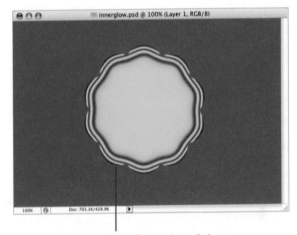

Inner Glow style applied

Creating Customized Layer Styles

PS 4.5, 4.6

Layer styles can be one style or a combination of many styles. For example, you could create a layer style that includes a Stroke, Bevel, Emboss, and Gradient Overlay. Once you create a layer style, it's possible you might want to use it again. If that's the case, Photoshop gives you an easy way to create a layer style directly from the Layer Style dialog box, or by using the Styles panel. Creating customized styles is a great time-saving feature, and not only speeds up the process of applying a style to a layer, but ensures that the style is applied in exactly the same way every time. That gives your designs a consistent look and feel.

Create Customized Layer Styles

1. Select the **Layers** panel.

2. Click the layer to which you want to apply a layer style.

3. Click the **Add Layer Style** button, and then click a style.

4. To add a style to an existing style, select the style from the styles list.

5. To modify an existing style, select from the various style options.

Did You Know?

You can combine elements of one layer style with another. Drag from one layer style into another. If you have two layers, both containing layer styles, and you want the drop shadow from one layer style added to the second layer, simply drag the drop shadow layer element to the other layer to create a copy of the drop shadow. In addition, you can drag layer styles between two open documents.

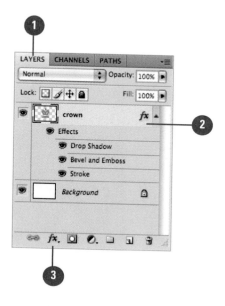

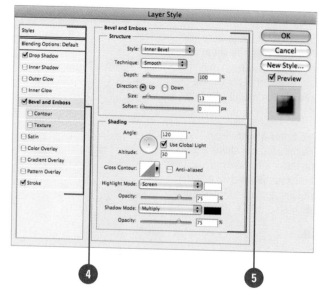

6 Click **New Style**, and then select from the following options:

◆ **Name.** Enter a name for the new layer style.

◆ **Include Layer Effects.** Select the check box to include any layer effects applied to the style.

◆ **Include Layer Blending Options.** Select the check box to include any blending mode options applied to the style.

7 Click **OK**.

8 Click **OK**.

If you open the Styles panel, you'll see the new style is added to the bottom of the current list.

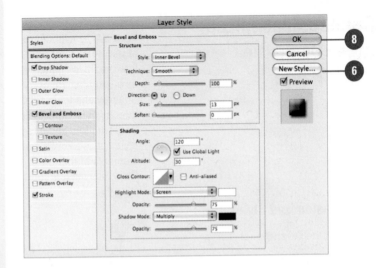

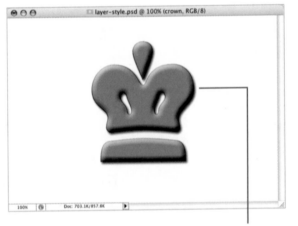

Newly created style applied

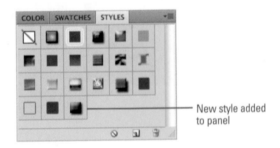

New style added to panel

Creating Customized Styles Using the Styles Panel

PS 4.5, 4.6

Creating customized styles using the Styles panel requires that you have a layer with an applied style and you would like to save the style to use again later. You're only a button click away from saving the style into the Styles panel. When you create a layer style, the style appears as a sub-element of the layer. For example, when you create a Drop Shadow and Inner Glow layer style, two sub-elements are created directly below the layer to which the styles are attached—one for the Drop Shadow and one for the Inner Glow. When you save a customized style, you select a layer, not an individual style, and save all the sub-elements of that layer. To save a customized style with only the Inner Glow, you must first drag the Drop Shadow to the Delete Layer button.

Create Customized Styles

① Select the **Layers** panel.

② Select a layer that contains a layer style.

③ Select the **Styles** panel.

④ Move to the bottom of the Styles panel, and then click your mouse when you see the cursor change to a paint bucket.

Did You Know?

You can download additional styles from Adobe. In your web browser, go to *www.adobe.com* and navigate to Adobe Studio Exchange for more styles.

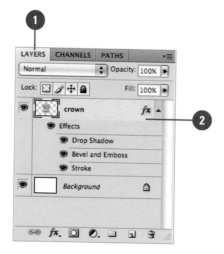

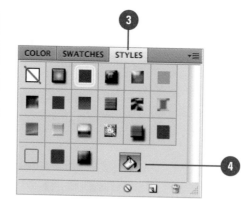

5 Select from the following options:

◆ **Name.** Enter a name for the new layer style.

◆ **Include Layer Effects.** Select the check box to include any layer effects applied to the style.

◆ **Include Layer Blending Options.** Select the check box to include any blending mode options applied to the style.

6 Click **OK**.

If you open the Styles panel, you'll see the new style is added to the bottom of the current list.

Did You Know?

You can share your styles with other Photoshop users. First click the Styles Options button, and then click Save Styles. The styles are now a file that can be e-mailed to any other Photoshop user. All the user has to do is click the Styles Options button, and then click the Load Styles option to load and use the new styles.

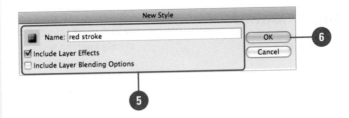

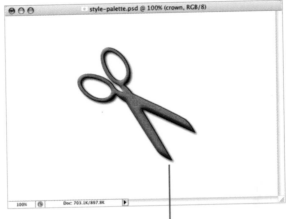

Customized style applied

Moving Existing Layer Styles

Once a layer style is applied to a layer, it can be moved to other layers, or into another document. This kind of flexibility and control lets you create specific layer styles and then apply them effortlessly to other layers or move them into other documents. In most cases it would make sense to save the style in the Styles panel. However, there are times when you will only use the style once or twice. In that case, a quick drag-and-drop is more efficient.

Move Existing Layer Styles

① Select the **Layers** panel.

② Click a layer that contains a layer style.

③ Click the **triangle** to expand the grouped layer styles.

④ Press the Alt (Win) or Option (Mac) key, and drag the grouped layer styles over another layer.

Photoshop makes a copy of all the styles and applies them to the new layer.

Did You Know?

You can move individual styles between layers. Drag the named style, instead of the Effects group, to move a single layer style instead of the entire group. When you release your mouse, the single layer style will be copied and applied to the new image.

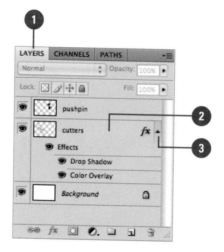

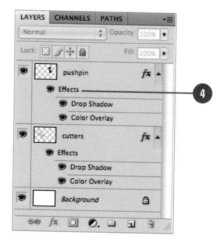

Getting Creative with Type

13

Introduction

The Type tool in Adobe Photoshop has advanced far beyond its humble beginnings. When Photoshop first appeared, the most you could expect from the Type tool was just the creation of text. Today it's a powerful and creative tool. Not only can you place text into any open Photoshop image, you can also use text as a mask, path, or even warp text into any shape you desire. In addition, Photoshop now preserves type without rasterizing. That means you can create type in Photoshop of comparable quality to type created in Adobe Illustrator, or Adobe InDesign, regardless of the image's resolution. When you work in Photoshop, type becomes as creative a design element as any other available feature.

Working with the Character panel gives you the ability to select a specific font, style, and size, as well as expand or contract the space between letters with tracking and kerning, or you can simply increase or decrease the physical width of the text. Baseline shifting even gives you the ability to raise or lower text off its original line. In addition, the Paragraph panel lets you create automatic breaks between paragraphs, and align rows of text to the left, center, or right, or to justify them to the margins.

When you're working with large blocks of text, Photoshop's Check Spelling command lets you identify and correct any misspelled words, and the Find and Replace Text feature makes quick work of identifying and replacing words or formats. You can isolate image pixels with a type mask to create words out of pictures. For example, you could type the phrase "Fall is Coming," along with an image of leaves. The Type mask would make the words appear as if they were spelled out in colorful fall leaves. In addition, you could use a type mask in combination with Photoshop's layer styles to create text that almost leaps off the page. Working with text in Photoshop is more than just typing words; it's a process every bit as creative as working with graphic images.

What You'll Do

Use Standard Type Tools

Work with Type Options

Work with the Character Panel

Work with the Paragraph Panel

Set Anti-aliasing Options

Use the Warp Text Option

Use Spell Check

Find and Replace Text

Use the Rasterize Type Command

Create Work Paths and Shapes from Type Layers

Create Shape Layers

Create a Type Mask

Isolate Image Pixels Using a Type Mask

Create Chiseled Type with a Type Mask

Use Masks to Generate Special Effects

Create and Modify Text on a Path

Using Standard Type Tools

 PS 6.4

Use Standard Type Tools

1. Click and hold the **Type** tool on the toolbox, and then select the **Horizontal Type** tool.

2. Click in the document window and begin typing.

   Photoshop creates a Type layer and places the text in the layer.

   IMPORTANT *When you work with the Type tools, the normal shortcut functions of the keyboard will not work. For example, holding down the Spacebar to access the Hand tool will only create a space at the insertion point of the text.*

3. Move your cursor to a point away from the text, and then drag to move the text.

Did You Know?

You can create type on a path. Create a path using Photoshop's Pen tool. Select the Type tool, and then click on the path. Photoshop creates an insertion point and when you type, the text follows the path.

Photoshop comes with a set of standard typing tools, which are controlled in much the same way typing tools are in any word processing program. However, the creative possibilities go far beyond those of a standard word processing program. When you work with the Type tools, you begin by typing some text and then controlling the text through the toolbox and the Options bar. Photoshop helps you maintain control over the text by automatically placing it in a separate type layer.

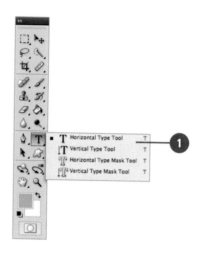

Text layer

4 Double-click to select a specific word, or drag across the text to select groups of words.

5 Change the text color by clicking the Options bar color swatch, and then choosing a new color from the Color Picker dialog box, or use the Swatches or Color panels to select a new color.

6 Delete the text by clicking within the text and pressing the backspace key to erase one letter at a time, or select a group of text and press the Backspace (Win) or Delete (Mac) key.

7 Insert text by clicking within the text to create an insertion point, and then type.

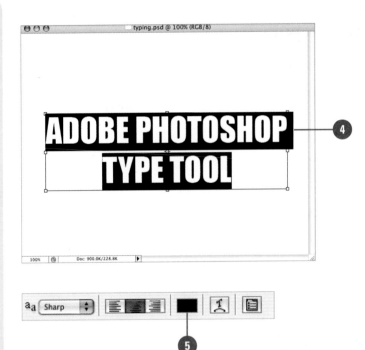

Did You Know?

You can edit type on a path. To edit text at any time in the creative process, double-click on the Type layer thumbnail, or select the Type tool, and then click on the text.

See Also

See "Creating a New Layer" on page 100 for more information on creating layers.

For Your Information

Preserving Text to Print

Photoshop lets you preserve the vector attributes of text when printing. Photoshop's type options give you control over text much the same way as high-end layout programs do, and even allow you to save the vector nature of text. This allows you to print Photoshop images with crisp text that's not dependent on the resolution of the document.

To save a Photoshop document and preserve the text vector data, click the File menu, point to Save As, and then choose the EPS (Encapsulated PostScript) format. Click the Include Vector Data option, and then save the file. The EPS document holds the type information and lets you print the document from any program, including layout programs like Adobe InDesign and QuarkXPress.

Working with Type Options

PS 6.4

Photoshop lets you control text through the Type options, located on the Options bar. To access the Type options you must have one of Photoshop's Type tools selected. It is not necessary to change Type options after typing. If you know what you're after, you can set the options, and then commence typing. However, if the need arises to change the text, Photoshop comes to the rescue with a host of type options, such as font family, size, color, justification, even high-end type processing controls like leading and kerning. You can preview font families and font styles directly in the Font menu. Font names appear in the regular system font, and a sample word ("Sample") appears next to each font name, displayed in the font itself.

Work with Type Options

1. Open a document.

2. Select the **Type** tool on the toolbox.

3. To toggle between horizontal and vertical type, click the **Change Text Orientation** button on the Options bar.

   If this option is selected on a preexisting type layer, the text switches between horizontal and vertical.

4. Click the **Font Family** list arrow, and then select from the fonts available on your computer.

5. Click the **Font Style** list arrow, and then select a font style, such as Regular, Bold, Oblique, or Italic. If the font family you select does not have any additional styles, this box will be grayed out.

6. Click the **Font Size** list arrow, and then select from the preset font sizes, measured in points (6 to 72).

   Photoshop uses a standard PostScript measuring system of 72 points to the inch.

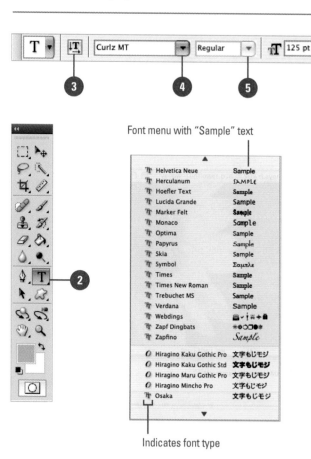

Font menu with "Sample" text

Indicates font type

7 Click the **Anti-aliasing** list arrow, and then select from the available options.

Anti-aliasing creates text that is visually smoother to the eye.

8 Click the **Left**, **Center**, or **Right Justification** button.

Justification balances text created on two or more vertical or horizontal lines.

9 Click the **Color Swatch** button, and then select a color from the Color Picker dialog box.

10 Click the **Warped Text** button to apply special warped effects to text.

11 Click the **Toggle the Character and Paragraph Panels** button to show the panels or to turn them off.

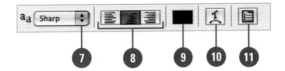

Anti Aliased - ON

Anti Aliased - OFF

Did You Know?

You can use non-preset font sizes from the Options bar. Select the current point size on the Options bar, type any point size, and then press Enter (Win) or Return (Mac).

You can change font attributes with the Character panel. Click the Character panel, select the text you want to change, and then use the options on the Character panel.

See Also

See "Using the Warp Text Option" on page 304 for information on warping text in your document.

For Your Information

What's the Difference Between the Fonts?

Everything you type appears in a specific font, with a unique type-face design and size for letters, numbers, and other characters. Usually, each typeface, such as Times New Roman, is available in four variations: normal, bold, italic, and bold italic. There are two basic types of fonts: scalable and bitmapped. A **scalable font** (also known as **outline font**) is based on a mathematical equation that creates character outlines to form letters and numbers of any size. The two major scalable fonts are Adobe's Type 1 PostScript and Apple/Microsoft's TrueType or OpenType. Scalable fonts are generated in any point size on the fly and require only four variations for each typeface. A **bitmapped font** consists of a set of dot patterns for each letter and number in a typeface for a specified type size. Bitmapped fonts are created or prepackaged ahead of time and require four variations for each point size used in each typeface. Although a bitmapped font designed for a particular font size will always look the best, scalable fonts eliminate storing hundreds of different sizes of fonts on a disk.

Working with the Character Panel

PS 6.4

Each version of Photoshop brought it closer to becoming a true type-setting application, and with the ability to preserve text layers, and work with high-end type controls, that time has finally arrived. You can access the Character options without having any Type layers active. However, if you select the text in a Type layer, any changes you've made to the options will impact the selected text. Changes made to the active type layer do not impact any other type layers, and only the text actually selected in the type layer will be changed.

Use the Character Panel

1. Open a document.

2. Select the **Type** tool on the toolbox.

3. Click the **Toggle the Character and Paragraph Panels** button on the Options bar.

4. Select the **Character** panel.

5. Select from the following options:

   ◆ **Font Family.** Click the list arrow, and then select a font family from the fonts available on your computer.

   ◆ **Font Style.** Click the list arrow, and then select a font style, such as Regular, Bold, Oblique, or Italic. If the font family you select does not have any additional styles, this box will be grayed out.

   ◆ **Font Size.** Click the list arrow, and then select from the preset font sizes, measured in points (6 to 72). Photoshop uses a standard PostScript measuring system of 72 points to the inch.

   ◆ **Kerning.** Click the list arrow, and then select from the preset values for kerning. Kerning adds or subtracts space between character pairs.

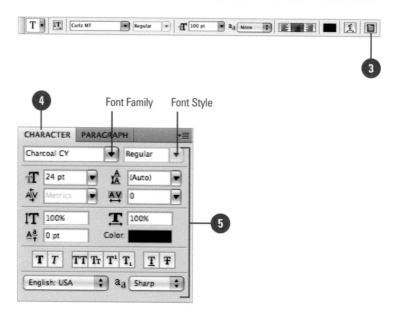

Font Family   Font Style

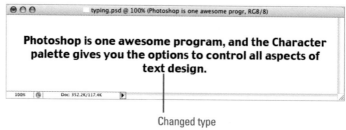

Changed type

- ◆ **Leading.** Click the list arrow, and then select from the preset values for leading. Leading adds or subtracts space vertically between lines of text.

- ◆ **Tracking.** Click the list arrow, and then select from the preset values for Tracking. Tracking adds or subtracts space between words.

- ◆ **Vertical Scale.** Enter a value to change the vertical scale. Vertical Scale increases or decreases the height of the text.

- ◆ **Baseline Shift.** Enter a value to set the Baseline Shift. Baseline Shift raises or lowers selected text, using the baseline as a reference.

- ◆ **Horizontal Scale.** Enter a Value to change the Horizontal Scale. Horizontal Scale increases or decreases the width of the text.

- ◆ **Font Color.** Click the color swatch, and then select a color from Photoshop's Color Picker dialog box.

- ◆ **Font Attributes.** Click the buttons to select additional font attributes, such as Underline and Strikethrough.

- ◆ **Spelling and Hyphenation.** Click the list arrow, and then select a language reference for Spelling and Hyphenation.

- ◆ **Anti-aliasing.** Click the list arrow, and then select from the available options. Anti-aliasing creates text that is visually smoother to the eye.

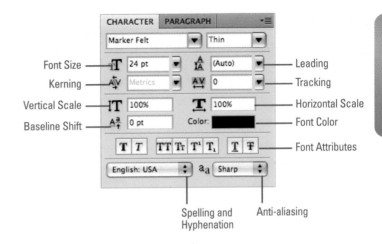

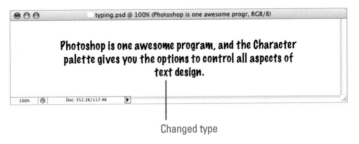

Changed type

For Your Information

Using the Paragraph Panel

The function of the Paragraph panel is to give you precise control over the elements of a paragraph. Unlike the Character panel, it is not necessary to select a paragraph to change it; you only need to have the insertion point of the cursor inside the paragraph you want to change. Photoshop, as well as other type and layout programs, defines a paragraph as the text between each activation of the Enter (Win) or Return (Mac) key. For example, you press the Enter key and type several sentences; when you press the Enter key again, the cursor jumps to the next line and you continue typing. The pressing of the Enter (Win) or Return (Mac) key defines the end of one paragraph and the beginning of another.

Working with the Paragraph Panel

 PS 6.4

Each version of Photoshop brought it closer to becoming a true type-setting application, and with the ability to preserve text layers, and work with high-end type design options, that time has finally arrived. You can access the Paragraph options without having any Type layers active. However, since paragraph styles are applied to paragraphs of type, not individual letters or words, if you select a Type layer, the changes made with the Paragraph panel will be applied to the text within the layer without the necessity of making a selection.

Use the Paragraph Panel

1. Open a document.

2. Select the **Type** tool on the toolbox.

3. Click the **Toggle the Character and Paragraph Panels** button on the Options bar.

4. Select the **Paragraph** panel, and then select from the following options:

   ◆ **Justification.** Click to choose from the various Justification methods.

   ◆ **Indent Left Margin.** Enter a value to indent the left margin (values from -1296 to 1296).

   ◆ **Indent First Line.** Enter a value to indent the first line of the paragraph (values from -1296 to 1296).

   ◆ **Indent Right Margin.** Enter a value to indent the right margin (values from -1296 to 1296).

   ◆ **Space Before Paragraph.** Enter a value to increase or decrease the space before each new paragraph (values from -1296 to 1296).

   ◆ **Space After Paragraph.** Enter a value to increase or decrease the space after each paragraph (values from -1296 to 1296).

   ◆ **Hyphenate.** Select the check box to hyphenate long words at the end of text lines.

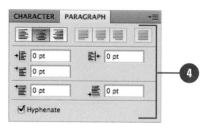

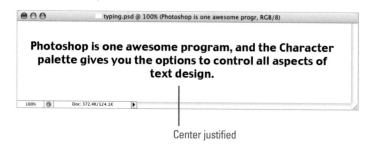

Center justified

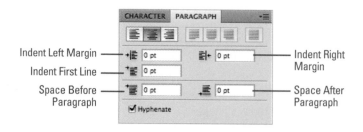

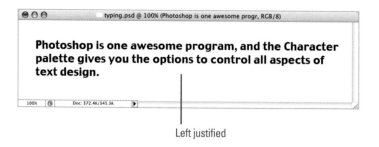

Left justified

Setting Anti-aliasing Options

Photoshop's Anti-aliasing option helps to make text appear smoother by painting the edges of the text with semi-transparent colors. When text is displayed on a computer monitor, the text is built using pixels, and since pixels are essentially bricks, the edges of curved type have a tendency to look ragged. By painting the edges of the text with semi-transparent pixels, the type blends into the background, creating a smoother look. Unless you apply a gradient or mask, text is typically one color; activating anti-aliasing can increase the colors (at the edge) by about 6-10 pixels. While this works to make the text smoother, it will also make small text (under 12 points) harder to read. The trick with anti-aliasing is to experiment with the various options to determine which one works the best, and that means occasionally turning anti-aliasing off.

Set Anti-aliasing Options

1. Open a document that contains a type layer.

2. Select the **Type** tool on the toolbox.

3. Select the **Layers** panel, and then select the layer containing the text.

4. Click the **Anti-aliasing** list arrow on the Options bar, and then select from the following options:

   ◆ **None.** Turns off anti-aliasing.

   ◆ **Sharp.** Creates visually sharp type in the active layer.

   ◆ **Crisp.** Creates crisp type (not as sharp as the Sharp option).

   ◆ **Strong.** Creates a heavier (bolder) type.

   ◆ **Smooth.** Creates type with a smooth appearance.

   IMPORTANT *The anti-aliasing option is only applied to the type in the active type layer.*

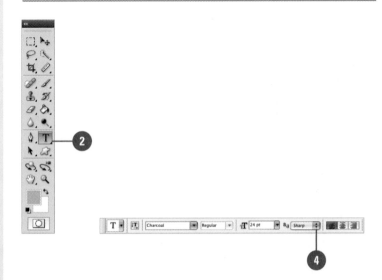

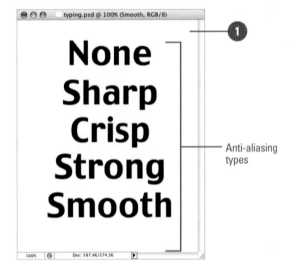

Anti-aliasing types

Using the Warp Text Option

PS 6.4

Photoshop's Warp Text option gives you creative control over the look of text. No longer are you confined to straight vertical or horizontal text. In the Photoshop world, text can be created in almost any size and shape. As an additional bonus, warping text does not require converting the text into raster data. So days later, you can access the warped text and change its font family, size, and color. It's all about control…in this case, controlling text.

Use Warp Text

1. Open a document.
2. Select the **Type** tool on the toolbox, and then select a type layer in the Layers panel or create a new type layer.
3. Click the **Warp Text** button.
4. Click the **Style** list arrow, and then select from the following style options:
   - Arc
   - Arc Lower
   - Arc Upper
   - Arch
   - Bulge
   - Shell Lower
   - Shell Upper
   - Flag
   - Wave
   - Fish
   - Rise
   - Fisheye
   - Inflate
   - Squeeze
   - Twist

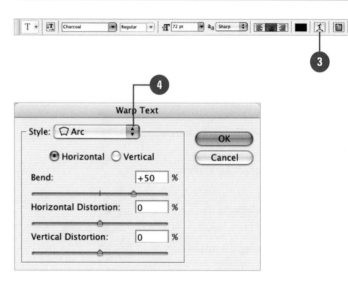

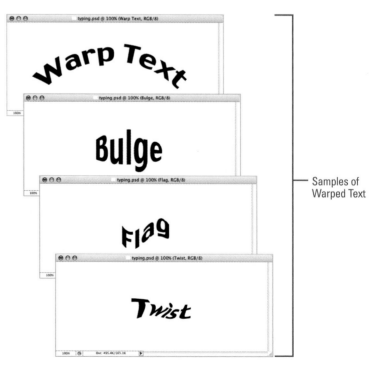

Samples of Warped Text

5 Click the **Horizontal** or **Vertical** option to warp the text in a horizontal or vertical direction.

6 Enter a percentage value in the Bend box, or drag the slider left or right (-100% to 100%). Bend controls the physical amount of bend applied to the text, based on warp style.

7 Enter a percentage value in the Horizontal Distortion box, or drag the slider left or right (-100% to 100%). Horizontal Distortion controls the amount of distortion on the horizontal axis applied to the text, based on warp style.

8 Enter a percentage value in the Vertical Distortion box, or drag the slider left or right (-100% to 100%). Vertical Distortion controls the amount of distortion on the vertical axis applied to the text, based on warp style.

9 Click **OK**.

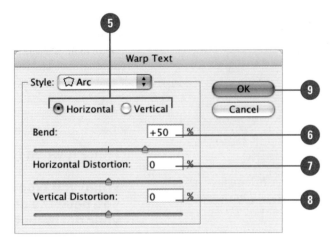

For Your Information

Designing with Warped Text

The Warp Text option is a great way to draw attention to a heading or word within a Photoshop document. However, warped text can be extremely hard to read, so use it sparingly. Think of the overall design of the image, and then ask yourself if the warped text supports the mood and message of the image. If it doesn't, then don't use it. Don't fall into the designer's trap of using every new feature you come across. If it doesn't support the message, use something else, like a layer style gradient, or Bevel and Emboss.

Using Spell Check

There's nothing more embarrassing than creating a document that contains misspelled words. Although you wouldn't use Photoshop if all you needed to do was create a text document, Photoshop includes a fully functional spell checking system, which at least lets you make sure all of your words are spelled correctly.

Use Spell Check

1. Open a document that contains one or more Type layers.

   You do not need to have the Type tool selected to perform a spell check.

2. Click the **Edit** menu, and then click **Check Spelling**.

3. When Photoshop encounters a word not in its dictionary, it displays that word in the Not in Dictionary box, and allows you to choose one of the following options:

   - **Ignore.** Ignore this word one time.

   - **Ignore All.** Ignore all instances of this word.

   - **Change.** Photoshop will give you a list of possible alternative spellings. Select one from the Suggestions box, and then click Change.

   - **Change All.** Change all occurrences of the word, based on the selected suggestion.

   - **Add.** Add the word to Photoshop's dictionary.

   Photoshop continues to highlight misspelled words until the document is completely scanned.

4. When you're finished, click **Done**.

The highlighted word has been identified by spell checker.

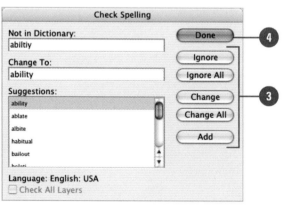

Finding and Replacing Text

In the editing process, it is sometimes helpful to find and replace a particular word or phrase because the text needs to be changed, either in one spot or globally throughout the document. The Find and Replace Text command makes it easy to locate and replace specific text in a document.

Use Find and Replace

1. Open a document that contains one or more type layers.

2. Click the **Edit** menu, and then click **Find and Replace Text**.

3. Enter the text to locate in the Find What box.

4. Select from the following **Find and Replace Text** options:

   ◆ **Search All Layers.** Select the check box to search all type layers.

   ◆ **Forward.** Select the check box to search forward through the document.

   ◆ **Case Sensitive.** Select the check box to search for the word in the same case as typed in the Find What box.

   ◆ **Whole Word Only.** Select the check box to search for whole words as typed in the Find What box.

5. Enter the replacement text in the Change To box.

6. Click **Find Next** to locate the next occurrence of the word:

   ◆ Click **Change** to change the word.

   ◆ Click **Change All** to change all occurrences of the word.

   ◆ Click **Change/Find** to automatically change the word and locate the next occurrence.

7. When you're finished, click **Done**.

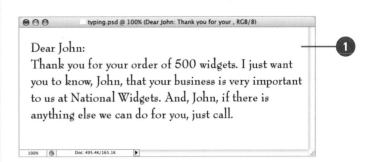

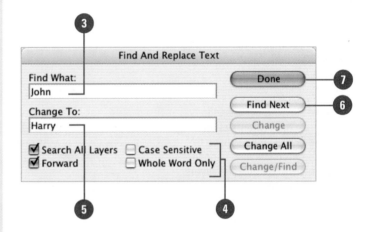

Using the Rasterize Type Command

When you are working with type, some commands, filters, and painting tools are not available. If you want to use Photoshop's whole arsenal of image adjustment tools, you must first rasterize the type layer. When you rasterize a type layer, you're converting the type into pixels, and once the rasterize operation is complete, the text within the type layer is no longer an editable font. Therefore, make sure you like the font family, and your text is spelled correctly before rasterizing. Once the text is rasterized, you can apply commands and filters normally reserved for images.

Use Rasterize Type

1. Open a document containing one or more type layers.

2. Select the **Layers** panel, and then select one of the type layers.

3. Click the **Layer** menu, point to **Rasterize**, and then select from the following commands:

   ◆ **Type.** Click the command to rasterize the type in the active layer.

   ◆ **Layer.** Click the command to rasterize the contents of the active layer (does not have to be type). You can also choose All Layers to rasterize all layers in your document.

   The Type layer is converted into a standard layer, and all of Photoshop's painting tools, filters, and commands will work on the information in the layer.

Did You Know?

You can rasterize other types of data. Rasterize other types of data, such as: Shape, Fill Content, Vector Mask, Smart Object, Video, and 3D.

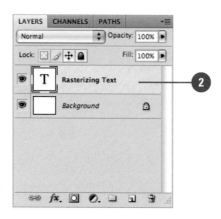

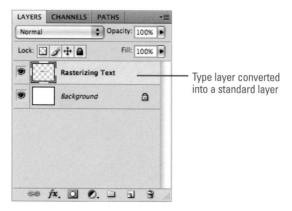

Type layer converted into a standard layer

Rasterize Type applied

Creating Work Paths and Shapes from Type Layers

PS 6.3

When you work with type, there are certain restrictions to what you can do. You can't apply filter effects to type, and many of Photoshop's commands do not work with type layers. One solution is to rasterize the type layer. However, rasterized type is converted to pixels. What if you want the text converted into a vector path? Once type is saved as a path, you can manipulate it like any other vector path. A text path is no longer considered text; however, the original type layer is intact and editable. Creating a path and at the same time preserving the original type layer gives you the best of both creative worlds.

Create Work Paths

1. Open a document containing a type layer.

2. Select the **Layers** panel, and then select one of the type layers.

3. Click the **Layer** menu, point to **Type**, and then click **Create Work Path**.

    IMPORTANT *Paths cannot be created from fonts that do not contain outline data, such as bitmap fonts.*

4. Select the **Paths** panel.

5. Select any of Photoshop's Pen tools to modify the path.

See Also

See Chapter 11,"Using the Paths Panel," on page 253 for more information on the Paths panel.

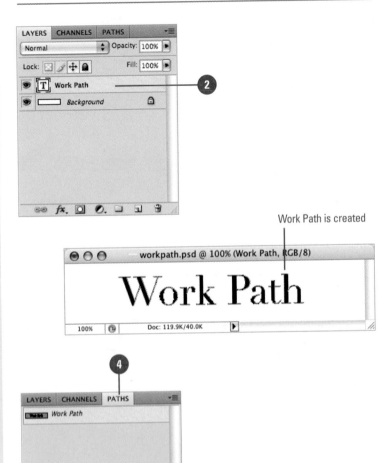

Work Path is created

Work Path is modified

Creating Shape Layers

PS 5.4

Create Shape Layers

1. Open a document containing a type layer.

2. Select the **Layers** panel, and then select one of the type layers.

3. Click the **Layer** menu, point to **Type**, and then click **Convert To Shape**.

    IMPORTANT *When you convert a type layer into a shape layer, Photoshop removes the type layer and replaces it with the shape layer. You gain the ability to manipulate the image as a vector shape; however, you lose the ability to edit the type.*

4. Click the **Vector Mask** thumbnail in the Layers panel, and then edit the mask using any of Photoshop's Pen tools.

Did You Know?

You can change the fill color of the text in your document. Click the Image Thumbnail, and then fill the area with a color, pattern, or gradient.

When you convert a type layer into a shape layer, the type layer is converted into a layer with a vector mask. In essence, Photoshop fills the layer with the color of the text, and then creates a vector mask to define the type. Once created, the vector mask can be edited just like any other vector shape. You gain the ability to manipulate the image as a vector shape; however, you lose the ability to edit the type.

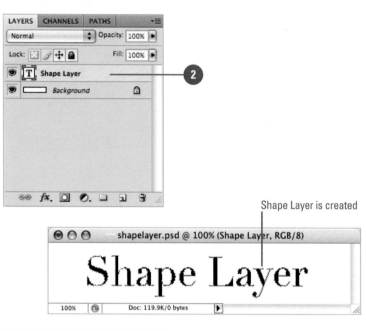

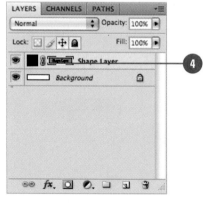

Shape Layer is created

Shape Layer is modified

Creating a Type Mask

Photoshop has two type tools—the Horizontal or Vertical Type tools and the Horizontal or Vertical Mask tools. The former creates regular type, using the fonts available on your computer system. When you add type to the screen, the color of the font defaults to the current foreground color. When you use the type masking tools, Photoshop creates a mask in the size and shape of the selected font with the mask appearing as a red overlay. Once the mask is created, you can modify it just like any normal text layer, by changing the font, size, or even using the Warp feature. Unlike the normal type tools, Photoshop does not create a type layer for the mask; the mask simply appears in the active layer. Being able to create a mask from a font opens up all kinds of creative possibilities. For example, you could use a mask in conjunction with a photograph to create a unique fill or you could use a mask to create a chiseled look for your text.

Create a Type Mask

1 Open a document.

2 Select the **Horizontal Type Mask** tool on the toolbox.

3 Click in the document window to place an insertion point, and then type.

As you type, Photoshop creates a mask in the size and shape of the current font.

4 Use the editing tools on the mask to change its font family, style, and size.

IMPORTANT *Masks, like regular text, must be selected before any of the above changes are applied.*

5 Select the **Marquee** tool on the toolbox, or any other of Photoshop's selection tools.

The mask converts from a red overlay into a traditional selection.

6 Move into the interior of one of the letters, and then drag to move the selection.

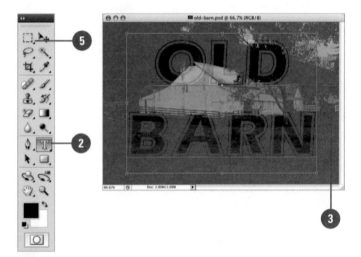

Isolating Image Pixels Using a Type Mask

One of the advantages to a mask is that you can create type using any fill you desire. For example, you're doing an advertising piece for a real estate company in California, and you want something unique for the text, so you get an image of a sunset, create a type mask with the word SUNSET and then use the image and mask to create a unique fill.

Isolate Image Pixels

① Open a document containing the image you want to mask.

② Select the **Layers** panel, and then select the layer containing the image.

③ Select the **Horizontal Type Mask** tool on the toolbox.

④ Click in the document window to place an insertion point, and then type.

As you type, Photoshop creates a mask in the size and shape of the current font.

IMPORTANT *If you want a lot of the image to show through the mask, use a large, thick mono-weight font, like Impact.*

⑤ Use the editing tools on the mask to change its font, style, and size.

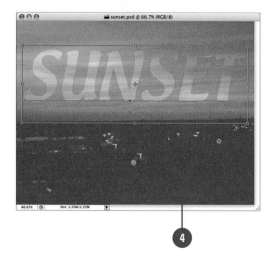

Did You Know?

You can move the mask after you've converted it into a selection. Click any selection tool, and then drag from inside the selection. The selection area will move without modifying the actual image. In addition, you can use your arrow keys to gently nudge the selection left, right, up, or down.

6 Select the **Marquee** tool on the toolbox, and then position the mask directly over the portion of the image you want inside the text.

7 Click the **Select** menu, and then click **Inverse**.

8 Press the Backspace (Win) or Delete (Mac) key to delete the inverse selection.

The Inverse command reverses the selection and the deletion removes all the pixels outside the mask.

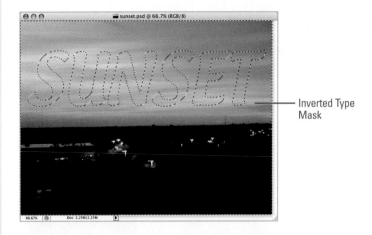

Inverted Type Mask

Did You Know?

You can use Photoshop's adjustment tools to control the selection. Instead of deleting the surrounding image, click the Image menu, point to Adjustments, and then click Levels. Move the middle gray slider left or right to increase or decrease the brightness of the surrounding pixels. That way the text will stand out against the original image background.

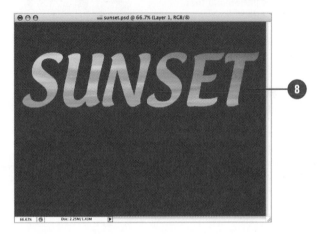

Creating Chiseled Type with a Type Mask

This technique is great for creating three-dimensional text on any image. For example, you could use this technique to create the raised text on a plastic credit card, or words chiseled in marble. The technique is simple, but the results are impressive. Using the Bevel and Emboss layer style creates the effect by darkening the upper left portions of the selection, while lightening the lower right portions. This creates the illusion of a light source falling across a convex or chiseled surface.

Create Chiseled Type

1. Open a document containing the image you want to use for the chisel effect.

2. Select the **Layers** panel, and then select the layer containing the image.

3. Select the **Horizontal Type Mask** tool on the toolbox.

4. Click in the document window to place an insertion point, and then type.

   As you type, Photoshop creates a mask in the size and shape of the current font.

5. Use the editing tools on the mask to change its font, style, and size.

   IMPORTANT *You'll need a thick sans serif font, like Arial Black, or Impact.*

6. Select the **Marquee** tool on the toolbox, and then position the mask directly over the portion of the image where you want the words to appear.

7. Press Ctrl+J (Win) or ⌘+J (Mac).

   Photoshop creates a copy of the image pixels inside the type mask, and then places them in a layer directly above the active layer.

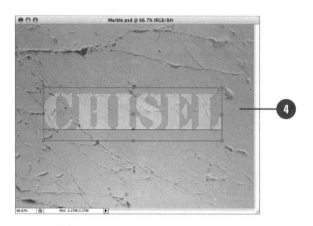

4

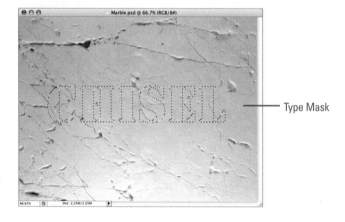

Type Mask

8. Click the layer containing the copied image pixels.

9. Click the **Add Layer Style** button, and then click **Bevel and Emboss**.

10. Select from the following options that will give the text the appearance of being chiseled:

   ◆ **Style.** Inner Bevel

   ◆ **Technique.** Chisel Hard

   ◆ **Depth.** ~150%

   ◆ **Direction.** Down

11. Click **OK**.

See Also

See Chapter 12, "Working with Layer Styles," on page 273 for more information on using layer styles.

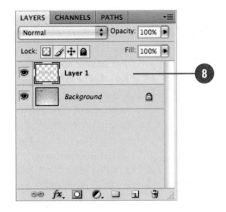

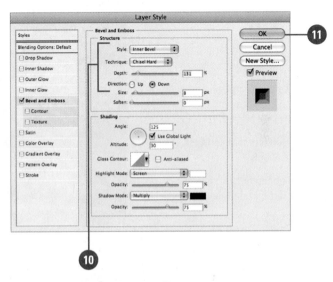

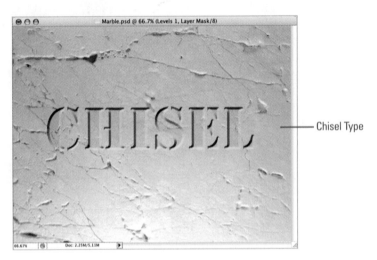

Chisel Type

Using Masks to Generate Special Effects

Using Type masks to generate unique fills or three-dimensional text are great features. However, the shape of the text is always predictable. The mask created with the Type Mask tool will always follow the curve and shape of the font used to create the mask, but not if you combine a Type Mask with a Layer Mask. For example, you create a marketing piece where you are using the word RADICAL, and you want the edges of the word to be more dramatic. You've looked at some of Photoshop's Brush Stroke filters, but you don't want to apply the filter to the image, just to the edges of the word. That's where Type masks and Layer masks do their magic. By combining a Type and Layer mask, you can achieve exactly what you want using an image to fill type, and modifying the edges of the type without distorting the image.

Use Masks for Special Effects

1. Open a document containing the image you want to use for the type effect.

2. Select the **Layers** panel, and then select the layer containing the image.

3. Select the **Horizontal Type Mask** tool on the toolbox.

4. Click in the document window to place an insertion point, and then type.

   As you type, Photoshop creates a mask in the size and shape of the current font.

5. Use the editing tools on the mask to change its font, style, and size.

   IMPORTANT *Sans serif fonts, like Impact, always work best when you're using images to mask text; however, experiment with different fonts.*

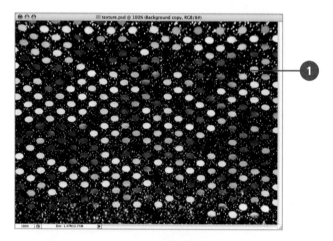

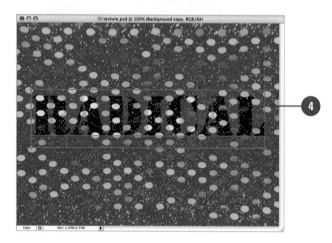

6 Select the **Marquee** tool on the toolbox, and then position the mask directly over the portion of the image you want inside the text.

7 Select the **Layers** panel.

8 Click the **Add Layer Mask** button.

Photoshop creates a layer mask from the type mask, and then selects the layer mask.

IMPORTANT *The Background cannot hold a layer mask. If the layer designated as the masking layer is Background, move into the Layers panel and double-click on the Background thumbnail, give it a new name, and then click OK.*

9 Click the **Filters** menu, point to **Brush Strokes**, and then click **Spatter**.

10 Modify the Brush Stroke options until you are happy with the results.

◆ Spray Radius (from 0-25)

◆ Smoothness (from 1-15)

11 Click **OK**.

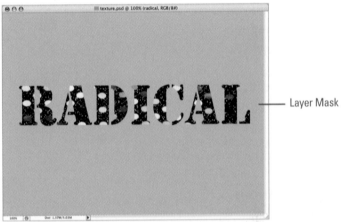

Layer Mask

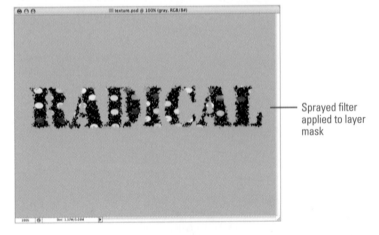

Sprayed filter applied to layer mask

Creating and Modifying Text on a Path

Using the type options, you can enter type that flows along the edge of a work path created by the Pen or Shape tool. When you enter type along a path, it flows in the direction in which anchor points were added to the path. For example, creating horizontal type on a path creates type that is perpendicular to the baseline, while creating vertical type on a path creates type parallel to the baseline. Once the type is created, selecting the Direct Selection tool allows you to reshape the path, and the type will change to fit the new form of the path.

Create and Modify Text on a Path

1. Select a **Pen** or **Shape** tool on the toolbox, and then create a path.

2. Select a typing tool (horizontal, vertical, or mask type tools) on the toolbox.

3. Position the pointer directly over the path, and then click once.

   The path now has an insertion point added to the line.

4. Type the text you want. As you type, the words flow along the curve of the path.

5. Select the **Direct Selection** tool on the toolbox to access and modify the path by controlling the position and shape of the anchor points.

6. Select the **Path Selection** tool and click at the front of the text to move the text forward and backward on the path.

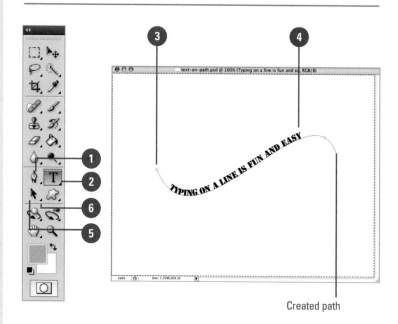

Created path

For Your Information

Printing Type on a Path

The path does not appear when the document is printed. If you want to see how the image will appear without the path, click the View menu, point to Show, and then click to uncheck the Target Path. To view the path, recheck the Target Path option.

Manipulating Images with Filters

14

Introduction

Adobe Photoshop filters are a designer's dream come true. With filters you can turn a photograph into an oil painting or a watercolor; you can even change night into day. Photoshop's Filter menu includes no less than 105 highly creative filters, which can be applied once, reapplied, or combined with other filters to create any effect your imagination can dream up.

The potential combination of filters and images literally runs into the millions. This means that Photoshop filters are truly an undiscovered territory. As a matter of fact, the Filter Gallery lets you view the effects of one or more filters on the active document. This level of power gives you unbelievable creative control over your images.

Other commands, such as the Fade command, let you reduce the effect of the applied filter. You can even apply a blending mode to the final image. In addition, you can utilize a channel mask to control how the filter is applied to the image. You could also use a black to white gradient channel mask to slowly fade the effects of the filter from left to right.

Photoshop even lets you protect your intellectual property by embedding a customizable watermark into the image that is almost invisible to see, and virtually impossible to remove. In fact, you can print an image that contains a watermark, run it off on a copy machine and rescan it, and the watermark is still there. Now that's protection.

Take a moment to view some of the various filter effects that Photoshop offers. Because there are 105 filters available, we can't show you all of them, but we think you'll enjoy viewing the selection at the end of the chapter.

What You'll Do

Work with the Filter Gallery

Create and Work with Smart Filters

Apply Multiple Filters to an Image

Modify Images with Liquify

Work with Liquify Tool Options

Work with Liquify Mask Options

Work with Liquify View Options

Create a Liquify Mesh

Apply a Liquify Mesh

Use the Lens Blur Filter

Work with Photo Filters

Blend Modes and Filter Effects

Build Custom Patterns

Use the Fade Command

Control Filters Using Selections

Use a Channel Mask to Control Filter Effects

Protect Images with Watermarks

View Various Filter Effects

Working with the Filter Gallery

 PS 2.6

The Filter Gallery enables you to maintain complete and total control over Photoshop's filters. In essence, the Filter Gallery gives you access to all of Photoshop's filters and lets you apply the filters to any raster image, while viewing a large preview of the results. The Filter Gallery dialog box is composed of three sections—Image Preview, Filter Selection, and Filter Controls. When you use the Filter Gallery to modify the image, you see exactly how the image will look; there is no guess-work involved. When you apply a filter to an image, you are physically remapping the pixel information within the image. Photoshop contains 105 filters and the combinations of those filters are astronomical. If you are a math wizard, you know there are over 100 million combinations available, and that means no one has yet discovered all the ways you can manipulate an image in Photoshop...have fun trying.

Work with the Filter Gallery

1. Open a document.

2. Select the **Layers** panel, and then select the layer you want to modify with a filter effect.

3. Click the **Filter** menu, and then click **Filter Gallery**.

4. Change the image preview by clicking the plus or minus zoom buttons, or by clicking the black triangle and selecting from the preset zoom sizes.

5. If necessary, drag the lower right corner in or out to resize the Filter Gallery dialog box.

6. Click the **expand triangle**, located to the left of the individual categories, to expand a filter category. Filter categories include:

   ◆ Artistic

   ◆ Brush Strokes

   ◆ Distort

   ◆ Sketch

   ◆ Stylize

   ◆ Texture

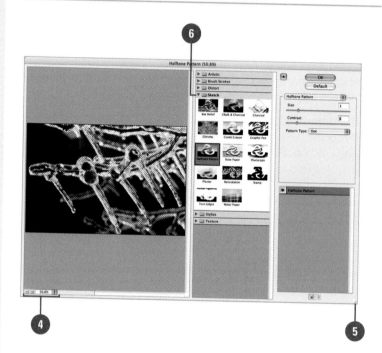

7 Click a filter from the expanded list to view its default effects on the image.

8 Modify the effects of the filter using the filter controls.

9 To temporarily hide the Filter Selections, click the **Show/Hide Filter Thumbnails** button, located to the left of the OK button.

10 Click **OK**.

Did You Know?

You can reapply a specific filter effect using a shortcut. Press Ctrl+F (Win) or ⇧⌘+F (Mac) to reapply the last filter to the image.

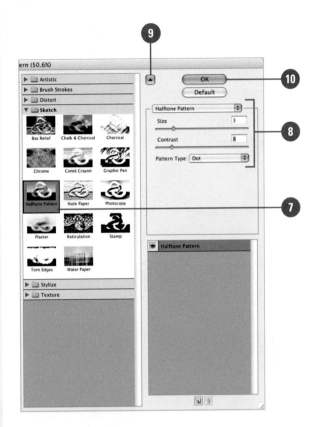

Creating and Working with Smart Filters

Create and Work with Smart Filters

1. Open a document.

2. Use one of the following to create a Smart Filter:

   ◆ **Smart Object layer.** Select a Smart Object layer, click the **Filter** menu, select a filter, then specify the options you want.

   ◆ **Normal layer.** Select the layer, click the **Filter** menu, click **Convert for Smart Filters**, and then click **OK**.

3. Select the layer with the Smart Filters in the Layers panel.

4. Click the arrow to the right of the layer to display the filter effects.

5. Select from the following:

   ◆ **Show or Hide.** Click the eye icon.

   ◆ **Move.** Drag the effect up or down the list.

   ◆ **Delete.** Drag the effect to the Delete icon at the bottom of the Layers panel.

   ◆ **Duplicate.** Hold down Alt (Win) or Option (Mac), and then drag the Smart Filter from one Smart Object to another, or to a new location in the Smart Filters list.

When you apply a filter to a Smart Object, the filter becomes a nondestructive Smart Filter. If you don't have a Smart Object, you can convert a normal layer for Smart Filters. Smart Filters appear in the Layers panel below the Smart Object layer, where you can show or hide them independently. You can apply any filter to a Smart Object except Liquify and Vanishing Point.

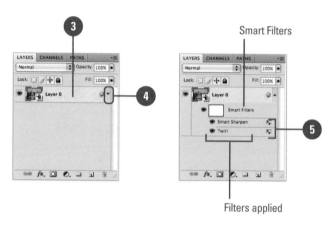

Filters applied

Filters applied to Smart Object

Applying Multiple Filters to an Image

 PS 2.6

Not only does Photoshop's Filter Gallery let you apply and view a filter effect, it lets you view the multiple effects of two or more filters. The Filter Gallery has its own Layers panel, and you can have multiple filter layers. The order of the filters influences their impact on the image, so when you use more than one filter, try dragging the filter layer up or down in the stack to see the different possibilities. Experiment with different stacking orders to create unique, eye-popping special effects.

Apply Multiple Filters to an Image

1. Open a document.

2. Select the **Layers** panel, and then select the layer you want to modify with a filter effect.

3. Click the **Filter** menu, and then click **Filter Gallery**.

4. Select the filter you want.

5. Adjust the filter as necessary.

6. Click the **New Layer Effect** button, located at the bottom of the Filter Adjustments section. You can add as many effects layers as needed.

7. Select and adjust a second filter (repeat steps 4 and 5).

8. Adjust each individual effect by clicking on the effect layer you want to change.

9. To change the filter's influence on the image, drag an effect layer to another position in the stack.

10. To temporarily show or hide the effect on the image, click the **Show/Hide** button.

11. To delete a selected effect layer, click the **Delete** button.

12. Click **OK**.

   IMPORTANT *Once you click the OK button, the effects are permanently applied to the active image, unless it's a Smart Object.*

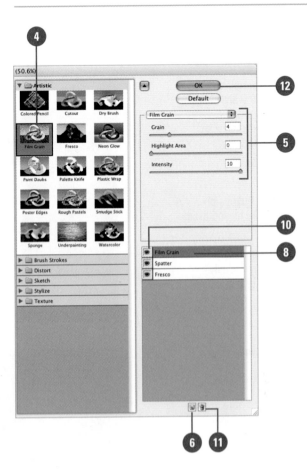

Modifying Images with Liquify

The Liquify filter gives you amazing control over an image. For example, you can distort the image pixels almost as if the image were an oil painting that had yet to dry. In addition, you can magnify specific areas of an image or reduce them in size. The Liquify filter lets you push, pull, rotate, reflect, pucker, and bloat any area of an image. The distortions you create can be subtle or drastic, which makes the Liquify command a powerful tool for retouching images as well as for creating artistic effects.

Modify Images with Liquify

1. Open a document.

2. Select the **Layers** panel, and then select the layer you want to liquify.

3. Click the **Filter** menu, and then click **Liquify**.

4. Select from the following Liquify tools:

   ◆ **Forward Warp.** Pushes pixels in front of the brush as you drag.

   ◆ **Reconstruct.** Drag inside the image, using a specific brush size to restore previously modified areas of the image.

   ◆ **Twirl Clockwise.** Click in an area to twirl the pixels (contained inside the brush tip) clockwise. To twirl counter clockwise, hold down the Alt (Win) or Option (Mac) key.

   ◆ **Pucker.** Click and hold to move pixels towards the center of the brush tip.

   ◆ **Bloat.** Click and hold to move pixels away from the center of the brush tip.

   ◆ **Push Left.** Drag to push pixels to the left of the brush tip. For example, dragging straight up pushes pixels to the left, and dragging to the right pushes pixels up.

Forward Warp

Twirl Clockwise

- **Mirror.** Drag to copy pixels to the left of the stroke.

- **Turbulence.** Smoothly scrambles the pixels in an image. Creates realistic waves or fire.

- **Freeze.** Paints a mask over an area of the image, and then protects that area from change.

- **Thaw.** Erases the protective mask created with the Freeze tool.

- **Hand.** Drag to move the visible image. Useful if the image is larger than the physical document window.

- **Zoom.** Click to zoom in on a specific area of the image. Click and drag to define an area to zoom in on. Hold down the Alt (Win) or Option (Mac) key and click to zoom out.

5 Click **OK**.

Bloat

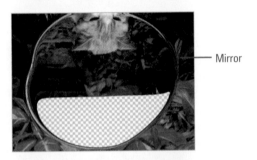

Mirror

Turbulence

Working with Liquify Tool Options

The Liquify Tool options control the brush tip. Since all the Liquify commands are executed with a brush, it's important to understand how you control the brush tip. When you apply the brush stroke, the faster you drag the mouse, the less effect is applied to the image; if you drag slowly, you gain more control and the effect is more intense. Practice dragging the cursor over the image to produce different effects, and if you make a mistake, don't forget the undo key—Ctrl+Z (Win), ⌘+Z (Mac).

Work with Liquify Tool Options

1. Open a document.

2. Select the **Layers** panel, and then select the layer on which you want to use the liquify tool.

3. Click the **Filter** menu, and then click **Liquify**.

4. Select from the following Liquify Tool options:

   ◆ **Brush Size.** Select a value (1 to 600).

   ◆ **Brush Density.** Select a value (0 to 100). Brush Density controls how much the brush feathers at the ends. Lower values equal increased feathering.

   ◆ **Brush Pressure.** Select a value (1 to 100). Determines how quickly a liquify effect is applied to the image when the brush is moving. The lower the value, the slower the effect.

   ◆ **Brush Rate.** Select a value (0 to 100). Determines how quickly a liquify effect is applied to the image when the brush is stationary. The lower the value, the slower the effect.

   ◆ **Turbulent Jitter.** Select a value (1 to 100). Controls how tightly the Turbulent Jitter tool distorts the image. The higher the value, the more distortion.

Liquify Tool options

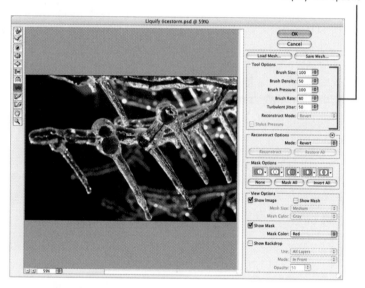

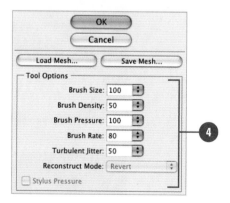

♦ **Reconstruct Mode.** Determines how the Reconstruct tool restores the image. Click the list arrow, and then select from the available options:

♦ Revert

♦ Rigid

♦ Stiff

♦ Smooth

♦ Loose

♦ **Reconstruct.** Click the button to reconstruct the image stage by stage.

♦ **Restore All.** Click the button to restore the image to its original state.

♦ **Stylus Pressure.** Select the check box if you're using a drawing tablet. The pressure you apply to the drawing tablet will now control the pressure applied with the Liquify brush.

5 Click **OK**.

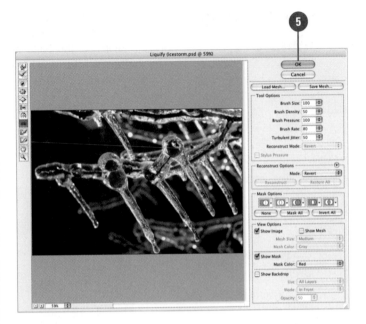

Working with Liquify Mask Options

When you work with an image that contains a selection or mask, you can use that information to control how the Liquify command adjusts the image. Think of the mask as a visual representation of the work areas of the image. Creating a mask gives you precise control over what portions of the image are modified.

Work with Liquify Mask Options

1. Open a document.

2. Select the **Layers** panel, and then select the layer containing a selection or mask.

3. Click the **Filter** menu, and then click **Liquify**.

4. Select from the following Liquify Mask options:

   ◆ **Replace Selection.** Shows the selection, transparency or layer mask in the original image.

   ◆ **Add To Selection.** Shows the mask in the original image, so you can then add to the selection using the Freeze tool.

   ◆ **Subtract From Selection.** Subtracts pixels in selection from current protection created with the Freeze tool.

   ◆ **Intersect With Selection.** Uses only pixels that are selected and currently frozen.

   ◆ **Invert Selection.** Uses your selection to invert the currently frozen area.

5. Click **OK**.

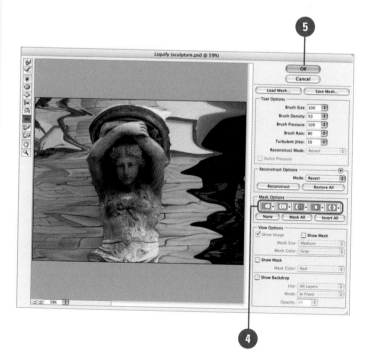

Working with Liquify View Options

The Liquify View Options control what you see in the preview window. For example, you can choose to view or hide a mask, or even change its color. If the image you're working on is in a transparent layer you can even choose to view the image with or without the other image layers. How you view the image is up to you; however, having choices gives you greater control over the final results.

Work with Liquify View Options

① Open a document.

② Select the **Layers** panel, and then select the layer containing a selection or mask.

③ Click the **Filter** menu, and then click **Liquify**.

④ Select from the following Liquify View options:

◆ **Show Image.** Shows/hides the active image preview.

◆ **Show Mesh.** Displays a mesh (grid) over the image preview.

◆ **Mesh Size.** Select between a Small, Medium, or Large mesh.

◆ **Mesh Color.** Select a color for the mesh.

◆ **Show Mask.** Shows/hides the mask.

◆ **Mask Color.** Select a color for the mask.

◆ **Show Backdrop.** Shows/hides the backdrop.

◆ **Use.** Select what layers are displayed in the image preview.

◆ **Mode.** Displays the active layer either In Front, Behind, or Blended with the other layers.

◆ **Opacity.** Determines the blending opacity between the individual layers.

⑤ Click **OK**.

Creating a Liquify Mesh

You may have noticed the Load Mesh and Save Mesh buttons, located at the top of the Liquify dialog box. A **mesh** is a predefined Liquify operation. When you activate the mesh option, a mesh or grid is placed over the image, and then as you use the Liquify tools, the mesh distorts and bends. After applying a lot of work to a particular image, it's quite possible you might want to use that exact mesh on another image. That's where the Load Mesh and Save Mesh options come into play. With the click of a button you can create a mesh and use it over and over again.

Create a Liquify Mesh

1. Open a document.

2. Select the **Layers** panel, and then select the layer on which you want to use the Liquify tool.

3. Click the **Filter** menu, and then click **Liquify**.

4. Select the **Show Mesh** check box.

5. Use the Liquify tools to adjust the image.

6. Click **Save Mesh**.

7. Enter a descriptive name for the mesh.

8. Click **Save**.

9. Click **OK**.

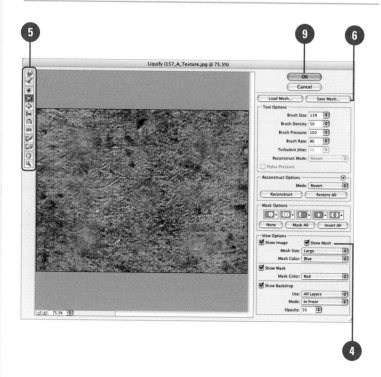

Did You Know?

You can display the distortion created by the Liquify tools. Check this option to display a mesh (grid) over the image preview. When you select the Show Mesh check box, a mesh is applied to an image, which distorts as you apply the Liquify tools. When you clear the Show Image check box (dimming the image), you get a visual grid that represents the distortion values applied to the image.

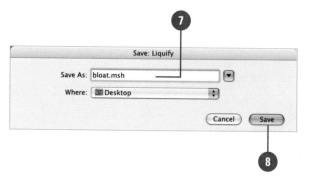

Applying a Liquify Mesh

Applying a mesh to an image is a lot easier than redoing a particular Liquify operation and to be honest, it would be virtually impossible to reproduce a Liquify adjustment from scratch. That's why Adobe gives you the option of creating, saving, and loading your very own personalized meshes.

Apply a Liquify Mesh

1. Open a document.

2. Select the **Layers** panel, and then select the layer on which you want to use the Liquify tool.

3. Click the **Filter** menu, and then click **Liquify**.

4. Select the **Show Mesh** check box.

5. Click **Load Mesh**.

6. Select a mesh.

7. Click **Open**.

   The distortions generated by the mesh are applied to the image.

8. Click **OK**.

Did You Know?

You can modify a loaded mesh. Open a mesh, and then use the Liquify options to further distort the mesh pattern. That way you can create a generic mesh pattern and modify the pattern to fit any design need.

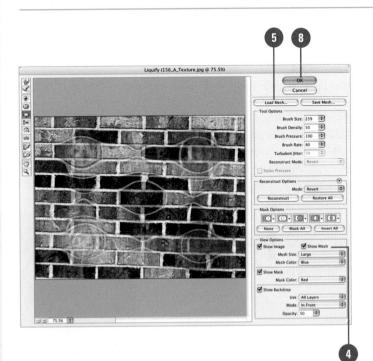

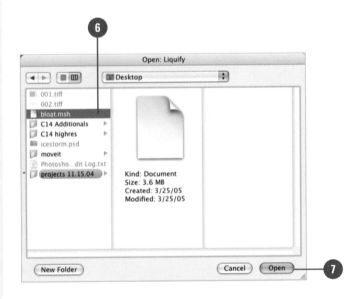

Using the Lens Blur Filter

The Lens Blur filter creates a varying depth of field so that certain objects stay in focus and other areas become blurred. What stays in focus and what is blurred is determined by a user-defined selection or alpha channel. When the filter is activated, a depth map is created to determine the three-dimensional position of the pixels in an image. If you use an alpha channel, the black areas in the alpha channel are at the front of the photo, and the white areas are in the distance. Experiment with selections and alpha channel masks to see how precisely you can control the visual effect of blurring in an image.

Use the Lens Blur Filter

1. Open a document.

2. Select the **Layers** panel, and then select the layer to which you want to apply the Lens Blur.

3. Create a selection or alpha mask to control the blur.

4. Click the **Filter** menu, point to **Blur**, and then click **Lens Blur**.

   The Lens Blur dialog box opens.

See Also

See "Using the Gaussian Blur and Despeckle Filters" on page 154 for information on using filters.

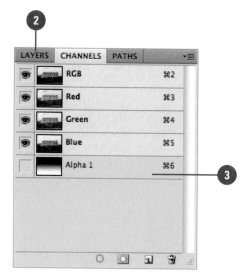

5 Select from the following options:

◆ **Preview.** Select Faster to generate quicker preview, or More Accurate to view the image with the filter applied.

◆ **Depth Map.** Select a source from the Source list arrow.

◆ **Blur Focal Distance.** Drag the slider to set the depth at which pixels are in focus. The higher the value, the greater the effect.

◆ **Invert.** Inverts the selection or alpha channel.

◆ **Shape.** Select an iris option from the Shape list arrow.

◆ **Radius.** Drag the slider to add more blur.

◆ **Blade Curvature.** Drag the slider to smooth out the edges of the iris.

◆ **Rotation.** Drag the slider to rotate the iris.

◆ **Brightness.** Drag the slider to increase the brightness of the highlights.

◆ **Threshold.** Drag the slider to select a brightness cutoff so that all the pixels that are brighter than that value are treated as highlights.

◆ **Amount.** Drag the slider to add or remove noise.

◆ **Uniform or Gaussian.** Select one method to add noise to an image.

◆ **Monochromatic.** Adds noise without affecting the color in your image.

6 Click **OK**.

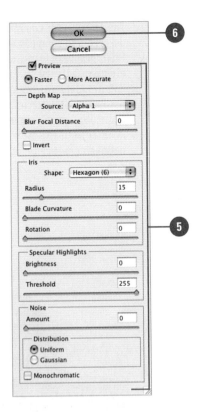

Image with Lens Blur filter applied

Working with Photo Filters

The Photo Filter command reproduces the same effect of placing a colored filter in front of the camera lens when you take a picture. Photographers place colored filters in front of a camera lens to adjust the color balance of the image and control the color temperature of the light transmitted through the lens. In addition to simulating a color filter, the Photo Filter command also lets you select a color preset and apply a specific hue adjustment to an image. If you want to apply a custom color adjustment, the Photo Filter command lets you specify a user-defined color using the Adobe Color Picker.

Work with Photo Filters

1. Open a document.

2. Select the **Layers** panel, and then select the layer to which you want to apply the Photo Filter.

3. Click the **Image** menu, point to **Adjustments**, and then click **Photo Filter**.

4. Select the **Preview** check box to view the results of the color filter directly in the active document window.

5. Select from the following options:

   ◆ **Filter.** Click the list arrow, and then select from the available filter presets.

   ◆ **Color.** Click the color box, and then select a color using the Color Picker dialog box.

   ◆ **Density.** Drag the slider to increase or decrease the impact the color has on the image.

   ◆ **Preserve Luminosity.** Select the check box to prevent the image's lightness values from being changed as a result of adding a color filter (recommended).

6. Click **OK**.

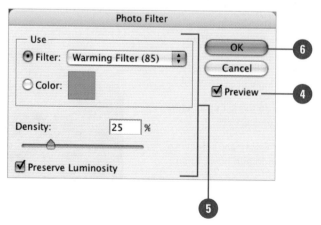

Blending Modes and Filter Effects

PS 4.4

When Adobe introduced the Filter Gallery in Photoshop CS, it finally gave designers the ability to view the effects of multiple filters applied to a single image. While this changed forever how we apply filters to an image, there is one more creative way to work—Blending Modes. For example, you can make a copy of an image, apply a separate filter effect to each layer, and then use the Blending Modes option to create a totally different image. While this is not a new technique, the results of combining two or more layers together, each with a different filter effect, can produce quite stunning results.

Work with Blending Modes and Filter Effects

1. Open an image.

2. Select the layer containing the image you want to modify.

3. Press Ctrl+J (Win) or ⌘+J (Mac) to create a copy of the selected layer.

4. Select the layers one at a time and apply a different filter to each layer.

5. Select the top layer.

6. Click the **Blending Modes** list arrow and experiment with the various blending options.

   In this example, the Cutout and Find Edges filters were used on the separate layers, and then combined with the Linear Light Blending Mode.

Did You Know?

You can use the Opacity option to further control the final image. If the blending effect appears a bit too intense, simply lower the opacity of the top or bottom layer to change the intensity of the filter effects.

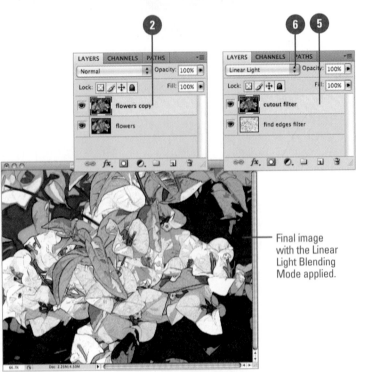

Final image with the Linear Light Blending Mode applied.

Building Custom Patterns

PS 2.5

The Pattern Maker filter lets you create your own distinctive patterns, based on image information in the active document, or clipboard memory. Since the pattern is based on sample data, it shares the visual characteristics of the sample. For example, if you sample an image of a cloudy sky, the Pattern Maker generates a tile-like pattern that is different from the sample but still retains the elements of a cloudy sky. You can even generate multiple patterns from the same sample.

Build Custom Patterns

① Open a document.

② Select the **Layers** panel, and then select the layer you want to use to create a pattern.

③ Click the **Filter** menu, and then click **Pattern Maker**.

If the filter is not available, go to *www.adobe.com*, search for the filter, and then download it.

④ Select the **Rectangular Marquee** tool on the toolbox, and then select a portion of the image.

⑤ Select the portion of the image you want to use to generate an image.

⑥ Click **Generate** to create a random pattern based on the selected sample.

⑦ Click **Generate Again** to generate another random pattern.

IMPORTANT *All the generated patterns are stored in the Tile History box, located on the bottom right of the Pattern Maker dialog box.*

⑧ Select from the available Tile Generation options:

◆ **Use Clipboard As Sample.** Uses the pixel information contained in the Clipboard as the tile-generating pattern.

◆ **Use Image Size.** Creates a tile pattern the size of the original image.

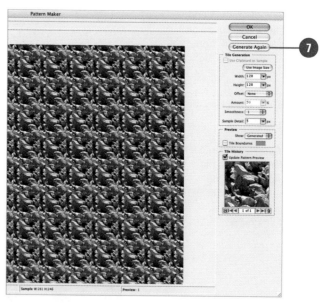

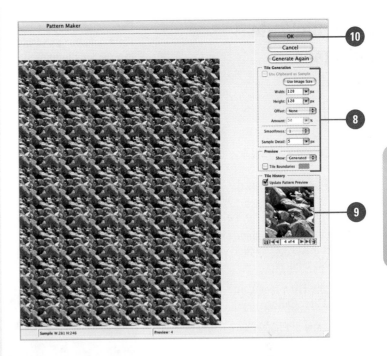

◆ **Width.** Enter a value (1 to 800), or click the black triangle and drag the slider left or right to define a width.

◆ **Height.** Enter a value (1 to 800), or click the black triangle and drag the slider left or right to define a height.

◆ **Offset.** Click the list arrow, and then click None, Horizontal, or Vertical.

◆ **Amount.** Enter a percentage value (1% to 100%), or click the black triangle and drag the slider left or right.

◆ **Smoothness.** Click the list arrow, and then select a value of 1, 2, or 3.

◆ **Sample Detail.** Enter a value from 3 to 21, or click the black triangle and drag the slider left or right.

◆ **Show.** Click the list arrow, and then select between the generated sample and the original image.

◆ **Tile Boundaries.** Select the check box to view the tile edges in the preview window. Click on the color box, and then select an alternate color.

⑨ Scroll through your tile patterns using the left/right arrow keys underneath the Tile History preview. Stop when you see the pattern you want.

⑩ Click **OK**.

IMPORTANT *When you click OK, the Pattern Maker filter over-writes the original image, so it's a good idea to make a copy of the image in a separate layer before using the Pattern Maker filter.*

For Your Information

Using Pattern Maker

Custom patterns can be generated from any RGB, Grayscale, CMYK, or Lab Color mode graphic image. In addition, when you create a pattern, the original image is overwritten with the new pattern, so you can use the generated pattern, reopen the Pattern Maker filter, and then create new patterns from the pattern you just created.

Using the Fade Command

Photoshop's Fade command is a one-shot chance to change your mind. For example, you've just applied the Find Edges filter to an image. You like the look but the effect is too dramatic. What you really want to do is tone down the effect. Unfortunately, filter effects don't fade like a gradient; they are simply applied, all or nothing, to the image. You could create a copy of the original layer, apply the effect to the copy, and then use Layer transparency and blending mode options to merge the effect with the image, but there's an easier way. Just use the Fade command.

Use the Fade Command

1. Open a document.

2. Select the **Layers** panel, and then select the layer to which you want to apply a filter.

3. Click the **Filter** menu, and then click **Filter Gallery**.

4. Apply any of Photoshop's filters to the active image.

5. Click **OK**.

6. Click the **Edit** menu, and then click **Fade**. The Fade command includes the name of the applied filter.

   IMPORTANT *The Fade command must be executed before performing any other command. Once you execute another command, the ability to modify the last filter is lost.*

7. Change the Opacity and Mode settings until you see the effect you're after.

8. Click **OK**.

Did You Know?

You can use the Fade command with almost any filter or drawing tool. Every time you draw, use a command or use a filter, the Fade command gives you a one-shot chance to fade and blend.

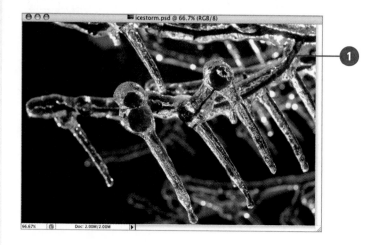

Filter effect and Fade applied

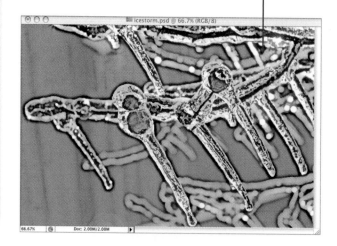

Controlling Filters Using Selections

When you apply a filter to an image, Photoshop applies the filter equally to the entire image. Unfortunately, that might not be what you had in mind. For example, you might want to apply the Gaussian Blur filter to a portion of the image. In that case, Photoshop's selection tools come to the rescue. The primary purpose of making a selection is to define a work area, and when you select an area before applying a filter, the only area impacted by the filter will be the selected area.

Control Filters Using Selections

1. Open a document.

2. Select the **Layers** panel, and then select the layer to which you want to apply a filter.

3. Click one of the selection tools on the toolbox, and then create a selection in the document window.

4. Click the **Filter** menu, and then click **Filter Gallery**.

5. Select any of Photoshop's filters.

6. Adjust the filter options until you see the effect you want.

7. Click **OK**.

    The filter is only applied to the selected areas of the image.

See Also

See Chapter 4, "Mastering the Art of Selection," on page 77 for more information on creating selections.

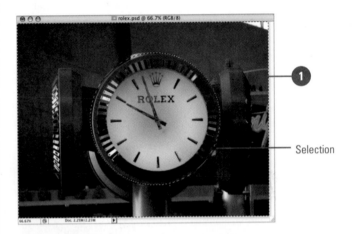

Selection

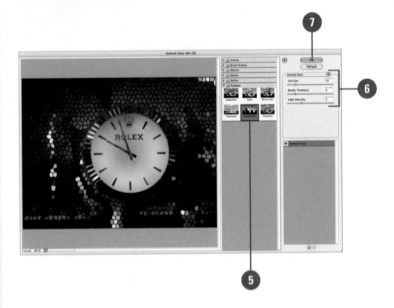

Using a Channel Mask to Control Filter Effects

Photoshop's filters can be applied to any raster image. In addition, filters can be controlled with the use of selections. You can use any of Photoshop's selection tools to define a working area. However, simple selections are limited in what they can do. Although the edge of selections can be modified by feathering, the inside area of the selection is completely selected. What if you want to apply a filter in a completely different way? For example, what if you want to apply a filter that is stronger on the right side of the image, and slowly tapers off from left to right? In that case a simple selection won't help, but a Channel mask will do exactly what you need.

Use a Channel Mask to Control Filter Effects

1. Open a document.

2. Click the **Channels** panel, and then click the **Add New Channel** button.

3. Select the **Gradient** tool on the toolbox, click a linear gradient, select the default foreground and background colors of black and white, and then drag left to right across the new channel mask.

   Photoshop creates a horizontal, black to white channel mask.

4. Select the **Layers** panel, and then select the layer containing the image you want to modify.

See Also

See Chapter 10, "Creating Layer and Channel Masks," on page 231 for information on using Channel Masks.

340

5　Click the **Select** menu, and then click **Load Selection**.

6　Click the **Channel** list arrow, select the new channel, and leave the other options at their default values.

7　Click **OK**.

8　Click the **Filter** menu, and then click **Filter Gallery**.

9　Click any of the available filters, and then adjust the options until you are satisfied with the result.

10　Click **OK**.

The gradient mask (black to white) creates a ramped percentage selection. The white area of the mask is fully selected and the black area is fully masked. As the mask moved to black, the image became less and less selected. When the filter was applied, it lost strength from left to right (matching the shades of gray in the mask).

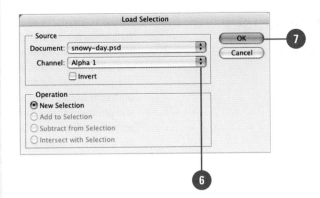

Protecting Images with Watermarks

Digital watermarks are designed to protect your intellectual property. When you embed a digital watermark, it actually inserts the watermark information as visible noise into the image. This means that someone can copy your image, scan it, and the watermark is still part of the image. To embed a digital watermark, you must first register with Digimarc Corporation, which maintains a database of artists, designers, and photographers along with their contact information. You can then embed the Digimarc ID in your images, along with information such as the copyright year or a restricted-use identifier.

Protect Images with Watermarks

1. Open the image you want to watermark.

   IMPORTANT *The Embed Watermark filter won't work on an image that has been previously watermarked.*

2. If you're working with a layered image, you should flatten the image before watermarking it; otherwise, the watermark will affect the active layer only.

3. Click the **Filter** menu, point to **Digimarc**, and then click **Embed Watermark**.

4. If you're using the watermark for the first time, click **Personalize**. Get a Digimarc ID by clicking Info to launch your Web browser and visit the Digimarc Web site at *www.digimarc.com*.

   Enter a Digimarc ID and any other necessary information, and then click OK.

   The Personalize button becomes a Change button, allowing you to enter a new Digimarc ID.

5. Click the **Image Information** list arrow, select an option, and then enter a copyright year, Transaction ID, or Image ID for the image.

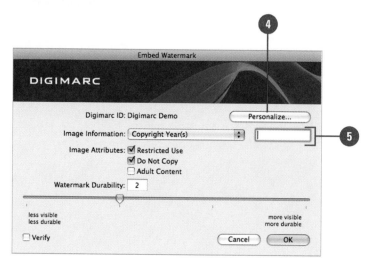

6 Select any of the following Image Attributes check boxes:

◆ **Restricted Use.** Select the check box to limit the use of the image.

◆ **Do Not Copy.** Select the check box to specify that the image should not be copied.

◆ **Adult Content.** Select the check box to label the image contents as suitable for adults only.

7 Choose a level of durability (visibility) for the watermark.

8 Drag the slider, or enter a value (1 to 4). The higher the number, the more aggressive the watermark.

9 To automatically assess the watermark's viability after it's embedded, select the **Verify** check box.

10 Click **OK**.

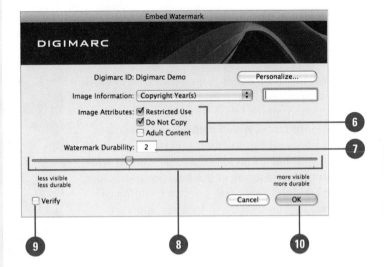

Viewing Various Filter Effects

Photoshop provides a bountiful selection of filters, 105 to be exact. Take a moment to view some of the various filter effects that Photoshop offers. The original image is shown to the right, and we've displayed some common filters on the following pages. A good thing to think about when using filters is your original image. Look at the background colors, and see if they will look good with some of the filters. The best thing to do is open an image that has a lot of varied details, and then apply some filters to see what looks good to you.

Various Filter Effects

Cutout

Dry Brush

Fresco

Palette Knife

Accented Edges

Glass

Diffuse Glow

Note Paper

Stamp

Glowing Edges

Grain

Spatter

Mosaic Tiles

Stained Glass

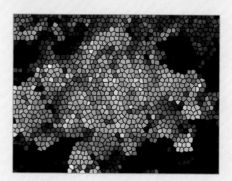

Graphic Pen

Plastic Wrap

Automating Your Work with Actions

15

Introduction

Actions are only one of the Adobe Photoshop Automate commands; however, they're so important to consistency and efficiency, they deserve their own chapter. Actions are Photoshop's way of relieving you of the mind-numbing task of repeating an operation over and over again. For example, you're recovering 55 images from your digital camera, and each image needs to be converted to a specific size and resolution. Instead of repeating the conversion process 55 times, you perform the conversion process once, and save it as a repeatable action.

Actions are similar to recording information on a tape; they record Photoshop commands and, like a tape recorder, can be played back at any time. Actions can be applied to any number of images. You can modify existing actions, and save them into a user-defined set. It's even possible to save them and send them to another Photoshop user. Actions have been a part of Photoshop since version 5, and each evolution of the Actions panel has seen new features and abilities. In Photoshop, it's now possible to create an action out of almost any command, filter, or adjustment, including blending mode changes to layers. This chapter is dedicated to all the Photoshop users who are tired of doing something over and over again. If you have ever considered using actions as a part of your design workflow, then you're in for a wonderful journey of discovery.

You can also enhance your actions by creating a droplet. A **droplet** is an action that appears as a file on your hard drive. For example, you could create a droplet that performs a generic color correction operation. To perform the operation on a Photoshop document, you would not even have to open Photoshop; you would simply drag the image file over the droplet, and release—the droplet does the rest.

Examining the Actions Panel

The Actions panel is where you create, save, modify, and store all of your actions. The analogy of a tape recorder is often used in describing the Actions panel, and it's actually a good way to think of actions. The action itself is a recording, and the Actions panel is the tape recorder. When you begin an action, the panel records each step in the process, saves them, and then lets you play them back on another image. In order to record and play actions, you need to understand how to use the Actions panel.

Examine the Actions Panel

1. Select the **Actions** panel.

2. Check the toggle box to toggle an action on or off.

3. Click the dialog box to toggle the dialog function on or off.

4. Click the **expand triangle** to expand or contract an action or set.

5. Click the **Actions Options** button to access all of the Actions panel options.

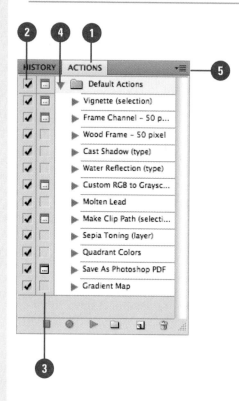

Did You Know?

You can use the Window menu to display the Actions panel. Click the Window menu, and then click Actions.

6 The following buttons are accessible at the bottom of the Actions panel, from left to right:

◆ **Stop.** Click to stop recording and save an action.

◆ **Record.** Click to begin recording an action.

◆ **Play.** Click to begin execution of the selected action.

◆ **Create New Set.** Creates a new action set.

Sets are like file folders; they store individual actions.

◆ **Create New Action.** Starts the process of creating a new action.

◆ **Delete.** Click to delete the selected action or set.

Did You Know?

You can convert your Actions into single-click buttons. Click the Actions Options button, and then click Button Mode. When the Actions panel is in Button Mode, you cannot access or edit the steps in the individual actions. To access the standard Actions panel, click the Actions Options button, and then click Button Mode to uncheck the option.

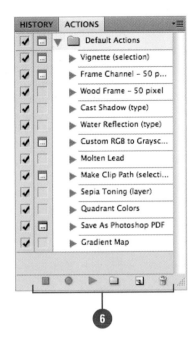

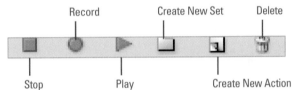

Record   Create New Set   Delete

Stop   Play   Create New Action

Building a New Action

 PS 8.1

Building an action is almost as simple as clicking the record button on a tape recorder. Actions are simply a series of program instructions. When you build an action, you're instructing Photoshop what to name the action, where to store it, and what shortcut keys, if any, will be used to activate the action. Since an action is simply a record of the work performed on an image, it's a good idea to plan out what you intend to do, and then build the action. Remember, actions are designed for tasks you plan to do repeatedly. It wouldn't make sense to create an action for a one-time use.

Build a New Action

① Open a document.

② Select the **Actions** panel.

③ Click the **Create New Action** button.

④ Enter a name for the action in the Name box.

⑤ Click the **Set** list arrow, and then select in which set to save the Action.

⑥ Click the **Function Key** list arrow, and then click F1 - F12 to assign your new action to a function key.

⑦ Select the **Shift** or **Command** check boxes to require the pressing of the Shift key, or the Ctrl (Win) or ⌘ (Mac) key in conjunction with the function key.

For example, F1, or Shift+F1, or Ctrl+F1, or Shift+Ctrl+F1.

⑧ Click the **Color** list arrow, and then select from the available colors.

⑨ Click **Record** to begin creating the action.

IMPORTANT *If you choose a color for the action, it will only be visible if the actions are viewed in Button Mode.*

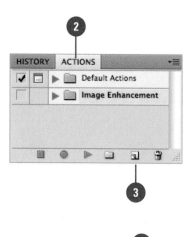

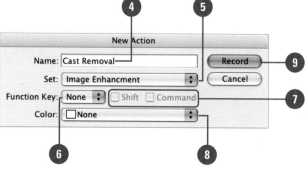

Recording an Action

Once you've planned the steps of your action, it's a simple matter of clicking the Record button and applying a predetermined set of commands to the image. Photoshop watches you like a hawk, faithfully recording each step in the process. When you end the action, Photoshop stores the step-by-step instructions of the action in a file, which is available in the Actions panel whenever you want to use it again. All of your loaded actions are displayed by name in the Actions panel. It's a simple matter of finding the action you want and clicking the Play button to apply the recorded instructions to another document.

Record an Action

1. Open a document.

2. Select the **Actions** panel.

3. Specify the action settings.

4. Click **Record**.

5. Edit the image. Each time you perform an edit, such as applying a filter, adjustments, or commands, the operation is listed as a step in the Actions panel.

   IMPORTANT *The Actions panel doesn't record the time it takes you to perform a command, only that you performed it. So take your time, and work carefully through the process. Creating an action right the first time saves editing hassles later.*

6. Click the **Stop** button on the Actions panel.

   The action is saved and listed in the current Action Set.

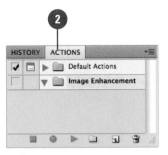

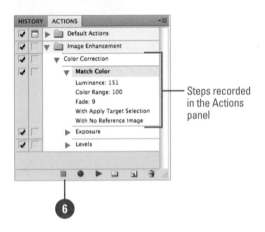

Steps recorded in the Actions panel

Adding a Stop to an Action

PS 8.1

There are times when you want to make changes to individual files during the playback of an action. For example, you create an action to balance the contrast in an image, and one of the commands you use is a Levels adjustment. Although none of the other commands need user modification during playback, an optimum Levels adjustment is specific to individual images. What you want is the action to perform (automatically) all of the steps, except Levels. When the action reaches the point where the Levels adjustment would be applied, you want the action to stop and let you make changes that are appropriate for that particular image and then move on to complete the rest of the steps when you've finalized the Levels adjustment by clicking OK.

Add a Stop to an Action

1. Open a document, and then select the **Actions** panel.

2. Click the **expand triangle** of the action you want to modify.

3. Click the command directly above where you want to place the action.

4. Click the **Actions Options** button, and then click **Insert Stop**.

5. Enter a text message associated with the purpose of the stop action.

6. Select the **Allow Continue** check box to add a Continue button to the stop alert box.

7. Click **OK**.

8. Click the **Play** button on the Actions panel to run the action.

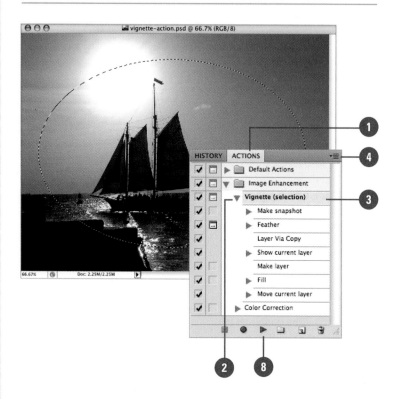

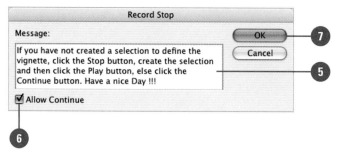

Controlling the Playback of a Command

Control the Playback of a Command

1. Open a document, and then select the **Actions** panel.

2. Click the **expand triangle** of the action you want to modify.

3. Uncheck the command or commands you do not want to execute.

4. Click the **Play** button on the Actions panel to run the action without executing the unchecked command(s).

5. Recheck the command(s) to return them to executable status.

See Also

See "Working with Batch File Processing" on page 398 for information on applying an action to multiple files at once.

Not all actions are created perfectly. Sooner or later, you'll work through the process of action building only to find out (after the action is saved), that you forgot a step, or you need to remove or modify an existing step. You might even need to change the order of the commands in the action. Fortunately, Photoshop doesn't make you recreate the action; all you have to do is modify it. When you create an action, all of the commands execute in the order they appear in the list of action steps. However, it's possible you might occasionally want to skip one of the steps in the list, without permanently deleting it.

Adding a Command to an Action

Actions are very versatile; in fact, almost anything that can be done to an image can be placed into an action. You might find that as you perform an action, you need to add an additional command. You can do this with ease; that's why actions are so great to work with. For example, you might create an action to convert an image from the RGB to the CMYK mode, and after you save the action, you decide it would be great to include a Curves adjustment. You don't have to throw away the previous action and start all over; all you have to do is select where the command will be inserted, restart the action, and perform the new step. The Actions panel is a powerful time-saving tool, and if you forget a step, it's also a breeze to modify.

Add a Command to an Action

1. Open a document, and then select the **Actions** panel.

2. Click the **expand triangle** of the action to which you want to add the command.

3. Click the command directly above where you want to insert the new command.

4. Click the **Actions Options** button, and then click **Start Recording**.

5. Add the additional command by selecting a filter, adjustment, or any other Photoshop option.

6. When you're finished adding commands, click the **Stop** button on the Actions panel.

   The next time the action is run, the additional command will be performed.

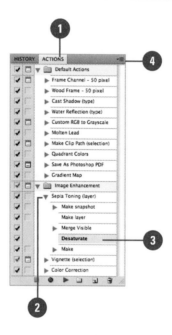

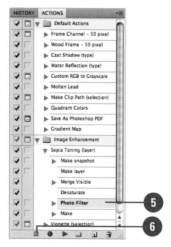

Deleting a Command from an Action

Adobe Certified Expert PS 8.1

Occasionally, you may want to permanently delete a command from an existing action. If that's the case, Photoshop makes the process quick and easy. An action consists of a group of steps. As the action executes, each step is completed in the order in which it appears within the action list. No one step is dependent upon another, so if you want to remove a step, it's a simple process of deletion. Once the command is removed, the action will perform as if the deleted command never existed.

Delete a Command from an Action

1. Open a document, and then select the **Actions** panel.

2. Click the **expand triangle** of the action from which you want to delete the command.

   IMPORTANT *You cannot delete a command from a running action.*

3. Click the command you want to delete.

4. Select from three deletion methods:

   ◆ Drag the command over the **Delete** button.

   ◆ Click the command, click the **Delete** button, and then click **OK** in the Delete the Selection alert box.

   ◆ Click the command, and then hold down the Alt (Win) or Option (Mac) key, and then click the **Delete** button to delete the command without the alert box message.

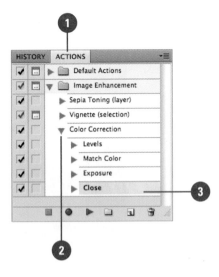

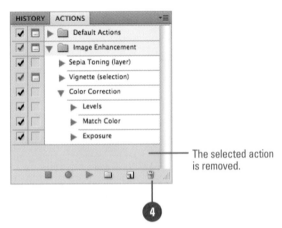

The selected action is removed.

Working with Modal Controls in an Action

PS 8.1

Modal controls are pauses in an action that allow you to modify a command before proceeding. Modal controls are available for every Photoshop command that utilizes a dialog box, or any command that requires the pressing of the Enter/Return key to process the effect. For example, you create an action that utilizes a Levels adjustment, and you want the option to specify a particular Levels adjustment each time the action is run.

Work with Modal Controls

1. Open a document, and then select the **Actions** panel.

2. Click the **expand triangle** of the action you want to modify.

3. Click the second column from the left to activate the Modal Control button.

4. Click an existing modal control button to deactivate the control.

5. Click the **Play** button on the Actions panel to run the action.

    The action stops and lets you control the command.

6. Adjust the image using the Exposure dialog box.

7. Click **OK** to continue the action.

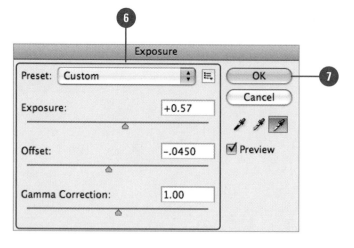

Changing the Order of Commands in an Action

PS 8.1

When an action runs, it performs each command in the order in which it appears in the action list. Since the order in which a filter or adjustment is applied to an image determines the document's final appearance, it's important to be able to adjust the order in which the commands are executed. For example, if you create an action that contains a Curves adjustment followed by a Gaussian Blur filter, and you move the Gaussian Blur filter above the Curves adjustment, it will totally change the look of the final image. The Actions panel gives you the ability to change the order in which commands are executed so that you will be in control of the end result.

Change the Order of Commands

1. Open a document, and then select the **Actions** panel.

2. Click the **expand triangle** of the action you want to change.

3. Drag the command you want to change up or down in the actions stack.

4. Release the mouse when you see a dark line underneath the command where you want the dragged one to be placed.

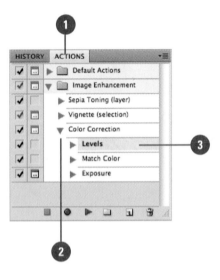

Copying an Action

PS 8.1

What if you create an action with several commands, and you need a similar, but not identical, action? Perhaps you have made an action that performs several commands and ends with the Curves adjustment. Then you find you need a new action that performs the same initial commands but ends with the Levels adjustment. If that's the case, there is no need to reinvent the wheel; just create the first action, make a copy, and then modify the copy.

Copy an Action

① Open a document, and then select the **Actions** panel.

② Click the **expand triangle** of the action you want to change.

③ Select how you want to duplicate the action:

   ◆ Drag the action over the **Create New Action** button on the Actions panel.

   ◆ Select the action, click the **Actions Options** button, and then click **Duplicate**.

Actions Options button

Copied action

Running an Action Inside an Action

 PS 8.1

You can make an action run within another action, thus reducing action complexity. For example, you could create an action that performs a dozen or more commands (it's not unusual), or you could create two simpler actions, and have one action load and run the other action. That way, when it comes time to modify the action, you have a smaller list of commands to deal with. You can also call actions from more than one source, giving you the ability to create small action codes that can be used over and over again.

Run an Action Inside an Action

1. Open a document, and then select the **Actions** panel.

2. Click the **expand triangle** of the action you want to modify.

3. Click the command directly above where you want to insert the run step for the other action.

4. Click the **Record** button.

5. Click the action to be added.

6. Click the **Play** button to record the second action into the first action.

7. Click the **Stop** button.

   The second action is recorded inside the first action.

   IMPORTANT When you click the Play button, the action executes on the active document, so you might want to perform this on a duplicate image.

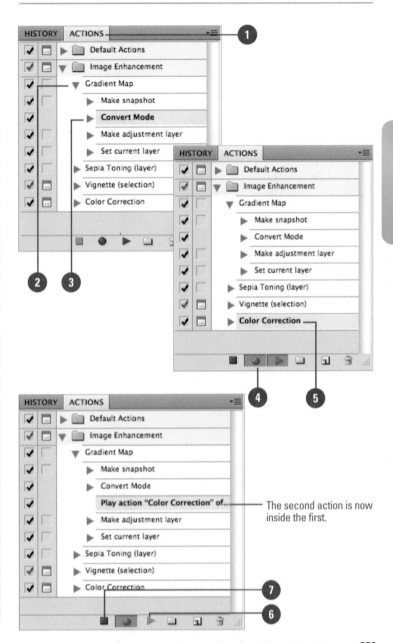

The second action is now inside the first.

Saving Actions into Sets

PS 8.1

Once you discover the advantages of using actions, you'll be creating actions for all those dull, boring, repetitive tasks, and life inside Photoshop will never be the same again. As the days go on, you'll see your list of actions growing longer and longer. Sooner or later (probably sooner), you'll develop so many actions that scrolling down the Actions panel to find your favorite actions becomes a job in itself. The Actions panel can hold as many actions as you need, and it also gives you the ability to organize those actions into sets. Action sets are like file folders; they hold groups of actions. For example, you might have a group of actions that perform image restoration, and another group for color correction. Using the Actions panel, you can create an action set for each different group of actions. Once a set is created, it can be removed from the Actions panel, and reloaded when needed. Action sets can also be distributed to other users.

Save Actions into Sets

1. Open a document, and then select the **Actions** panel.

2. Click the **Create New Set** button.

3. Enter a name for the new set.

4. Click **OK**.

   The new set is added to the Actions panel.

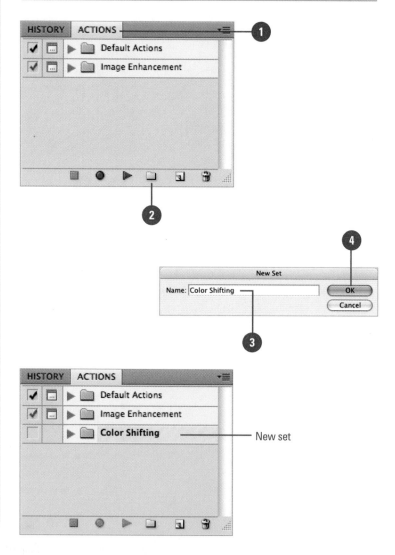

Saving Actions as Files

 PS 8.1

When you create a new set of actions, Photoshop displays the actions in the Actions panel, but the actions are not permanently saved to the hard drive. That means if you delete an unsaved action or action set, they will be gone forever. To stop that from happening, you need to save the sets. Not only does this give you the ability to save your precious actions, it lets you share your actions with other Photoshop users. For example, you have a friend who's having trouble performing color correction to an image. You'd like to help her, but she lives 800 miles away. So you create an action that performs the color correction, save the action as a file, and e-mail her the file. Now, all she has to do is click the Actions Options button, and then click Load Actions. She now has the action to color correct her images.

Save Actions as Files

1. Select the **Actions** panel.

2. Click the set you want to save.

3. Click the **Actions Options** button, and then click **Save Actions**.

4. Enter a name for the action set.

   The default name will be the original name of the set.

5. Click the **Save In** (Win) or **Where** (Mac) list arrow, and then click where to save the set.

6. Click **Save**.

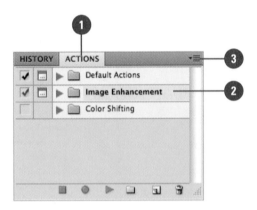

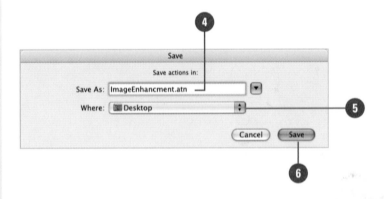

Did You Know?

You can access your new Action Set directly from the Actions dialog box. If you save the new action set in the Photoshop Actions folder, the set appears at the bottom of the Actions Options dialog box.

Moving and Copying Actions Between Sets

 PS 8.1

Once you've created an action set, it's a simple matter to organize all of your time-saving actions. Think of an action set as a file drawer. When you need a specific action, you expand the set, and then locate the proper action. You might want to create sets with names such as Color Correction or Special Effects, for easier retrieval. Then you can create new actions, or move existing actions, into your organized sets. Once the perfect action set is created it can be saved, and even e-mailed to other Photoshop users.

Move and Copy Actions Between Sets

1. Select the **Actions** panel.

2. Click a preexisting set, and then click the **expand triangle** to open the set.

3. Use the following move or copy method:

   ◆ To move an action, drag the action from one set to another.

   ◆ To copy an action, hold down the Alt (Win) or Option (Mac) key, and then drag the action from one set to another.

4. Release when your mouse hovers over the set into which you want to move or copy the selected set.

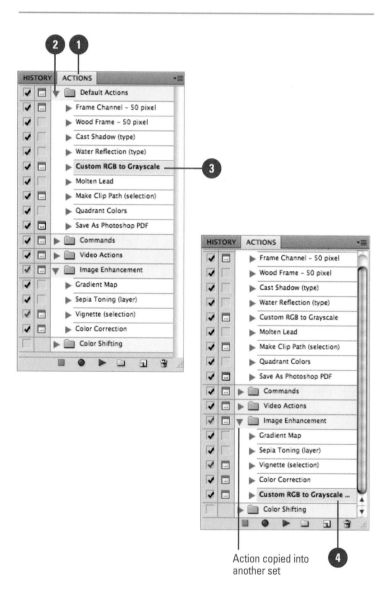

Action copied into another set

Inserting a Non-Recordable Command into an Action

PS 8.1

When you create an action, you cannot record mouse movements, such as a brush stroke, or any of the View and Window commands. However, you can insert many non-recordable commands into an action by using an Insert Menu Item command. The Insert Menu Item command can be used when recording an action or after it has been recorded. Inserted commands do not execute until the action is played, so the file remains unchanged when the command is inserted. This gives you the ability to experiment with different non-recordable commands without the risk of damaging a valuable image.

Insert a Non-Recordable Command into an Action

1. Select the **Actions** panel.

2. Click an action, and then click the **expand triangle**.

3. Click the name of the action to insert the item at the end of the action, or click a specific action step to insert the item after the selected step.

4. Click the **Actions Options** button, and then click **Insert Menu Item**.

5. Select a command from the available options (the command is selected by clicking and selecting an item from Photoshop's drop-down menu system).

6. Click **OK**.

The non-recordable command is added to the action steps.

IMPORTANT *When you use the Insert Menu Item command for a command that opens a dialog box, you cannot disable the modal control in the Actions panel.*

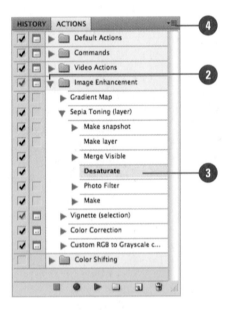

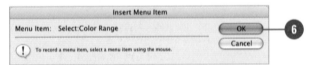

Using Enhanced Scripting

PS 8.5

A **script** is a series of commands that instructs Photoshop to perform a set of specified actions. These actions can be simple, affecting only a single object, or more complex, affecting many objects. The actions can call not only Photoshop, but also invoke other applications such as Adobe Illustrator. Scripts are useful for repetitive tasks and can be used as a creative tool to streamline tasks that are time consuming and boring. For example, you could write a script to access images on your digital camera. The script could process the images, and then create and save the documents in a folder that automatically includes the current date in the folder name, like Nikon 5700-12.12.2005. A scripting language lets you ask a question (an event), and use the answer to that question to perform any commands (an action) that are available in Photoshop. To create your own scripts you need a working knowledge of a scripting language like JavaScript, and either a script-editing application or a simple text editor, such as Notepad (Win), TextEdit (Mac) BBEdit or even Microsoft Word. The languages you can use to perform scripting are varied and include Visual Basic, AppleScript, and JavaScript, to name a few. As a matter of fact, the Scripts Events Manager lets you set JavaScript and Photoshop Actions to run automatically when a specified Photoshop event occurs.

Use Enhanced Scripting

1. Open a text editor, and then create the script using any approved scripting language.

2. Save the document with the correct extension, for example, ActiveLayer.js for JavaScript.

3. To access the script in Photoshop, click the **File** menu, point to **Scripts**, and then click **Browse**.

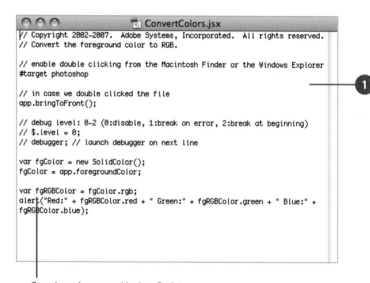

Sample script created in JavaScript

4 Click the **Look In** (Win) or **From** (Mac) list arrow, and then select your script file.

5 Click the script that you want to run.

6 Click **Open** to run the script.

Your script appears in a browser window.

See Also

For more information on Enhanced Scripting, open the Photoshop application folder, and then navigate to the Scripting Guide folder for access to several PDF tutorial files and sample scripts.

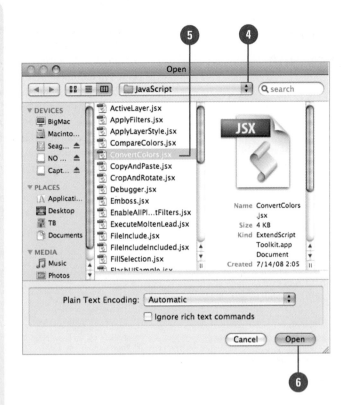

For Your Information

Using Built-in Scripts

You can save time by automating repeated tasks, such as outputting your layers to files or saving Layer Comps as separate pages of an Adobe PDF file, by using user-defined or Photoshop's own enhanced built-in scripts. Click the File menu, point to Scripts, and then select from the available option presets. For more information on how to write your own scripts, see the documentation available in your Adobe Photoshop CS4/Scripting Guide folder.

Enhancing the Process with Droplets

PS 8.2, 8.4

When you apply an action to an image, you open the document in Photoshop, open the Actions panel, select the action, and then click the Play button. While that process is easier than having to redo all the steps in a complicated action, there is a simpler way—create a droplet. Droplets apply Photoshop Actions to your images. They appear as files on your hard drive, or you can organize them within a specific folder. For example, you could create a droplet that performs a generic color correction operation. To perform the operation on a Photoshop document, you would not even have to open Photoshop; simply drag the image file over the droplet and release—the droplet does the rest.

Create a Droplet

1. Click the **File** menu, point to **Automate**, and then click **Create Droplet**.

   IMPORTANT *Droplets are created from existing actions.*

2. Click **Choose**, and then select a location to store the droplet.

3. Click the **Set** list arrow, and then select from the available sets.

4. Click the **Action** list arrow, and then select the action you want to convert into a droplet.

5. Select from the available Play options (see table).

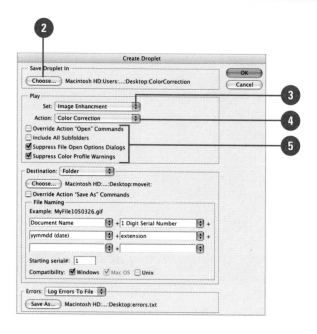

Available Play Options

Option	Purpose
Override Action "Open" Commands	Overrides the batch Open command and uses an embedded Open command in the Action. The Action MUST have an Open command as one of the steps.
Include All Subfolders	Opens any subfolders within the selected folder and performs the action on any files found within.
Suppress File Open Options Dialogs	Does not show any File Open dialog boxes.
Suppress Color Profile Warnings	When a color profile mismatch occurs, does not display a warning dialog box, but just continues.

6 Click the **Destination** list arrow, and then select from the following options:

- **None.** The file remains open after the droplet ends.

- **Save And Close.** The file is resaved (loss of original).

- **Folder.** The file is saved in a new folder (selected by user), with the option of renaming the file and extension.

7 Select from the following File Naming options:

- **Document Name.** Use the original name of the document, or click to choose from various naming schemes, including incrementing the files by a number (001, 002, etc).

- **Extension.** Use the original extension of the document, or click to choose from extension options such as using the date or a sequenced serial number.

- **Starting Serial Number.** If you select to use a serial number, you can select a starting value for the sequence.

- **Compatibility.** Select the check boxes you want from Windows, Mac OS, or Unix or any combination of the three.

8 To create an error log file, click the **Errors** list arrow, and then click **Log Errors To File**.

The error log records any problems associated with applying the droplet to the image file.

9 To specify an error log file name and location, click **Save As**.

10 Click **OK**.

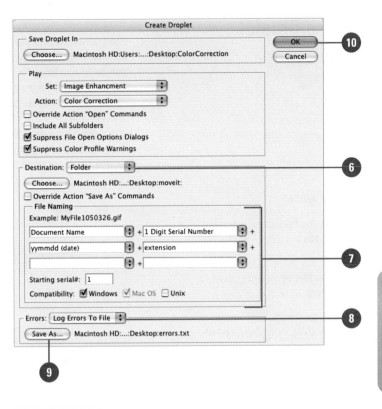

Droplet icon

Using a Droplet

 PS 8.2, 8.4

Once you've created a droplet, it's a simple matter to use it to streamline your workload. For example, you've created a droplet that converts an image into the grayscale color mode, and reduces the image resolution to 72 ppi. To convert an image file to those specifications, just drag the file and drop it on to the droplet. Droplets are files that hold action instructions. Once a droplet is created, you can store them anywhere that you can store a file. It's not a bad idea to create file folders that hold specific types of droplets, such as color-correction droplets, or image-enhancement droplets. To use a droplet, it's as easy as clicking an image file, dragging, and then dropping it over the droplet.

Use a Droplet

1. Open the folder that contains your droplets.

2. Open the folder that contains the image file, or files you need to convert.

3. Drag an image file directly over the droplet, and then release.

    Photoshop automatically opens and applies the selected droplet.

Did You Know?

You can use droplets with more than one file. To use a droplet on more than one image file, hold down the Shift key, select all the image files to which you want to apply the single droplet, and then drag over the droplet. Photoshop applies the droplet to all selected files.

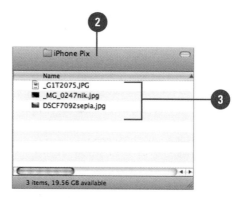

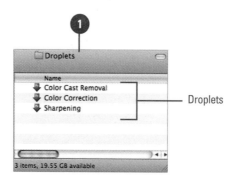

Controlling Image Output

16

Introduction

Once you create your Adobe Photoshop masterpiece, you will have to decide the output for the image file. This is not an easy decision. For example, an image created with a resolution of 72 ppi might be fine if output to the Web, but would not be of sufficient quality for output to a high-quality laser printer. In addition, images saved in the RGB color space would not work if the image were to be printed on a 4-color press, which uses the CMYK color space.

Raster images (such as Photoshop files) do not handle change very well, so it's important to design with a goal in mind. Designers call this process a workflow. When you start a Photoshop project you should have a good idea of where the project is headed—to a press or inkjet printer, a copy machine, or a monitor. Knowing this information helps you design with the end in mind. That's not to say you can't make changes to a Photoshop document; however, when it comes to color space and resolution, the less change, the better the output quality.

When preparing images for the Web, it's important to understand that file size and format are important considerations. People aren't very patient when it comes to downloading web pages. Creating good-looking, yet fast-loading images keeps visitors on your web site, looking for more. Photoshop gives you the ability to perform image compression using formats such as the JPEG (Joint Photographic Experts Group), and GIF (Graphics Interchange Format) formats. Those formats will make your images as small as possible, while still retaining great quality. In image preparation it's all about control, and Photoshop gives you the tools to make the job easy.

Working with Page Setup in Macintosh

Photoshop images can be printed out to virtually any device. For example, an image could find its way to a laser or inkjet printer, or a 4-color press. Even run-of-the-mill copy machines have options to print using information from Photoshop or similar applications used to design the image. What you need is Photoshop, an open image, and a good idea of where you want the image displayed. This may seem easy; however, a few careful adjustments will make all the difference in the world.

Work with Page Setup in Macintosh

1. Open a document.

2. Click the **File** menu, and then click **Page Setup**.

3. Click the **Settings** list arrow, and then click **Page Attributes**.

4. Select from the various Page Attributes options:

   ◆ **Format For.** Click the list arrow, and then select a printer from the available options. If your printer is not accessible from the list, click the Edit Printer List, and then add your printer (you may need the printer disc, or access to the Internet, to load the latest drivers).

   ◆ **Paper Size.** Click the list arrow, and select from the available options. The default printer will determine the available paper sizes.

   ◆ **Orientation.** Click the Portrait or Landscape button; options vary depending on the printer.

   ◆ **Scale.** Enter a percentage value to increase (over 100%) or decrease (under 100%) the size of the printed document.

5. Click **OK**.

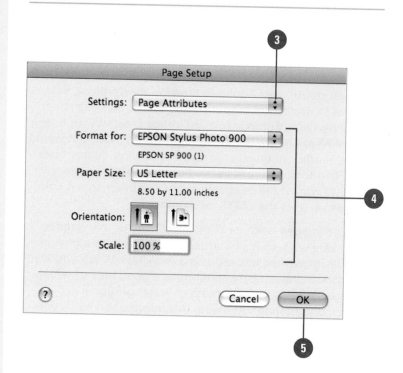

Working with Page Setup in Windows

You can use the Page Setup dialog box in Windows to select the size and location in the printer of the paper you want to use. You can also select the page orientation (portrait or landscape) that best fits the entire document or any selection. **Portrait** orients the page vertically (taller than it is wide) and **landscape** orients the page horizontally (wider than it is tall). When you shift between the two, the margin settings automatically change. **Margins** are the blank space between the edge of the page and the printable area. The printer does not print within these margins. Different printer models support different options and features; available options depend on your printer and print drivers.

Work with Page Setup in Windows

1. Open a document.

2. Click the **File** menu, and then click **Page Setup**.

3. Select from the various Page Setup options:

    - **Size.** Click the list arrow, and then select from the available options. The default printer will determine the available paper sizes.

    - **Source.** Click the list arrow, and then select from the available options.

    - **Orientation.** Click the Portrait or Landscape option.

    - **Margins.** Enter Top, Bottom, Left, and Right paper margins for a customized document.

4. Click **Printer** if you have more than one printer, and then choose which one you will be using for the job.

5. Click **OK**.

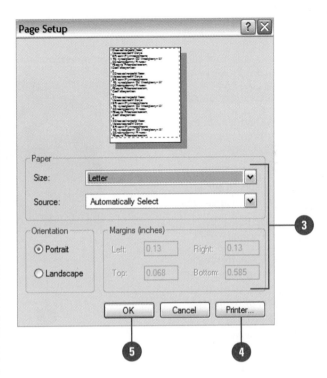

Setting Document Print Options

PS 11.1, 11.2, 11.3

When you select the Print command, Photoshop displays a preview dialog box , which gives you the opportunity to view the image (on screen), and decide whether to print or return to the drawing board. The white area in the image preview is the printable area, while the shaded border at the edge shows the paper margins. You can adjust the position and scale of the image and see the results. The size of the image is determined by the document size settings in the Image Size dialog box. When you scale an image in the Print dialog box, the changes only affect the printed image, not the actual image. If you want to use the same print settings the next time you print, Photoshop can remember your settings.

Set Document Print Options

1. Open a document.

2. Click the **File** menu, and then click **Print**.

   Choose from three output options:

   - **Match Print Colors.** Select to show the soft-proofed printed colors in the Preview.

     If Match Print Colors is turned on, you will be able to add one or both of the following options:

   - **Gamut Warning. (New!)** Will highlight out of gamut colors.

   - **Show Paper White. (New!)** Sets image whites to the color of the paper being used to compensate for off-white or beige paper stock.

3. To change the image orientation, click the **Portrait** or **Landscape** button next to Page Setup.

4. Select from the various Position options:

   - **Center Image.** Select to instruct the output device to center the image on the paper.

   - **Top.** Instructs the output device to print the image from the top of the page.

   - **Left.** Instructs the output device to print the image from the left of the page.

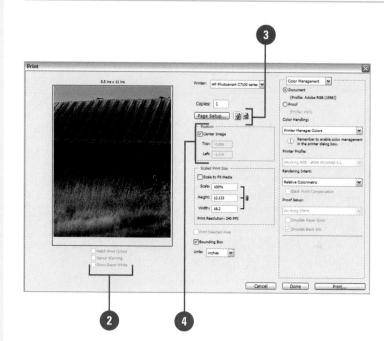

5 Select from the various Scaled Print Size options:

♦ **Scale to Fit Media.** Select to scale the document to the selected paper size.

♦ **Scale.** Enter a percentage value.

♦ **Height.** Enter an image height.

♦ **Width.** Enter an image width.

6 Select the check boxes for the various options:

♦ **Print Selected Area.** Select to print only the selected area of the image.

♦ **Bounding Box.** Select to add a bounding box around the image.

♦ **Units.** Specifies the units of measure for size settings.

7 Click **Page Setup** to choose setup options.

8 Click **Print** to open the Print dialog box.

♦ To print one copy without displaying the Print dialog box, hold down Alt (Win) or Option (Mac), and then click **Print One**.

9 Click **Done** to return to your document without printing.

Preview of active image

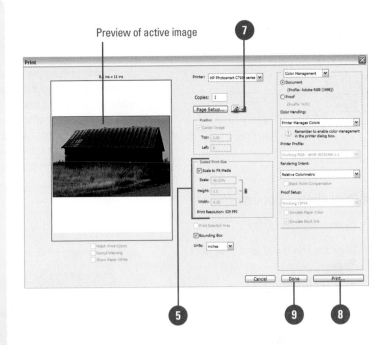

Did You Know?

You can manually scale and position an image. Select the Show Bounding Box check box, and then clear the Scale To Fit Media and Center Image check boxes. Then simply drag the image in the View window to reposition, and then click and drag a corner to resize.

For Your Information

Displaying vs. Printing an Image

Although the image is displayed on a monitor, you still get to see an accurate representation of how the graphic and all its associated layers and effects will appear. Remember, a monitor uses additive color (RGB), and most output devices, such as printing presses, use subtractive color (CMYK). However, if you have a good, color-calibrated monitor, you should have a good idea of how the image will look.

Setting Print Output Options

PS 11.1, 11.3

On the right side of the preview Print dialog box, Photoshop not only gives you access to its powerful color management tools, it also lets you create calibration bars, add file name labels, and even place a custom border around the image. Click the Color Management list arrow, and then click Output. Photoshop displays a listing of all the options available, including the ability to print vector data or change the document's encoding. For example, if you want to print a vector image that includes shapes and type with optimal results, you can use the Include Vector Data option to send the image to a PostScript printer. It's just one more way that Photoshop gives you control over document output.

Set Print Output Options

1. Open a document.

2. Click the **File** menu, and then click **Print**.

3. Click the list arrow at the top right of the Print dialog box, and then click **Output**.

4. Select from the various Printing Marks options:

   ◆ **Calibration Bars.** Prints a gradient tint bar to compare color ranges.

   ◆ **Registration Marks.** Prints marks to align color separations.

   ◆ **Corner Crop Marks.** Prints marks where the page is to be trimmed.

   ◆ **Center Crop Marks.** Prints marks to identify the center of the page.

   ◆ **Description.** Prints text provided in the File Info dialog box.

   ◆ **Labels.** Prints the file name at the top of the page.

   ◆ **Emulsion Down.** Prints images to film. Use to make type readable when printing to photographic paper facing away from you.

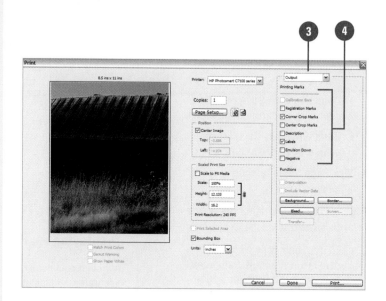

◆ **Negative.** Prints an inverted image. Use if you want to print separations directly to film.

5. Select from the various Functions options:

◆ **Interpolation.** Resamples the image to reduce the jagged appearance of a low-resolution image.

◆ **Include Vector Data.** Select to print a vector image. If the option is grayed, the image doesn't contain vector data.

◆ **Send 16-bit Data.** Select to have 16-bit per color channel data sent to the printer (Mac only).

◆ **Background.** Selects a background color to be printed outside the image area.

◆ **Border.** Prints a black border around the image.

◆ **Bleed.** Prints crop marks inside rather than outside the image.

◆ **Screen.** Sets the print screen frequency and dot shape.

◆ **Transfer.** Adjusts the dot gain or loss, which can be used to compensate for a poorly calibrated output device.

6. Click **Print** to open the Print dialog box.

7. Click **Done** to return to your document without printing.

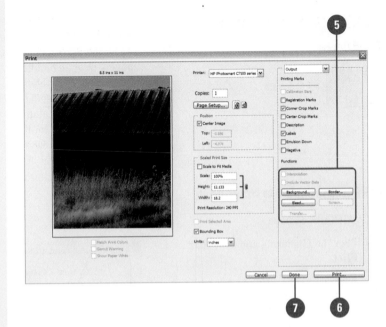

See Also

See "Setting Document Print Options" on page 372 for information on using the preview Print dialog box.

Printing a Document in Macintosh

PS 11.1, 11.3

The Print command is probably the most used of all Photoshop's print options. In addition to normal printing functions, such as Copies and Pages, the Print command gives you other menus that let you control specific printing functions, such as output ink and color management. Understand that the options available for the Print command will be partially determined by your default printer. For example, if your default printer uses more than one paper tray, you will see options for selecting a specific tray for the current print job. In spite of the differences, there are some universal options for all print jobs, and these are covered here.

Print a Document in Macintosh

1. Open a document.

2. Click the **File** menu, and then click **Print**.

   A print preview dialog box opens.

3. Specify the print options you want, and then click **Print**.

4. Click the **Expand/Collapse** button to expand the dialog box, if necessary.

5. Click the **Printer** list arrow, and then select from the available printer descriptions.

   IMPORTANT *Changes made here override any changes made in the Page Setup dialog box.*

6. Click the **Presets** list arrow, and then select from the available preset options.

7. Select from the various options: Number of copies, Collated, Print All or Range of pages. Options vary between Windows and Macintosh.

8. Click the **Print Options** list arrow, click **Layout**, and then select the various options: Pages Per Sheet, Layout Direction, and if you want a Border.

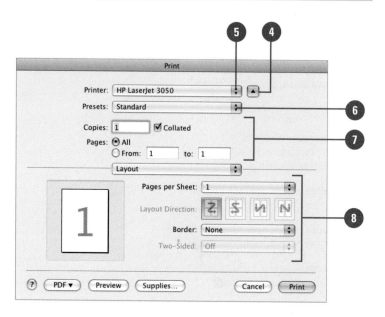

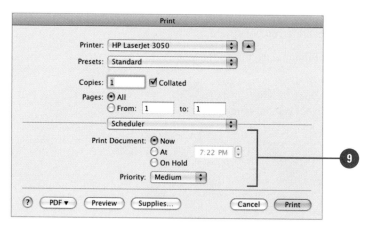

9 To print the document at a later time, click the **Print Options** list arrow, click **Scheduler**, and then select the options you want.

10 To set paper-related options, click the **Print Options** list arrow, click **Paper Handling**, or **Cover Page**, and then select the options you want.

11 To set color-related options, click the **Print Options** list arrow, click **Color Management**, and then select the color options you want.

12 Click the **Print Options** list arrow, click **Summary**, and then view the summary of settings.

13 Click the following options to finalize your print: **PDF**, **Preview**, **Supplies**, **Cancel**, or **Print**.

  ◆ **PDF.** From the menu, select the PDF option you want.

14 If you need additional help along the way, click the **Help** button.

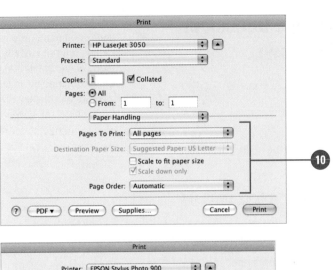

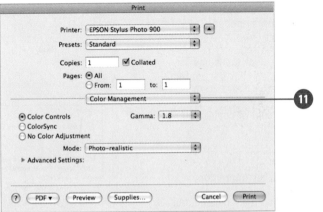

Did You Know?

You can save print options as a preset (Mac). In the Print dialog box, select the options you want, click the Presets pop-up menu, click Save As, type a name, and then click OK.

See Also

See "Setting Document Print Options" on page 372 for information on setting print options.

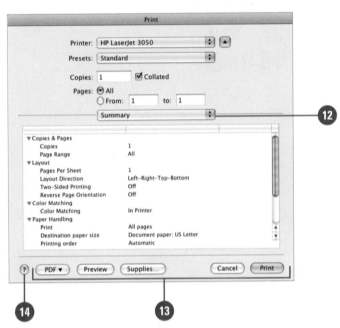

Printing a Document in Windows

Printing a paper copy is the most common way to preview and share your documents. You can use the Print dialog box to set how many copies to print, specify a range of pages to print, and print your document. Understand that the options available for the Print command will be determined by your default printer and operating system. Different printers will display different options. There are some options that are fairly universal, however, and these options are covered here.

Print a Document in Windows

1. Open a document.

2. Click the **File** menu, and then click **Print**.

   A print preview dialog box opens.

3. Specify the print options you want, and then click **Print**.

4. If necessary, click the **Name** list arrow, and then click the printer you want.

5. Type the number of copies you want to print.

6. Specify the pages to print:

   ◆ **All.** Prints the entire document.

   ◆ **Selection.** Prints the selected item.

   ◆ **Current Page.** Prints only the active page.

   ◆ **Pages.** Prints the specified pages.

7. Click **Print**.

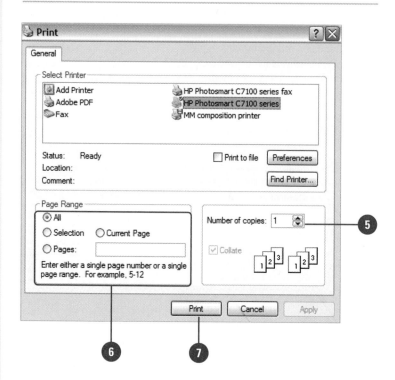

See Also

See "Setting Document Print Options" on page 372 for information on setting print options.

Printing Part of a Document

 Adobe Certified Expert PS 11.1

Print Part of a Document

1. Open a document.

2. Select the **Rectangle Marquee** tool on the toolbox.

3. Select a section of the image you want to print.

4. Click the **File** menu, and then click **Print**.

5. Select the **Print Selected Area** check box.

6. Click **Print**.

Did You Know?

You can scale an image if it's larger than the printable area of the paper. If a warning appears indicating your image is larger than the printable area, click Cancel, click the File menu, click Print, select the Scale To Fit Media check box, and then click Print. You can also click the File menu, and then click Page Setup to change your paper size.

If you only want to print part of an image in a Photoshop document, you can use the Print Selected Area option in the Print dialog box to quickly perform the task. All you need to do is select which part of the image you want to print, select the Print command on the File menu, select the Print Selected Area check box, and then send it to the printer.

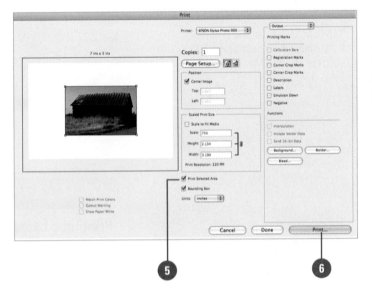

Printing One Copy

If you want it quick without any questions, then the Print One Copy command is for you. There's no hassle; you just get a printed copy of the image, using Photoshop's default print settings. The Print One Copy command does not open a dialog box, so when the option is selected, the printing process starts and an attempt is made to print the document. If you try to print an image that is larger than the paper's printable area, an alert dialog box appears. If this happens, you have the option of continuing the printing process, or canceling. Otherwise, the Print One Copy command is a one-click way to get a fast printed copy of your active document.

Print One Copy of a Document

1 Open a document.

2 Click the **File** menu, and then click **Print One Copy**.

Photoshop prints a single copy of the image without a dialog box.

IMPORTANT *If you have made any changes to Page Setup, or modified the printer settings in any way, Photoshop will ignore its default settings and print using your modified settings.*

TIMESAVER In the preview Print dialog box, hold down Alt (Win) or Option (Mac) to display Print One.

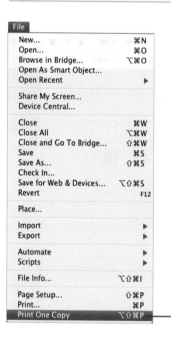

Printing a Larger Image

Occasionally, when printing a document, you will see an alert dialog box informing you that the image is larger than the paper's printable area. When this happens, you have the choice of continuing or canceling. If you choose to continue, the image will be clipped. In most cases it's best to cancel the Print command, and then adjust the image size to match the printable area of the image.

Understanding File Formats

 PS 1.7

File Formats

Format	Usage
Photoshop	Uses the PSD (Photoshop) format (the default), which saves layers, channels, notes, and color profiles.
BMP	Uses the BMP (Bitmap) format.
CompuServe GIF	Uses the GIF (Graphics Interchange Format) format, primarily used for clip art and text for the Web. A format for images on the Web that only uses 256 colors. GIF's compress image information by selectively disregarding color and repeating simple patterns. This format supports transparency and animation.
Dicom	Uses the DICOM (Digital Imaging and Communications in Medicine) format. This format is commonly used for the transfer and storage of medical images, such as ultrasounds and scans.
Photoshop EPS	Uses the EPS (Encapsulated PostScript) format, which saves vector information (i.e. paths).
Photoshop DCS 1.0 & 2.0	Uses the DCS (Desktop Color Separations) format. This format is used by press operators to create the plates used in 4-color printing.
JPEG	Uses the JPG or JPEG (Joint Photographic Experts Group) format. A compression method used to reduce the size of image files primarily for the Web.
Large Document Format	Uses the PSB (Photoshop) format (for Photoshop CS and later), which is used for saving documents up to 300,000 pixels in any dimension; this format is useful for saving High Dynamic Range images.
PCX	Uses the PCX (PC Paintbrush bitmap) format, which is used primarily in PC formats.
Photoshop PDF	Uses the PDF (Portable Document Format) format, which creates a file that can be read by anyone who has a PDF reader program (such as Adobe).
Photoshop RAW	Uses the RAW format that is used for saving and transferring files between programs and computer platforms.
PICT File	Uses the PICT or PICT Resource format that is used by the Macintosh operating system.
Pixar	Uses the Pixar format for images used in high-end animation and 3-D rendering programs.
PNG	Uses the PNG (Portable Network Graphics) format. This format is used for saving images onto the Web; it supports up to 16 million colors and 256 levels of transparency.
PBM	Uses the PBM (Portable Bit Map) format, which supports monochrome bitmaps (1 bit per channel), and is part of a family of bitmap formats supported by most applications.
Scitex CT	Uses the SCT (Scitex Continuous Tone) format in high-end Scitex image-rendering computers.
Targa	Uses the Targa format for high-end image editing on the Windows platform.
TIFF	Uses the TIFF (Tagged-Image File Format) format. These files can be opened by almost any image-editing or layout program. TIFF is a common format for printing and saving flattened images without losing quality.

Saving a Document with a Different File Format

 PS 9.6, 11.4

After all your hard work, you now need to save your document. The saving process involves selecting a specific file format, naming the file, and choosing a destination. Choose a file name that will help identify the document (looking in a folder of 100 images and seeing file names such as image_a, image_b, really doesn't help). Select a destination, such as a hard drive, removable media, or even a rewritable CD or DVD. Determine the format of the document file. While name and location are important, the file format is crucial to the future of the image. The file format determines how the document is stored, and what information is saved with the file. Choosing the wrong format may even prevent you from correctly outputting the file.

Save a Document with a Different File Format

1. Open a document.

2. Click the **File** menu, and then click Save As.

3. Enter a name in the **File Name** (Win) or **Save As** (Mac) box.

4. Click the **Format** list arrow, and then select a format.

   See the table on the previous page for assistance.

5. Click the **Save In** (Win) or **Where** (Mac) list arrow, and then select a location in which to save the document file.

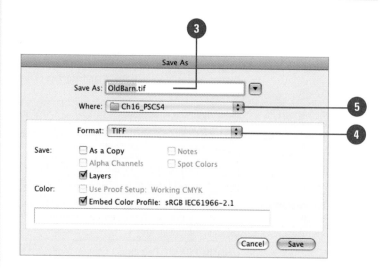

See Also

See "Understanding File Formats" on page 381 for information on the different file formats.

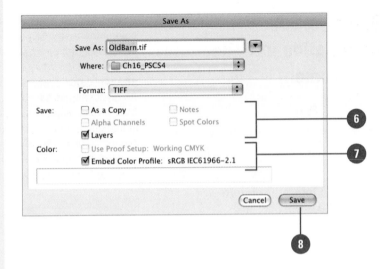

6 Select from the following Save options:

- **As a Copy.** Select the check box to save a copy of the file, while leaving the original open.

- **Alpha Channels.** Select the check box to save any alpha channel information.

- **Layers.** Select the check box to preserve all layers within the document.

- **Notes.** Select the check box to save any note annotations with the document.

- **Spot Colors.** Select the check box to save any spot channel information.

7 Select from the following Color options:

- **Use Proof Setup.** Select the check box to create a color-managed document.

- **Embed Color Profile (Mac).** Select the check box to create a color-managed Macintosh document.

- **ICC Profile (Win).** Select the check box to create a color-managed Windows document.

8 Click **Save**.

For Your Information

Organizing Documents

Organization is a big part of any Photoshop project. For example, you might be working on several images, along with a dozen supporting images and text. When you work on a project, create a project-specific folder and save all the different files you need for that project in the same folder. That way everything is in one place, so it's easy to access, easy to move, and easy to store.

Inserting File Information into a Document

 PS 1.5

When you save a document, you have the ability to save more than just color information. You can save copyright, camera, and even image category information. This data is saved with the file as metadata in the XMP format (Extensible Metadata Platform), and can be accessed by any application that reads XMP data. In addition, if the image is a photograph, you can save data specifying the type of image, where it was shot, or the camera used. You can even get information on shutter speed and f-stop. That information will not only protect your intellectual property, but will supply you with vital statistics on exactly how you created that one-of-a-kind image.

Insert File Information into a Document

1. Open a document.

2. Click the **File** menu, and then click **File Info**.

3. Click **Description**, and then enter information concerning the author and any copyright information.

4. Click **Camera Data**, which reveals information about the camera that took the image.

   These are read-only fields and include information such as camera model, ISO, aperture, metering, shutter speed, and pixel dimensions.

5. Click **History** to view historical information about the active document, such as dates last opened and saved, and a list of adjustments performed on the image.

6. Click **IPTC**, and then **IPTC Contact**, **IPTC Image**, **IPTC Content**, and **IPTC Status** to enter information concerning the image's creator, description and keywords, location where photograph was taken, date created, copyright, and usage terms.

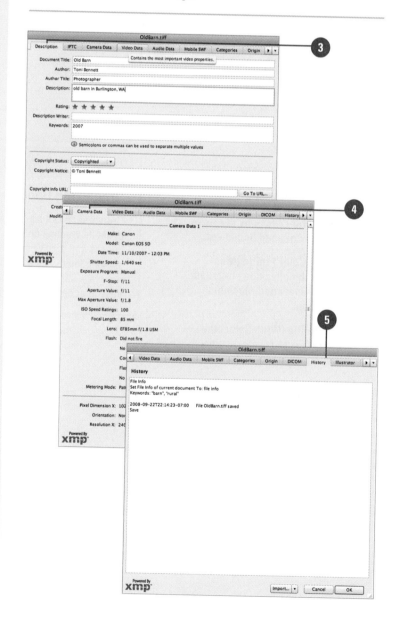

7 Click **Origin**, and then enter data pertaining to the origin of the image.

8 Click **Advanced** to view additional information on the active document, such as EXIF, and PDF document properties.

9 Click **OK**.

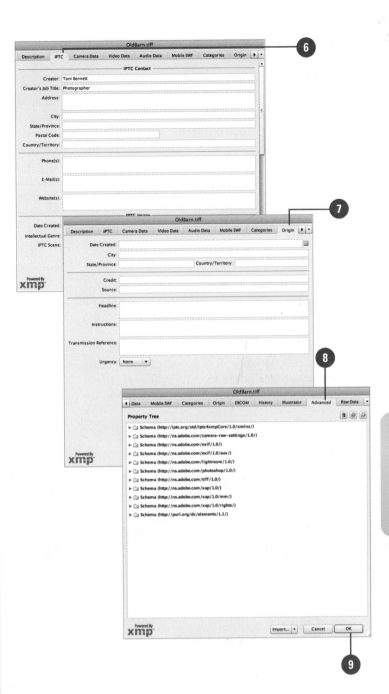

Understanding File Compression

Compression is Photoshop's way of reducing the size of a document file, kind of like the ultimate weight-loss program. Just click a button, and the file can be reduced to half its original size. Photoshop employs two types of compression schemes: lossy and lossless. **Lossy** compression reduces the size of the file by removing color information—information that can never be restored to the saved document. Lossy compression schemes can achieve file reductions of 80% or greater.

The **Lossless** method reduces file size by using compression algorithms that reduce the size of a file without removing image information. Lossy methods are used primarily for images displayed in browsers (images for the Web). The relatively slow speed of the Internet forces web designers to employ lossy compression methods to reduce images down to

their smallest values. Lossless methods are used when the reduction of a file is important, but not so much that you would consider removing information. For example, you might want to reduce the size of a group of high-quality TIFF images so they fit on a rewritable CD. Lossless compression methods can reduce files sizes up to 50%, or even a bit more.

Both methods compress documents based on the actual image information. For example, images that contain a lot of solid color information would compress quite well using the GIF (Graphics Interchange Format) or PNG-8 formats, whereas an image with a lot of continuous tone colors, such as a photograph, would be best compressed using the JPEG (Joint Photographic Experts Group) format.

Lossy

Lossless

Format Type, Compression Type, and Output Uses

Format	Compression	Output Use
JPEG	Lossy	**Web/Slide Presentations.** PDFs, photographs, and images that contain lots of colors that softly blend together.
GIF	Lossless	**Web.** Clip art, text, and any images that contain solid colors and images with hard edges.
PNG-8	Lossless	**Web.** Clip art, text, and any images that contain solid colors and images with hard edges.
PNG-24	Lossless	**Web/Slide Presentations/PDF/Print.** Photographs and images that contain lots of colors that softly blend together. Because the PNG-24 format is lossless, it can not compress images as small as the JPEG format. Therefore, the JPEG format is still the format of choice for compressing images for the Web.
ZIP	Lossless	**Used on all image types for image storage and transfer.** The Zip compression application lets you compress images without affecting image quality. To open a Zip image, you must have the Unzip application.
LZW	Lossless	**Used primarily on TIFF images for image storage and transfer.** The LZW compression scheme lets you compress images without affecting image quality. To open an LZW image, the opening application must have the proper LZW decompress utility.

Preparing Clip Art for the Web

Clip art is defined as non-photographic image information, with a lot of solid-color areas. When saving this type of file, the GIF or PNG-8 formats would work best. The GIF (Graphics Interchange Format) and PNG (Portable Network Graphics) formats use an RLE (Run Length Encoding) scheme. When the file is saved, areas of solid color are compressed into small units and then restored to the file when it is opened. The GIF format supports a maximum of 256 colors. While that may not seem like much, most GIF images, such as clip art and text, contain far less color information. By reducing the number of colors available for the GIF color table, you can significantly reduce the image's file size. For example, a GIF image composed of black text might only require a maximum of 2 colors (black and white). Experiment with the GIF Colors option to produce small, fast-loading image files. Since the GIF format has been around for a long time, using it almost guarantees that the image will open on a visitor's browser. The PNG format is newer, and has some new encoding schemes that make even smaller files, but it is not supported by all web browsers.

Prepare Clip Art for the Web

1. Open a clip art document.

2. Click the **File** menu, and then click **Save As**.

3. Enter a name for the file in the Save As box.

4. Click the **Save In** (Win) or **Where** (Mac) list arrow, and then select a location in which to save the file.

5. Click the **Format** list arrow, and then click **CompuServe GIF**.

6. Click **Save**.

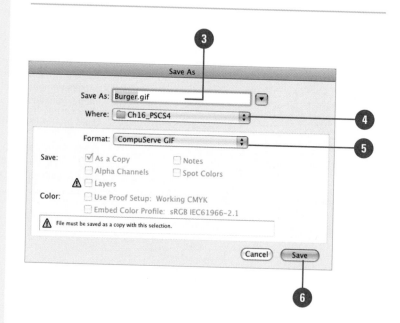

7 Select from the following Indexed
   Color options:

   ◆ **Palette.** Click the list arrow, and
     then select from the available
     color palette options, including
     Web (Safe), Mac, and Win
     System panels.

   ◆ **Colors.** If you selected a local
     color, or custom panel, click to
     select the number of colors
     saved with the image. The
     maximum number of colors
     is 256.

   ◆ **Forced.** Click the list arrow, and
     then select what colors will be
     retained in the image.

   ◆ **Transparency.** Select the check
     box to preserve any transparent
     areas.

   ◆ **Matte.** If the image contains
     transparent areas, clicking this
     list arrow lets you select a color
     to fill the areas. For example,
     you could fill all transparent
     areas of the image with black to
     match the black background of
     a Web document.

   ◆ **Dither.** Click the list arrow, and
     then select how you want the
     remaining image's color to mix.

   ◆ **Amount.** Enter an Amount
     percentage to instruct the GIF
     format how aggressively to
     dither the image colors.

   ◆ **Preserve Exact Colors.** Select
     the check box to force the
     preservation of the original
     image colors (based on how
     many colors were chosen using
     the Palette option).

8 Click **OK**.

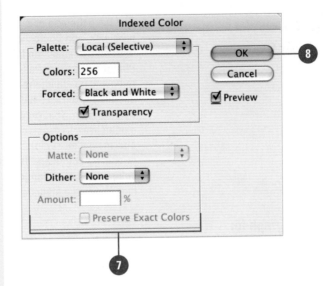

Preparing a Photograph for the Web

Reducing the size of a photograph presents its own particular set of problems, and Photoshop comes to the rescue with solutions. For photographic images, the best format to use is the JPEG (Joint Photographic Experts Group) format. This format reduces file size by removing image information (lossy compression). For example, a 1 MB uncompressed TIFF file can be reduced to 20 KB or 30 KB using JPEG compression. That reduces the download time of the image on a 33 KB modem from15 minutes to 10 seconds. While that is quite a reduction, it also means most of the image colors have been removed and the remaining colors are dithered (simulated) to fool the eyes into seeing colors that are no longer in the image. Highly compressed JPEG images look good on a monitor, but fare poorly when sent to a printer.

Prepare a Photograph for the Web

① Open a photographic document.

② Click the **File** menu, and then click **Save As**.

③ Enter a name for the file in the Save As box.

④ Click the **Save In** (Win) or **Where** (Mac) list arrow, and then select a location in which to save the file.

⑤ Click the **Format** list arrow, and then click **JPEG**.

⑥ Click **Save**.

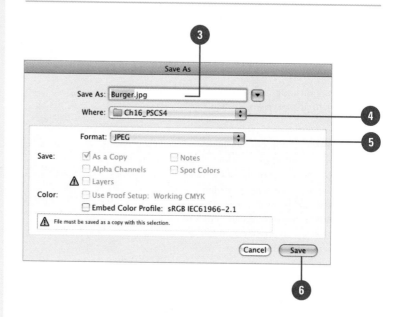

7 Select from the following JPEG Options:

- ◆ **Matte.** The JPEG format does not support transparency. Click the Matte list arrow, and then select the color with which to fill transparent areas within the active document.

- ◆ **Quality.** The Quality option determines the amount of image information loss. Enter a value from 1 to 12; the higher the value, the more information is retained, thus creating a larger file.

- ◆ **Baseline (Standard).** The format is recognized by most browsers.

- ◆ **Baseline Optimized.** Produces optimized color, and a slightly smaller file size, but is not supported by older browsers.

- ◆ **Progressive.** Displays a series of increasingly detailed scans as the image downloads. The visual impression is of a blurred image slowly coming into focus (not supported by older browsers).

- ◆ **Scans.** If Progressive is selected, select the number of scan passes for the image.

8 Click **OK**.

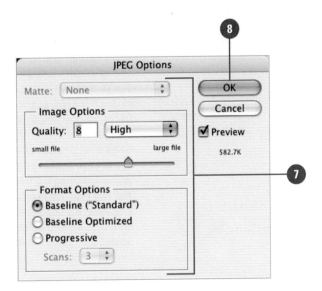

For Your Information

Using the JPEG 2000 Format

JPEG 2000 is a file format that provides more options and greater flexibility than the standard JPEG format. It produces images with better compression and quality for both web and print publishing. The optional JPEG 2000 format plug-in can be found on the Photoshop CS4 installation CD in Goodies/Optional Plug-Ins/Photoshop Only/File Formats. Currently, only computers with the necessary plug-in can view a JPEG 2000 file on the Web.

Preparing an Image for the Press

Images saved for press printing are in another world. For example, images displayed on a monitor use the RGB (additive) color space, while images sent to a press use the CMYK (subtractive) color space. The format of choice is the DCS (Desktop Color Separations) format. The DCS format is a version of the standard EPS format that lets you save color separations of CMYK images. DCS comes in two flavors, DCS 1.0 and DCS 2.0. Both create five separate files: one is for each of the four color plates, Cyan, Magenta, Yellow, and Black, and one is for a combined, or composite image. However, the DCS 2.0 format allows you to save alpha and spot-color channels, as well as giving you the option of saving the five separate files under one combined file name. You can also use the DCS 2.0 format to export images containing spot channels. It's important to understand that the only device that can print a DCS file is a PostScript printer. As with anything related to press operations, always contact your friendly press operator and ask what format to use.

Prepare an Image for the Press

1. Open a document.

2. Click the **File** menu, and then click **Save As**.

   IMPORTANT *Images saved in the DCS format must be in the CMYK color mode.*

3. Enter a name for the file in the Save As box.

4. Click the **Save In** (Win) or **Where** (Mac) list arrow, and then select a location in which to save the file.

5. Click the **Format** list arrow, and then click **Photoshop DCS 2.0**.

6. Click **Save**.

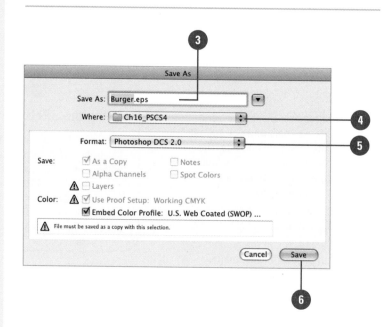

7 Select from the following DCS 2.0 Format options:

- **Preview.** Click the list arrow, and then select what type of low-resolution image to use in the layout application.

- **DCS.** Click the list arrow, and then select how you want the color plate information saved.

- **Encoding.** Click the list arrow, and then select how the image data is encoded for delivery to the output device (contact your service bureau).

- **Include Halftone Screen.** Select the check box to include any halftone screens.

- **Include Transfer Function.** Used with high-end commercial production jobs.

- **Include Vector Data.** Select the check box to include any vector data contained within the active image.

- **Image Interpolation.** Select the check box to create an anti-aliased version of the Preview image (does not impact printing).

8 Click **OK**.

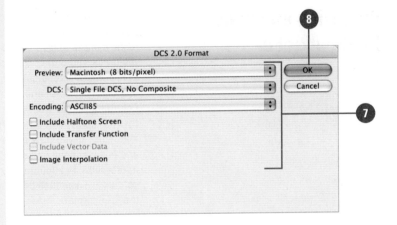

Preparing an Image for an Inkjet or Laser Printer

 PS 11.3

While not everyone has access to a 4-color press, even casual computer users have or have access to, an inkjet or laser printer. Inkjet and laser printers apply color to the paper using dots of ink. In fact, one of the measurements of quality for this type of output is its printing resolution. For example, a photo-quality inkjet or laser printer can have a resolution of 1,400 dpi and higher, or one thousand four hundred dots of color information per linear inch. There are several file format options to print this type of output; however, none is as versatile as the TIFF format. The Tagged-Image File Format uses lossy or lossless compression, and lets you save multiple Photoshop layers, as well as alpha channel information. In addition, there is hardly a layout application in the marketplace, Macintosh or Windows, that will not open an image saved in the TIFF format.

Prepare an Image for an Inkjet or Laser Printer

1. Open a document.

2. Click the **File** menu, and then click **Save As**.

3. Enter a name for the file in the Save As box.

4. Click the **Save In** (Win) or **Where** (Mac) list arrow, and then select a location in which to save the file.

5. Click the **Format** list arrow, and then click **TIFF**.

6. Click **Save**.

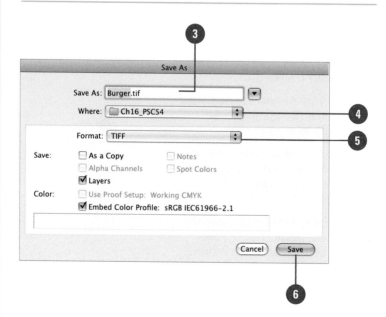

7 Select from the following TIFF Options:

◆ **None.** No compression is performed to the image.

◆ **LZW.** Performs lossless compression to the image. When this method is used, the receiving application must have the corresponding LZW option or it will not be able to decompress the file.

◆ **Zip.** Performs a standard Zip (lossless) compression to the image. Receiving application must have an unzip utility.

◆ **JPEG.** Performs lossy (image loss) compression to the image.

◆ **IBM PC.** Select PC if the image is to be used on an IBM system. Works also on Macintosh systems.

◆ **Macintosh.** Select Macintosh if the image is to be used on a Macintosh system.

◆ **Save Image Pyramid.** Check to save the image using several image resolutions. Lets you decide what resolution to use when reopening the image.

◆ **Save Transparency.** Check to preserve any transparent areas in the active image.

◆ **RLE.** Run Length Encoding (RLE) helps to compress solid areas of color across multiple layers.

◆ **ZIP.** Uses the Zip format to compress multiple layers.

◆ **Discard Layers and Save a Copy.** Creates a copy of the file without the layers, essentially saving a composite image file.

8 Click **OK**.

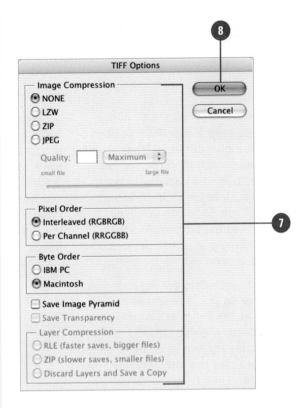

For Your Information

Getting the Best Results on an Inkjet or Laser Printer

Since your monitor displays an image using light and a desktop printer reproduces an image using inks, dyes, or pigments, it is impossible for a desktop printer to reproduce all the colors that can be displayed on a monitor. However, by incorporating certain procedures (such as color management) into your workflow, you can achieve predictable results when printing your images to a desktop printer. For more information on getting the best color results, see Chapter 18, "Managing Color from Monitor to Print."

Understanding Monitor, Image, and Device Resolution

 PS 1.4

Remember that raster images are all about resolution. Images have a specific scanned resolution (spi, samples per inch). Your monitor also has a native resolution (ppi, pixels per inch), as does output devices such as inkjet printers (dpi, dots per inch), and high-end presses (lpi, lines per inch). While all these terms may seem a bit complicated, they're not; they simply explain how much information is contained within the image.

Most computer monitors are set to a fixed resolution of 72 or 96 ppi. Say you scan a 4 by 4 inch image at 288 spi (that's 4 times the resolution of a 72-ppi monitor). If you attempted to display the image at 100% view, the monitor would take the image pixels and adjust the width and height to match its resolution, so the image would be 16 by 16 inches (288 divided by 72 = 4). If the display of the image doesn't fit the size of your monitor and you attempt to reduce the magnification of the image to make it fit the monitor size, Photoshop will have to remove pixels from the image to make it fit. This typically causes the image to generate jagged lines, especially around angles. The moral of this story is: when adjusting an image for viewing on a monitor (for example, when preparing a slide presentation), never change the zoom of the image to fit the monitor; always adjust the resolution by selecting the Image menu, and then clicking Image Size.

When it comes to output, such as to an inkjet printer, the rules are a bit more forgiving. Many output devices have print resolutions of 1,440 or higher. However, we're not talking about fixed monitor pixels (ppi), we're talking about dots of ink hitting a piece of paper (dpi). Most inkjet printers, because of the dot gain of the inks (that's the amount of space over which a dot of ink spreads when it hits the paper), do not need image resolution greater than 300 spi. Although image quality suffers when you enlarge an image beyond its original size for viewing on a monitor, if you use higher resolutions than needed when you print, the image won't be degraded; you'll just be printing an image with a larger file size. However, that can be a waste of time. For example, a 300 spi, 8 by 10 inch image will have a file size of about 20 MB; the same image scanned at 1,200 spi will produce a 329 MB file size. When you print the two images, you will probably not notice any difference in quality; however, it will take, on average, 6 minutes longer to print the 1,200 spi document on most mid-range printers.

The bottom line is that resolution represents the amount of information contained within a linear inch; however, various devices handle that same resolution differently. The good news is that understanding those differences helps you to create a useable workflow. Knowledge is power.

Working with Automate Commands

17

Introduction

It's great when you hear about new tips and tricks that will save time. But it's never a good policy to shave time if it means sacrificing quality. Adobe Photoshop has come to the rescue with some great time-savers that will help you. The Automate commands give you the ability to streamline your workflow, and make short work of repetitive tasks.

Think of an automation as a batch of actions all rolled up into one powerful command. In the busy world of graphic design, with all the image processing you need to do on a daily basis, Photoshop's Automate commands give you the ability to deliver consistent results, over and over again, with the click of a button.

The Automate commands let you process—through batch file processing—hundreds of image files with the click of a button. In addition, you can use commands to crop and straighten photos, resize photos, and merge photos together to create a panoramic or HDR (High Dynamic Range) image. Photoshop also gives you the ability to convert a multi-page PDF file into a Photoshop document.

In addition to using the automation commands in Photoshop, you can also use them in Adobe Bridge. The Tools menu in Bridge contains commands available with different Adobe Creative Suite programs, such as Photoshop or Illustrator. The Photoshop automation commands appear under the Photoshop submenu in Bridge's Tools menu.

What You'll Do

Work with Batch File Processing

Work with Conditional Mode Change

Use the Crop and Straighten Photos Command

Convert a Multi-Page PDF to PSD

Create a PDF Document

Use Photomerge

Merge Images to HDR

Process Multiple Image Files

Use the Fit Image Command

Working with Batch File Processing

PS 8.2, 8.3, 8.4

There is nothing more exciting than working on a new creative project, and watching your designs come to life. Conversely, there is nothing more tiresome than having to apply a new creative concept or correction individually to 50 separate images. For example, you just spent three hours coming up with a procedure to color-correct an heirloom photograph, and the process took two filters and three adjustments. The photo looks great; however, you now have 50 other images with the exact problem. You could create an action, but you would still have to open each image and apply the action 50 times. The solution is to batch process the images after you have created the action. Batch file processing lets you apply an action to an entire folder of images, and all you have to do is click a button. Now, what could be simpler than that?

Work with Batch File Processing

1. Create a new folder, and then move all the images into the folder.

   IMPORTANT *These files must be image files. There should not be any other files, such as text files, inside this folder.*

2. Create a second folder to hold the modified images (optional).

3. Open Photoshop (you do not need to open a document).

4. Click the **File** menu, point to **Automate**, and then click **Batch**.

5. Select from the following Play options:

   ◆ Click the **Set** list arrow, and then select the Set containing the Action you want to apply to the images.

   ◆ Click the **Action** list arrow, and then select the correct Action.

6. Click the **Source** list arrow, and then select an image source from the following: Folder, Import, Opened Files, or Bridge.

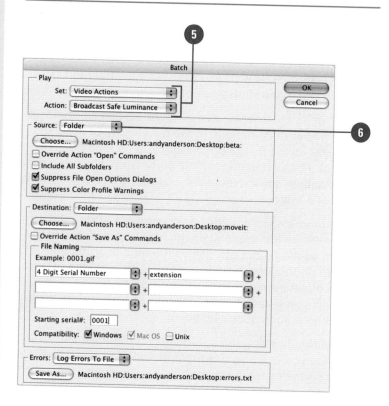

7 Click **Choose** (available if Folder is selected as the source), and then select the location of the image folder.

8 Select the check boxes for any options you want:

- ◆ **Override Action "Open" Commands.** Select to use an open command embedded into the Action.

- ◆ **Include All Subfolders.** Select to batch process any images located in folders embedded in the main image folder.

- ◆ **Suppress File Open Options Dialogs.** Select to disable the File Open dialog box.

- ◆ **Suppress Color Profile Warnings.** Select to disable the Color Profile Mismatch dialog box.

9 Click the **Destination** list arrow, and then click **None**, **Save and Close**, or **Folder**.

10 Click **Choose** (available if Folder is selected as the source), and then select the destination of the modified images.

11 Select the **Override Action "Save As" Commands** check box to use a save command embedded into the Action.

12 If Folder is selected as destination, the File Naming options allow you to rename the modified files, and then select the Compatibility options you want: Windows, Mac OS or Unix, or any combination of the three.

13 Click the **Errors** list arrow, select an errors option, and then click **Save As** to save your error information, if necessary.

14 Click **OK**.

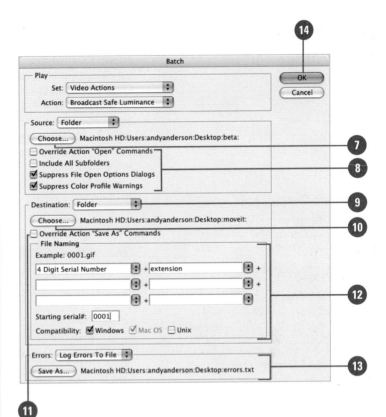

For Your Information

Things to Remember About Batch File Processing

There are many settings and requirements in order to make your batch file processing a success. Remember that before you begin, you need to have a created action. For more information on actions, you can refer to Chapter 15. After your action is created, and all the kinks are worked out, you can then set up your batch file processing. Knowing ahead of time where the source images are, where you'll be storing them (destination), having a naming convention, and other similar details will help reduce your setup of the batch file processing to a few easy steps.

Working with Conditional Mode Change

The Conditional Mode Change command lets you specify the conditions for changing the mode of an image in an action. When you create an action that changes modes, it can cause a problem when you run the action. For example, you create an action and one of the commands is to convert the image from RGB to Grayscale. Running the action on a file that is not RGB will cause an error. But, what if you want to use the same action to convert a CMYK image to Grayscale? You can if you make the mode change within the action using Conditional Mode Change. Using this option guarantees that you will never have a problem using an action to change the mode of an image.

Work with Conditional Mode Change

1. Open a document.

2. Start recording an Action.

   IMPORTANT *To make a conditional mode change, you must have a document open and an available Action to change.*

3. Click the **File** menu, point to **Automate**, and then click **Conditional Mode Change**.

4. Select the check boxes with the possible modes for the source image; you can click **All**.

5. Click the **Mode** list arrow, and then select the Target mode to which you want the image converted.

6. Click **OK**.

7. Add any additional commands to the action.

8. Click the **Stop Recording** button, and then save the action.

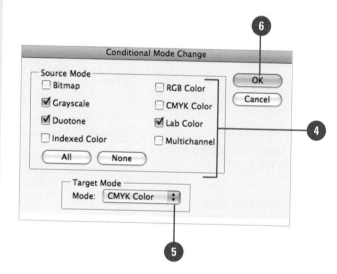

See Also

See "Building a New Action" and "Recording an Action" on pages 350-351 for information on action recording.

Using the Crop and Straighten Photos Command

The Crop and Straighten Photos command is a nifty way to quickly straighten multiple scanned images or make separate image files out of one image. For example, you have a photograph of two people standing side-by-side, and you want a separate image of each person. Or you have several scanned images that weren't quite straight on the platen. The Crop and Straighten Photos command works best when the images in the document are separated by some white space. When you apply the command to an image, it looks for areas to divide based on shifts in color; no selection is required.

Use the Crop and Straighten Photos Command

1. Open a document.

2. Click the **File** menu, point to **Automate**, and then click **Crop and Straighten Photos**.

   Photoshop automatically creates separate images from the available image information in the active document, and then places the images into individual files.

Did You Know?

You can control the Crop and Straighten Photos command through selection. Use the Rectangular Marquee tool to select a portion of the image before using the Crop and Straighten Photos command, and then Photoshop will work only within the selection.

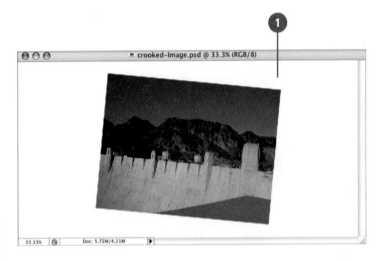

Image cropped and straightened

Converting a Multi-Page PDF to PSD

 PS 8.3

Photoshop's list of automation features is impressive, and it gets longer and better with each new version of the program. One of the features that will come in handy is the ability to convert a multi-page PDF directly into multiple Photoshop image files. For example, you have this great Adobe PDF document that contains images you want to use in a Photoshop design. The PDF format is a versatile file format that can contain both vector and bitmap data, as well as electronic document search and navigation features. Some PDF files contain a single image, while other PDF files contain multiple pages and images. When you open a PDF file, you can choose which pages to open, as well as specify a specific rasterization process (how to convert the image from vector to raster). Although Adobe moved this process from the Automation panel to the Open dialog box, it still rates a spot in automation.

Work with Multi-Page PDF to PSD

1. Open Photoshop (it is not necessary to open a document).

2. Click the **File** menu, and then click **Open**.

3. Select a document in the Photoshop PDF format, and then click **Open**.

4. Click the **Pages** or **Images** option to display PDF pages or images extracted from the PDF pages.

5. Select from the following Page Options:

   ◆ **Name:** Enter a name for the new document.

   ◆ **Crop To:** Click the list arrow, and then select from the various cropping options.

Selected PDF file

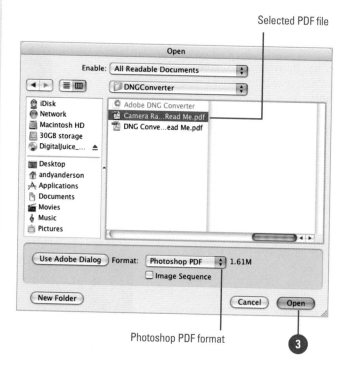

Photoshop PDF format

3

- ◆ **Anti-aliased.** Select the check box to use anti-aliasing smoothing techniques during the conversion.

- ◆ **Width and Height.** Specify the width and height for the image size in the measurement system you want. Select the Constrain Proportions check box to maintain proportions.

- ◆ **Resolution.** Choose a resolution for Photoshop to use when it rasterizes the PDF document.

- ◆ **Mode.** Click the list arrow, and then select a color mode for the output document.

- ◆ **Bit Depth.** Click the list arrow and then select 8- or 16-bit color depth.

6 Select the **Suppress Warnings** check box to prevent the operation from stopping on alert dialog boxes.

7 Shift+click to select contiguous pages, or Ctrl+click (Win) or ⌘+click (Mac) to select separate pages.

8 Click **OK**.

Photoshop creates separate PSD files from each specified page within the PDF document, and places the text and/or images on a transparent layer.

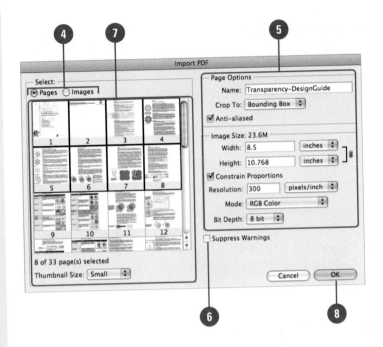

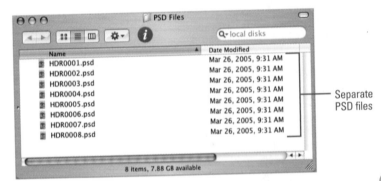

Separate PSD files

Did You Know?

You can convert Photoshop images into PDF documents. Photoshop gives you the option to save the document in the Photoshop PDF file format. Photoshop documents saved as PDF files preserve shape information as vector data, and you have the option of preserving type layers.

Creating a PDF Document

The **PDF** (Portable Document Format) format from Adobe lets you create individual documents that can be opened by literally any computer or operating system using Adobe Acrobat Reader (free at *www.adobe.com*). Photoshop recognizes two types of PDF files: Generic PDF (multiple pages and images) and Photoshop PDF (single image only). If you need to create specialized PDFs, you can create your own PDF presets to make the job easier. Adobe provides standard presets to make PDF creation quick and easy, and you can even create your own customized presets.

Create a PDF Document

1. Click the **File** menu, and then click **Save**.

2. Enter a name for the file in the File Name (Win) or Save As (Mac) box.

3. Click the **Format** list arrow, and then click **Photoshop PDF**.

4. Click the **Save In** (Win) or **Where** (Mac) list arrow, and then choose where to store the image.

5. Select the save options that you want.

6. Click **Save**.

7. Select from the general options:

   ◆ **Adobe PDF Preset.** Select from predefined compression options (Smallest File Size, recommended).

   ◆ **Standard.** Select from various PDF standards with which the file should be compliant (None, recommended).

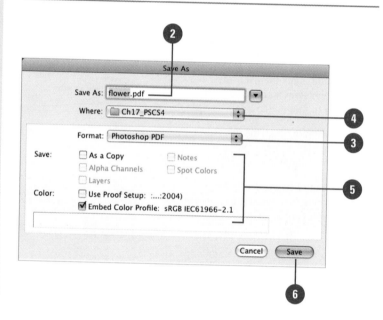

See Also

See "Saving a Document" on page 28 for information on the save options in the Save As dialog box.

- **Compatibility.** Select a version of the PDF reader application with which the file should to be compatible (5.0, recommended).

- **Description.** Enter a new description, if desired.

8 Select from the other PDF options:

- **Preserve Photoshop Editing Capabilities.** Disabled for PDF presentations.

- **Embed Page Thumbnails.** Check to add thumbnails to the presentation (optional; creates larger files).

- **Optimize For Fast Web Preview.** Check to optimize for viewing on the Web (recommended).

- **View PDF After Saving.** Check to view the presentation after it's created.

9 Click **Compression** to modify compression values (typically not required), **Output** to set color management and PDF/X (for prepress) options, **Security** to set passwords and print options, and **Summary** to review your settings.

10 To create your own presets, click **Save Preset**, enter a name, and then click **Save**.

- You can access the Adobe PDF Presets dialog box from the Edit menu. Click the **Edit** menu, and then click **Adobe PDF Presets**.

11 Click **Save PDF** to save your PDF document.

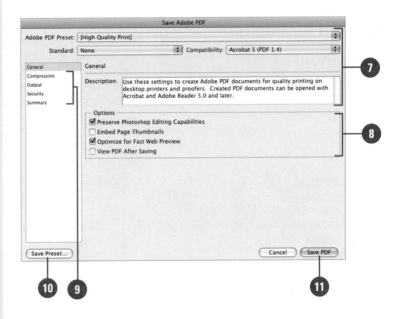

For Your Information

Creating and Working with Custom PDF Presets

If you need to create specialized PDFs, you can create your own PDF presets to make the job easier. Click the Edit menu, click Adobe PDF Presets, click New to create a preset, or select a preset and click Edit (you can't edit the default presets). In the Save Adobe PDF dialog box, select the options you want (see steps 7-11 for details), name the file and save (if necessary), and then exit the dialog boxes. Adobe PDF presets are saved as files with a ".joboptions" extension, which can be accessed by all CS4 programs using the Load button.

Creating a PDF Presentation

There are times when you want to create a slide show of your latest summer vacation and distribute it via e-mail or DVD. You have the entire image collection in a folder; it's ready to go, but you need a format in which to save all of the images so that your relatives, can open them. The answer is PDF (Portable Document Format). Open Adobe Bridge, display the Output workspace, select the files that you want to put into your presentation, click the PDF button, select a template, click the Document option, select a background (White, Gray, or Black), specify how long you want each image to appear on the screen, determine whether to loop after the last page, select transition options, and then click Save. Follow steps 7-11 (in this topic) to complete the process.

Using Photomerge

Ever wanted to create a panoramic photograph? Panoramas are those great-looking images that incorporate a wide view into one photograph. For example, you want to create a single photograph of the Grand Canyon, but the lens on your camera doesn't go that wide. So you start at the left of the canyon wall, and take a photo. Then you move slightly to the right and take another photo, and another, until you have reached the far right canyon wall. So, now you have four or five separate images of the Grand Canyon, and you want to stitch them together into a single panoramic view. If you have Photoshop, you have what you need to make it happen.

Use Photomerge

1. Click the **File** menu, point to **Automate**, and then click **Photomerge**.

2. Click the **Use** list arrow, and then select from the following options:

   ◆ **Files.** Click the Browse button, and then select the images.

   ◆ **Folder.** Click the Browse button, and then select the folder containing all the images.

3. To quickly add currently opened files to the list, click **Add Open Files**.

4. To remove any images from the list, click the file name, and then click **Remove**.

5. Click one of the layout options:

   ◆ **Auto.** Analyzes the images and uses the Perspective, Spherical, or Cylindrical layout.

   ◆ **Perspective.** Creates a stretched or skewed effect on the side images.

   ◆ **Cylindrical.** Creates a bow-tie effect like an unfolded cylinder.

   ◆ **Spherical.** (New!) Aligns the layers as if mapped inside a sphere. Great for images that cover 360 degrees.

   ◆ **Collage.** (New!) Matches overlapping content and transforms source.

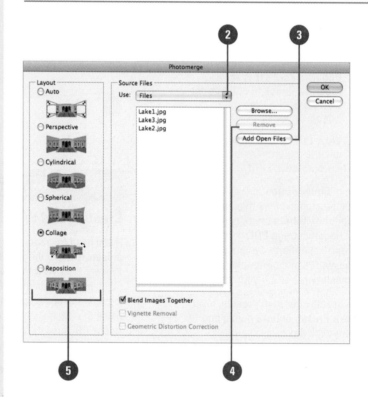

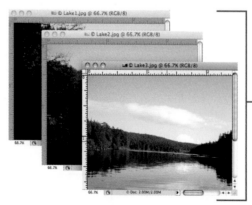

3 separate images used as sources for Photomerge.

◆ **Reposition.** Aligns the layers and matches overlapping content without transforming source.

6 Select the **Blend Images Together** check box to create seams between the image borders and match the image color. Clear the checked box to apply a simple rectanglar blend to the images.

◆ **Vignette Removal. (New!)** To compensate for darkened corners, usually when using wide-angle lenses.

◆ **Geometric Distortion Correction. (New!)** Allows Photoshop to fix problems caused by wide-angle and fisheye lenses.

7 Click **OK**.

Photoshop merges the images into a single, panoramic document file.

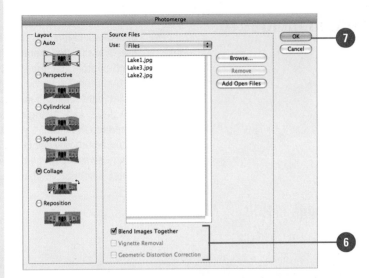

Did You Know?

You can use the following hints for the best results with Photomerge. For the best results, use the following rules of thumb when you take pictures. Overlap images by approximately 25% to 40%, don't change the zoom distance, keep the camera level, stay in the same position, maintain the same exposure, and avoid using distortion lenses.

You can start the Photomerge command from Bridge. In Adobe Bridge, select the images you want, click the Tools menu, point to Photoshop, and then click Photomerge.

Assembled image using the Collage option

Single panoramic document

Merging Images to HDR

 PS 10.5

The Merge to HDR (High Dynamic Range) command allows you to combine multiple images or different exposures of the same image or scene (i.e., a bracketed exposure). This command takes the best elements of each photograph and combines them to create a single HDR image with more dynamic range than is possible with a single image, creating 32-bit high-quality digital images. Since several photos will be combined to create a single image, it's important to place the camera on a tripod (so the camera won't move between shots), and then take enough photographs (a minimum of 3) at different exposures to capture all the dynamic range of the scene. HDR enhancements in CS4 include faster, smoother exposure adjustments (**New!**).

Use the Merge To HDR Command

1. Click the **File** menu, point to **Automate**, and then click **Merge To HDR**.

2. Click the **Use** list arrow, and then select from the following options:

   ◆ **Files.** Click the Browse button, and then select the images.

   ◆ **Folder.** Click the Browse button, and then select the folder containing all the images.

3. To quickly add currently opened files to the list, click **Add Open Files**.

4. To remove any images from the list, click the file name, and then click **Remove**.

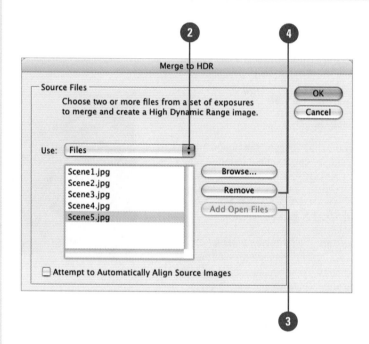

Did You Know?

You can start the Merge To HDR command from Bridge. Select the images you want, click the Tools menu, point to Photoshop, and then click Merge To HDR.

5 Select the **Attempt To Automatically Align Source Images** check box to let Photoshop try to align the images together (always try this option first).

6 Click **OK**.

7 If you did not check the option in step 4, specify any of the following options, and then click **OK**.

◆ **Select Files.** Select or clear the check box under each thumbnail to specify which images to use.

◆ **Bit Depth.** Click the **Bit Depth** list arrow, and then select a bit depth for the merged image.

◆ **Histogram.** Drag the slider to set the white point for previewing the merged image.

◆ **Response Curve.** Click the **Automatic** option to use tone curves to fine-tune HDR images after you have made the main adjustments you want.

   Click **Save Response Curve As** to save current settings. If you have a saved file with response curve presets, click **Load From File** to select the file you want.

Photoshop attempts to combine the elements of all the images.

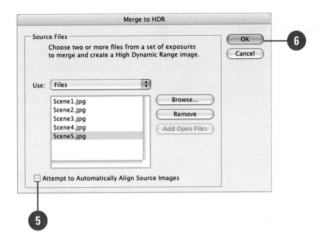

Select to include or clear to exclude from the merge

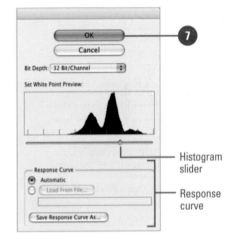

Histogram slider

Response curve

Merge to HDR image

Processing Multiple Image Files

PS 1.4, 1.5, 8.4

The Image Processor command in Photoshop allows you to convert and process multiple files without first creating an action, which is something you need to do with the Batch command. The Image Processor options make it easy to convert a set of files to either JPEG, PSD, or TIFF, or all three formats at the same time. When you take a lot of digital pictures, you can process the raw files all at once using the same options. If you are working on a collage with specific size and color requirements, you can use Image Processor to resize images to specific dimensions and embed a color profile or change the color mode to sRGB (the default working space for most Adobe color settings and the one recommended for web and digital camera images). In addition, you can include copyright metadata into any of the converted images.

Use the Image Processor Command

1. Click the **File** menu, point to **Scripts**, and then click **Image Processor**.

2. Click the **Use Open Images** option or click **Select Folder** to select the images or folder to process. You now also have the option to choose to include sub-folders. (**New!**)

3. Select the **Open First Image To Apply Settings** check box to apply the same settings to all the images.

    This allows you to adjust the settings in the first image, and then apply the same settings to the rest of the images.

4. Click the **Save in Same Location** option or click **Select Folder** to select the location in which to save processed images. You also now have the option to keep the original folder structure when saving. (**New!**)

    If you process the same file multiple times and save it to the same location, each file is saved with a unique file name so it's not overwritten.

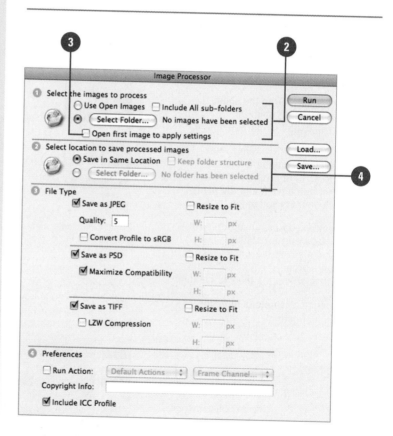

5 Select from the following options:

- **Save As JPEG.** Saves image in JPEG format.

- **Quality.** Enter a quality value between 0 and 12 (3 or 4 recommended for web graphics).

- **Resize To Fit.** Resizes the images to fit the width and height in pixels.

- **Convert Profile To sRGB.** Converts the color profile to sRGB; select the Include ICC Profile check box to save it.

- **Save As PSD.** Saves images in the PSD Photoshop format.

- **Maximize Compatibility.** Saves a composite of a layer image for programs that can't read layered images.

- **Save As TIFF.** Saves images in the TIFF format.

- **LZW Compression.** Saves TIFF files using the LZW compression scheme.

6 Select from the following Preferences options:

- **Run Action.** Runs a selected Photoshop action.

- **Copyright Info.** Includes file information entered in the IPTC copyright metadata.

- **Include ICC Profile.** Embeds the color profile with the saved image files.

7 To save your settings, click **Save**, enter a name, and then click **Save**.

8 To load saved settings, click **Load**, select the settings file, and then click **Open**.

9 Click **Run**.

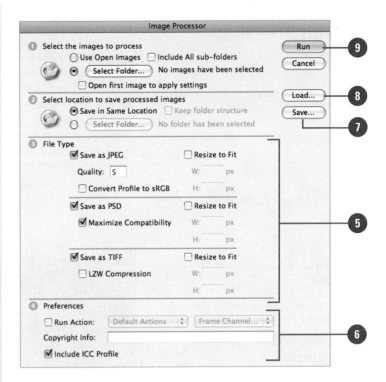

For Your Information

Batch Renaming Files with Adobe Bridge

You can rename files and folders in a batch, or group, to save time. With Bridge, you can select the same settings for all the files you want to process. Launch Adobe Bridge, select the files you want to rename or select a folder in the Folders panel that contains the files you want to rename. Launch the Batch Rename command from the Bridge Tools menu. You will need to decide whether to rename in the same folder, move, or copy the files and choose a destination folder if you choose to move or copy them. Then you can choose how the new file names will look by choosing options from drop-down menus or entering your own text to create file names (click plus (+) to add and minus (-) to remove data options). You can also choose to preserve the original file name in the XMP Metadata and choose your preferred operating system compatibility.

Using the Fit Image Command

 PS 1.4

The Fit Image command is a quick way to adjust an image to a specific width and height without changing its current aspect ratio. While the same process can be accomplished using Photoshop's Image Size dialog box, this way is quicker and works more reliably when used to change the size of an image within an action. Like another one of the Automate commands called Conditional Mode Change, the Fit Image command is designed to work best when incorporated into an action. When the action is executed, the Fit Image command will adjust the image size without opening any dialog boxes or requiring you to answer any formatting questions.

Use the Fit Image Command

1. Open a document.

2. Click the **File** menu, point to **Automate**, and then click **Fit Image**.

3. Enter a Width and Height for the transformation.

    Photoshop maintains the image's aspect ratio.

4. Click **OK**.

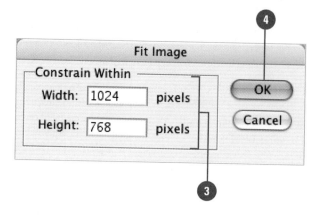

Managing Color from Monitor to Print

18

Introduction

Color management has changed a lot in the last few years. New standards have been defined, and Adobe is at the forefront of this new technology. No longer do you have to fear color management, because Adobe Photoshop has taken all (or at least most) of the guesswork out of the equation. Adobe's color management system (CMS), provides different rendering intents, or ways to translate color definitions between the input device and the output device using color profiles to avoid color-matching problems.

When you work on a computer monitor, you're viewing color information in the RGB (Red, Green, and Blue), additive color space. When you move into the world of the 4-color press, you're viewing color information in the CMYK, or subtractive color space. While a standard color press is called a 4-color press, in reality, only three colors are used—CMY (Cyan, Magenta, and Yellow—the opposites of RGB). To generate a true black, a printer must use the "K" plate (K stands for black, or key plate). Monitors display RGB colors very differently; when you factor in monitor resolutions, and the different types of monitors in the marketplace, what you see on a computer monitor is seldom what anyone else sees on their monitors. And that's not all; everyone who owns a computer has the ability to adjust or calibrate the colors on their monitors differently, further confusing the issue.

While nothing is perfect, the world of professional printing is more controlled. For example, when you're working on a color document that is moving to press, you can use a predetermined set of colors, such as the Pantone Matching System. The Pantone colors come printed on special card stock. When you're looking for a specific color, you choose it from the card stock, and then that information is given to the press operator. This type of control, even including the type of paper, keeps you in charge of the process of moving from monitor to print.

Producing Consistent Color

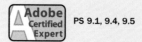 PS 9.1, 9.4, 9.5

Producing Consistent Color

You can create consistent color in Photoshop by following some basic steps:

1 If you are working with a production company, consult with them to make sure they provide you with any necessary software and hardware configuration and color management settings.

2 Calibrate and profile your monitor. See "Calibrating a Monitor" on this page.

3 Add color profiles to your computer for your input and output devices, such as a printer or scanner. Color profiles are typically added to your computer when you install the device. Photoshop uses the profile to help determine how the device produces color in a document.

4 Set up color management in Adobe programs. See "Working with Color Management" on page 422.

5 Preview colors using a soft proof (optional). See "Setting Up Soft-Proof Colors" on page 416.

6 Use color management when printing and saving files. See "Saving a Document" on page 28 and "Setting Document Print Options" on page 372.

Calibrating a Monitor (Manually)

Photoshop comes with its own color management system; however, before you can successfully use color management, you must first calibrate your monitor to a predefined standard. There are several methods available to you for monitor calibration. One is to purchase a third-party calibration system, while another is to use the operating system's built-

in color calibrator. While this section deals with manual calibration of your monitor, it is highly recommended that you purchase calibration equipment, or hire someone to calibrate your system, because the human eye is not the best device to color manage a system.

Before beginning the calibration process, let your monitor warm up for thirty minutes to an hour, and calibrate under the same lighting system that you'll be using when you work. To manually calibrate your computer monitor, on Windows, select the Adobe Gamma utility located in the Control Panel. For Macintosh users, select the Calibrate Utility by opening System Preferences, clicking the Display tab, and then clicking the Color tab. After you launch the calibration application, you will be instructed to manually balance the monitor for various shades of red, green, and blue, or to pick from a set of predetermined calibration settings. Since the human eye is not the best device for adjusting color, this method produces less-than-desirable results.

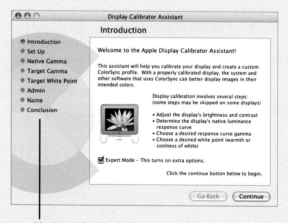

Macintosh Calibrate Utility

Calibrating Using Hardware and Software

The digital tools available today are so sophisticated that just 10 years ago, no one would have thought them possible. Color calibration falls into three categories: Input (digital cameras, scanners), Processing (monitors), and Output (printers, presses). Each category requires calibration to create a workflow between devices. Remember a few things before you calibrate your system: Let monitors warm up for 30 minutes to an hour before doing the calibration, and calibrate the system using the same lighting levels in which you will be designing. Once the calibration of all your devices is complete, you can expect the best color consistency that technology can provide. Several companies market color calibration hardware and software; one of them is ColorCal at *www.colorcal.com*.

Calibrate a Monitor (Processing)

To calibrate a monitor, you will need to purchase a digital device called a colorimeter, or spectrophotometer. When you launch the calibration software, it typically displays a color target in the middle of the monitor. You would then attach the device to the monitor, directly over the color patch, and follow the step-by-step instructions. When complete, the software creates a digital color profile for the monitor and PostScript output devices use that profile to accurately print color images.

Calibrate a Scanner and Digital Camera (Input)

Calibration of a scanner and digital camera requires the scanning or photographing of a reference color target with known color values. For example, the Kodak Q-60 IT8 color target has 240 color patches, a 24-step

grayscale, and reproduction of flesh tones. The calibration software reads the scanned colors and compares them to known color values to create a table of how the camera or scanner performs. Scanning a color target is easy. You lay the target on the scanner, close the lid and push the button. Digital cameras are a bit more difficult because you have to deal with the lighting conditions at the time the target was shot. With studio cameras this isn't a problem; however, taking photographs in ambient lighting involves different times of day, sunny versus cloudy, and incandescent versus fluorescent lighting. Yet, even factoring in the potential problems, calibrating your camera goes a long way in stabilizing color information on a digital camera.

Calibrate a Printer

To calibrate a printer, you will need a digital target file. The file is sent directly to the printer. Once printed, the results are checked with a spectrophotometer, and then the software measures the colors against the target values and creates a profile. There are many variables involved in the printing process, such as the type of inks used, and the type of paper used for printing. Therefore, calibration is performed based on the fact that you will be using the same ink and paper combination, so the calibration process should be performed each time you purchase new ink cartridges and/or change the paper type.

Setting Up Soft-Proof Colors

PS 9.4, 9.6, 11.5

When you work with a printer, you traditionally print a hard proof of your document, and visually preview how the colors look. Then you sign off on the proof, and the press operator begins the run. In Photoshop, you can use color profiles to soft-proof the document. Color profiles are a way to display the colors of a specific device directly on your monitor. While not as exact as a hard proof, it can go a long way to getting the colors of a CMYK document into the range of the output device. It's important to understand that the results of the soft proof compared to a hard proof is directly dependent on the quality of your monitor and monitor profiles. When you soft-proof a document, you're temporarily assigning a color profile to the document.

Understand How to Soft-Proof Colors

1. Open a document (to use soft proofing, the document does not have to be in the CMYK color mode).

2. Click the **View** menu, point to **Proof Setup**, and then click **Custom**.

3. Click the **Custom Proof Condition** list arrow, and then select from the available customized setups (check with your press operator).

4. Click the **Device to Simulate** list arrow, and then select from the available color output devices.

5. Select the **Preserve Numbers** check box to simulate how the colors will appear without conversion.

6. Click the **Rendering Intent** list arrow, (available if Preserve Numbers is unchecked), and then select from the available options to view how the colors will convert using the proof profile colors, and not the document profile.

7. Select the **Black Point Compensation** check box to map the full dynamic range of the source space (recommended).

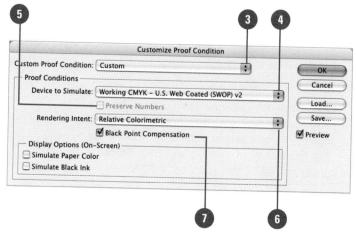

416

8 Select the **Simulate Paper Color** check box to simulate the visual conditions of white paper as defined by the current profile.

9 Select the **Simulate Black Ink** check box to map the full dynamic range of black as defined by the current profile.

10 To save a customized profile setup, click **Save**.

11 To load a previously saved profile setup, click **Load**.

Check with your press operator; in many cases they have profiles set up to match the dynamic range of their presses.

12 Click **OK**.

13 Click the **View** menu, and then click **Proof Colors** to view the color profile for the active document.

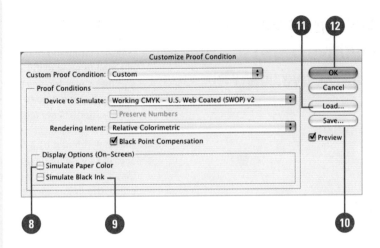

For Your Information

Understanding Soft-Proof Colors

If your monitor is properly calibrated and you have accurate profiles of your output devices, you can use Photoshop's soft-proof capabilities to preview how your image will look when printed to your desktop printer, sent to a printing press, or even when viewed on a particular computer operating system. The viewing capabilities of the Proof Setup option are only limited by the availability of output device profiles. If you don't have a specific profile, check with the manufacturer; many times they will have the device profiles available and, in most cases, for free.

Changing from Additive (RGB) to Subtractive (CMYK) Color

 PS 9.1, 9.4

RGB (Red, Green, and Blue) is defined as an additive color space, in which primary colors are added together to produce other colors. RGB is the color space of computer monitors, televisions, and most PDAs and cell phones with built-in color screens. A monitor uses pixels (small square or rectangular bricks), and each pixel mixes a combination of red, green, and blue to project a specific color to your eyes. Pixels use (on average) 24 switches to hold color information, and can produce 1 of 16,777,216 separate colors. CMYK (Cyan, Magenta, Yellow, and Black) is defined as a subtractive color space. CMYK is the color space of high-end inkjet, laser, and professional presses. A press uses plates that define each of the 4 colors; as a piece of paper passes through the press, the colors are applied from each plate. The term subtractive comes from the fact that the inks used in printing absorb or "subtract" a portion of the spectrum in order to produce other colors. Since a press cannot generate the intense saturation of an electronic pixel, the number of possible colors is reduced into the thousands. However, when used correctly, you can produce some stunning results. It's a simple matter to convert a Photoshop document into the CMYK mode; however, good planning will ensure the colors you want will be the colors you get.

Change from RGB to CMYK Color

1. Open a document.

   IMPORTANT *You cannot convert a Bitmap or Multichannel document directly into CMYK mode. Convert a Bitmap image to Grayscale, and then to CMYK; convert a Multichannel to RGB, and then to CMYK.*

2. Click the **Image** menu, point to **Mode**, and then click **CMYK**.

   Photoshop converts the RGB image into CMYK.

   If the RGB colors are not supported by the CMYK color space, they will be converted into the closest subtractive color values.

Image converts to CMYK

Working with Rendering Intents

PS 9.4, 9.5, 9.6, 11.3

Rendering Intents define how the selected color profile is converted from one color space into another. When you choose a rendering intent you are specifying how the colors should be displayed, even at the expense of the original gamut (range of colors) within the active document. The rendering intent you choose depends on which colors are critical in an image and on your preference of what the overall color appearance of an image should be. Many times the intent of the image's color gamut is different than how the original image was shot.

Work with Rendering Intents

1. Open a document.

2. Click the **View** menu, point to **Proof Setup**, and then click **Custom**.

3. Click the **Rendering Intent** list arrow, and then select from the following options:

   - **Perceptual.** Preserves the natural colors of an image, as viewed by the human eye, sometimes at the expense of the true color values. Good for photographic images.

   - **Saturation.** Produces vivid colors in an image, without paying attention to the original color values of the image. Good for business graphics, and charts where you want the colors to pop.

   - **Relative Colorimetric.** Shifts the color space of the document to that of the maximum highlight values of the destination. Useful for photographic images, and preserves more of the original color than Perceptual.

   - **Absolute Colorimetric.** Clips any colors in the destination image that do not fall into the color gamut of the destination. Use to proof images sent to devices such as 4-color presses.

4. Click **OK**.

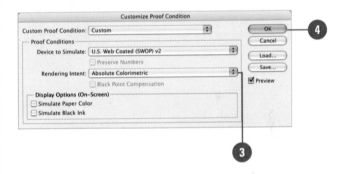

Image with a Web Coated profile.

Printing a Hard Proof

 PS 9.4, 9.6, 11.3, 11.5

In the language of the print world, a soft proof is viewed on a monitor, and a hard proof (sometimes referred to as a match print) is viewed on a piece of paper, typically printed on a device such as an inkjet or laser printer, that is less expensive than producing a hard proof from a printing press. In the last few years, many inkjet printers now have the resolution necessary to produce inexpensive prints that can be used as hard proofs, which previously had to be printed on high-end printing presses, or expensive high-resolution laser printers. A hard proof gives you something you can hold in your hands, and is not only useful for viewing colors, but even evaluating the layout. Since a monitor typically displays a document at a different size than your printed document dimensions, you now have an exact size to match to your final document and review before going ahead with the final printing.

Print a Hard Proof

1. Open a document.

2. Click the **View** menu, point to **Proof Setup**, and then click **Custom**.

3. Click the **Device To Simulate** list arrow, and then select a specific proof set.

4. Click **OK**.

5. Click the **File** menu, and then click **Print**.

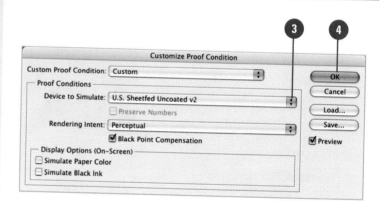

See Also

See "Setting Up Soft-Proof Colors" on page 416 for information on using color profiles.

6 Click the **Proof** option (it should display your chosen proof setup).

7 Click the **Color Handling** list arrow, and click **Photoshop Manages Colors**.

8 Click the **Printer Profile** list arrow, and then select your output device from the available options.

9 Click the **Rendering Intent** list arrow, and then select from the available options (disabled when you select the Proof option, step 6).

10 Click the **Proof Setup** list arrow, and then click **Current Custom Setup**.

11 Click **Print**.

See Also

See "Working with Rendering Intents" on page 419 for more information on using rendering intent options.

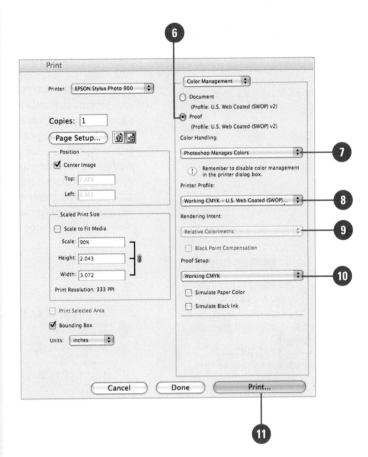

Working with Color Management

 PS 9.1, 9.2, 9.3, 9.4, 11.3

Colors in an image will often look different when you view them using different monitors. They may also look very different when printed on your desktop printer or when printed on a professional printing press. If your work in Photoshop requires you to produce consistent color across different devices, managing color should be an essential part of your workflow. Photoshop gives you a group of predefined color management systems, which are designed to help you produce consistent color. These management systems are recognized by other Adobe products, and by most professional printing services. In most cases, the predefined sets are all you will need to manage color workflow or, as you become more adept at managing color, they can be used as a basis for creating your own customized sets. The power of color management lies in its ability to produce consistent colors with a system that reconciles differences between the color spaces of each device.

Work with Color Management

1. Open Photoshop (it is not necessary to open a document).

2. Click the **Edit** menu, and then click **Color Settings**.

3. Click the **Settings** list arrow, and then select from the available options:

    ◆ **Custom.** Create your own customized set (requires a good knowledge of color management and color theory).

    ◆ **Monitor Color.** For creating content for video and onscreen presentations.

    ◆ **North America General Purpose 2** (default). For creating consistent workflow with Adobe applications used in North America.

    ◆ **North America Prepress 2.** The defaults for common prepress operations in the U.S.

    ◆ **North America Web/Internet.** Manages color-space content for documents published on the Web.

    ◆ **More Settings.** Click the More Options button, and then click

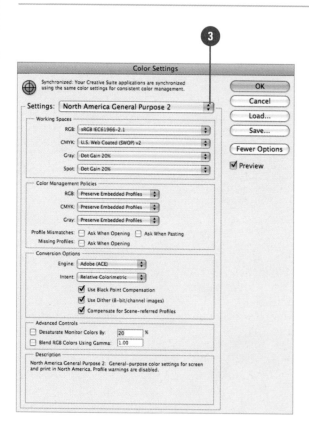

Settings list arrow to see more options for Japan and Europe.

④ Create your own customized color sets using the following options:

◆ **Working Spaces:** Defines the working color profiles for each color model. Working Spaces can be used for images that were not previously color-managed, or for newly created color-managed documents.

◆ **Color Management Policies:** Defines how the colors in a specific color model are managed. You can choose to embed or convert the selected profile, or to ignore it.

◆ **Conversion Options:** Defines exactly how you want the conversion process handled using a color-defined Engine, and color conversion Intent. You can adjust for black point when converting color spaces, dither color channel information when converting between color spaces and compensate for Scene-referred Profiles (**New!**).

◆ **Advanced Controls:** Desaturate Monitor Colors gives you the ability to control the viewing of a color space on different monitors; however, if activated, images will print differently than viewed. You can also decide what Gamma level is used when blending RGB values.

⑤ To save color settings as a preset, click **Save**, and then save the file in the default location.

⑥ To load a Color Settings preset not saved in the standard location, click **Load**.

⑦ Click **OK**.

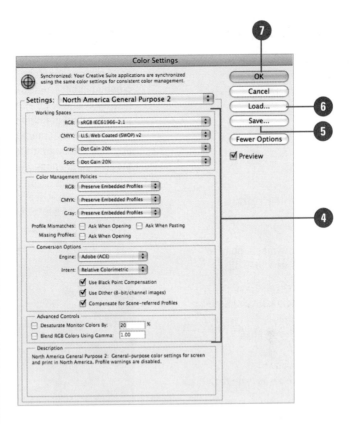

Embedding ICC Color Profiles

When you work on a color document, you're viewing the image using your own computer, with a specific version of Photoshop, and a unique monitor calibration. What you need is a way to preserve the visual settings of the document. In other words, you want someone else to see what you see. The ICC (International Color Consortium) color profiles provide a universal way of saving (called tagging or embedding) a mathematical definition of a particular color space, and gives you a reasonable certainty that the document will display correctly on other devices. Although there are several file modes that accept ICC profiles, the two most common are RGB and CMYK.

Embed ICC Color Profiles

1. Open a document.

2. Click the **View** menu, point to **Proof Setup**, and then click **Custom**.

3. Click the **Device To Simulate** list arrow, and then select a color profile for the image.

4. Click **OK**.

5. Click the **File** menu, and then click **Save As**.

6. Enter a file name.

7. Click the **Format** list arrow, and then select one of the following formats: Photoshop PSD, Photoshop EPS, JPEG, Photoshop PDF, Photoshop DCS, or TIFF.

    IMPORTANT *To save the file with the newly created custom profile, the file must be saved as an EPS, DCS, or PDF.*

8. Click the **Save As** (Win) or **Where** (Mac) list arrow, and then select a location in which to save the file.

9. Select the **ICC Profile** (Win) or **Embed Color Profile** (Mac) check box.

10. Click **Save** to save the file as a copy and embed the new profile.

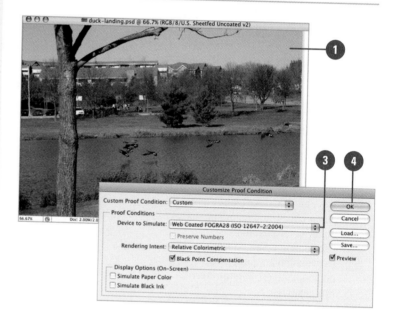

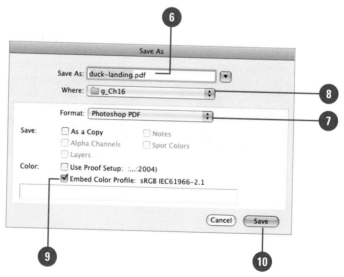

424

Assigning a Different Profile to a Document

PS 9.1, 9.4

Photoshop's color management system must know the color space of your document so it can decipher the meaning of the color values in the image. When assigning a profile to an image, the image will be in the color space described by the particular profile. For example, a document's profile can be assigned by a source device, like a digital camera or a scanner, or assigned directly in Photoshop. When using the Assign Profile command, color values are mapped directly into the new profile space.

Assign or Remove a Profile

1. Open a document.

2. Click the **Edit** menu, and then click **Assign Profile**.

3. Select from the following options:

   ◆ **Don't Color Manage This Document.** Select this option to remove any assigned profile (the document becomes untagged).

   ◆ **Working RGB.** Select this option to tag the document with the current working space profile.

   ◆ **Profile.** Select this option, click the list arrow, and then select a new color profile, which removes the old one.

4. Click **OK**.

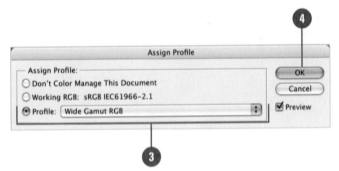

See Also

See "Changing from Additive (RGB) to Subtractive (CMYK) Color" on page 418 for more information on using and working with CMYK images.

Converting the Color Space to Another Profile

There are times when you will open a document that contains an embedded profile, and you need to convert it. Photoshop gives you the option of tagging the document with another profile without converting the colors, or removing the old profile and converting the color space. Photoshop's Convert to Profile command gives you the ability to change the profile in a document. In addition, you may want to prepare a document for a different output destination, such as an inkjet printer or 4-color press.

Convert the Color Space to Another Profile

1. Open a document.

2. Click the **Edit** menu, and then click **Convert to Profile**.

3. Click the **Profile** list arrow, and then select a new color profile.

   The document will be converted and tagged with the new color profile.

4. Click the **Engine** list arrow, and then select:

   ◆ **Adobe (ACE).** Adobe color management (default).

   ◆ **Microsoft ICM.** Windows color management.

   ◆ **Apple CMM.** Mac OS color management. (Depending on your operating system, your options may vary.)

5. Click the **Intent** list arrow, and then select an option.

See Also

See "Working with Rendering Intents" on page 419 for more information on using rendering intent options.

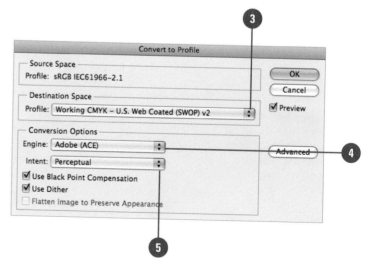

6 Select the **Use Black Point Compensation** check box to map the full color range of the source to the full color range of the destination profile.

7 Select the **Use Dither** check box to use with 8-bit color images; if you select this option, Photoshop dithers color pixels when converting between source and destination color profiles.

8 Select the **Flatten Image to Preserve Appearance** check box to flatten a multi-layered document.

9 Click **OK**.

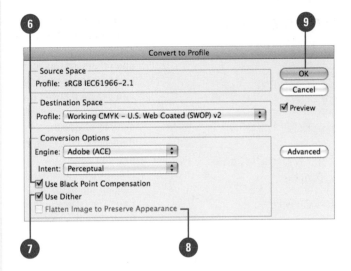

Printing a Target Image

PS 9.4

When you work in the world of computer monitors and output devices, what you see on your monitor is seldom what you get when you print. The color spaces are different—monitors are based on additive color, and printing on paper is based on subtractive color. In addition, monitors use pixels to generate colors, and printers use inks. However, you can create a target print, and then use that to generate a custom profile. A target document with specific color swatches and information is used to create the target document and is usually supplied as part of a third-party color management software package. When printing a target, you want to turn off all color management in both Photoshop and the print driver. Once the target is printed, it is scanned by a third-party measuring instrument to create the custom profile. Companies such as Color Cal (*www.colorcal.com*) provide electronic measurement systems to analyze the image and create the profile. If you have more than one output device, you will have to print a target for each document.

Print a Target Image

1. Open a color target document.

2. Click the **File** menu, and then click **Print**.

3. Click the list arrow, and then select **Color Management**.

4. Click the **Document** option.

   This reproduces colors as interpreted by the profile currently assigned to the document.

5. Click the **Color Handling** list arrow, and then click **No Color Management**.

6. Click **Print**.

7. Click the **Printer** list arrow, and then select the correct output device.

8. Select any other print-related options as needed.

9. Click **Print**.

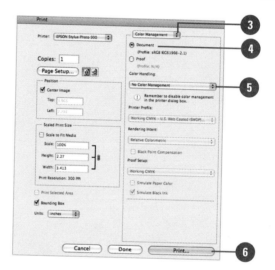

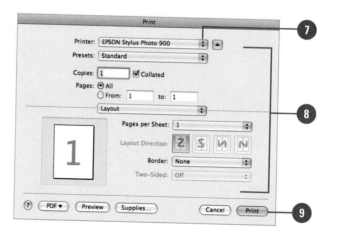

Working with the Out-Of-Gamut Warning

Adobe Certified Expert PS 9.4

One of the biggest problems with images displayed on a computer monitor is that they don't accurately represent the color space of a 4-color press. There are ways that we can reduce the possibility of colors not printing correctly, but in the end the RGB and CMYK color spaces are different—in fact, they're exactly the opposite of each other. Photoshop understands this, and gives you a way to view before printing which colors will be out of gamut. The term **Gamut** refers to the colors that a particular device can display or print; in the case of a 4-color press, it would describe a color that could be reproduced on that press. The out-of-gamut test is performed on an image before the conversion into the CMYK mode. Once you convert an image to CMYK it's too late to test, because Photoshop has already made the conversion.

Work with the Out-Of-Gamut Warning

① Open an RGB image.

② Click the **Edit** (Win) or **Photoshop** (Mac) menu, point to **Preferences**, and then click **Transparency & Gamut**.

③ Select a Gamut Warning color, and then enter an Opacity percentage value (1% to 100%).

Gamut Warning refers to the color Photoshop uses to mask the out-of-gamut areas of the image.

④ Click **OK**.

⑤ Click the **View** menu, and then click **Gamut Warning**.

Photoshop displays any color outside the CMYK gamut with a predefined color mask.

Did You Know?

There are other ways to identify out-of-gamut colors. In the Info panel, when you point to an out-of-gamut color, an exclamation point appears. In the Color Picker and the Color panel, an alert triangle appears.

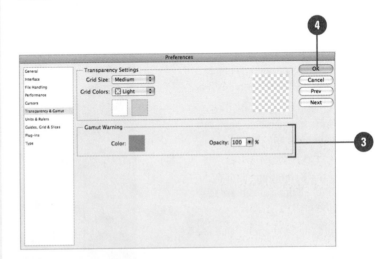

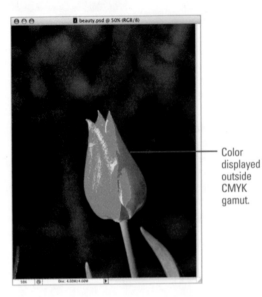

Color displayed outside CMYK gamut.

Using Hue/Saturation for Out-Of-Gamut Colors

PS 9.4

Once you've established that your document contains colors outside the CMYK color space, it's up to you to decide exactly how to correct the problem. There are as many ways to correct color problems as there are tools, and each Photoshop user has their favorites. Two methods that are simple and powerful are using the Hue/Saturation Adjustment and Photoshop's Sponge tool. Understand that the primary reason a color won't translate correctly into the CMYK color space is due to the saturation values of the ink. A monitor can produce more saturation in a pixel than a 4-color press can produce by mixing inks.

Use the Hue/Saturation Adjustment

1. Open an RGB image.

2. Click the **View** menu, and then click **Gamut Warning**.

   Photoshop displays any colors outside the CMYK gamut with a predefined color mask.

3. Click the **Image** menu, point to **Adjustments**, and then click **Hue/Saturation**.

4. Drag the **Saturation** slider to the left until all the masked areas disappear.

5. Record the Saturation Value used.

6. Click **Cancel**.

7. Click the **Select** menu, and then click **Color Range**.

Did You Know?

You can select the closest CMYK equivalent of an out-of-gamut color in the Color Picker or the Color panel. Display the Color Picker or the Color panel, select the out-of-gamut color you want to change, which displays the closest CMYK equivalent, and then click the triangle or the color patch.

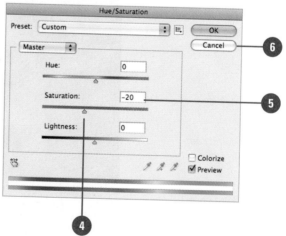

8 Click the **Select** list arrow, and then click **Out Of Gamut**.

9 Click **OK**.

The out-of-gamut areas of the image are now selected and isolated from the rest of the image.

10 Click the **Select** menu, and then click **Refine Edge**.

11 Enter a Feather value of .5.

This softens the desaturation of the out-of-gamut areas of the image.

12 Click **OK**.

13 Click the **Image** menu, point to **Adjustments**, and then click **Hue/Saturation**.

14 Enter the Saturation value you recorded from step 5.

15 Click **OK**.

16 Press Ctrl+D (Win) or ⌘+D (Mac) to deselect the image areas.

The image is now ready for conversion to CMYK.

Did You Know?

Photoshop can automatically convert all out-of-gamut colors to be within the gamut area. Simply convert an RGB image to CMYK. Open an RGB image, click the Image menu, point to Mode, and then click CMYK Color.

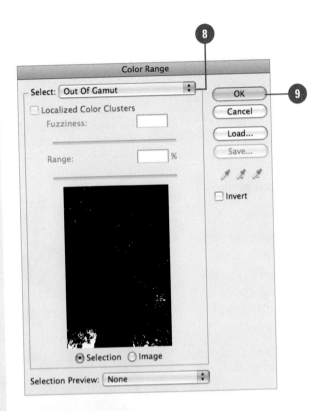

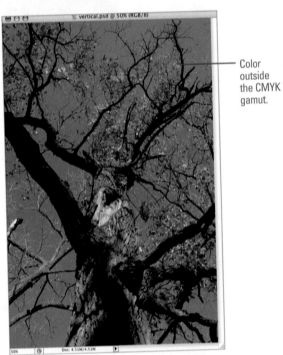

Color outside the CMYK gamut.

Using the Sponge Tool for Out-Of-Gamut Colors

 PS 9.4

The Sponge tool method is a bit more work intensive; however, it gives you precise control over each out-of-gamut area of the image. Since the Sponge tool decreases saturation values from the colors based on the speed with which the tool is dragged across the image, the key to successfully using the Sponge tool to restore out-of-gamut colors is to choose a soft-edged brush, and use smooth, even strokes. Practice is the key to effective image restoration and color correction, and using a drawing tablet as opposed to a mouse will help in the control of the tool.

Use the Sponge Tool Method

1. Open an RGB image.

2. Click the **View** menu, and then click **Gamut Warning**.

   Photoshop displays any color outside the CMYK gamut with a predefined color mask.

3. Select the **Sponge** tool.

4. Click the **Brush** list arrow, and then select a soft, round brush tip with a small diameter from the brush tip options.

5. Click the **Mode** list arrow, and then click **Desaturate**.

6. Enter a Flow value of 60%, and then use the **Vibrance** box to minimize clipping of strongly saturated or desaturated colors (**New!**).

7. Click the **Select** menu, and then click **Color Range**.

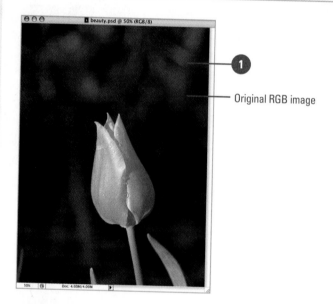

Original RGB image

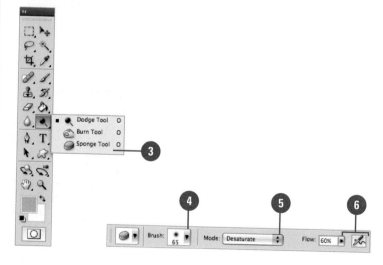

8 Click the **Select** list arrow, and then click **Out Of Gamut**.

9 Click **OK**.

The out-of-gamut areas of the image are now selected and isolated from the rest of the image.

10 Click the **Refine Edge** menu, and then click **Feather**.

11 Enter a Feather value of .5.

This softens the desaturation of the out-of-gamut areas of the image.

12 Click **OK**.

13 Slowly drag the **Sponge** tool over an out-of-gamut area until the color mask disappears.

Continue through the document until all the areas have been corrected.

14 Press Ctrl+D (Win) or ⌘+D (Mac) to deselect the image areas.

The image is now ready for conversion to CMYK.

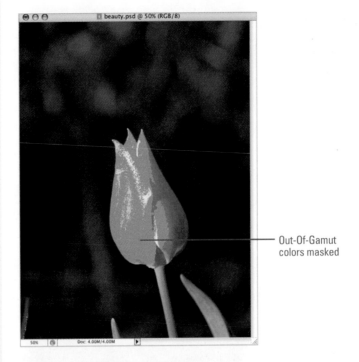

Out-Of-Gamut colors masked

Out-Of-Gamut colors removed with the Sponge tool

Did You Know?

You can hide selection marquees. If the selection marquee is getting in the way of seeing small out-of-gamut areas, press Ctrl+H (Win) or ⌘+H (Mac) to temporarily hide the selection marquee, and then repeat the command to restore the marquee.

Designing for the Web and Devices

19

Introduction

If you need to manipulate a photographic image to place it on the Web, there's not a better program on the market than Adobe Photoshop that will do the job for you. You can prepare images for the Internet all right from Photoshop.

Photoshop uses various document formats such as JPEG, GIF, PNG, and WBMP (Wireless BMP), to save images for the Web. For example, the JPEG format is used primarily for compressing photographic images, while the GIF format is used for compressing clip art and text. Each format is designed to serve a purpose, and knowing when to use a specific format will help you design fast-loading, dynamic web documents.

However, saving files in a specific file format is not the only way Photoshop helps you create web-friendly images; you can also slice images. When you slice an image, you're cutting the image into several pieces. Since the Internet handles smaller packets of information more efficiently than one large piece, slicing an image makes the whole graphic load faster, and Photoshop helps you slice images with ease.

Saving for the Web

PS 1.5, 12.1, 12.2

Photoshop's Save For Web & Devices command is a dream come true for preparing images for the Internet, or even for saving images in a quick-loading format for Microsoft PowerPoint slide presentations, and you don't even have to leave Photoshop. The Save For Web & Devices command lets you open any Photoshop document, and convert it into a web-friendly format using the GIF, JPEG, PNG, or WBMP formats. You can even try different optimization settings or compare different optimizations using the 2-Up or 4-Up panes. In addition, the dialog area below each image provides optimization information on the size and download time of the file.

Save for the Web

1. Open a document.

2. Click the **File** menu, and then click **Save For Web & Devices**.

3. Click the **Original**, **Optimized**, **2-Up**, or **4-Up** tabs to view the document using different layouts.

4. Click one of the sample images to change its default format.

   IMPORTANT *If you're viewing the document using 2-Up or 4-Up, the first image is the original. You can't change the original; you can only edit one of the sample images.*

5. Click the **Optimized File Format** list arrow, and then select from the following options:

   ◆ **GIF.** The Graphics Interchange Format is useful for clip art, text, or images that contain a large amount of solid color. GIF uses lossless compression.

   ◆ **JPEG.** The Joint Photographic Experts Group format is useful for images that contain a lot of continuous tones, like photographs. JPEG uses lossy compression.

   ◆ **PNG-8.** The Portable Network Graphics 8-bit format functions like the GIF format. PNG uses lossless compression.

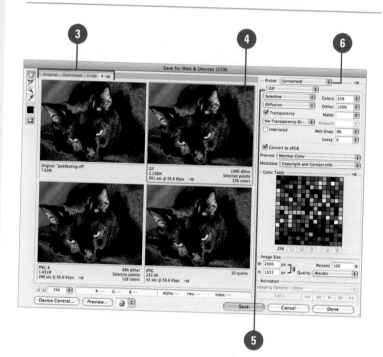

◆ **PNG-24.** The Portable Network Graphics 24-bit format functions like the JPEG format. PNG-24 uses lossless compression.

◆ **WBMP.** The Wireless Bitmap format converts an image into black and white dots, for use on output devices like cell phones and PDAs.

6 Click the **Preset** list arrow. Select a template from the available options, if you want to use some timesaving default options.

7 Select from the various options that will change based on your File Format selection. Select **Convert to sRGB** if you want the image converted, and choose your preferred viewing style and amount of metadata to be included in the file. (**New!**)

8 Click the **Color Table** section (available for the GIF and PNG-8 formats), and add, subtract, or edit colors in the selected document.

9 To change the selected image's width and height, make desired adjustments from the Image Size section.

10 To move the selected image directly into the Device Central application, click the **Device Central** button.

11 Click **Save**.

12 Enter a name, and then select a location in which to save the image file.

13 Click **OK**.

Photoshop saves the modified file and returns you to the original image.

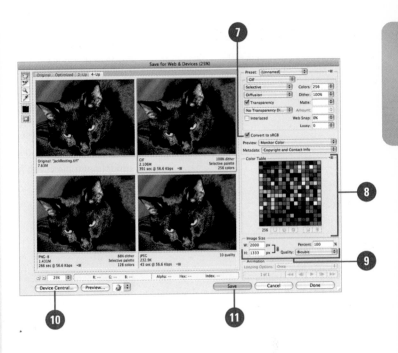

For Your Information

Working with Matte and Transparency

The Matte option, when available, specifies the background color used to fill anti-aliased edges that lie adjacent to transparent areas of the image. When the Transparency option is selected, the matte is applied to edge areas to help blend the edges with a web background of the same color. When the Transparency option is not selected, the matte is applied to transparent areas. Choosing the None option for the matte creates hard edges if Transparency is selected; otherwise, all transparent areas are filled with 100% white. The image must have transparency for the Matte options to be available.

Working with Save For Web Options

 PS 12.1, 12.2

When you choose Save For Web & Devices, you are able to save your image in one of four web formats: GIF, JPEG, PNG, or WBMP. The Save For Web & Devices dialog box comes with options that will help you through the process. For example, if you choose the JPEG format, you can select the amount of compression applied to the image or, if you select the GIF format, you can choose how many colors are preserved with the image. The PNG format lets you save images in an 8-bit (256 colors) or a 24-bit (millions of colors) format. The options available with Save For Web & Devices give you the control you need to produce small image files with high quality.

Work with Save For Web Options

1. Open a document.

2. Click the **File** menu, and then click **Save For Web & Devices**.

3. Select from the various Save For Web & Devices tools:

   ◆ **Hand Tool.** Drag the image to change the view of a document.

   ◆ **Slice Selection Tool.** Select a predefined image slice.

   ◆ **Zoom Tool.** Click on the image to expand the view size.

   ◆ **Eyedropper Tool.** Drag within the image to perform a live sampling of the colors.

4. Click the **Thumbnail Options** button, and then select bandwidth options for the selected document.

5. Click the **Zoom** list arrow, and then select a view size for the sample images.

6. Click the **Toggle Slices Visibility** button to show or hide the image slices.

7. Click the **Preview** button to choose from browser options or view in the default browser, and then select the image.

8. Click **Save**.

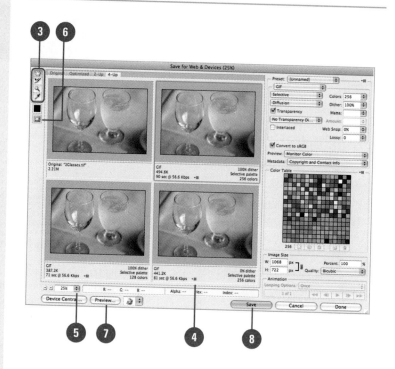

For Your Information

New save options in Photoshop CS4 include:

Convert to sRGB. You can choose to have image colors converted to sRGB in the Save process.

Preview. Select from four preview options: Monitor Color (default), Macintosh or Windows with no color management, or Use Document Profile.

Metadata. Select from five options to include no metadata (very helpful for stripping out metadata you don't want others to see), copyright only, copyright and contact info, all metadata except camera info, or all metadata.

Optimizing an Image to File Size

PS 12.1, 12.2

The Save For Web & Devices dialog box has many options to help you create the exact image you need—including helping you compress an image down to a specific file size. For example, you've just created an image you want to display on the Web, but the maximum file size you can use is 35 KB. You could experiment with compression options in the Save For Web & Devices settings, or you could use the Optimize to File Size option.

Optimize an Image to File Size

1. Open a document.

2. Click the **File** menu, and then click **Save For Web & Devices**.

3. Click the **2-Up** tab, and then select the sample image to the right.

4. Click the **Optimize** menu, and then click **Optimize To File Size**.

5. Enter a file size in the Desired File Size data box.

6. Click the **Current Settings** option or the **Auto Select GIF/JPEG** option to let Photoshop choose between the JPEG or GIF format.

7. Click the following Use options:

   ◆ Current Slice

   ◆ Each Slice

   ◆ Total of All Slices

8. Click **OK**.

   Photoshop compresses the selected sample.

9. Click **Save** to save the compressed image.

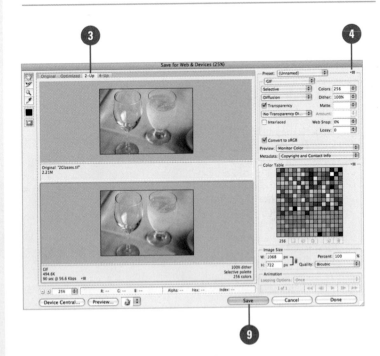

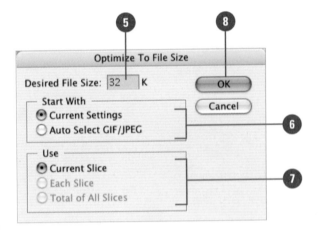

Working with Web File Formats

PS 12.1, 12.2

If you design web documents, you know that the size of your images is very important. Photoshop gives you the option of compressing images in one of four formats appropriate for use on the Web: GIF, JPEG, PNG, and WBMP. The GIF format compresses images that contain solid colors with sharp, definable edges, such as clip art and text. The JPEG format reduces the size of image files that contain a lot of soft transitional colors, such as photographs. The PNG format is a hybrid format designed to take the place of the GIF and JPEG format. Finally, the WBMP format was created to display images on low-resolution devices like cell phones and PDAs by converting the image into dots of black and white. Photoshop will help you transform your images into whatever format you need in order to create stunning web images.

Work with Web File Formats

1. Open a document.

2. Click the **File** menu, and then click **Save For Web & Devices**.

3. Click the **Original**, **Optimized**, **2-Up**, or **4-Up** tabs to view the document using different layouts.

4. Select one of the samples.

5. Click the **Optimized File Format** list arrow, and then select a format from the available options.

6. Select the options you want to use to change the image compression, and specify your desired color profile options.

7. Click **Save**.

   The Save Optimized As dialog box appears.

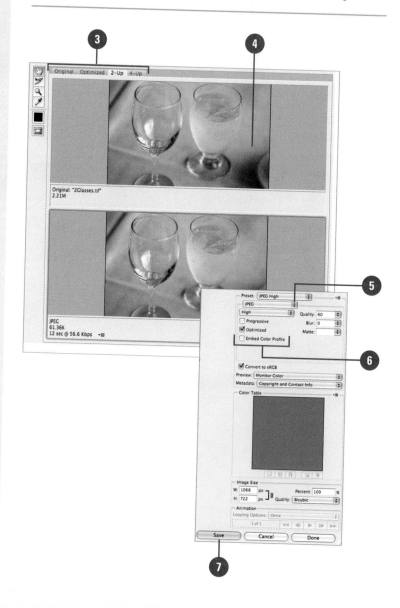

8 Enter a file name in the Save As box.

9 Click the **Save as Type** (Win) or **Format** (Mac) list arrow, and then select to save the image in HTML and Images, Images Only, or HTML Only.

10 Click the **Save As** list arrow, and then select the location in which to save the file.

11 Click the **Settings** and **Slices** list arrows to further define the output files (if you save a single image without slices, you can leave these settings at their default values).

12 Click **Save**.

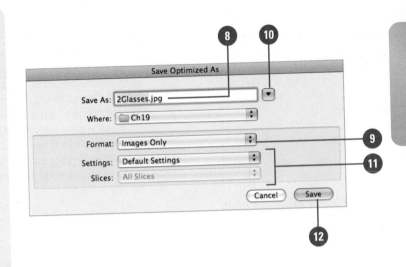

For Your Information

Creating an HTML File for an Image

When you save an optimized file using the Save Optimized As command, you can choose to generate an HTML file for the image. This file contains all the necessary information to display your image in a web browser.

Optimizing a JPEG Document

Photoshop comes complete with everything you will need to properly compress any JPEG Document. The Internet can generally be slow to navigate, and your visitors typically do not have much patience. When you compress a JPEG image, you're essentially removing information from the image to reduce its file size and speed up the loading time. The unfortunate result of that reduction is loss of image quality. Internet graphics are not always the best quality; however, reducing file size is a necessary evil to keep visitors from clicking off your site and moving to another. To keep visitors happy, your JPEG images must load fast, and Photoshop is just the application to help you accomplish that goal.

Optimize a JPEG Document

1. Open a document.

2. Click the **File** menu, and then click **Save For Web & Devices**.

3. Click the **Original**, **Optimized**, **2-Up**, or **4-Up** tabs to view the document using different layouts.

4. Click one of the sample images to change its default format.

5. Click the **Optimized File Format** list arrow, and then click **JPEG**.

6. Select from the following Quality options:

   ◆ **Compression Quality.** Click the list arrow, and then select a preset JPEG quality from Low (poor quality) to Maximum (best quality).

   ◆ **Quality Amount.** Enter a JPEG quality compression value (0 to 100). The lower the value, the more information (color) is sacrificed for image size.

   ◆ **Blur.** JPEG images compress better when the image has soft edges. Apply the Blur option to increase the softness of the image (at a sacrifice of image quality).

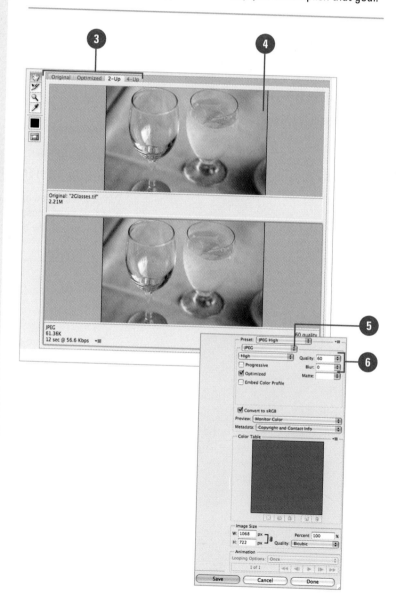

7 Click the **Matte** list arrow, and then select from the available options.

JPEG images do not support transparency. If your image contains transparent areas, use the Matte option to fill them in using a specific color.

8 Select the **Optimized** check box to further compress the image. Choose from two additional options:

◆ **Progressive.** Select the check box to load a JPEG in three progressive scans. Not supported by all browsers.

◆ **Embed Color Profile.** Select the check box to embed an ICC color profile into the JPEG image. This increases file size but helps maintain color consistency between monitors and operating systems.

9 Choose from three new options to apply to your saved file:

◆ **Convert to sRGB.** You can choose to have image colors converted to sRGB in the Save process.

◆ **Preview.** Select from four preview options: Monitor Color (default), Macintosh or Windows with no color management, or Use Document Profile.

◆ **Metadata.** Select from five options to include no metadata, copyright only, copyright and contact info, all metadata except camera info, or all metadata.

10 Click **Save** to open the **Save Optimized As** dialog box where you can choose a location for your saved file.

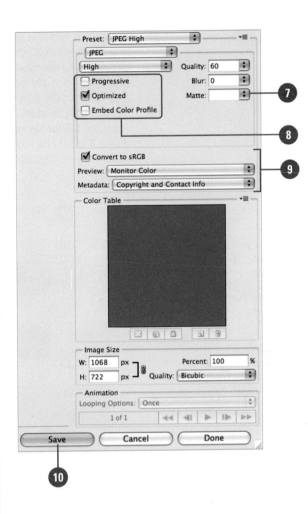

Optimizing a GIF Document

The GIF file format is used primarily for images that contain solid colors with sharp edges, such as clip art, text, line art, and logos. Since the Internet can generally be slow to navigate, using the GIF format for images significantly reduces their file size, and will create fast-loading graphics. The GIF format supports 8-bit color, and creates a document with a maximum of 256 colors (the fewer colors, the smaller the file size). The GIF format has been around long enough for it to be considered a "native" Internet format. A **native format** is one that does not require a specific plug-in for the browser to display the file.

Optimize a GIF Document

1. Open a document.

2. Click the **File** menu, and then click **Save For Web & Devices**.

3. Click the **Original**, **Optimized**, **2-Up**, or **4-Up** tabs to view the document using different layouts.

4. Click one of the sample images to change its default format.

5. Click the **Optimized File Format** list arrow, and then click **GIF**.

6. Select from the following options:

   Color Options:

   ◆ **Reduction.** Click to select a visual reduction method for the image's colors. (Selective is the default)

   ◆ **Colors.** Enter or select a value from 2 to 256 maximum colors.

   ◆ **Web Snap.** Enter or select a value from 0% to 100% to instruct the GIF compression utility how many of the image colors should be web-safe.

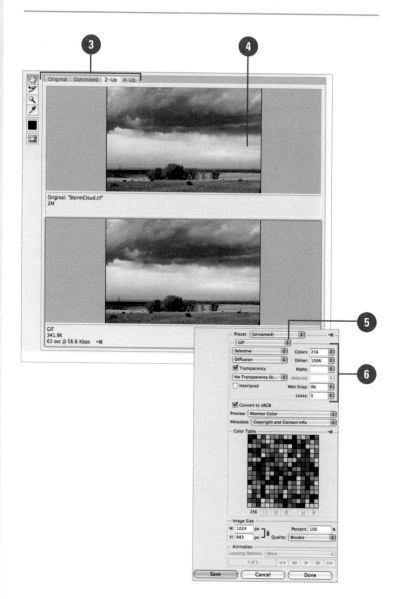

Dither Options:

◆ **Method.** Click the list arrow, and then select from the available dithering schemes (No Dither, Diffusion, Pattern, or Noise). Dithering refers to how the GIF format mixes the available colors in the image.

◆ **Amount.** Enter or select a value from 0% to 100% to instruct the GIF compression utility how many of the image's colors should be dithered.

Transparency Options:

◆ **Transparency.** Check to keep the transparent areas of a GIF image transparent and choose type of transparency dither (None, Diffusion, Pattern, or Noise) (**New!**).

◆ **Matte.** Click to fill the transparent areas of a GIF image.

◆ **Dither.** Click to select a dithering scheme (None, Diffusion, Pattern, Noise) and enter an amount for the mixing of the matte color.

Other Options:

◆ **Interlaced.** Check to have the GIF image load in three scans.

◆ **Lossy.** Enter or select a value from 0 to 100 to instruct the GIF compression utility how much image loss is allowed.

7 Click **Save** to save the current image using the Save Optimized As dialog box.

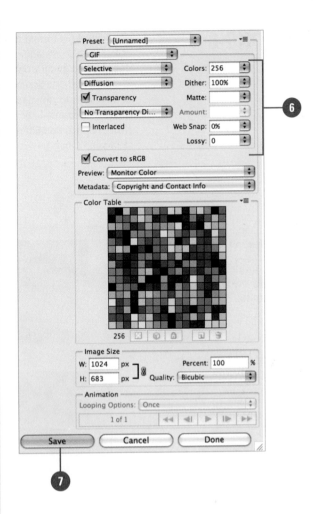

Optimizing a PNG-8 Document

The PNG-8 file format is used primarily for images that contain solid colors with sharp edges—clip art, text, line art, and logos—and was designed as an alternative to the GIF file format. Since the PNG-8 format generates an image with a maximum of 256 colors, it significantly reduces an image's file size. While similar to the GIF file format, the PNG-8 format is not completely supported by older browsers. However, it is considered a native format for the creation of Flash animation movies.

Optimize a PNG-8 Document

1. Open a document.

2. Click the **File** menu, and then click **Save For Web & Devices**.

3. Click the **Original**, **Optimized**, **2-Up**, or **4-Up** tabs to view the document using different layouts.

4. Click one of the sample images to change its default format.

5. Click the **Optimized File Format** list arrow, and then click **PNG-8**.

6. Select from the following options:

   Color Options:

   ◆ **Reduction.** Click to select a visual reduction method for the colors in the image (Selective is the default).

   ◆ **Colors.** Enter or select a value from 2 to 256 maximum colors.

   ◆ **Web Snap.** Enter or select a value from 0% to 100% to instruct the PNG-8 compression utility how many of the image's colors should be web-safe.

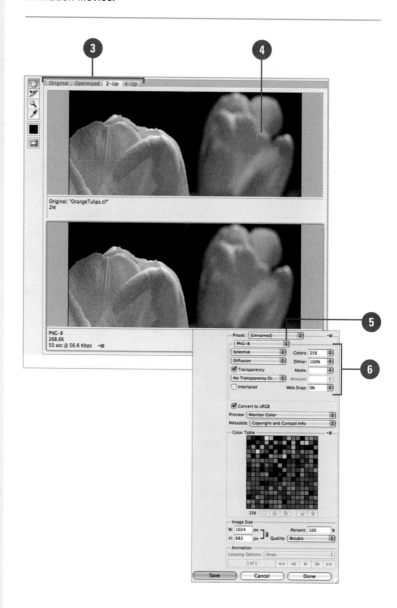

Dither Options:

◆ **Method.** Click the list arrow, and then select from the available dithering schemes (None, Diffusion, Pattern, or Noise). Dithering is how the PNG-8 format mixes the available image's colors.

◆ **Amount.** Enter or select a value from 0% to 100% to instruct the PNG-8 compression utility how many of the image's colors should be dithered.

Transparency Options:

◆ **Transparency.** Check to keep the transparent areas of a PNG-8 image transparent.

◆ **Matte.** Click to fill the transparent areas of a PNG-8 image.

◆ **Dither.** Click to select a dithering scheme (None, Diffusion, Pattern, or Noise) and enter an amount for the mixing of the matte color.

Other Options:

◆ **Interlaced.** Check to have the PNG image load in three scans.

7 Click **Save** to save the current image using the Save Optimized As dialog box.

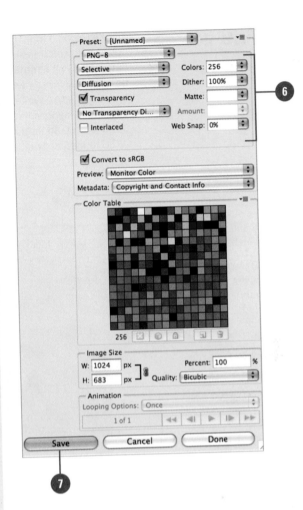

Optimizing a PNG-24 Document

The PNG-24 file format is used primarily for images that contain lots of colors with soft transitional edges, such as photographs, and was designed as an alternative to the JPEG file format. The PNG-24 format generates an image with millions of colors, and still manages to reduce the size of a file. While similar to the JPEG file format, the PNG-24 uses lossless compression, and does not compress files as small as the JPEG format. So for the time being, most designers are still using the JPEG format for creating faster-loading web graphics.

Optimize a PNG-24 Document

1. Open a document.

2. Click the **File** menu, and then click **Save For Web & Devices**.

3. Click the **Original**, **Optimized**, **2-Up**, or **4-Up** tabs to view the document using different layouts.

4. Click one of the sample images to change its default format.

5. Click the **Optimized File Format** list arrow, and then click **PNG-24**.

6. Select from the following options:

   Transparency Options:

   ◆ **Transparency.** Check to keep the transparent areas of a PNG-24 image transparent.

   ◆ **Matte.** Click to fill the transparent areas of a PNG-24 image.

   Other Options:

   ◆ **Interlaced.** Check to have the PNG-24 image load in three scans.

7. Click **Save** to save the current image using the Save Optimized As dialog box.

Optimizing a WBMP Document

 PS 12.1, 12.2

The WBMP file format is used for images that are displayed on small hand-held devices such as PDAs and cell phones. The WBMP format generates an image with only 2 pixel colors (black and white), which significantly reduces the file size of the image. The WBMP format is new to the world of wireless devices, and while it creates small images, using only black and white pixels results in very low-quality images.

Optimize a WBMP Document

1. Open a document.

2. Click the **File** menu, and then click **Save For Web & Devices**.

3. Click the **Original**, **Optimized**, **2-Up**, or **4-Up** tabs to view the document using different layouts.

4. Click one of the sample images to change its default format.

5. Click the **Optimized File Format** list arrow, and then click **WBMP**.

6. Select from the following options:

    ◆ **Method.** Click the list arrow, and then select from the available dithering schemes (None, Diffusion, Pattern, or Noise). Dithering is how the WBMP format mixes the available colors in the image.

    ◆ **Amount.** Enter or select a value from 0% to 100% to instruct the WBMP compression utility how many of the image's colors should be dithered.

7. Click **Save** to save the current image using the Save Optimized As dialog box.

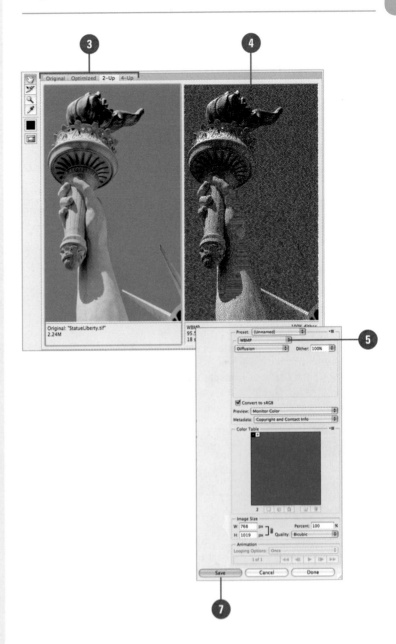

Creating an Animated GIF

PS 12.3

Create an Animated GIF from Scratch

1. Open Photoshop.

2. Click the **File** menu, and then click **New**.

3. Enter a name in the Name box.

4. Click the **Preset** list arrow, and then select from the available presets, or enter in a customized Width, Height, and Resolution.

5. Click the **Color Mode** list arrow, and then select a color mode for the image.

6. Click the **Bit Size** list arrow, and then choose a bit depth for the image (8 bit recommended).

7. Click the **Background Contents** list arrow, and then click **White**, **Background Color**, or **Transparent** (animated GIF files look best using transparency).

8. Click **OK**.

9. Create the first image for the animated GIF.

An **animation** is a sequence of images, or frames, that vary slightly to create the illusion of movement over time. One of the most Internet-compatible animation formats is the animated GIF. The original designation, GIF89a, gives you an idea of how long this format has been around. The GIF file format (Graphics Interchange Format) is used primarily for clip art, text, and line art, or for images that contain areas of solid color. Once the image is created, you can open and use it in any application that supports the GIF file format.

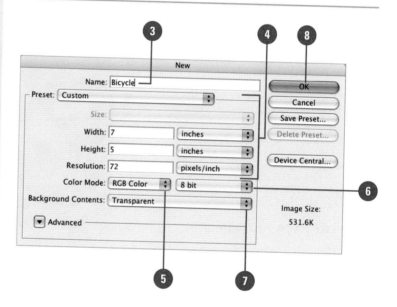

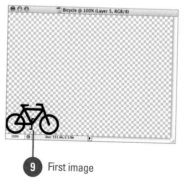

9 First image

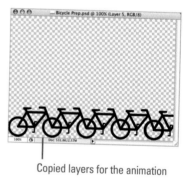

Copied layers for the animation

10 Press Ctrl+J (Win) or ⌘+J (Mac) to create a copy of your first animation in a separate layer.

11 Modify the second image (animations are essentially the same image, modified slightly between each animation frame or, in this case each layer).

12 Repeat steps 10 and 11 until you have enough layers for the animation.

13 Click the **Window** menu, and then click **Animation**.

14 Click the **Animation Options** button on the Animation panel, and then click **Make Frames From Layers**.

15 Click the **Play** button to view your animation in the document window.

16 Click the **File** button, and then click **Save For Web & Devices**.

17 Fine-tune the image using the available options.

18 Click **Save** to save the current image using the Save Optimized As dialog box.

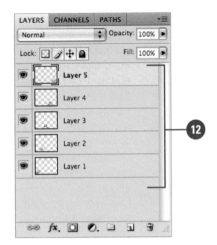

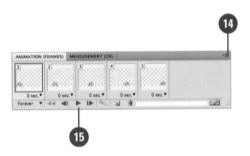

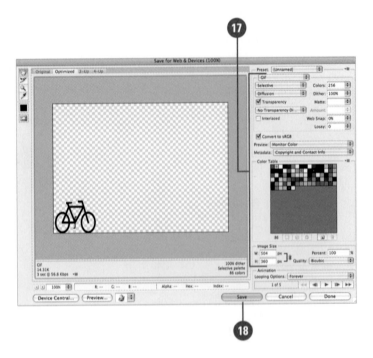

See Also

See Chapter 9, "Using the Paint, Shape Drawing, and Eraser Tools," on page 205 for more information on using the various drawing tools.

Working with Animation

After you create an animation using the Animation panel, you can use controls at the bottom of the panel to work with the animation. You can use controls to select frames, play back the animation, and specify how many times you want to play it back. If you need to quickly copy or remove frames, you can use the Duplicate Selected Frames or Delete Selected Frames buttons. Animation is all about creating motion, which can be time intensive to do on a frame-by-frame basis. In Photoshop, it's not necessary to create every frame. You can use the Tweens Animation Frames button to help you create frames between one frame and another. **Tweening** allows you to quickly animate objects. The animation appears by default in the Frames view; however, you can also display it in Timeline view (Extended). In **Timeline view**, you can see how each layer within the animation plays. In this view, you can also use **Onion Skin** mode, which allows you to view multiple frames simultaneously.

Work with an Animation

1. Open a document with an animation.

2. Click the **Window** menu, and then click **Animation**.

3. Select any of the following options to play and select frames in the animation:

   ◆ **First Frame.** Selects the first frame.

   ◆ **Previous Frame.** Selects the previous frame.

   ◆ **Play.** Plays the animation.

   ◆ **Next Frame.** Selects the next frame.

4. Click the **Loop Count** list arrow, and then select the option you want.

   ◆ **Once/3 Times.** Plays the animation one time or three times.

   ◆ **Forever.** Plays the animation over and over again in a continuous loop.

   ◆ **Other.** Opens the Loop Count dialog box where you can select a specific number of times to loop the animation.

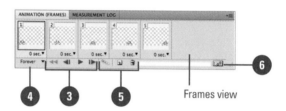

Frames view

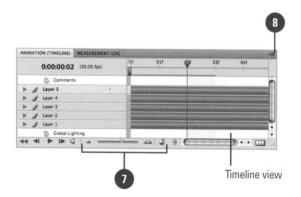

Timeline view

5 Select any of the following options to work with frames:

◆ **Tween Frames.** Creates motion tween between frames.

◆ **Duplicate Frames.** Duplicates the selected frames.

◆ **Delete Frames.** Deletes the selected frames.

6 To switch to Timeline view (Extended), click the **Convert to Timeline Animation** button.

◆ This is a toggle button that switches back and forth between Timeline and Frames animation view.

7 Select any of the following options to play and select frames in the animation:

◆ **Zoom In and Zoom Out.** Changes the Timeline view to see more or less of the animation window.

◆ **Onion Skinning.** Displays multiple frames simultaneously.

8 To display other commands and options, click the **Animation Options** button.

9 To switch to Frames view, click the **Convert to Frame Animation** button.

Options menu for Frames view

Options menu for Timeline view

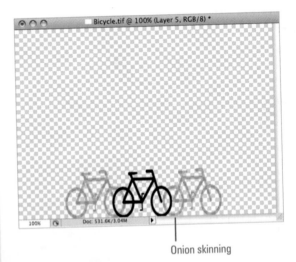

Onion skinning

Slicing Images the Easy Way

PS 12.5

Photoshop allows you to slice a document into smaller pieces. You might want to slice an image to create interactive links; however, the best reason is speed. You gain speed by compressing individual slices to reduce the image size. There are two types of slices: user-defined and layer-based. You can draw directly on an image to create a **user slice** using the Slice tool, or create a layer and then change it into a **layer-based slice**. When you create a slice, Photoshop also creates **auto slices**, which fill the space in the image that is not defined by a user-defined slice. User-defined and layer-based slices are identified by a solid line with blue symbols, while auto slices are identified by a dotted line with gray symbols. The slices also are numbered from left to right and top to bottom. A layer-based slice uses all the data in the layer to make up the slice. If you want to make changes to the slice, you need to edit the layer, which makes it a little more difficult to use than a user slice. When you edit or move the layer contents, the slice is automatically changed too.

Create a User Slice

1. Open a document.

2. Select the **Slice** tool on the toolbox.

   IMPORTANT To make slicing a little easier, drag a few guides from the Ruler bar to help guide your slicing tool.

3. Click the **Style Setting** list arrow on the Options bar, and then select the style you want:

   - **Normal.** Specifies the slice size as you drag.
   - **Fixed Aspect Ratio.** Specifies a ratio for the slice height and width.
   - **Fixed Size.** Specifies the slice height and width in pixels.

4. Drag and release the slice tool in the document to create a rectangular or square slice.

   - To constrain the slice to a square, hold down Shift as you drag. To create a circle, hold down Alt (Win) or Option (Mac).

5. Continue to drag and release until you have the image correctly sliced.

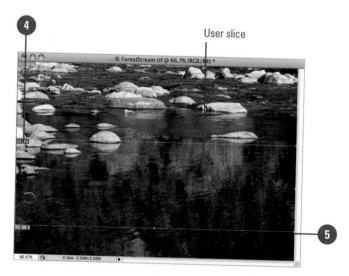

User slice

Create a Layer-based Slice

1. Open a document.

2. Select the layer you want in the Layers panel.

3. Click the **Layer** menu, and then click **New Layer Based Slice**.

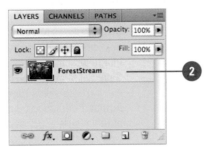

2

Did You Know?

You can convert an auto or layer-based slice to a user slice. Select the slice using the Slice Select tool, and then click Promote on the Options bar.

You can create slices from guides. Add guides to the image, select the Slice tool on the toolbox, and then click Slices From Guides in the Options bar. To create a new guide, click the View menu, click New Guide, click the Horizontal or Vertical option, specify the position in inches, and then click OK.

You can lock guides. To keep a guide from being moved, click the View menu, and then click Lock Guides.

You can remove guides. To remove guides, click the View menu, and then click Clear Guides.

You can show and hide guides. Click the View menu, point to Show, and then click Guides. The command toggles the guides' visibility on and off.

Layer-based slice

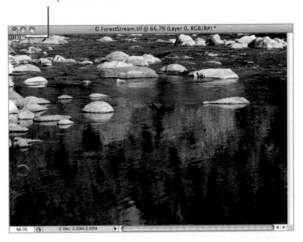

For Your Information

What's a Subslice?

The subslice is a type of auto slice that is automatically created when you create overlapping slices. They are created as a stack, one on top of the other, which you can rearrange. The subslice shows you how the image is divided when you save the optimized file. Subslices appear with a number and a slice symbol. When you make changes to a slice related to a subslice, the subslice automatically gets recreated.

Working with Slices

After you create slices within an image, you can use the Options bar or the Save For Web & Devices dialog box to work with slices. You can select options to show or hide slices, select one or more slices, delete or duplicate slices, and view or change slice settings. If you have an image with more than one slice, you need to optimize the slices in the Save For Web & Devices dialog box. You can use the Optimize menu to link multiple slices together. For linked slices in the GIF and PNG-8 format, Photoshop uses the same color panel and a dithering pattern to hide the seams between slices.

Work with Slices in the Photoshop Window

1. Open a document with slices.

2. Use any of the following:

   ◆ **Show or Hide Slices.** Click the View menu, point to Show, and then click Slices.

   ◆ **Show or Hide Auto Slices.** Select the Slice Select tool, and then click Show Auto Slices or Hide Auto Slices in the Options bar.

   ◆ **Select Slices.** Click the Slice Select tool, and then click the slice you want. Use Shift+click or drag to select multiple slices.

   ◆ **Delete Slices.** Select the slices, and then press Delete.

   ◆ **Duplicate Slices.** Select the slices, and then Alt (Win) or Option (Mac) and drag the selection.

   ◆ **View Slice Options.** Click the Slice Select tool, and then double-click the slice you want.

See Also

See "Working with Guides, Grid & Slices" on page 64 for information on setting preferences to show or hide slice numbers and change the slice border color.

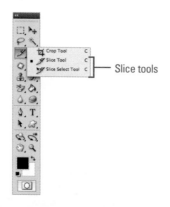

Slice tools

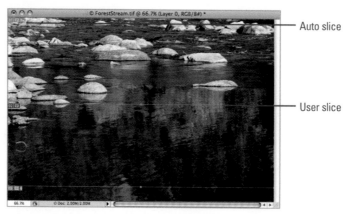

Auto slice

User slice

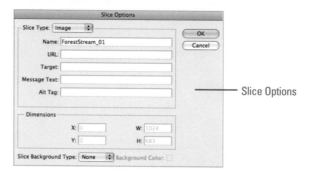

Slice Options

456

Work with Slices in the Save For Web & Devices Dialog Box

1. Open a document with slices.

2. Click the **File** menu, and then click **Save For Web & Devices**.

3. Select the file type you want, select any options, and then make any adjustments you want.

   ◆ **Show or Hide Slices.** Click the Toggle Slices Visibility button.

   ◆ **Select Slices.** Click the Slice Select tool, and then click the slice you want. Use Shift+click or drag to select multiple slices.

   ◆ **View Slice Options.** Click the Slice Select tool, and then double-click the slice you want.

   ◆ **Link Slices.** Select the slices you want to link, click the Optimize menu double-arrow (Win) or arrow (Mac) button, and then click Link Slices.

     A link icon appears on the slices.

   ◆ **Unlink Slices.** Select the slice, click the Optimize menu double-arrow (Win) or arrow (Mac) button, and then click Unlink Slice or Unlink All Slices.

4. When you're done, click **Save** to save the image or click **Done** to save your settings.

   TIMESAVER *Hold down Ctrl (Win) or Command (Mac) to switch between the Slice tool and the Slice Select tool.*

Toggle Slices Visibility button

Slice Select button   Linked slices   Optimize menu

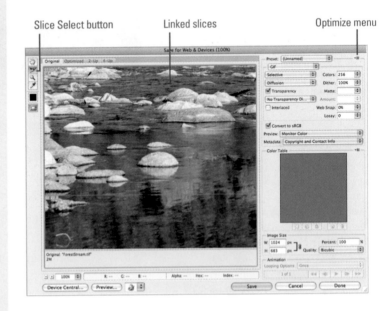

Arranging Slices

Moving and resizing objects in Photoshop is a common task. You can move or resize slices in the same basic way you do other objects. In addition to moving slices, you can also align them along an edge or to the middle, and evenly distribute them horizontally or vertically. When you align and distribute slices, you can reduce the amount of unnecessary auto slices, thereby creating smaller files and faster load times. When you have slices overlapping each other, you can change the stacking order to move them up or down in the order. For example, if you have one slice behind another, you can bring the slice forward one level at a time or to the top (front).

Move or Resize Slices

1. Open a document with slices.

2. Select the slices you want to move or resize.

3. To move a slice selection, drag the slice to a new location. You can press Shift to constrain movement up, down, or diagonally.

4. To resize a slice, drag the side or corner handle of the slice. When you select adjacent slices with common edges, the slices resize together.

   ◆ You can also click Options in the Options bar to set exact slice position or size.

Options button

Did You Know?

You can copy and paste a slice. You can copy and paste a slice like any other object using the Copy and Paste commands. If you copy a slice from Dreamweaver, it retains information from the original file in Photoshop.

You can snap slices to a guide, user slice, or other object. Click the View menu, point to Snap To, and then select the elements you want. Click the View menu, and then click Snap to display a check mark. When you move a slice toward an element, the slice snaps to the elements within 4 pixels.

Align, Distribute, or Stack Slices

1. Open a document with slices.

2. Select the slices you want to arrange.

3. To align slices, select the alignment button on the Options bar you want: Top, Vertical Centers, Bottom, Left, Horizontal Centers, or Right.

4. To evenly distribute slices, select the distribute button on the Options bar you want: Top, Vertical Centers, Bottom, Left, Horizontal Centers, or Right.

5. To change the slice stacking order, select the stack button on the Options bar you want: Bring To Front, Bring Forward, Send Backward, or Send To Back.

Did You Know?

You can combine user and auto slices. Right-click the selected slices, and then click Combine Slices.

You can divide user and auto slices. Select the slice using the Slice Select tool, and then click Divide on the Options bar. In the Divide Slice dialog box, select options to divide the slice horizontally or vertically, up or down in equal parts, or enter an exact size in pixels, and then click OK.

Saving a Sliced Image for the Web

PS 12.5

After you create slices within an image, you can export and optimize each slice using the Save For Web & Devices command, which saves each slice as a separate file and creates the code to display them on a web page. After you click Save in the Save For Web & Devices dialog box, the Save Optimized As dialog box appears. You can use this dialog box to access the Output Settings dialog box and set output options to control the format of HTML files, the names of files and slices, and the way Photoshop saves background images.

Save a Slice for the Web

1. Open a document with the slice you want to save.

2. Click the **File** menu, and then click **Save For Web & Devices**.

3. Select the file type you want, select any options, and then make any adjustments you want.

4. Click **Save**.

5. Click the **Save as Type** (Win) or **Format** (Mac) list arrow, and then select whether to save the images in **HTML and Images**, **Images Only**, or **HTML Only**.

6. Click the **Settings** list arrow, and then select the output settings you want. Default Settings is recommended for normal use.

   See the next page for details about selecting output settings.

7. Click the **Slices** list arrow, and then click **All Slices**, **All User Slices**, or **Selected Slices**.

8. Click **Save**.

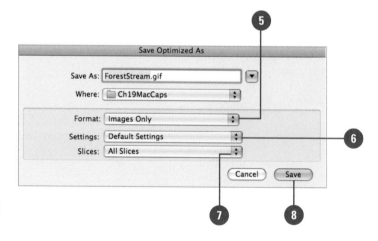

Set Output Options for Slices

1. Open a document with the slice you want to save.

2. Click the **File** menu, and then click **Save For Web & Devices**.

3. Click **Save**.

4. Click the **Save as Type** (Win) or **Format** list arrow, and then select the format you want.

5. Click the **Settings** list arrow, and then click **Other**.

6. Click the **Output Type** list arrow, and then click **Slices**.

7. Select the following options:

   ◆ **Generate Table.** Uses an HTML table to display slices.

   ◆ **Empty Cells.** Specifies the way to convert empty slices to table cells.

   ◆ **TD W&H.** Specifies whether to include width and height for table data.

   ◆ **Spacer Cells.** Specifies when to add empty spacer cells.

   ◆ **Generate CSS.** Creates a Cascading Style Sheet (CSS) to display the slices.

   ◆ **Referenced.** Specifies how to reference slice positions using CSS.

   ◆ **Default Slice Naming.** From the list menus, select the options to specify a slice naming scheme.

8. Click **OK**.

9. Click the **Slices** list arrow, and then select the slices option you want.

10. Click **Save**.

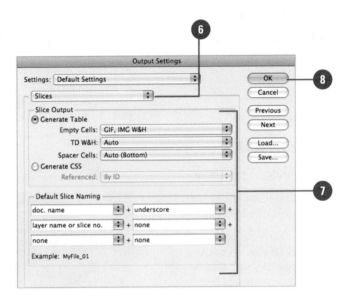

For Your Information

Saving Output Settings for Future Use

If you frequently use the same settings to save a file, you can save your output settings as a preset for future use. In the Output Settings dialog box, specify the settings you want to save for HTML, Slices, Background, or Saving Files, click Save, type a name, use the default folder location (the Optimized Output Settings folder), and then click Save. The Output Setting file is saved with the ".iros" file extension. By saving the Output Settings files in the Optimized Output Settings folder, you can quickly select the custom output setting file from the Save Optimized As dialog box. If you didn't store the Output Settings file in the default folder, you can also use the Load button in the Output Settings dialog box to find it.

Adding HTML Text or an URL Link to a Slice

 PS 12.5

If you want to include text within a slice for use on the Web, you can enter plain or formatted text with standard HTML tags directly on a slice with the type **No Image**. The text doesn't show up in Photoshop; you need to use a web browser to see it. Don't enter too much text as it might affect the exported layout. You can add text using the Slice Select tool on the toolbox, or in the Save For Web & Devices dialog box. If you want to create a hyperlink out of a slice for use on the Web, you can add an URL to a slice with the type **Image**.

Add HTML Text to a Slice

1. Open a document with the slice.

2. Open the Slice dialog box to add text using one of the following:

   ◆ **Toolbox.** Select the **Slice Select** tool on the toolbox, and then double-click the slice to which you want to add text.

   ◆ **Save For Web & Devices dialog box.** Click the File menu, click Save For Web & Devices, and then double-click the slice to which you want to add text.

3. Click the **Slice Type** list arrow, and then click **No Image**.

4. Enter the text you want.

5. Click the **Background Color** or **Slice Background Type** list arrow, and then select a color: **None**, **Matte**, **White**, **Black**, or **Other**.

   ◆ **Eyedropper.** Only in the Save For Web & Devices dialog box.

6. For Save For Web & Devices, select the **Text is HTML** check box to include HTML formatted tags.

7. For Save For Web & Devices, select the horizontal and vertical cell alignment options you want.

   ◆ To line up text in cells in the same row, set a common baseline for all cells in the row.

8. Click **OK**.

Double-click the slice to open the Slice dialog box.

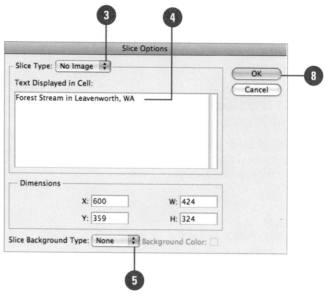

Add an URL Link to a Slice

1 Open a document.

2 Select the **Slice Select** tool on the toolbox.

3 Double-click the slice to which you want to add an URL link.

4 Click the **Slice Type** list arrow, and then click **Image**.

5 Enter an URL address or select a previously created one from the list. Be sure to use the complete URL address, such as *http://www.perspection.com*.

6 If you want to enter a target frame:

◆ **_blank**. Displays the linked file in a new window.

◆ **_self**. Displays the linked file in the same frame as the original file.

◆ **_parent**. Displays the linked file in its own original parent frameset.

◆ **_top**. Replaces the entire browser window with the linked file, removing all current frames.

7 Click **OK**.

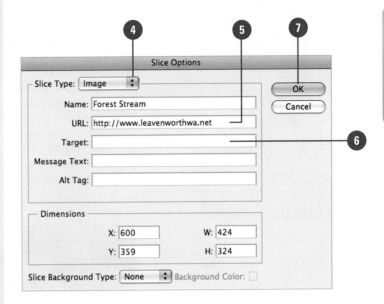

Defining and Editing Web Data Variables

When you work with images in Photoshop, you can define variables to drive the graphics in your web document. Data-driven graphics make it possible to create multiple versions of an image quickly and precisely. For example, you need to produce several web banners using the same template. Instead of creating each banner, one at a time, you can use data-driven graphics to generate web banners using variables and data sets. Any image can be converted into a template for data-driven graphics by defining variables for layers in the image. A **data set** is a collection of variables and associated data. You can switch between data sets to upload different data into your template. When you combine a Defined layer with a data set, you can use the information to swap images based on input variables.

Define a Data-Driven Graphic

1. Open a document.

2. Select the layer in which you want to define variables.

3. Click the **Image** menu, point to **Variables**, and then click **Define**.

4. Select from the available options:

   ◆ **Visibility.** Select to show or hide the content of the layer.

   ◆ **Pixel Replacement.** Select to replace the pixels in the layer with pixels from another image file.

   ◆ **Text Replacement.** Select to replace a string of text in a type layer (available when a text layer is selected).

   ◆ **Name.** Enter names for the variables. Variable names must begin with a letter, underscore, or colon.

5. To define variables for an additional layer, choose a layer from the Layer list arrow.

6. Prepare a .txt document from your word editing program with names of your variables and a list of the variable text and names/locations of variable images.

7. Click **OK**.

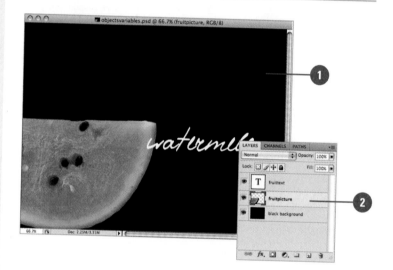

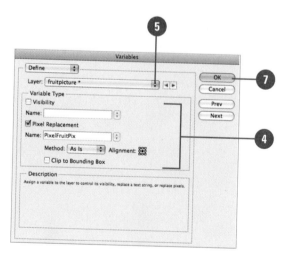

Create a Data Set

1. Open a document.

2. Select the layer in which you want to define variables (fruitpicture, in this example).

3. Click the **Image** menu, point to **Variables**, and then click **Data Sets**.

4. Click **Import** to choose the .txt file you just made or choose a predefined data set from the list arrow.

5. Select a variable from the available listed objects.

6. Edit the following variable data (each available when selected as the definition for the file):

   ◆ **Visibility.** Select Visible or Invisible to show or hide the layer's content.

   ◆ **Value.** Click **Select File**, and then select a replacement image file or choose Do Not Replace if you do not want the original pixels replaced.

   ◆ **Text Replacement.** Enter a text string in the Value box.

7. Repeat Steps 5 and 6 for each variable in the template.

   Image visibility, the text in a type layer, or exchanging one image for another, can now be controlled through changing variables.

8. Click **OK**.

9. Click the **Image** menu, point to **Apply Data Set**, and you will be provided with a dialog box from which you can choose the data you want to replace the existing data.

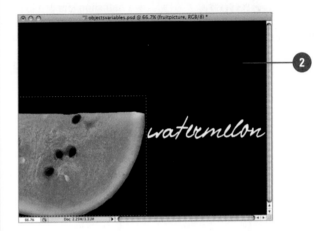

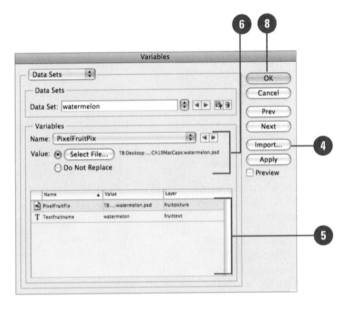

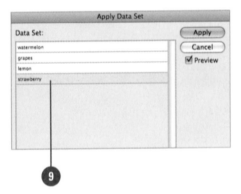

Exporting Directly to Video

Photoshop lets you export a document with animation as a QuickTime movie or an image sequence. The video formats include: 3G, FLC (also known as FLI), iPod (on the 320 x 240 screen), QuickTime movie, AVI (for Windows), DV Stream, Image Sequence, or MPEG-4 (Extended). If you have FLV QuickTime encoder installed on your computer, you can export to the Adobe Flash Video format (FLV). You can also export an animation to separate image files. The file formats include: BMP, Cineon, Dicom, JPEG, OpenEXR, Photoshop, PNG, Targa, and TIFF.

Export Directly to Video

1. Open a document.

   If the document is an animation, the frames will be visible in the Animation panel.

2. Click the **File** menu, point to **Export**, and then click **Render Video**.

3. Type a name for the video or use the one provided.

4. Click **Select Folder**, select the folder where you want to store the file, and then click **OK**.

5. Click the **QuickTime Export** option.

6. Click the **QuickTime Export** list arrow, and then click the video format you want.

7. To select options related to the format you selected, click **Settings**, make your selections, and then click **OK**; options vary depending on the format.

8. Select the option with the range of frames you want to include.

9. If available, select the alpha channel option and specify the frames per second (fps) you want.

10. Click **Render**.

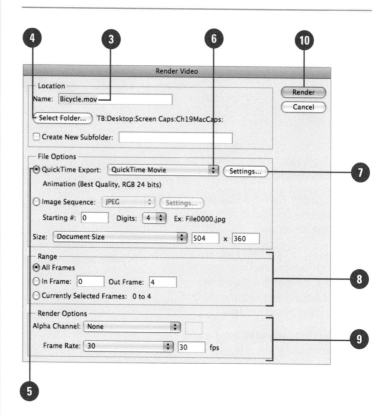

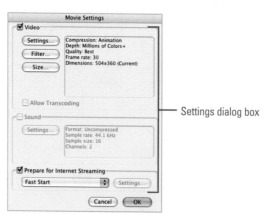

Settings dialog box

Export Directly to an Image Sequence

① Open a document.

   If the document is an animation, the frames will be visible in the Animation panel.

② Click the **File** menu, point to **Export**, and then click **Render Video**.

③ Type a name for the video or use the one provided.

④ Click **Select Folder**, select the folder where you want to store the file, and then click **OK**.

⑤ Click the **Image Sequence** option.

⑥ Click the **Image Sequence** list arrow, and then click the video format you want.

⑦ Specify the start number and number of digits you want in the file name, and then select the size you want.

⑧ To select options related to the format you selected, click **Settings**, make your selections, and then click **OK**; options vary depending on the format.

⑨ Select the option with the range of frames you want to include.

⑩ If you want, specify the frames per second (fps) you want.

⑪ Click **Render**.

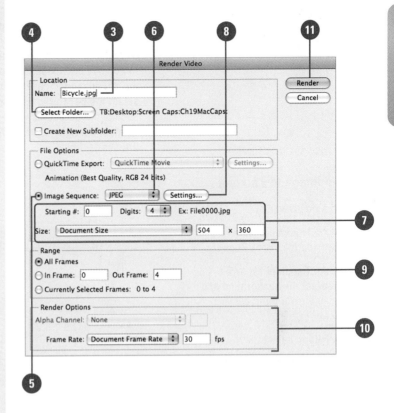

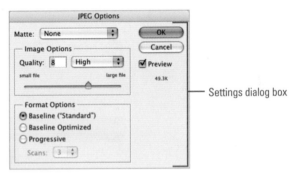

Settings dialog box

Exporting an Image to Zoomify

 PS 1.3

Exporting an image to Zoomify allows you to display high-resolution images on the Web that users can zoom into and pan around in order to view more detail. When you export to Zoomify, Photoshop exports JPEG files and HTML that you can put on your web server. An image exported to Zoomify downloads in the same time as a regular image, yet you get the added magnification benefits. During the export process, you can select the background and navigation for the image using a template, specify the output location, specify image quality, set the base image width and height for web browsers, and open the image in your browser.

Export an Image to Zoomify

1. Open a document.

2. Click the **File** menu, point to **Export**, and then click **Zoomify**.

3. Click the **Template** list arrow, and then select the background and Zoomify Viewer template you want.

4. Click **Folder**, select the output location you want, and then click **OK**.

5. Specify the Image Tile Options you want; drag the slider to adjust the quality settings.

6. Specify the desired base image width and height in pixels.

7. To open the image in your web browser, select the **Open In Web Browser** check box.

8. Click **OK**.

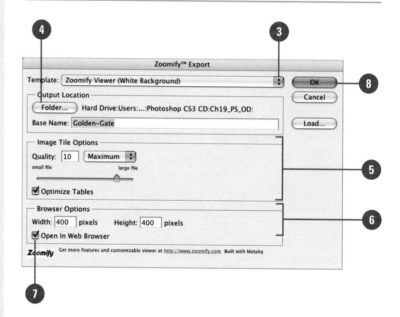

Image with Zoomify

468

Extending Photoshop

20

Introduction

Adobe Photoshop comes in two editions: Photoshop CS4 and Photoshop CS4 Extended. Photoshop CS4 is a subset of the Extended edition. Photoshop CS4 Extended edition has all the same features included in the standard edition. However, the Extended edition also contains additional features that are geared towards creating more sophisticated content.

If you need to count objects in an image for statistical purposes, you can use the Count tool. The Count tool allows you to manually click an image and track the number of times you do it. If you need to physically count the number of elements that appear in a photo, you can click the image to add numbers, so you don't have to remember them. If you need to measure an area in an image and track the measurement data for statistical purposes, you can use the Measurement feature. You can measure any area defined with one of Photoshop's selection tools, Ruler tool, or Count tool. The Measurement feature allows you to compute and track data points, such as width, height, area, and perimeter.

Photoshop Extended allows you to create a timeline-based animation. If you want to add video to a document, you can create a new video layer. You can create a video layer from a file, or create a blank one and add a video file to it later. After you insert a video layer, you can modify it using the Animation panel in Timeline view. You can change the start and stop points (also known as In and Out points), trim frames, add a fade-in or fade-out, or add animation using keyframes.

Counting Objects in an Image

If you need to count objects in an image for statistical purposes, you can use the Count tool in Photoshop Extended. The Count tool allows you to manually click an image and track the number of times you do it. If you need to physically count the number of elements that appear in a photo, you can click the image to add numbers, so you don't have to remember them. After you manually count by clicking, you can record the count in the Measurement Log. The count numbers are not saved with the document. If you have multiple selections in an image, Photoshop can automatically count them and record the results in the Measurement Log panel.

Count Objects in an Image Manually

1. Open a document.

2. Select the **Count** tool on the toolbox, now in the same section as the Eyedropper tool (**New!**).

3. To change the color, click the **Color** box on the Options bar, select a color, and then click **OK**.

4. Click in the image to add numbers in sequential order.

5. To work with the numbers, do any of the following:

   ◆ **Move.** Drag the existing number.

   ◆ **Remove.** Press Alt (Win) or Option (Mac) and click an existing number.

   ◆ **Reset.** Click **Clear** in the Options bar to reset the count to 0.

   ◆ **Show or Hide.** Click the **View** menu, point to **Show**, and then click **Count**.

6. To view the measurement data, click the **Window** menu, and then click **Measurement Log**.

7. To record the count to the Measurement Log, click **Record Measurements** in the Measurement Log panel.

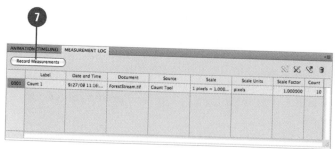

Count Objects in an Image Automatically

1. Open a document.

2. Select the **Magic Wand** tool on the toolbox, or click the **Select** menu, and then click **Color Range**.

   ◆ **Magic Wand.** You may need to adjust the Tolerance level to select the objects you want.

   ◆ **Color Range.** You may need to set Fuzziness and choose specific colors to select the objects you want.

3. Click the **Analysis** menu, point to **Select Data Points**, and then click **Custom**.

4. Click the **Deselect All** button, and then select the **Count** check box in the Selections area.

5. Click **OK**.

6. Click the **Window** menu, and then click **Measurement Log** to open the Measurement Log panel.

7. Click **Record Measurements** in the Measurement Log panel.

   Photoshop counts the selection areas and enters the number in the Custom column in the Measurement Log.

See Also

See "Working with Guides, Grid & Slices" on page 64 for information on changing the color of the count number.

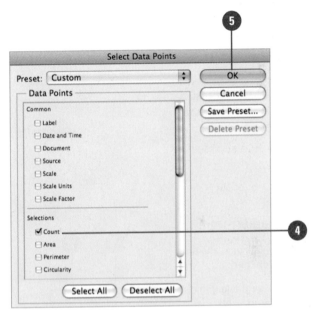

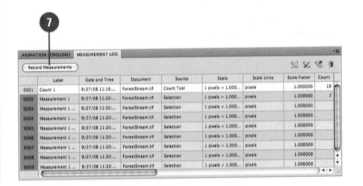

Taking Measurements in an Image

If you need to measure an area in an image and track the measurement data for statistical purposes, you can use the Measurement feature in Photoshop Extended. You can measure any area defined with one of Photoshop's selection tools, Ruler tool, or Count tool. The measurement feature allows you to compute and track **data points**, such as width, height, area, and perimeter. Photoshop tracks the measurement data in the Measurement Log panel, which you can customize to display the information you want. Before you start measuring, it's important to set the measurement scale to specify what you want a specific number of pixels to represent in units, such as inches, millimeters, microns, or pixels. To make it easier to measure, you can place scale markers on an image to display the measurement scale.

Set Measurement Scale

1. Click the **Analysis** menu, point to **Set Measurement Scale**, and then click **Custom**.

2. Specify the pixel and logical length, and then specify the logical units.

3. To save the measurement scale as a preset for later use, click **Save Preset**, type a name, and then click **OK**.

4. Click **OK**.

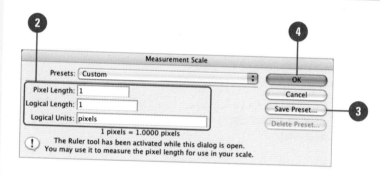

Place a Scale Marker

1. Click the **Analysis** menu, and then click **Place Scale Marker**.

2. Enter a number for the length of the scale marker in pixels.

3. To show the logical length and units for the scale marker, select the **Display Text** check box and choose specific font and font size.

4. Click the **Bottom** or **Top** option to specify where you want the text caption.

5. Click the **Black** or **White** option to set the scale marker and caption color.

6. Click **OK**.

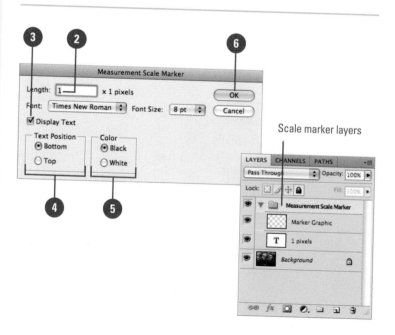

Scale marker layers

Perform a Measurement

1 Open a document.

2 Click the **Analysis** menu, point to **Select Data Points**, and then click **Custom**.

3 Select the check boxes next to the data points you want to measure and track for the different tools.

4 Click **OK**.

5 Use any of the following methods to specify what you want to measure:

◆ **Selection.** Create one or more selections.

◆ **Ruler.** Select the Ruler tool in the toolbox, and then drag the tool to measure what you want.

◆ **Count.** Select the Count tool in the toolbox, and then click to count items.

6 Click the **Window** menu, and then click **Measurement Log** to open the Measurement Log panel.

7 Click the **Analysis** menu, and then click **Record Measurements** to record the count to the Measurement Log.

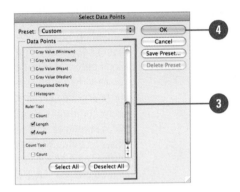

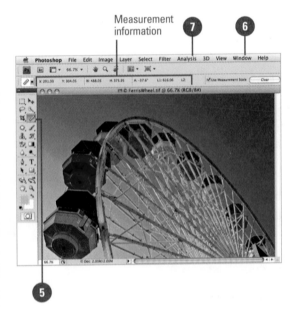

Measurement information

Did You Know?

You can delete a scale marker. In the Layers panel, select the Measure Scale Marker Layer group for the scale you want to delete, right-click the layer group, and then click Delete Group.

You can add or replace scale markers. Click the Analysis menu, click Place Scale Marker, click Remove or Keep, specify settings for the new marker, and then click OK.

For Your Information

Exporting Measurement Log Data

After you collect the measurement data you want, you can export the Measurement Log as a tab delimited text file (.txt) that you can import into a spreadsheet or database. To export data, click the Window menu, click Measurement Log to open the panel, select one or more rows of data in the log, click the Export button at the bottom of the panel, type a file name, specify a location, and then click Save.

Aligning and Combining Layers

Ever wanted to replace or delete parts of an image that have the same background or combine images that share overlapping content? In Photoshop, you can do it with the Auto-Align Layers and Auto-Blend Layers commands. The Auto-Align Layers command automatically aligns different layers that contain similar content. One layer is assigned to be the reference layer and all other layers are aligned to the reference layer in order to match everything up. You can manually set the reference layer, or let Photoshop automatically choose it for you. Sometimes when you align images, a visible stitching appears between them. You can use the Auto-Blend Layers command with RGB or grayscale images to create a smooth appearance between the aligned images. Auto-Blend Layers uses layer masks to remove content differences between the images.

Original image

Align Layers

1. Open a document.

2. Duplicate or place the images you want to align on different layers.

3. To set a reference layer, select the layer you want, and then click the **Lock** button on the Layers panel.

    ◆ If you don't have a locked layer, Photoshop will create one for you.

4. Select the layers you want to align in the Layers panel.

5. Click the **Edit** menu, and then click **Auto-Align Layers**.

6. Click one of the layout alignment options:

    ◆ **Auto.** Analyzes the images and uses either the Perspective, Spherical, or Cylindrical layout.

    ◆ **Perspective.** Creates a stretched or skewed effect on the side images.

    ◆ **Collage.** Retains object shapes while aligning layers and matching overlapping content (**New!**).

    ◆ **Cylindrical.** Reduces a bow-tie effect by displaying images as if they were on an unfolded cylinder.

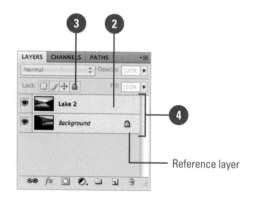

Reference layer

◆ **Spherical. (New!)** Transforms images spherically using wide fields of view.

◆ **Reposition.** Aligns the layers and matches overlapping content.

⑦ Select **Vignette Removal (New!)** to remove unwanted lens vignette and **Geometric Distortion** to automatically correct for fisheye lenses.

⑧ Click **OK**.

⑨ To fine-tune the alignment or make tonal changes, click the **Edit** menu, and then click **Free Transform**.

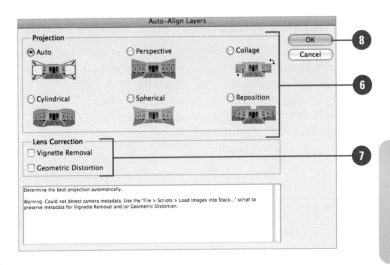

Combine and Blend Layers

① Select the layers you want to combine in the Layers panel.

② Click the **Edit** menu, and then click **Auto-Blend Layers**.

③ Select the **Panorama** or **Stack Images** option.

④ Click **OK**.

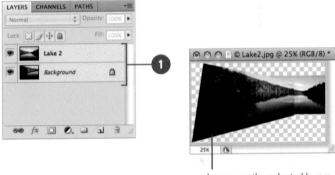

Images on the selected layers

Did You Know?

You can create an image stack (Extended). If you have images with a similar size, you can create an image stack. Create a document with each image as a separate layer. Select the all the layers, use the Auto-Align Layers command with the Auto option, convert the layers to Smart Objects, and then create an image stack. Click the Layer menu, point to Smart Objects, point to Stack Mode, and then select a stack mode from the submenu. To remove a stack, click None on the submenu. You can edit an image stack like any other Smart Object.

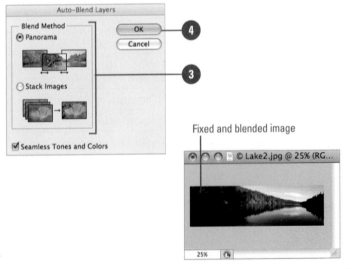

Fixed and blended image

Opening Video Files and Image Sequences

In Photoshop Extended, you can open video files and image sequences using the Open command from the File menu in the formats listed in the table below. Video layers can contain files with the following color modes and bits per channel (bpc):

- ◆ **Grayscale**. 8, 16, or 32 bpc
- ◆ **RGB**. 8, 16, or 32 bpc
- ◆ **CMYK**. 8 or 16 bpc
- ◆ **Lab**. 8 or 16 bpc

Video and Image Sequence Formats

Format	Usage
MPEG-1	Uses the Moving Picture Experts Group (MPEG) format; a video format with quality slightly below the quality of conventional VCR videos.
MPEG-4	Uses the Moving Picture Experts Group (MPEG) format; a video format that transmits over a narrower bandwidth and can mix video with text, graphics and 2-D and 3-D animation layers.
MOV	Uses the QuickTime (MOV) format; a video and animation format developed by Apple Inc.
AVI	Uses the Audio Video Interleave (AVI) format; a video format developed by Microsoft for storing video and audio information.
FLV	Uses the Adobe Flash Video (FLV) format from QuickTime; supported with Flash 8 installed.
MPEG-2	Uses the Moving Picture Experts Group (MPEG) format; a video format with quality equal to TV standards, including NTSC, and even HDTV; supported with an MPEG-2 encoder installed.
BMP	Uses the Bitmap format; an image format.
Dicom	Uses the DICOM (Digital Imaging and Communications in Medicine) format; an image format used for the transfer and storage of medical images, such as ultrasounds.
JPEG	Uses the JPEG (Joint Photographic Experts Group) format; an image format that uses a compression method to reduce the size of image files primarily for the Web.
OpenEXR	Uses the HDR (High Dynamic Range) format; a film format used to produce images for use in motion picture production.
PNG	Uses the PNG (Portable Network Graphics) format; an image format used to save images for the Web. Supports up to 16 million colors and 256 levels of transparency.
PSD	Uses the PSD (Photoshop) format, which saves layers, channels, notes, and color profiles.
Targa	Uses the Targa format; an image format for high-end image editing on the Windows platform.
TIFF	Uses a TIFF (Tagged-Image File Format) format; an image format commonly used for printing and saving flattened images without losing quality.
Cineon	Uses the Cineon Digital Film System format; a digital format developed by Kodak. Supported with the plug-in installed.
JPEG 2000	Uses an advanced JPEG format; an image format that produces images with better compression and quality for use on the Web or in print; supported with the plug-in installed.

Creating a Video Layer

If you want to add video to a document, you can create a new video layer in Photoshop Extended. You can create a video layer from a file, or create a blank one and add a video file to it later. If you want to open a video later, you can use the Open command from the File menu. Photoshop opens a variety of video files and image sequences. You can even play the video with sound by either clicking Alt (Win) or Option (Mac) when you hit the Play button, or toggle the sound icon on the bottom of the panel (**New!**).

Create a Video Layer

1. Open a document.

2. Click the **Window** menu, and then click **Animation** to display the Animation panel.

3. Click the **Convert to Timeline Animation** button to switch to Timeline view.

4. Click the **Layer** menu, point to **Video Layers**, and then click the layer type you want:

   ◆ **From File.** Click **New Video Layer from File**, select a video or image sequence, and then click **Open**.

   ◆ **Blank.** Click **New Blank Video Layer**.

5. If you want to open a video file and add it to a layer, click the **File** menu, click **Open**, select the video file you want to open, and then click **Open**.

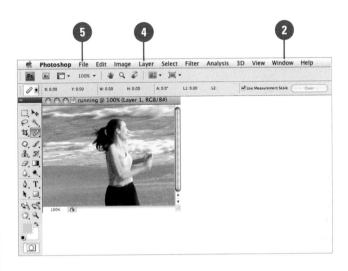

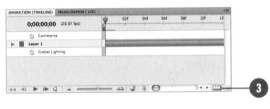

New video layer

Did You Know?

You can create a still frame from a video layer. If you want a still image from a video, you can rasterize the video layer, creating a flattened composite of the current frame. Select the video layer you want, move the playback head to the frame you want, click the Layer menu, point to Rasterize, and then click Video or Layer.

Modifying a Video Layer

After you insert a video layer, you can modify it in Photoshop Extended using the Animation panel in Timeline view. You can zoom in and out to display the Timeline the way you want, and then drag the playhead, also known as the current-time indicator, to the time or frame number in the video where you want to start your modifications. You can change the start and stop points (also known as In and Out points), trim frames, add a fade-in or fade-out, or add animation using keyframes. A keyframe defines the location of a property change to the video layer. When you set at least two keyframes that change properties, such as position, opacity, or style, you create animation.

Modify a Video Layer Duration

1. Open a document with a video.

2. Click the **Window** menu, and then click **Animation** to display the Animation panel.

3. Click the **Convert to Timeline Animation** button to switch to Timeline view.

4. Use any of the following methods to change the duration of the video:

   ◆ **Start and End Work Area.** Point to the ends of the work area bar, and then drag to change the position.

   ◆ **In and Out Points.** Point to the beginning or end of the layer duration bar (cursor changes to a double-arrow), and then drag to change the points.

   ◆ **Move duration.** Point to the duration bar, and then drag to move the duration to start and stop at a new position.

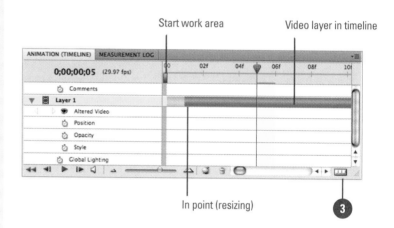

Start work area

Video layer in timeline

In point (resizing)

3

Did You Know?

You can delete a section of video. In the Animation panel in Timeline view, drag the ends of the work area bar to select the footage you want to delete, click the Animation Options button, and then click Lift Work Area.

Use Keyframes to Animate Layer Properties

1. Open a document.

2. Click the **Window** menu, and then click **Animation** to display the Animation panel.

3. Click the **Convert to Timeline Animation** button to switch to Timeline view.

4. Click the down arrow for a video layer to display layer properties.

5. Click the **Time-Vary Stopwatch** icon to enable shape animation for the layer property.

6. Position the playhead where you want to set a keyframe, and then make the property changes you want, such as Opacity, in the Layers panel.

7. Use any of the following methods to change the keyframe:

   ◆ **Select.** Click the keyframe icon.

   ◆ **Move.** Drag to change the position.

   ◆ **Delete.** Right-click the keyframe icon, and then click Delete Keyframes.

   ◆ **Method.** The diamond keyframe icon animates the property change evenly over time (known as a Linear Keyframe). If you want an instant property change, you can change the interpolation method to a Hold Keyframe, which appears as a square keyframe icon. Right-click a keyframe icon, and then click Hold Interpolation or Linear Interpolation.

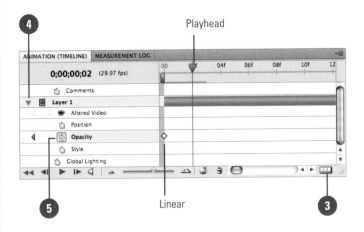

For Your Information

Changing the Video Playback Speed

If you want to speed up or slow down a video, you need to adjust the frames per second (fps). To change the fps, display the video in the Animation panel in Timeline view, click the Animation Options button, click Document Settings, set the frames per second (fps) you want (the higher the number, the faster the speed), and then click OK.

Splitting a Video Layer

In addition to modifying a video layer, you can split it into two new video layers at the specific point you want in Photoshop Extended. You can zoom in and out to display the Timeline the way you want, and then drag the playhead to the time or frame number in the video where you want to split it. The video layer is duplicated and appears above the original in the Animation panel. The original layer contains the video from the start to the current time or frame, and the duplicate layer contains the video from current time or frame to the end.

Split a Video Layer

1. Open a document with a video layer.

2. Click the **Window** menu, and then click **Animation** to display the Animation panel.

3. Click the **Convert to Timeline Animation** button to switch to Timeline view.

4. Drag the playhead to the time or frame number where you want to split the video layer.

5. Click the **Animation Options** button, and then click **Split Layers**.

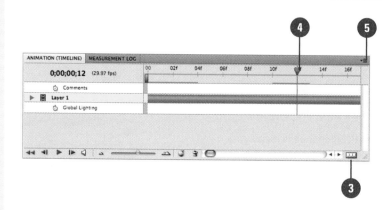

Did You Know?

You can preview video or timeline animation. You can preview a video or animation in the document window. Drag the playback head to the point where you want to play the video or animation. Click the Play button at the bottom of the Animation panel. You can also press the spacebar to play or stop the playback. Photoshop caches it to memory for faster playback.

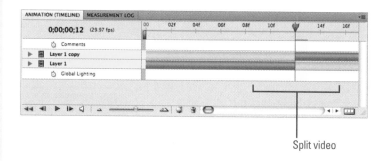

Split video

Cloning Video Layer Content

If you have video or animation frames that you want to retouch or duplicate, you can use the Clone Stamp and Healing Brush tool in Photoshop Extended. The Clone Stamp tool allows you to sample content from one area of a frame (known as the **source**) and paint it over another area of the same or a different frame (known as the **target**). The Healing Brush tool allows you to blend the sampled content from the source with the target to fix a problem. You can use the Clone Source panel to set several samples from one part of a video frame and clone or blend them in another video frame.

Clone Parts of a Video Layer

1. Open a document with a video layer, and then select it in the Layers panel.

2. Click the **Window** menu, and then click **Animation** to display the Animation panel.

3. Click the **Convert to Timeline Animation** button to switch to Timeline view.

4. Drag the playhead to the time or frame number that is the source of the sample you want.

5. Select the **Clone Stamp** tool on the toolbox.

6. To set a sample point, Alt (Win) or Option (Mac), and click where you want the sample.

7. To set another sample point, select a **Clone Stamp** button on the Clone Source panel, adjust the playhead, and then repeat Step 6.

8. Select the target video layer and move the playhead to the frame you want to paint.

9. If you set multiple samples, click the source in the Clone Source panel.

   TIMESAVER *Use Shift+Alt (Win) or Shift+Option (Mac) to show the clone overlay temporarily.*

10. Drag the area you want to paint.

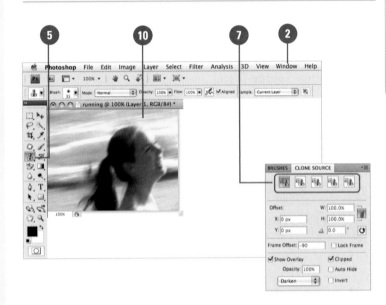

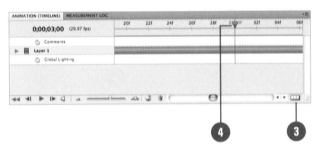

Setting Up Multiple Clone Sources

 PS 2.4

The Clone Source panel allows you to set up to five different sample sources for the Clone Stamp or Healing Brush tools in Photoshop. The Clone Source panel contains five clone buttons to which you can assign samples. Simply open the Clone Source panel, click a Clone Stamp button, and then select the sample you want. The Clone Source panel saves the samples until you close the document. To help you clone the source in a specific location, you can overlay your sample source and show the overlay on the screen. The overlay allows you to view your changes and helps you visualize where to paint. You can show or hide the overlay and change its appearance. In addition, you can scale and rotate the sample source to clone the sample at a specific size and orientation. If you need to paint in a very specific location relative to the sampling point, you can use the x and y pixel offset.

Use the Clone Source Panel

1. Open a document.

2. Click the **Clone Source** button to display the Clone Source panel.

3. To determine if a Clone Stamp button is in use, point to it to display a Screen Tip.

4. Click a Clone Stamp not in use, or one you want to replace.

5. To set a sample point, Alt (Win) or Option (Mac), and click where you want the sample.

6. To show the overlay, select the **Show Overlay** check box.

7. Select overlay options:

   ◆ **Opacity.** Specify a percentage value.

   ◆ **Clipped.** (New!) Check this box to clip the overlay to the brush size.

   ◆ **Auto Hide.** Select to hide the overlay while you paint.

   ◆ **Invert.** Select to invert the overlay.

   ◆ **Blend.** Click the list arrow, and then select a blending mode.

8. To scale or rotate the sample source, enter the values you want.

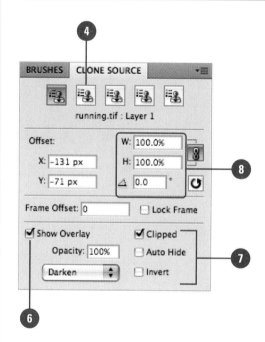

Creating 3D Model Files

Photoshop CS4 Extended provides vast improvements to the way you work with 3D files. To start with, there is a 3D menu (**New!**) with an assortment of commands and there are now two slots in the toolbox entirely dedicated to 3D, for a total of 10 easy-to-reach tools (**New!**). And, artists can paint directly on 3D objects (**New!**) without having to render them in another program. Photoshop includes support for three-dimensional files (.u3d, .3ds, .obj, .kms, and Collada file formats) created by programs like Adobe Acrobat 3D Version 8, 3D Studio Max, Alias, Maya, and Google Earth. You can open 3D files into a new document or insert 3D files into an existing document in Photoshop. When you open a 3D file, Photoshop places the 3D model on a separate 3D layer. You can add multiple 3D layers to an image. If your Photoshop document contains one or more 2D layers (typical images), you can combine any one of them with a 3D layer, or convert a 3D layer to a 2D layer.

Add a 3D Model to a 2D Image

1. Open a document.

2. Click the **3D** menu, and then click **New Layer from 3D File**.

3. Navigate to drive or folder where the 3D file is located, and then select the 3D file.

4. Click **Open**.

   A new 3D layer appears in the document.

5. To add a 3D layer to an image, drag the 3D layer from one layer in the Layers panel to another layer.

6. Select the 3D layer in the new location.

7. Use the 3D tools on the toolbox to position or scale the 3D model.

   ◆ **Change 3D position and scale.** Use the following 3D tools: **3D Rotate Tool, 3D Roll Tool, 3D Pan Tool, 3D Slide Tool, or 3D Scale Tool**.

   ◆ **Change 3D view.** Use the following 3D tools: **3D Orbit Tool, 3D Roll View Tool, 3D Pan View Tool, 3D Walk View Tool, and 3D Zoom Tool**.

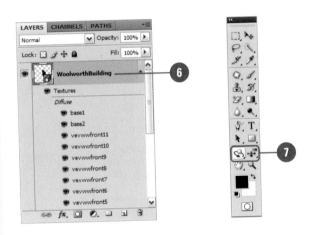

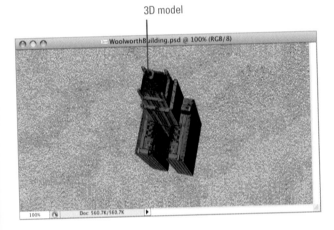

3D model

Working with 3D Model Files

After you have opened a 3D file or created a new 3D layer from a 2D file, you can use Photoshop 3D tools (**New!**) to move or scale the 3D model, change the camera view, change the lighting (to daylight or interior light, for example), or change render modes (to solid or wireframe). If you have a texture layer, you can edit it using standard Photoshop tools and reapply the texture to the 3D model.

Create a 3D Model from a 2D Image

1. Open a 2D image.

2. Click the **3D** menu, point to **New 3D Shape from Layer**, and then select a shape option in which to wrap your 2D image around.

   Some of the shapes include soda can, cube, cone, pyramid, and hat.

3. Select one of the navigation tools from the toolbox or Options bar, such as 3D Rotate to move the image in a 3D space.

4. Or, use the **Axis Widget** (**New!**). The three colored areas represent the three axes (x, y, z) of the object.

   ◆ You can also highlight parts of the widget to isolate the movements or scaling of the object to specific axes.

5. Click the **Window** menu, and then click **3D** to open the 3D panel.

   From the 3D panel, you can access four areas to change properties of your new 3D object (Scene, Mesh, Materials, and Lights).

6. When you're done, you can rasterize, render for final output, export the 3D layer and even browse other 3D content online from the 3D menu.

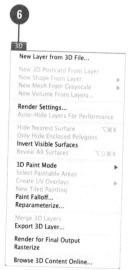

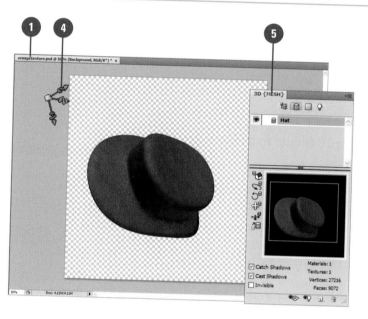

Edit a 3D Model

1. Open a document with the 3D model you want to edit.

2. Click the **Window** menu, and then click **3D** to open the 3D panel.

3. Click any of the following buttons in the 3D panel to change a 3D model:

   ◆ **Scene.** Choose from 17 render settings, view cross sections, and save your own presets.

   ◆ **Mesh.** Shows the object mesh pieces, which you can edit.

   ◆ **Materials.** Select properties of the 3D object environment, such as reflections, highlights, and bump maps.

   ◆ **Lights.** Select the lighting mode you want.

4. To move and view the object in different ways, you can use the 3D tools from the toolbox, which are replicated on the Options bar:

   ◆ **Move, rotate, or scale.** Click a 3D tool in the toolbox or on the Options bar, and then drag to change the rotation, roll, pan, slide, or scale.

   ◆ **Camera.** Click a camera editing tool in the toolbox, and then drag to change the orbit, roll, pan, walk, or zoom.

   ◆ **Create and View 3D animations.** Click the **Window** menu, point to **Animation**, and then click **Timeline** to animate your 3D objects and play the animations.

5. When you're done, you can rasterize, render for final output, export the 3D layer and even browse other 3D content online from the 3D menu.

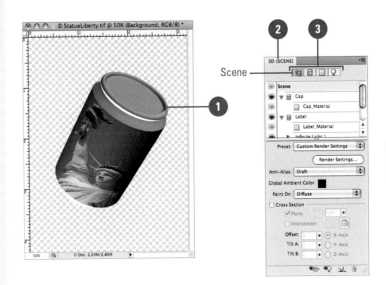

Scene

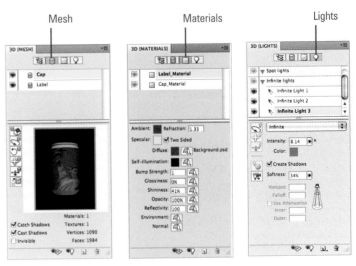

Mesh · Materials · Lights

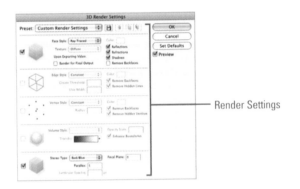

Render Settings

Exploring Other Photoshop Extended Features

If you want to explore additional Photoshop Extended features, you can get started in Photoshop CS4 Help. Click the Help menu, click Photoshop Help, click in the Search box, type **Photoshop Extended**, and then press Enter (Win) or Return (Mac). A list of all Photoshop Extended features appears, where you can select the ones you want to use. Part of the list is included here:

- About Photoshop and MATLAB
- MATLAB commands
- Set up MATLAB and Photoshop
- DICOM metadata
- Connect/disconnect to Photoshop from MATLAB
- About image stacks
- Use scale markers
- Use the Measurement Log
- Extract work area
- Performing a measurement
- Switch animation modes
- Transform video layers
- Lift work area
- Animate DICOM files
- Set a work area
- 3D files in Photoshop
- Keys for using Measurement
- Interpret video footage
- Rasterize video layers
- Import image sequences
- Choose interpolation method

- Remove footage from a layer
- Paint on HDR images
- Open a DICOM file
- Specify QuickTime Movie settings
- Reload footage in a video layer
- Set the measurement scale
- Convert frame and timeline animations
- About the HDR Color Picker
- Save 3D files
- Creating an image stack
- About straight and premultiplied channels in video
- Open or import a video file
- Group layers in a video or animation
- Keys for working with DICOM files
- Restore frames in video layers
- Set the timeline area to be previewed
- Previewing video or timeline animations
- Replace footage in a video layer
- Use a script to create an image stack
- Paint on 3D objects in Photoshop

Working Together with Adobe Programs

21

Introduction

Adobe programs are designed to work together so you can focus on what you need to do, rather than on how to do it. In fact, the Adobe programs share tools and features for your most common tasks so you can work uninterrupted and move seamlessly from one program to another. Adobe Creative Suite is an integrated collection of programs that work together to help you create designs in print, on the Web, or on mobile devices. When you install Adobe Creative Suite or a stand-alone Adobe program, you also get additional Adobe programs—Bridge, Version Cue, Drive, ConnectNow, Device Central, and Extension Manager—to help you perform specific jobs, such as locating, downloading, and modifying images for projects, managing files and program extensions and testing files for different mobile devices.

Adobe Bridge is a program that lets you view, open, modify, and manage images located on your computer from any Adobe Creative Suite program. Adobe Bridge is literally the glue that binds Adobe Creative Suite programs together into one cohesive unit with shared tools. Bridge allows you to search, sort, filter, manage, and process image files one at a time or in batches. You can also use Bridge to do the following: create new folders; rename, move, delete and group files; edit metadata; rotate images; create web galleries and contact sheets; and run batch commands. You can also import files from your digital camera and view file information and metadata.

Exploring Adobe Programs

Adobe Creative Suite 4

Adobe Creative Suite 4 is an integrated collection of programs that work together to help you create designs in print, on the Web, or on mobile devices. Adobe's Creative Suite 4 comes in different editions with different combinations of Adobe programs. The main programs for print design include InDesign and Acrobat Professional; for graphic design the programs include Photoshop, Illustrator, and Fireworks; for video and sound design the programs include Premiere, After Effects Professional, Encore, and Soundbooth; and for web design the programs include Flash Professional, Dreamweaver, Fireworks, and Contribute.

Working Together with Adobe Programs

When you install Adobe Creative Suite 4 or a stand-alone Adobe program, you also get additional Adobe programs—Bridge, Version Cue, Drive, ConnectNow, Device Central, and Extension Manager—to help you perform specific jobs such as managing files and program extensions and testing files for mobile devices.

Adobe Bridge

Adobe Bridge CS4 is a file management/batching program that manages and processes images while you work in your other Adobe programs. To use Bridge, click Browse in Bridge on the File menu within an Adobe product, such as Flash, or from the desktop use the Start menu (Win) or go to the Applications folder (Mac).

Adobe Version Cue

Adobe Version Cue is a file tracking management program you can use to keep track of changes to a file as you work on it or if you work collaboratively on the same files with colleagues. You use Adobe Bridge as a central location from which to use Version Cue. You can track Adobe and non-Adobe program files.

Adobe Drive

Adobe Drive (**New!**) allows you to connect to and use Version Cue servers as if they were a local hard drive or mapped network drive. After you set up a connection, you can work with Version Cue files by using the Open, Import, Export, Place, Save, or Save As dialog boxes, and Explorer (Win) or Finder (Mac).

Adobe ConnectNow

The Share My Screen command (**New!**) on the File menu allows you to connect to Adobe ConnectNow, which is a secure Web site where you can start an online meeting. You can share and annotate your computer screen or take control of an attendee's computer. During the meeting, you can communicate by sending chat messages, using live audio, or broadcasting live video.

Adobe Device Central

Adobe Device Central CS4 allows you to test your content to see how it would look on a variety of mobile devices. You can interact with the emulated device in a way that allows you to test your content in real-world situations. Device Central provides a library of devices and each device includes a profile with information about the device, including media and content support types.

Adobe Extension Manager

Adobe Extension Manager CS4 allows you to install and delete added program functionality, known as extensions, to many Adobe programs.

Exploring Adobe Bridge

 PS 7.7

Quick Search (New!)
Search for file names, keywords, folder names.

Inspector panel
Displays or hides Version Cue panels.

Folders panel
Displays the folders on your computer in a tree structure.

Workspaces (New!)
Choose from common workspaces.

Preview panel
Displays a preview of the selected image.

File path (New!)
To trace file back to its folder.

Favorites panel
Displays links to common features and favorite places.

Filter panel
Displays files based on filter criteria.

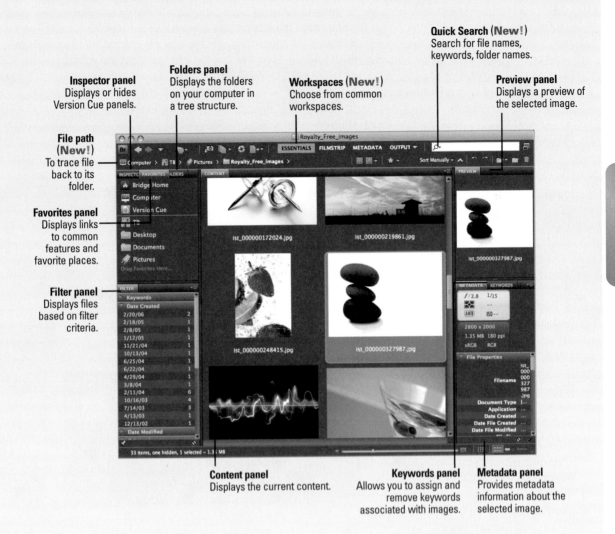

Content panel
Displays the current content.

Keywords panel
Allows you to assign and remove keywords associated with images.

Metadata panel
Provides metadata information about the selected image.

Getting Started with Adobe Bridge

Adobe Bridge CS4 is a stand-alone program that lets you view, open, and manage images located on your computer from any Adobe Creative Suite 4 program. Adobe Bridge is literally the glue that binds Adobe Creative Suite 4 programs and shared tools together into one cohesive unit. Adobe Bridge integrates with shared tools including Adobe Version Cue, a file tracking project management program. The Bridge program provides a set of panels that make it easy to find, view, and manage the files on your computer or network. As you work with Bridge, you'll open, close, and move (dock and undock) the panels to meet your individual needs. After you customize the workspace, you can save the location of the panels as a custom workspace, which you can display using the Workspace command on the Window menu. Bridge also provides some predefined workspaces.

Get Started with Adobe Bridge

1. Launch your Adobe product, click the **File** menu, and then click **Browse in Bridge**.

   ◆ You can also start Adobe Bridge CS4 from the Start menu (Win) or the Applications folder (Mac).

2. To open and close a panel, click the **Window** menu, and then click the panel name you want.

3. To move a panel, drag the panel tab you want to another location in the Bridge window.

4. To save a workspace, click the **Window** menu, point to **Workspace**, click **New Workspace**, type a name, and then click **OK**.

5. To display a workspace, click the **Window** menu, point to **Workspace**, and then click the workspace you want.

6. When you're done, click the **Close** button in the Bridge window.

1 The Launch Bridge button on the Application bar in Photoshop

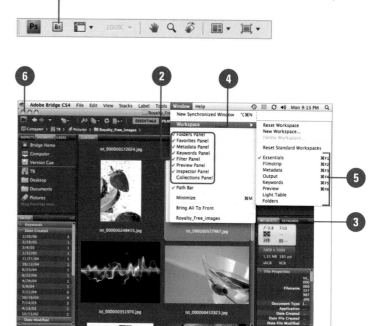

Getting Photos from a Digital Camera

 PS 1.5, 7.4

If you have raw or other images from your digital camera, you can use the Get Photos from Camera command in Adobe Bridge to retrieve and copy them to your computer. This allows you to specify where you want to store the files, rename them if you want, preserve metadata, or convert them to the DNG format. When you convert raw files to the DNG format, you specify preview size, compression, and whether to preserve the raw image data or embed the original raw file.

Import Raw and Other Files from a Camera

1. In Adobe Bridge, click the **File** menu, and then click **Get Photos from Camera** or click the camera icon on the Application bar. (**New!**)

2. Click the **Get Photos From** popup, and then select the source camera or memory card.

3. Create a new subfolder to store the images (optional).

4. To rename the files, select a method, and then enter file name text.

5. Select the options you want:

   ◆ **Preserve Current Filename in XMP.** Select to save the current filename as image metadata.

   ◆ **Open Adobe Bridge.** Select to open and display the files in Adobe Bridge.

   ◆ **Convert To DNG.** Select to convert Camera Raw files to DNG. Click Settings to set DNG conversion options.

   ◆ **Delete Original Files. (New!)** Select to delete original files from camera or memory card.

   ◆ **Save Copies To.** Select to save copies to another folder for backup.

6. To apply metadata to the files, click **Advanced Dialog**.

7. Click **Get Photos**.

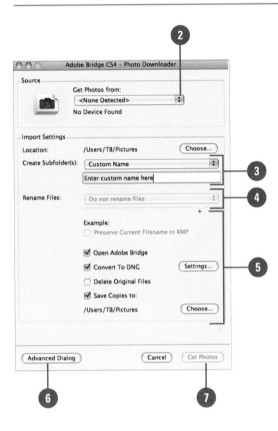

Working with Raw Images from a Digital Camera

PS 1.3, 7.1, 7.2, 7.3, 7.5

Raw image file formats are created by most mid- to high-end digital cameras and contain information about how the image was taken. The raw format turns off all camera adjustments, and simply saves the image information. Using the raw format is as close to using traditional film as a digital camera can get. Raw images are larger; however, the increase in file size gives you more information that can be used by Camera Raw to adjust the image. From Adobe Bridge, you can use Camera Raw to open raw files, JPEG, and TIFF files to make image enhancements. If you're not sure what to do, you can click Auto to have Camera Raw do it or drag color sliders to adjust options manually. Raw images can be converted into 16-bit images. When you use a 16-bit image, you have more control over adjustments such as tonal and color corrections. Once processed, raw images can be saved in the DNG, TIFF, PSD, PSB, or JPEG formats. After you make Camera Raw adjustments, you can save the settings so you can use them later.

Set Camera Raw Preferences

1. In Adobe Bridge, click the **Edit** (Win) or **Adobe Bridge** (Mac) menu, and then click **Camera Raw Preferences**.

2. Select the preferences you want:

   ◆ **General.** Specify where Camera Raw file settings are stored. Use Sidecar XMP files to store settings separately, or Camera Raw Database to store settings in a searchable database.

   ◆ **Default Image Settings.** Select options to automatically apply settings or set defaults.

   ◆ **Camera Raw Cache.** Set a cache size to shorten loading time for thumbnails and previews.

   ◆ **DNG File Handling.** Select options to ignore XMP files or update embedded content.

   ◆ **JPEG and TIFF Handling.** (New!) Automatically open JPEGs and/or TIFFs in Camera Raw.

3. Click **OK**.

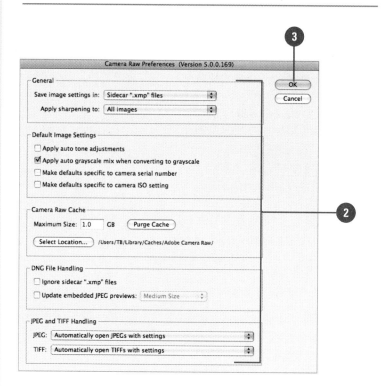

Modify a File in Camera Raw

1 Right-click the image, and then click **Open in Camera Raw**.

2 Use the **Zoom**, **Hand**, **Rotate**, **Crop**, and **Straighten** tools to change the size, orientation, and position of the image, or use the **White Balance** tool to set the white balance or the **Color Sampler** tool to sample a color, or use the **Retouch** and **Red Eye Removal** tools to correct the image. Use the **Adjustment Brush** and **Graduated Filter** for local adjustments.**(New!)**

3 Select from the available image view options:

- ◆ **Image Preview.** Displays the active image.
- ◆ **Zoom Level.** Changes the view of the active image.
- ◆ **Histogram.** Displays information on the colors and brightness levels in the active image.

4 Click the **Basic**, **Tone Curve**, **Detail**, **Lens**, **HSL/ Grayscale**, **Split Toning**, **Lens Corrections**, or **Camera Calibration** tabs, and then click **Auto** (Basic tab) or drag sliders to modify the color and tonal values of the image.

5 Click **Save Image** to specify a folder destination, file name, and format for the processed images.

6 Select the images you want to synchronize (apply settings) in the Filmstrip (if desired, click Select All), and then click **Synchronize**.

7 Click the **Camera Raw Menu** button to **Load**, **Save**, or **Delete** a specific set of Raw settings, or to modify dialog box settings.

8 Click **Done** to process the file, but not open it, or click **Open Image** to process and open it in Photoshop. Hold Alt (Win) or Option (Mac) to use **Open Copy** or **Reset**.

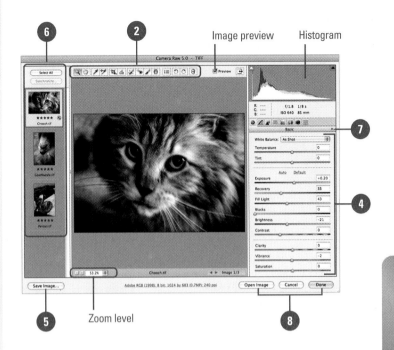

Image preview Histogram

Zoom level

For Your Information

What is the DNG File Format?

The DNG, or Digital Negative, format is an openly published raw file format from Adobe that stores "raw" pixel data captured by digital cameras before it has been converted to another format, such as TIFF or JPEG. In addition, it captures standard 'EXIF' metadata, such as date, time, camera used, and camera settings. Saving raw files in the DNG format provides several advantages. DNG files are smaller than uncompressed TIFFs, and they do not have the artifacts of compressed JPEGs. Many key camera parameters, such as white balance, can be modified even after the image is captured. You have access to 16-bit data for greater detail and fidelity, and the added flexibility of converting a single file using multiple conversion settings. When you convert raw images into the DNG format, you are using a format that is openly published by Adobe and usable by other software and hardware vendors, which makes it a safe format for the long-term storage and archiving of digital images. The raw format used by digital cameras is proprietary to the specific camera (e.g., NEF for Nikon, CR2 for Canon, RAF for Fuji), so the format might not be supported once that camera and its proprietary software is obsolete, which means at some point in the future, you might not be able to open any of your archived raw images. The DNG format solves that problem. To get a free copy of the DNG converter, go to *www.adobe.com* and then search for DNG converter.

Working with Images Using Adobe Bridge

PS 1.5, 7.5, 7.6, 7.7

With Adobe Bridge, you can drag assets into your layouts as needed, preview them, and add metadata to them. Bridge allows you to search, sort, filter, manage, and process image files one at a time or in batches. You can also use Bridge to create new folders; rename, move, delete and group files (known as stacking); edit metadata; rotate images; and run batch commands. You can also view information about files and data imported from your digital camera.

Work with Images Using Bridge

1 Launch your Adobe product, click the **File** menu, and then click **Browse in Bridge**, or click the **Launch Bridge** button (if available).

2 Click the **Folder** path, and then select a folder.

3 Click the **Folders** tab and choose a folder from the scrolling list.

4 Click the **Favorites** tab to choose from a listing of user-defined items, such as Pictures or Version Cue.

5 Click an image within the preview window to select it.

6 Click the **Metadata** tab to view image information, including date and time the image was shot, and aperture, shutter speed, and f-stop.

7 Click the **IPTC Core** arrow to add user-defined metadata, such as creator and copyright information, or captions.

8 Click the **Preview** tab to view a larger thumbnail of the selected image. Multiple images appear when you select them.

◆ Click the image in the Preview tab to display a Loupe tool for zooming. Drag magnified box to change positions. Click it to deactivate the tool.

9 Drag the **Zoom** slider to increase or decrease the thumbnail views.

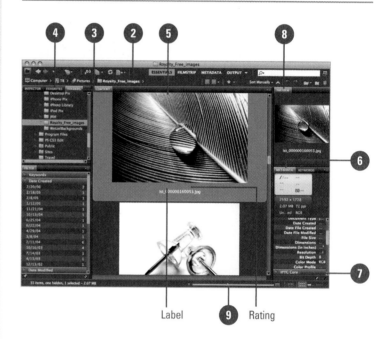

Label **9** Rating

10 Click the preview buttons to select a different view of the workspace you have chosen. If you want to view your images in filmstrip or metadata focus mode, choose that workspace from the Window menu.

◆ **View Content as Thumbnails.** Default view. Displays the images as thumbnails with the file name underneath.

◆ **View Content as Details.** Displays a thumbnail of each image with selected details about the image such as date created, document type, resolution.

◆ **View Content as List.** Displays a small thumbnail of each image with metadata information details, such as date created and file size.

11 Use the file management buttons to rotate or delete images, or create a new folder.

12 To narrow down the list of images using a filter, click the criteria you want to use in the Filter panel.

13 To add a label or rating to images, select the ones you want, click the **Label** menu, and then select the label or rating you want.

14 To group related images as a stacked group, select the images, click the **Stacks** menu, and then click **Group as Stack**.

◆ Use the Stacks menu to ungroup, open, expand, or collapse stacks.

15 Double-click on a thumbnail to open it in the default program, or drag the thumbnail from the Bridge into an open Adobe application.

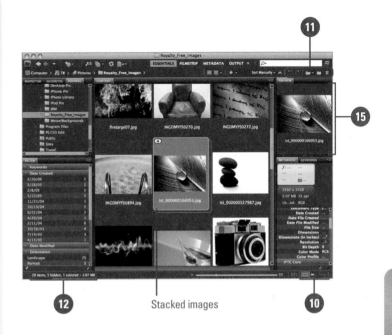

Stacked images

For Your Information

What is Metadata?

Metadata is information about an image file, such as its author, copyright, creation date, size, version, color space, resolution, and searchable keywords. This data is stored in the file or in a separate file known as a **sidecar file**, using a standard format called **Extensible Metadata Platform (XMP)**. Bridge and Version Cue use XMP files to help you organize and search for files on your computer. Metadata is also stored in other formats, such as EXIF (digital camera data), IPTC (photographer and image data), GPS (global positioning system data), and TIFF, which are all synchronized with XMP.

Applying Image Adjustments

 PS 7.5, 8.3

Adobe Bridge makes it easy to make adjustments to one image in Camera Raw and then apply those adjustments to other images directly from Bridge without going back into Camera Raw. For instance, you may be correcting the white balance for an image and have many other images that were shot at the same time, under the same lighting conditions. You can use the initial settings to correct the rest of your images right from Bridge. You can also make a preset from your favorite adjustments, which will then be available as a develop setting within Bridge.

Modify Images in Adobe Bridge

1 In Adobe Bridge, display and select the images that you want to adjust.

2 Use any of the following methods to modify an image:

◆ **Apply a Preset Adjustment.** Click the **Edit** menu, point to **Develop Settings**, and then select a preset adjustment.

◆ **Copy and Paste Settings.** Click the **Edit** menu, point to **Develop Settings**, and then click **Copy Settings**. Select the image(s) to which you want to apply the settings. Click the **Edit** menu, point to **Develop Settings**, and then click **Paste Settings**. Select the options to apply, and then click **OK**.

◆ **Apply the Most Recent Adjustment.** Click the **Edit** menu, point to **Develop Settings**, and then click **Previous Conversion.**

Did You Know?

You can use Photoshop automation commands in Adobe Bridge. You can use the Batch or Image Processor commands on the Tools menu under Photoshop in Bridge to automate the processing of your camera's raw files.

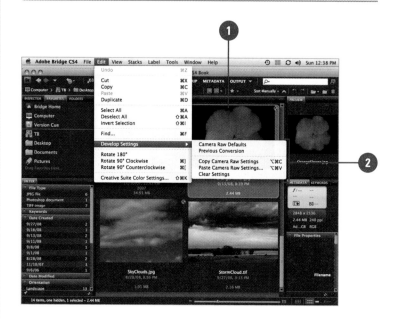

Paste Settings

Creating a Web Photo Gallery

 PS 12.4

Adobe Bridge takes the drudgery out of creating a Web Photo Gallery (**New!**) (thumbnail images on web pages). The pages generated with this command display small thumbnails of a group of images—when you click on an image, a larger version is displayed within another window or section of the page. If your goal is to show the world your photographs, but you don't want to write all the HTML code involved in making that happen, then the Web Photo Gallery is just what you need.

Create a Web Photo Gallery in Adobe Bridge

1. In Adobe Bridge, select a folder with the images that you want to use for the photo gallery.

2. Click the **Workspace** menu, and then click **Output**.

3. Click the **Web Gallery** button.

4. Click the **Template** list arrow, and then select a template.

   ◆ Click the **Refresh Preview** button to view your template choices or click the **Preview in Browser** button to see how it would look on the Web.

5. Use the following panels to customize the Web gallery:

   ◆ **Site Info.** Provide descriptive information about the Web Photo gallery.

   ◆ **Color Palette.** Select custom colors for screen elements.

   ◆ **Appearance.** Specify options to show file names, a preview and thumbnail size, slide duration, and a transition effect.

6. In the Create Gallery panel, enter a gallery name, and then select a creation option:

   ◆ **Save to Disk.** Click **Browse** to specify a location, and then click **Save**.

   ◆ **Upload.** Specify the FTP server location, user name, password, a folder, and then click **Upload**.

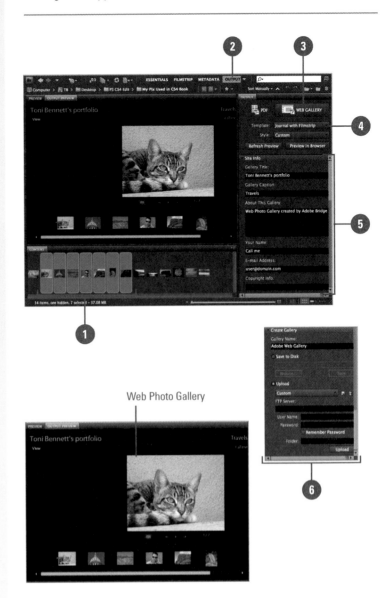

Web Photo Gallery

Automating Tasks in Adobe Bridge

The Tools menu provides commands you can use to automate tasks in Bridge. For example, you can automate the process of renaming a group of files using the Batch Rename command. If you use Photoshop, InDesign, or Version Cue, you can use commands on submenus to run automated tasks, such as adding and synchronizing files with Version Cue or processing raw images with Photoshop, or you can create a contact sheet of images in InDesign. You can also use the Tools menu to start other Adobe programs, such as Device Central and Acrobat Connect (Start Meeting) as well as create and edit Metadata templates, which you can use to append or replace metadata in Adobe InDesign or other XMP-enabled programs.

Rename Files Automatically in Adobe Bridge

1. In Adobe Bridge, select the files or folders you want to use.

2. Click the **Tools** menu, and then click **Batch Rename**.

3. Select the Destination Folder option you want: **Rename in same folder**, **Move to other folder**, or **Copy to other folder**, and then click **Browse** to specify a new folder location.

4. Click the **Element** drop-down, and then select options to specify how you want to name the files:

   ◆ Text, New Extension, Current Filename, Preserved Filename, Sequence Number, Sequence Letter, Date/Time, Metadata, or Folder Name.

5. Enter the text you want to use in conjunction with the Element selection to name the files.

6. Select the **Preserve Current File Name In XMP Metadata** check box to retain the original filename in the metadata.

7. Select the check boxes for the operating systems with which you want the renamed files to be compatible.

8. Click **Rename**.

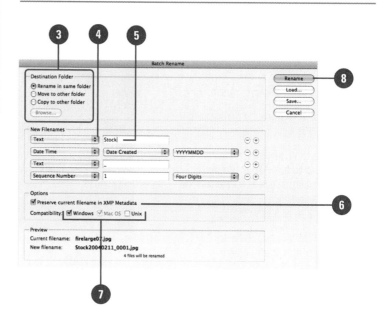

Sharing My Screen

The Share My Screen command (**New!**) on the File menu allows you to connect to Adobe ConnectNow, which is a secure Web site where you can start an online meeting and collaborate on any design project across platforms and programs. You can share and annotate your computer screen or take control of an attendee's computer. During the meeting, you can communicate by sending chat messages, using live audio, or broadcasting live video. In addition, you can take meeting notes, and share files.

Share My Screen

1. Click the **File** menu, and then click **Share My Screen**.

2. Enter your Adobe ID and password.

   ◆ If you don't have an Adobe ID and password, click the Create a Free Adobe ID link, and then follow the online instructions.

3. Click **Sign In**.

   ◆ If prompted, sign in to ConnectNow.

4. To share your computer screen, click the **Share My Computer Screen** button.

5. Use the ConnectNow toolbar to do any of the following:

   ◆ **Meeting.** Use to invite participants, share your computer screen, upload a file, share your webcam, set preferences, end a meeting, and exit Adobe ConnectNow.

   ◆ **PODS.** Use to show and hide pod panels.

   ◆ **Help.** Use to get help, troubleshoot problems, and set account and Flash Player settings.

6. Click the participant buttons at the bottom to specify roles, remove a user, or request control of a user's computer.

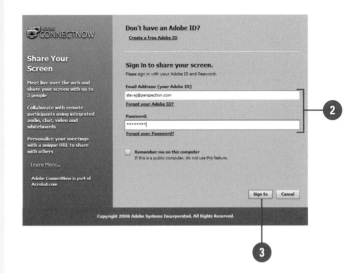

Exploring Adobe Device Central

 PS 12.6

Device Profiles tab
Displays detailed information about devices, including support details for Flash, bitmap, video, and Web.

Emulator tab
Displays a simulation of how content appears on specific mobile devices.

Device Sets panel
Displays sets of devices for testing; availability depends on the content type.

Online Library panel
Downloads specific mobile device specifications.

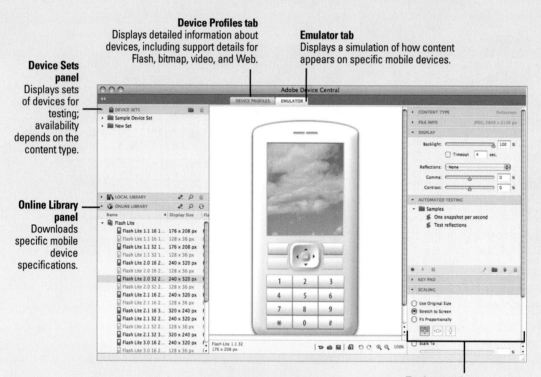

Testing panels
Displays a number of panels for testing content based on the selected options.

Checking Content Using Adobe Device Central

PS 12.6

Testing your content on as many different devices as possible allows you to reach a wider audience. Adobe Device Central makes it easy to test your content on a wide variety of different mobile devices in one place. Device Central provides a library of devices from which to choose, and each device includes a profile with information about the device, including media and content support types. Device Central uses an emulator to simulate the way your content will look on a selected device. An emulator is not the same as the real device. However, it allows you to quickly test devices to get initial results.

Check Content Using Adobe Device Central

1. Start Adobe Device Central from the Start menu (Win) or the Applications folder (Mac) or from the File menu in Photoshop and choose Device Central.

   ◆ In Bridge, right-click a file, and then click **Test in Device Central**.

2. From the Welcome screen or the File menu, select the option you want:

   ◆ **Open for Testing**. Opens a file for testing with the Emulator tab. Use the buttons on the mobile device to test your content.

   ◆ **Device Profiles**. Displays mobile device profiles. In the Available Devices panel, expand a folder with devices. On the Device Profiles tab, click links to display profile information.

   ◆ **Create New Mobile**. Creates a new mobile document for Flash, Photoshop, or Illustrator; select a mobile device, and then click **Create**.

3. Select the Online Library panel where you can download specific mobile device specifications.

4. If you're testing, select the options you want in the Testing panels.

5. When you're done, click the **Close** button in the Device Central window.

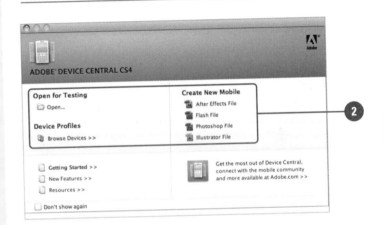

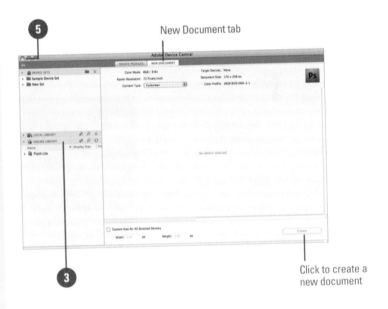

New Document tab

Click to create a new document

Using Adobe Extension Manager

The Adobe Extension Manager CS4 is a program you can use to install and delete added program functionality, known as extensions, to many Adobe programs. The Extension Manager is automatically installed when you install Flash, Dreamweaver, or Fireworks. You can use the Extension Manager to access the Adobe Exchange site, where you can locate, research, and download many different types of extensions. Some are free and some are not. After you download an extension, you can use Extension Manager to install it. Extension Manager only displays extensions installed using the Extension Manager; other extensions installed using a third-party installer might not appear. After you install an extension, you can find and display information about it.

Download and Install an Extension

1 Start Adobe Extension Manager CS4 from the Start menu (Win) or the Applications folder (Mac).

TIMESAVER *In Flash, Dreamweaver, or Fireworks, click the Help menu, and then click Manage Extensions.*

2 Click the **Exchange** button on the toolbar.

3 Select the extension you want to download, and then save it to your computer.

4 In Extension Manager, click the **Install** button on the toolbar.

5 Locate and select the extension (.mxp) you want to install, and then click **Install**.

6 You can perform any of the following:

 ◆ **Sort**. Click a column heading.

 ◆ **Enable or Disable**. Select or clear the check in the Enabled check box next to the extension.

 ◆ **Remove**. Select the extension, and then click **Remove**.

7 Click the **Close** button.

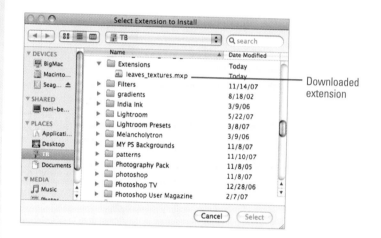

Downloaded extension

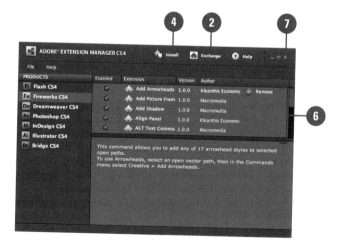

Workshops

Introduction

The Workshop is all about being creative and thinking outside of the box. These workshops will help your right-brain soar, while making your left-brain happy by explaining why things work the way they do. Exploring Photoshop's possibilities is great fun; however, always stay grounded with the knowledge of how things work. Knowledge is power.

Getting and Using the Project Files

Each project in the Workshop includes a start file to help you get started with the project, and a final file to provide you with the results so you can see how well you accomplished the task.

Before you can use the project files, you need to download them from the Web. You can access the files at *www.perspection.com*. After you download the files, uncompress them into a folder on your hard drive.

Project 1: Scaling an Image Using Content-Aware

Skills and Tools: Content-Aware Scale, Refine Edge, and Blending Mode

One of the exciting features in Photoshop CS4 is Content-Aware Scaling (**New!**). This command looks for the focal point in your image and then identifies pixel areas that are less important and adds or subtracts pixels in those areas as necessary as you scale the image, leaving the focal point unchanged (unless you go too far). You can use Content-Aware scaling on layers and selections with a variety of color modes (RGB, CMYK, Lab, and Grayscale). However, you can use it with adjustment layers, layer masks, individual channels, Smart Objects, 3D layers, Video layers, multiple layers, and layer groups.

The Project

In this project, you'll use the Content-Aware Scaling feature along with other refining tools to modify and enhance a photograph.

The Process

 Open the file Red_Rock_Canyon_start.psd in Photoshop and then save it as **my_Red_Rock_Canyon.psd**.

2 Be sure you're not working on a locked layer (like the Background). If necessary, double click the *Background* layer name and rename it. Duplicate the layer by dragging it on to the New Layer icon or using Ctrl+J (Win) or ⌘+J (Mac). Duplicating the layer enables you to compare your results to the original. Click the eyeball icon for Layer 0 to make it invisible while you work on Layer 0 copy.

3 If you want to protect your most important image elements from being squished or stretched, make a selection around the area you want to protect, using any selection tool. The selection does not have to be exact; a loose selection is fine. In this case, I've selected the large bush.

4 Click the **Refine Edge** button on the Options bar to open a dialog box where you can specify a Feather size and preview the result.

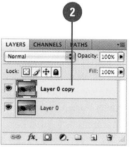

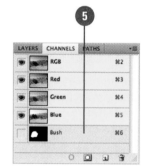

5 Save the selection as an alpha channel. Click the **Select** menu, click **Save Selection**, and then name it something descriptive. I've named this one *Bush*.

6 Deselect the selection. Click the **Select** menu, and then click **Deselect** or press Ctrl+D.

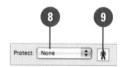

7 Click the **Edit** menu, and then click **Content-Aware Scale**.

8 If you've created an alpha channel representing a selection of an area, you want to force Photoshop to protect it. Click the **Protect** popup on the Options bar, and then select the channel now.

9 If there are people in your image, click the **Protect Skin Tones** button on the Options bar to protect flesh tones.

10 Point to one of the squares on the bounding box. When your cursor becomes a double arrow, drag towards the center of the image to change the orientation of your image.

11 As with any transform command, press Enter (Win) or Return (Mac) when you're done to commit to the change.

You can keep Layer 0 for comparison purposes (see Tweaking the Image below) or you can choose to discard Layer 0, Select All, Choose Trim from the Image menu and choose Based on Transparent Pixels to reduce your file to the new scaled size. Then choose the Save As command to save your new file.

Difference Blend Mode

The Results

Finish: Compare your completed project file with the image in **Red_Rock_Canyon_fnl.psd**. ☞

Tweaking the Image

To see how much pixel information change (loss) your image has incurred as a result of using the Content-Aware Scale command, turn back on the visibility for Layer 0, and change the blend mode to Difference. Then, using the Move tool, move the transformed layer directly over the same area on the bottom layer. If the areas you wanted protected are mostly black, that means there is little or no difference between the two layers (no change in the pixels) and you have made your transformation without altering the most important parts of your image.

Good to Know: As great as this new feature is, there are some limitations. It doesn't work on every image. There are limits as to how far you can scale the image before it starts to look strange. Also, you can't use it on adjustment layers, layer masks, channels, Smart Objects, 3D layers, or video layers. It will work on all bit-depths (16-bit, etc.) and will work on layers and selections in RGB, CMYK, Lab, and Grayscale image modes.

Project 2: Creating a Template Using Smart Objects

Skills and Tools: Multiple Documents, Smart Objects, Text Layers, and Guides

Smart Objects (**New!**) are essentially containers for image (either raster or vector) data. In the transformation of a file or a layer into a Smart Object, the original file remains intact, embedded within the file. This allows you to resize the image up or down (up to the maximum of the original file size) nondestructively, edit one layer to update multiple appearances of the same Smart Object, and bring vector artwork into Photoshop in a way that the original data is retained. One very handy trick that Smart Objects can do is allow you the ability to create a template and easily replace the contents of one layer's data with another.

The Project

In this project, you'll create a template for a 6" x 4" postcard to send to friends, family, or customers to show off your photos. You can use this template to swap out the photos and create more postcards without having to recreate the whole document. The text will stay the same in each new document.

The Process

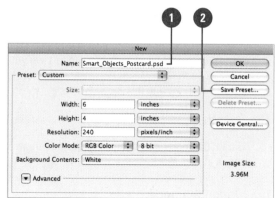

1 Click the **File** menu, click **New**, create a new blank image, 6" wide x 4" high at 240 dpi. Name the file **Smart_Objects_Postcard.psd**.

2 Click **Save Preset** in the New document dialog box and name it **6 x 4 Postcard Template**.

The background layer should be white by default.

3 Click the **View** menu, click **Rulers**, and then pull out vertical and horizontal guides at the .5" and 5.5" marks.

4 Select the **Rectangle** tool on the toolbox and draw a rectangle that conforms to the inside box (5" by 3"). This will create a new Shape layer.

5 Click the **Layer Style** button, click **Layer Effects**, and click **Stroke**. In CS4, the stroke color is now black by default instead of red (a welcome change!). Change the pixel size to 7 and select **Inside** from the Position options. The layer will be named "Shape 1," which you can rename.

6 Select the **Text** tool on the toolbox, and then click to create a text box on the top. This will create a new text layer. Add a heading or title for the postcard, such as a business name.

7 Select the **Text** tool on the toolbox, and then click to create a text box on the bottom. Add more text, such as a copyright line or a tagline, or maybe contact info. Position both text layers where you want them using the Move tool.

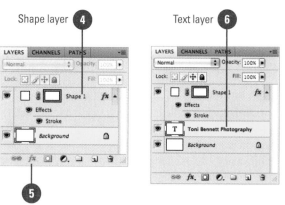

Shape layer 4

Text layer 6

8 Select the **Marquee** tool. Select **Fixed Size** from the Options bar and type in 5 in x 3 in. Your default may be pixels but you can type "5 in" and it will change to inches. Place the marquee over the picture box area. Drag the Shape 1 layer underneath the text layers.

9 Click the **File** menu, and then click **Place**. Choose an image. If you've already sized some images to the 5 x 3 size, they should fit right in. But no worries; after you place the image, you have transformation handles that you can use to resize your image to fit into the box. Hold the Shift key down as you transform so it will be resized proportionately. Press Enter (Win) or Return (Mac) to commit the transformation.

10 When you place an object, the new layer automatically becomes a Smart Object. You can convert other layers to Smart Objects by clicking the Layer menu, pointing to Smart Objects, and then clicking Convert to Smart Object.

11 To change the image, right-click (Win) or Control-click (Mac) the Smart Object layer, and then click **Replace Contents**. Then, browse to the picture you want to use as the new image within the box and choose it. If it doesn't fit exactly, select **Free Transform** from the Edit menu and resize it. Your Smart Object layer will still be named with the original image title; double click on it to change the layer name to reflect the new image contents.

12 Click the **View** menu, and then click **Clear Guides** to see your finished postcard in all its glory.

The Results

Finish: Compare your completed project file with the image in Smart_Objects_Postcard_fnl.psd.

Text layer **7**   **8**

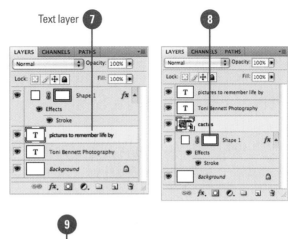

9

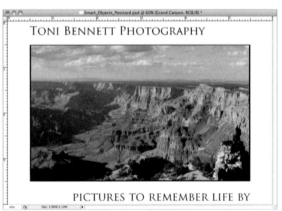

Good to Know: You could choose a folder full of images that you'd like to swap out on this postcard template and choose File/Scripts/ImageProcessor to size them all at one time to fit within your picture border. If you resize on the fly, bring in pictures that are larger than your border. Trying to enlarge pictures to fit within the border may cause noticeable degradation of the image.

Project 3: Creating a Sketch from Scratch

Skills and Tools: Multiple Layers, Gaussian Blur, and Blending Modes

Photoshop has a ton of filters. In fact, there are 105 filters located under the Filter menu. Filters perform a wealth of special-effects operations—everything from artistic, distort, and even sketch effects, and while filters are very creative and fun to use, there is a limit to what they can do. For example, Photoshop has no less than 14 Sketch filters, and while they do creative things to an image they can't do everything. What if you want to create what looks like a sketch effect and none of the sketch filters do what you want? If you don't know how to do things from scratch, you're stuck with the limitations of the filters. The technique you are about to learn will not only let you create an awesome sketch effect, but will give you a better understanding of how blending modes work with multiple layers.

The Project

In this project, you'll take a photograph and through the judicious use of multiple layers and blending modes, convert it into a beautiful colorized sketch. There are a lot of steps in this workshop, but the final results are more than worth the journey.

The Process

① Open the file **sketch_start.psd** in Photoshop, and then save it as **my_sketch.psd**.

② Create a duplicate of the image by dragging the layer over the Create a New Layer icon.

③ Click the **Image** menu, point to **Adjustments**, and then click **Desaturate**. The copied layer is converted into shades of gray.

④ Create a copy of the desaturated layer, and then select it.

⑤ Click the **Image** menu, point to **Adjustments**, and click **Invert**. The image layer becomes a grayscale negative (leave the negative image selected).

⑥ Click the **Blending Mode** list arrow on the Layers panel, and then click **Color Dodge**. The image appears to change to white.

Note: If you see areas of the image that do not change to white, but are pure black, don't worry; those areas of the image were originally pure black, and they will never convert to white.

7 Click the **Filter** menu, point to **Blur**, and then click **Gaussian Blur**.

8 Blur the image very slightly (just a few radius pixels) until you see a softly ghosted outline of the image.

9 Click **OK**.

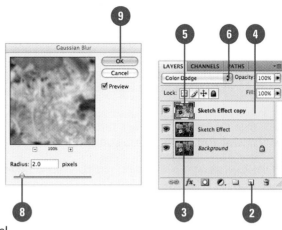

10 Select the top layer in the Layers panel, click the **Layers Options** button, and then click **Merge Down**, or press Ctrl+E (Win) or ⌘+E (Mac).

You should now be left with the original image (the bottom layer), and the softly ghosted image (the top layer), which I've named *Sketch Effect*.

11 Create a copy of the layer named Sketch Effect, and select it.

12 Click the **Blending Mode** list arrow on the Layers panel, and then click **Multiply**. The two copies combine to create a darker image.

13 Continue to make copies of the Sketch Effect layer until the image darkens to your taste (this might be 3 layers, or it might be 10).

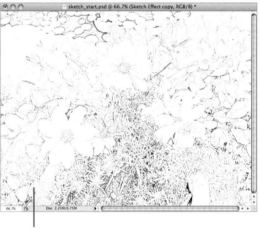

Softly ghosted image

14 Merge all the Sketch Effect layers together, but do not merge the original image layer into the Sketch Effect layers.

Note: You can quickly merge layers by using the Merge Down shortcut. Select the top layer, and then press Ctrl+E (Win) or ⌘+E (Mac). This merges the top layer into the layer directly underneath. Continue using the Merge Down shortcut until all the Sketch layers are merged.

15 Create another copy of the merged Sketch Effect layer, and select it.

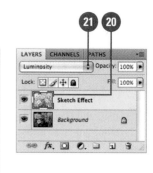

16 Click the **Blending Mode** list arrow on the Layers panel, and then click **Multiply**.

17 Click the **Filter** menu, point to **Blur**, and then click **Gaussian Blur**.

18 Add a small amount of Gaussian Blur to taste (1 or 2 Radius). This will soften the edges of the sketch image and create visually softer sketch lines.

19 Click **OK**.

20 Merge the two Sketch Effects layers together.

21 To colorize the image, select the top layer (Sketch Effect), click the **Blending Mode** list arrow, and then click **Luminosity**.

The Results

Finish: Compare your completed project file with the image in **sketch_fnl.psd**.

Tweaking the Image

The subjective items that will influence the final sketch image are how much you use Gaussian Blur on the image, and how many additional copy layers you create. Creating more blur enhances the sketch lines, and adding more copy layers increases the overall density of the final sketch image.

Good to Know: You can increase or decrease the intensity of the Sketch Effect by selecting the Sketch Effect layer and lowering its opacity.

Project 4: Creating a Sharper Image

Skills and Tools: Multiple Layers, Blending Modes, Layer Opacity, and Paintbrush

In the world of photography, not everything has to be in focus. In fact, smart photographers know that placing certain image elements out of focus will help to draw the eye to the focused areas. However, there are times when you will take a photograph and the image is accidentally, not intentionally, out of focus (I hate it when that happens). Photoshop has several filters that help you create a sharper image. As a matter of fact, Photoshop has five sharpen filters: Sharpen, Sharpen Edges, Sharpen More, Smart Sharpen, and Unsharp Mask. Of these filters, Smart Sharpen and Unsharp Mask are considered the two most powerful sharpening filters. Unfortunately, all the sharpening filters have one major flaw; they do not separate the sharpening effects from the image, as they would be in an adjustment layer. So, when you click the OK button, you're stuck with the results. That's not always a bad thing; however, there is another way. The technique you're about to learn for sharpening an image does not require any of the sharpening filters; its effect on the image creates a more believable sharpening result, and the changes to the image are contained within a separate layer. That gives you the control you need to be creative, and to get the most visibly pleasing sharpening results possible.

The Project

In this project, you'll take an out-of-focus image and sharpen it by creating an editable sharpening layer. Separating the sharpening adjustments from the image gives you creative control over the entire process.

The Process

1. Open the file lighthouse_start.psd in Photoshop, and then save it as my_lighthouse.psd.

2. Create a duplicate of the image by dragging the layer over the **Create a New Layer** button, or by selecting the layer and pressing Ctrl+J (Win), or ⌘+J (Mac).

3. Click the **Image** menu, point to **Adjustments**, and then click **Desaturate**. The copied layer is converted into shades of gray.

   Note: If the image is originally a grayscale image, you can skip step 3.

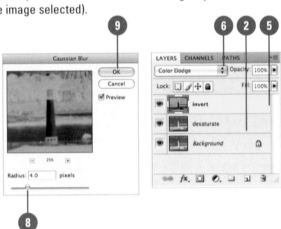

4. Create a copy of the desaturated layer and select it.

5. Click the **Image** menu, point to **Adjustments**, and then click **Invert**. The image layer becomes a grayscale negative (leave the negative image selected).

You now have the option of applying your selected adjustment from the new Adjustments panel (**New!**), which automatically creates an adjustment layer. This option makes all the image changes nondestructive.

6. Click the **Blending Mode** list arrow on the Layers panel, and then click **Color Dodge**. The image appears to change to white.

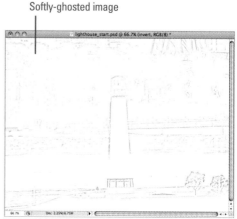

Note: If you see areas of the image that do not change to white, but are pure black, don't worry; those areas of the image were originally pure black, and they will never convert to white.

7️⃣ Click the **Filter** menu, point to **Blur**, and then click **Gaussian Blur**.

8️⃣ Blur the image very slightly (just a few radius pixels) until you see a softly ghosted outline of the image.

9️⃣ Click **OK**.

🔟 Select the top layer in the Layers panel, click the **Layers Options** button, and then click **Merge Down**, or press Ctrl+E (Win) or ⌘+E (Mac).

You should now be left with the original image (the bottom layer), and the softly ghosted image (the top layer), which I've named *Unsharp mask*.

1️⃣1️⃣ Click the **Blending Mode** list arrow on the Layers panel, and then click **Multiply**. The white areas of the ghosted image change to transparent, and the darker lines are blended in with the original image, creating the illusion of sharpness.

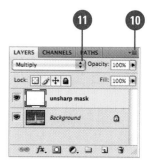

The Results

Finish: Compare your completed project file with the image in lighthouse_fnl.psd. 👉

Tweaking the Image

It's possible that the sharpening effect may be too intense. If that's the case, simply reduce the opacity of the top layer to reduce its effect on the image. If, however, the effect is less than you hoped for, simply create a copy of the top layer to double the effect. Additionally, if you want to remove some of the sharpening effects from portions of the image, just select your Paintbrush tool, and paint with white over the areas from which you want the effect removed.

Good to Know: It is actually impossible to sharpen a photograph. Photographs are two-dimensional representations of a three-dimensional world. Since there are no optics in a two-dimensional world, there can be no sharpening. What happens in this technique is that the Unsharp mask layer actually creates visible lines of contrast around the out-of-focus areas of the image, and the mind interprets the image as being sharper.

Project 5: Colorizing a Grayscale Image

Skills and Tools: Multiple Layers, Blending Modes, Layer Opacity, and Paintbrush

Have you ever wanted to colorize an old grayscale image? Well, if you've ever wanted to add color to an old image, or change the colors within a new color image, then you've come to the right place. There are a lot of ways to colorize an image, and Photoshop knows them all. The technique you are about to learn will help you control the colorization process through the use of layers, blending modes, and opacity. As a matter of fact, you will be able to control each color within the image and, later, change those colors with the click of a button. This method is so powerful that with a little bit of patience and care, the image won't just look colorized; it will look like an original color image. Just remember this simple item: every time you add a new color to the image, you will add a new layer. This means that a single image may contain twenty or more layers; however, the final results are worth it.

The Project

In this project, you'll take an old or new grayscale image, and through the use of multiple layers and blending modes create a colorized image that looks like it was taken with color film.

The Process

① Open the file colorization_start.psd in Photoshop, and then save it as my_colorization.psd.

② Click the **Create a New Layer** button, located at the bottom of the Layers panel, and name the layer to correspond to the area of the image you're coloring.

③ Click the **Blending Mode** list arrow, and then click **Color**.

④ Select the **Paintbrush** tool.

⑤ Select the color you want to use to paint a specific area of the image within the new layer.

⑥ Use the **Paintbrush** tool to paint an area of the image.

Note: Since you changed the blending mode of the layer to Color, the image retains its details, and only the color (Hue) of the information changes.

⑦ Depending on the color you chose, slightly lower the opacity of the layer to make it appear natural.

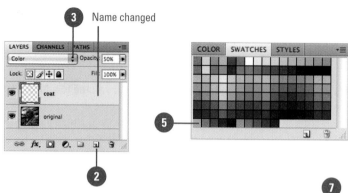

3 Name changed

5

2

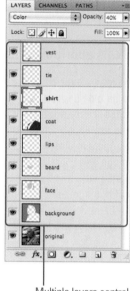

Multiple layers control color information

Note: Different colors require different opacity settings to appear natural because of the saturation of the color, and the detail within the areas you are painting. Experiment with opacity settings until the image looks correct.

8 Repeat steps 2 thru 7 for each individual color within the image.

7

The Results

Finish: Compare your completed project file with the image in colorization_fnl.psd.

☞

Tweaking the Image

Since you are using individual layers to control the colorization process, if you overpaint an area, it's a simple matter to use your eraser tool and remove the excess color information.

Smart Tip: When you change the opacity of a layer, it's not necessary to click the triangle button, located to the right of the Opacity input box, to access the triangular slider. All you have to do is click the word Opacity, and drag left or right. It's that simple.

Project 6: Managing Images with Masks

Skills and Tools: Multiple Images, Layer Masks, Paintbrush, and Selection

Layer masks are one of those powerful features in Photoshop that have been around for a long time. The technique you are about to learn will give you a greater understanding of Layer masks, and how they can be used to combine image elements from multiple images. Layer masks let you control the visible elements of a layer by simply painting on the mask. Think of the mask as a piece of black construction paper. You take a pair of scissors and cut a shape out of the construction paper, and lay it directly over the image. The area cut out of the construction paper becomes the visible elements of the image, and the black areas of the construction paper mask everything else. When you work with a Layer mask, you paint with black, white, and shades of gray. Areas of the mask painted black are hidden, areas painted white are visible (the cutout in the construction paper), and shades of gray produce various values of transparency. For example, painting with 50% gray produces 50% transparency. Each layer in an image can have its own layer mask, and the mask will control only the elements in the layer to which they're attached. As you can see, Layer masks are a very powerful and creative tool.

The Project

In this project, you'll learn the creative potential of using layer masks to control the visible portions of any layer in Photoshop.

The Process

1. Open the file **lake_start.psd** in Photoshop, and then save it as **my_lake.psd**.

2. Click the **Add Layer Mask** button, located at the bottom of the Layers panel.

   Photoshop creates a mask, and places it to the right of the image thumbnail.

3. Select the **Paintbrush** tool.

4. Select Black as your Foreground color by clicking the **Default Foreground and Background Colors** button.

   Important: A layer with an attached mask has two elements: The image thumbnail, and the mask thumbnail. If you want to edit the image, click the image thumbnail. If you want to edit the mask, click the mask thumbnail.

5. Click the mask thumbnail to select it.

6. Move into the document window, and begin painting. As you paint, the black color converts the image information to transparency.

   Note: Areas of the mask painted with white become 100% visible, and painting with shades of gray produces various percentages of transparency, depending on the shade of gray.

7. Continue painting using black, white, and shades of gray, until you have completely isolated the sky section of the image.

Smart Tip: You can create a mask by first using a selection. Open the image, and before creating the mask, use your selection tools to select the visible areas of the image. Now, when you click the Add Layer Mask button, the mask will be created for you.

In the Masks panel (**New!**), you can view pixel or vector masks, adjust their density (opacity), choose a feather size, invert the mask and even create new masks

Mask thumbnail

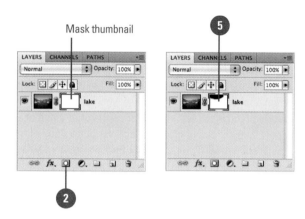

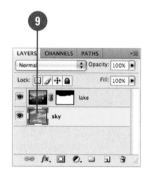

using Color Range. The Mask Edge option displays the Refine Mask dialog box where you can view the mask against different backgrounds, contract or expand the mask, and choose the radius and feather size.

8 Open the **sky.psd** image in Photoshop, save it as **my_sky.psd**, and then click in its document window.

9 Move to the Layers panel, and drag the sky layer into the document window of the image containing the mask. You have just made a copy of the sky layer in the masked image.

10 Close the sky image.

11 Click the sky layer in the Layers panel and drag it underneath the masked layer.

The image, which is now defined as a composite, appears with its new sky.

The Results

Finish: Compare your completed project file with the image in lake_fnl.psd_fnl.psd. ☞

Tweaking the Image

It's possible that the visible edge of the masked image and sky appear too sharp and, therefore, unnatural. To help blend the two layers together, simply select the mask thumbnail and apply a bit of Gaussian Blur to the mask. Click the Filter menu, point to Blur, and choose Gaussian Blur. The blur creates a band of gray pixels on the edge of the black/white areas of the image, and helps blend the two images together.

Good to Know: By default, a mask and image move and transform as a unit. If you want to adjust the mask independently of the image (or vice versa), click once on the chain icon located between the image and mask thumbnail. The icon will disappear, and the mask and thumbnail can be adjusted or transformed independently.

Icing on the Cake: If you really want to get fancy, you might want to create a reflection of the clouds on the water. To accomplish this, create a copy of the sky layer, select the Edit menu, point to Transform, and then click Flip Vertical. Now, create a mask that only reveals the areas of the water, use the Overlay Blending mode, and lower the opacity slightly. The lake_fnl.psd image contains a sample reflection in a separate layer.

Project 7: Getting Creative with Adjustment Layers

Skills and Tools: Adjustment Layers, Layer Masks, and Paintbrush

Adjustment layers are used extensively for image enhancement. For example, the Levels and Curves adjustment layers are excellent tools for restoring lost contrast, or rebalancing the colors in an old photograph. The technique you are about to learn will give you a greater understanding of how adjustment layers can be used to not only correct image problems, but to generate special effects. The key is in understanding that an adjustment layer can be controlled using its built-in layer mask. The adjustment layer mask functions like a normal layer mask; in other words, you can paint the mask with black, white, or shades of gray. However, the results are different. In a normal layer mask, areas of the mask painted black make the corresponding areas of the image transparent; when you paint with black on an adjustment layer mask, you mask out the effects of the adjustment. That means you can create a mask and isolate its effects on the image by using the mask. While this is a powerful way to control image enhancement, it's also a great way to use adjustment layers to produce special effects. In addition, when you use an adjustment layer, the changes to the image are contained within the adjustment layer, and the original image is never changed. This gives you the ability to precisely control the creative process nondestructively. In this example, you will completely change the mood of an image using an adjustment layer and mask to create the illusion of looking through window blinds. One of the most visible (and welcome) changes to Photoshop CS4 is the Adjustments panel (**New!**). From this one panel, you now have access to icons representing 15 adjustment types complete with preloaded presets and the flexibility to make your own presets for many of them.

The Project

In this project, you'll learn how to use Adjustment layers to precisely control the restoration and enhancement of any Photoshop image.

The Process

1 Open the file **mystery_woman_start.psd** in Photoshop, and then save it as **my_mystery_woman.psd**.

2 Select the **Rectangular Marquee** tool.

3 Create a long rectangular selection from left to right, across the image (like a window blind).

4 Hold the Shift key, and proceed to draw several more rectangular selections underneath the first.

Note: Holding the Shift key lets you create two or three additional selections within the document window.

5 Click the **Select** menu, and then click **Inverse** (this reverses the selection).

6 Click the **Hue/Saturation** icon from the Adjustments panel (2nd icon on 2nd row).

Photoshop creates the adjustment layer, and the mask is created based on the selected areas of the image.

7 Drag the **Lightness** slider to the left until the non-masked areas of the image have significantly darkened.

8 Drag the **Saturation** slider to the left and lower the saturation value to -20%.

Smart Tip: You now also have the option of using "on-image" tools in Hue/Saturation (also available for Curves and Black/White). Just put your cursor on the color in the image you want to adjust. The cursor turns into a hand with double-arrows. Just move to the right or left to increase or decrease saturation. Add the Ctrl (Win) or Command (Mac) key to change the hue.

3

4

8 **7**

9 Click **OK**.

10 Select the **Hue/Saturation** adjustment layer.

11 Click the **Filter** menu, point to **Blur**, and then click **Gaussian Blur**.

12 Drag the **Radius** slider to the right to slightly blur the adjustment layer mask (you're looking for the light areas of the mask to resemble sunlight streaming through window blinds).

13 Click **OK**.

14 Use the **Paintbrush** tool with white (in this example) to paint out the blinds on the right side where they expose the back wall.

The image has now completely changed, and even the mood of the woman seems to be more serious. This is an example of how you can use adjustment layers to change the very mood of a digital image.

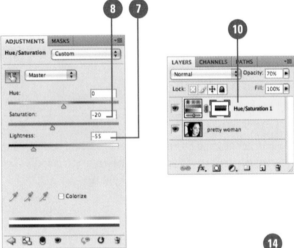

10

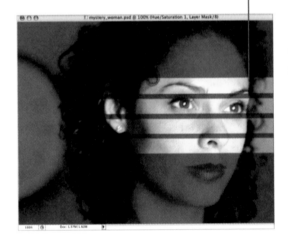

14

The Results

Finish: Compare your completed project file with the image in **mystery_woman_fnl.psd.** ☞

Tweaking the Image

The realism in this effect is all in the Gaussian Blur. Light streaming through blinds and falling on someone's face (in this example) would create a soft transition between dark and light tonal values. However, the amount of blur would be determined by the image and the resolution of the image. Therefore, don't look for a specific Radius; just look at the image and stop when you like what you see. Remember, being creative is not about adhering to a specific mathematical equation; it's about achieving that certain look you have imagined.

Good to Know: The reason we slightly lowered the saturation value of the image is to make it appear more natural. In the real world, when images darken, they have a tendency to lose some of their tonal values, and that effect can be replicated by slightly lowering the saturation of the darker areas.

Want More Projects

You can access and download more workshop projects and related files at *www.perspection.com*. After you download the files from the Web, uncompress the files into a folder on your hard drive to which you have easy access from Photoshop.

Get Everything on DVD

Instead of downloading everything from the Web, which can take a while depending on your Internet connection speed, you can get all the files used in this book and much more on a Photoshop CS4 On Demand DVD. The DVD contains task and workshop files, tips and tricks, keyboard shortcuts, and other goodies from the author.

To get the Photoshop CS4 On Demand DVD, go to *www.perspection.com*.

New! Features

n

Adobe Photoshop CS4

Adobe Photoshop CS4 means superior results faster, with new features and enhancements that help you create and manage your images more easily and efficiently. The indispensable new and improved features help graphic web designers, photographers, and video professionals create the highest quality images, with the control, flexibility, and capabilities that you expect from the professional standard in desktop digital imaging. Adobe Photoshop comes in two editions: Photoshop CS4 and Photoshop CS4 Extended. The new features list are organized by edition.

Only New Features

If you're already familiar with Photoshop CS3, you can access and download all the tasks in this book with Adobe Photoshop CS4 New Features to help make your transition to the new version simple and smooth. The Photoshop CS4 New Features as well as other Photoshop CS3 to Photoshop CS4 transition helpers are available on the Web at *www.perspection.com*.

What's New

If you're searching for what's new in Photoshop CS4, just look for the icon: New!. The new icon appears in the table of contents and throughout this book so you can quickly and easily identify a new or improved feature in Photoshop CS4. The following is a brief description of each new feature and its location in this book.

Photoshop CS4

◆ **CS4 Interface (p. 9, 26, 31, 41, 42-43, 45, 58, 72, 74)**   One of the big changes is the new Application Frame, just for Mac users. There is also an Application Bar, which puts commonly used tasks close at hand. The biggest difference in the toolbar is the ten new 3D tools and the new Rotate View tool. Workspaces are now readily accessible from the Application bar. Documents can appear with tabbed titles and there are new layout options to choose from when arranging your documents, as well as a new Match Rotation option. And, palettes have been renamed "panels."

- ◆ **Spring-loaded keys (p. 10, 41)** When you're using a tool and need to switch quickly to a different one, you can hold down the shortcut key for that tool, use the tool, then release the shortcut key and you will be automatically taken back to the tool you were previously using.

- ◆ **Camera Raw (p. 19, 492)** Exciting new features include the ability to make local adjustments with the Graduated Filter tool and the Adjustment Brush. The Spot Removal tool has a new Opacity slider that controls the strength of the healing or cloning. And now, you have the ability to retain vignetting choices after cropping the photo.

- ◆ **Smart Objects (p. 20-21)** You can now link Smart Objects with their layer mask so they can be moved together. There are also two transforming options that can now be used with Smart Objects: Perspective and Distort.

- ◆ **Help (p. 26)** Now there are additional Help resources with Adobe Community Help. You can search Adobe.com by using keywords or phrases. You'll be shown a list of possible answers, along with comments and ratings from users.

- ◆ **Navigation (p. 38-39)** Bird's Eye View offers a new way to quickly zoom in and out of your images. A new pixel grid appears when you are zoomed in to 500% or more to make pixel-specific changes easier. In the past, when you zoomed in or out of your image at odd percentages (such as 33.3%), the preview would be jagged. Now, you can view your documents at any zoom percentage and not lose any quality in the preview.

- ◆ **New panels (p. 45, 72, 99, 136, 144, 164-165, 233, 514-520)** Two new panels in CS4 that will probably become a daily part of your workflow are the Adjustments panel and the Masks panel. There is also a Notes panel, where you can view your notes and export them to a text document. As part of the enhancement of 3D functionality in Photoshop CS4, there is a new 3D panel.

- ◆ **Flash panels (p. 66)** There are two new Flash panels that come with Photoshop CS4. Kuler is an online, interactive way to build color schemes. Connections lets you manage all your Adobe accounts and check for new updates and panels.

- ◆ **Color Range (p. 87, 181)** There is a new option in the Color Range dialog box called Localized Color Clusters. You can use this to restrict your selection to a color that is contained within a certain physical area instead of grabbing that same color from all through the image.

- ◆ **Content-Aware Scaling (p. 96, 503-505)** The Content-aware Scale command automatically seeks out what it thinks are the most important parts of your image and protects them from being squished or stretched as you transform the image. You can also make your own protected selection.

- ◆ **Clone Source Panel (p. 158, 482)** You now have the option to use the "Clipped" option if you choose to see a source overlay, which limits the overlay to the brush cursor.

- ◆ **Specific Tool Enhancements (p. 159, 432)** The Dodge, Burn, and Sponge tools were enhanced in this version of Photoshop. The Dodge and Burn tools have a new option called "Protect Tones." The Sponge tool now has a Vibrance option for use when using the tool to increase saturation.

- ◆ **Vibrance option** (p. 169)   A new option has been added to the Adjustments menu and panel. Vibrance limits an increase of saturation to colors that are not already highly saturated. This option is also available for 32-bit images.

- ◆ **Adjustment presets** (p. 190, 201)   Many of the commonly used adjustments now come with preloaded presets. Adjustments that have presets are Levels, Curves, Exposure, Hue/Saturation, Black & White, Channel Mixer, and Selective Color.

- ◆ **On-image controls** (p. 204, 517-520)   Now available are on-image controls for use in Black/White adjustments, as well as Curves and Hue/Saturation. Just click in the image and drag left or right to make image adjustments to specific spots in the image.

- ◆ **Brushes** (p. 208)   There is an improved brush engine, resulting in quicker and more precise responses, especially with a drawing tablet. You can now do on the fly brush resizing by simply dragging with your mouse.

- ◆ **Mask Edge button** (p. 236)   In the new Masks panel, this button brings up the Refine Mask panel (the same as the Refine Edge panel) where you can feather, choose a radius, and view your mask on different backgrounds.

- ◆ **Printing and Proofing** (p. 372)   There are new output options in the Print command: Gamut Warning and Show Paper White. There is also a new information display above the preview area that shows your page size.

- ◆ **Photomerge** (p. 406-407, 474-475)   In the place of the Interactive Layout are two new options: the Spherical and the Collage layout. There are also two new features: the opportunity to remove fisheye lens distortion (Geometric Distortion Correction) and to remove vignettes caused by wide angle lenses (Vignette Removal).

- ◆ **Adobe Bridge** (p. 410, 488, 497)   General improvements include faster asset management and a Quick Search bar, from which you can search keywords, file names, and folder names. You also have a choice of commonly used Workspaces on the Application bar, as well as a "breadcrumb" file path so you can easily link back to the source folder for any file you're viewing. Bridge allows you to create PDF slideshows, contact sheets, PDF layouts for printing, and web galleries.

- ◆ **Saving for Web & Devices** (p. 437, 445)   There are new Transparency dither options in the dialog box. You can now choose options such as the ability to automatically convert the file to sRGB mode, the preview method, and the amount of metadata to be included in the saved file.

- ◆ **Compositing** (p. 474-475)   The Auto-Align command has been enhanced with automatic fisheye lens correction. It also compensates for lens vignetting in panoramic images so the individual images will fit together more seamlessly. You can use the Auto-Blend command to take a series of images with different focal points and blend them together so that everything is in focus (great for macro shots!).

- ◆ **ConnectNow** (p. 488, 499)   There's a new menu command in the File menu called "Share My Screen." This command opens ConnectNow, a secure web site where you can have others join you in an online meeting and collaborate on projects by sharing computer screens and files.

- **Version Cue (p. 488)** Version Cue is now accessed through Adobe Drive, a program that comes with CS4 that allows you to connect to servers as well as online services.

- **Adobe Drive (p. 488)** Adobe Drive allows you to connect to and use Version Cue servers as if they were a local hard drive or mapped network drive as well as connect to online services.

- **General** In this version of Photoshop, there is enhanced integration with Lightroom, smoother pans and zooms with GPU acceleration, and improved brush and print engines. If you're lucky enough to own one of the new MacBook Pro models, you can use "gestures" to navigate, rotate, and scale.

Photoshop CS4 Extended

- **3D Tools (p. 477, 483-484)** The biggest changes are in 3D, with ten tools in the toolbox, a separate menu, and a panel dedicated solely to 3D. From the menu, you can generate shapes, create 3D layers from files, and modify render settings. You can now paint directly on 3D objects, merge a 2D layer onto a 3D object, and animate 3D objects. One of the fun new features of 3D in CS4 is the Axis Widget. This object appears when you select a Rotate or Orbit tool and allows you to move the object more intuitively.

What Happened To

- **Automation** The Contact Sheet, Picture Package, PDF Presentation, and Web Photo Gallery commands are gone from the Photoshop Automate menu and from the Tools/Photoshop menu in Bridge. However, Bridge has a new Output Workspace, from which you can build PDF slideshows, contact sheets, PDF layouts for printing, and web galleries.

Adobe Certified Expert

About the Adobe Certified Expert (ACE) Program

The Adobe Certified Expert (ACE) program is for graphic designers, Web designers, systems integrators, value-added resellers, developers, and business professionals seeking official recognition of their expertise on Adobe products.

What Is an ACE?

An Adobe Certified Expert is an individual who has passed an Adobe Product Proficiency Exam for a specific Adobe software product. Adobe Certified Experts are eligible to promote themselves to clients or employers as highly skilled, expert-level users of Adobe software. ACE certification is a recognized worldwide standard for excellence in Adobe software knowledge. There are three levels of ACE certification: Single product certification, Specialist certification, and Master certification. To become an ACE, you must pass one or more product-specific proficiency exam and sign the ACE program agreement. When you become an ACE, you enjoy these special benefits:

- ◆ Professional recognition
- ◆ An ACE program certificate
- ◆ Use of the Adobe Certified Expert program logo

What Does This Logo Mean?

It means this book will prepare you fully for the Adobe Certified Expert exam for Adobe Photoshop CS4. The certification exam has a set of objectives, which are organized into broader skill sets. Throughout this book, content that pertains to an ACE objective is identified with the following Adobe Certified Expert logo and objective number below the title of the topic:

 PS 3.1

Photoshop CS4 ACE Exam Objectives

Objective	Skill	Page
1.0	**General knowledge**	
1.1	Describe how to arrange panels and save workspaces. (Includes: arranging and docking panels, customizing menus and shortcuts, and saving workspaces.)	7-9, 58, 72-75
1.2	Describe how to use tabbed documents and the application frame. (Includes: window management (not panel/workspace management), includes screen modes, canvas rotation, n-up views.)	10, 37, 41-43, 58
1.3	Describe options for changing the document view and zoom level. (Includes: GPU assisted pan and zoom techniques.)	34-35, 38-40, 55, 69, 468, 493
1.4	Given a scenario, describe the best way to resize an image. (Includes: Canvas Size dialog box, Image Size dialog box, resampling options, Free Transform, Options bar, resolution concepts.)	22-23, 94-95, 396, 410-412
1.5	Add metadata to an image in Adobe Photoshop.	384-385, 410-411, 437-438, 443, 491, 494-495
1.6	Explain the advantages of and when you would use 32-bit, 16-bit, and 8-bit images.	18-19, 168-169
1.7	Explain the advantages of different file format choices when saving a Photoshop document. (Includes: file formats, compression methods, color support.)	381, 386
2.0	**Correcting, painting, and retouching images**	
2.1	Explain how to correct tonal range and color in Photoshop by using the Adjustments panel. (Includes: setting black point and white point, using Curves/Levels, Hue/Saturation vs. Vibrance, Auto Color, new Curves interface, Selective Color, new color correction UI.)	136, 164-165, 191-193, 195-199, 204
2.2	Given a painting tool, adjust options appropriately and paint on a layer. (Includes: Brush tool, Pencil tool, blending modes, Options bar.)	208-210, 214-216, 223-226
2.3	Create, edit, and save a custom brush.	211-212
2.4	Given a scenario, explain which retouching tool would be most effective. (Includes: Healing, Spot healing, Patch tools and options, Clone Source panel.)	158, 160-162, 482
2.5	Create and use gradients and patterns.	198, 227-229, 336-337
2.6	Explain how to use filters and the Filter Gallery.	320-323
3.0	**Working with selections**	
3.1	Given a scenario, create a selection using the appropriate tool. (Includes: Quick Selection, Lasso tools, Magic Wand, Marquee tool, Color Range, Luminosity shortcut.)	78-87
3.2	Save and load selections.	243, 246-247
3.3	Move and transform selections.	89-91, 94-95

Photoshop CS4 ACE Exam Objectives *(continued)*

Objective	Skill	Page
3.4	Modify and preview a selection using Refine Edge.	88
4.0	**Creating and using layers**	
4.1	Create and arrange layers and layer groups.	100-103
4.2	Given a scenario, select, align, and distribute multiple layers.	102, 108-110, 113-114, 474-475
4.3	Explain the uses of layer comps, and compare to layer groups.	103, 116
4.4	Given a scenario, explain the use of layer Blending Options.	112, 142, 335
4.5	Create and edit layer effects.	219, 274-293
4.6	Create and edit layer styles.	274-293
4.7	Explain how to convert an image to black and white with the most control.	136, 204
5.0	**Working with masks and channels**	
5.1	Explain the uses of masks and channels.	99, 144, 170, 231-232, 240
5.2	Given a scenario, use the Masks panel and painting tools to create and edit a layer mask.	144, 233-239
5.3	Create, view, and edit channels.	92-93, 170, 241-249
5.4	Explain the difference between a layer mask and a vector mask.	99, 144, 232, 310
5.5	Explain why you would use a clipping mask.	91, 101, 140
5.6	Convert to or from a selection, a channel, a layer mask, a vector mask, and a Quick Mask.	92-93, 145, 235, 243, 250-252
6.0	**Working with vector tools**	
6.1	Create shape layers and paths using the Pen and Shape tools.	256-267
6.2	Explain the advantages of using vector drawing tools versus pixel-based tools.	254
6.3	Given a scenario, manage paths using the Paths panel.	255-258, 260-270, 309
6.4	Given a scenario, alter the properties of type.	296-305
7.0	**Using Camera Raw and Bridge**	
7.1	Describe the advantages of using Adobe Camera Raw to process digital Camera Raw files.	18-19, 21, 492-493
7.2	Given a Camera Raw adjustment setting, explain the purpose of that setting.	18-19, 492
7.3	Export files from Camera Raw.	19, 493

Photoshop CS4 ACE Exam Objectives *(continued)*

Objective	Skill	Page
7.4	Given a scenario, import files directly from a camera using Bridge. (Includes: Adobe Photo Downloader options.)	491
7.5	Given a scenario, describe the best way to apply one image's adjustments to many others. (Includes: Synchronize in Camera Raw, or copy and paste settings in Bridge.)	19, 492-493, 496
7.6	Apply keywords and metadata to images by using Bridge. (Includes: Keywords panel, Metadata panel, and metadata templates.)	494-495
7.7	Given a scenario, find a specific group of files out of a large collection.	489, 494-495
8.0	**Automating tasks**	
8.1	Create and use actions.	348-363, 400
8.2	Create and use a batch action.	366-368, 398-399
8.3	List and describe the automation features in Photoshop.	397-399, 402-403, 496
8.4	Given a scenario, describe the best way to process a large number of images through Photoshop.	366-368, 398-399, 410-411
8.5	Describe the difference between actions and scripting.	364-365
8.6	Create variables.	464-465
9.0	**Managing color**	
9.1	Describe the process and components of Photoshop color management. (Includes: profiles, working spaces, rendering intents, settings.)	207, 414-415, 418-419, 422-427
9.2	Configure the Color Settings dialog box.	422-423
9.3	Given a scenario, describe the proper color conversion to apply. (Scenarios include: To CMYK for prepress, to a different color space for Web or video.)	422-423, 426
9.4	Given a scenario about a color management problem, describe the proper action to take.	413-433
9.5	Discuss the relationship between color gamut and rendering intents.	414, 419
9.6	Explain the purpose and use of the Proof Setup command.	29, 383, 416-417, 419-421
10.0	**Advanced knowledge**	
10.1	Given a scenario, create and edit a Smart Object. (Scenarios include: create from Camera Raw files, imported vector objects, and layers.)	20-21, 322
10.2	Create and edit Smart Filters.	20-21, 322
10.3	Given a scenario, use Vanishing Point to edit in perspective.	148-149
10.4	Explain how to use features that handle images moving to and from video workflows. (Includes: Pixel aspect ratio, document presets, Video Preview.)	14-15

Preparing for an Adobe Certified Expert Exam

Every Adobe Certified Expert Exam is developed from a list of objectives, which are based on studies of how an Adobe program is actually used in the workplace. The list of objectives determine the scope of each exam, so they provide you with the information you need to prepare for ACE certification. Follow these steps to complete the ACE Exam requirement:

1 Review and perform each task identified with a Adobe Certified Expert objective to confirm that you can meet the requirements for the exam.

2 Identify the topic areas and objectives you need to study, and then prepare for the exam.

3 Review the Adobe Certified Expert Program Agreement. To review it, go online to *http://www.adobe.com/support/certification/ace_certify.html*.

You will be required to accept the ACE agreement when you take the Adobe Certified Exam at an authorized testing center.

4 Register for the Adobe Certified Expert Exam.

ACE testing is offered at more than a thousand authorized Pearson VUE and Thomson Prometric testing centers in many countries. To find the testing center nearest you, go online to *www.pearsonvue.com/adobe* (for Pearson VUE) or *www.2test.com* (for Prometric). The ACE exam fee is US$150 worldwide. When contacting an authorized training center, provide them with the Adobe Product Proficiency exam name and number you want to take, which is available online in the Exam Bulletin at *http://www.adobe.com/support/certification/ace_certify.html*.

5 Take the ACE exam.

Taking an Adobe Certified Expert Exam

The Adobe Certified Expert exams are computer-delivered, closed-book tests consisting of 60 to 90 multiple-choice questions. Each exam is approximately one to two hours long. A 15-minute tutorial will precede the test to familiarize you with the function of the Windows-based driver. The exams are currently available worldwide in English only. They are administered by Pearson VUE and Thomson Prometric, independent third-party testing companies.

Exam Results

At the end of the exam, a score report appears indicating whether you passed or failed the exam. Diagnostic information is included in your exam report. When you pass the exam, your score is electronically reported to Adobe. You will then be sent an ACE Welcome Kit and access to the ACE program logo in four to six weeks. You are also placed on the Adobe certification mailing list to receive special Adobe announcements and information about promotions and events that take place throughout the year.

When you pass the exam, you can get program information, check and update your profile, or download ACE program logos for your promotional materials online at:

http://www.adobe.com/support/certification/community.html

Getting More Information

To learn more about the Adobe Certified Expert program, read a list of frequently asked questions, and locate the nearest testing center, go online to:

http://www.adobe.com/support/certification/ace.html

To learn more about other Adobe certification programs, go online to:

http://www.adobe.com/support/certification

Index